...eing Key

0 km   1
0 miles   0.5

Museum of London

St Paul's Cathedral

THE CITY AND THE EAST END

Shakespeare's Globe

Tower of London

HMS Belfast

Thames

SOUTHWARK AND THE SOUTH BANK

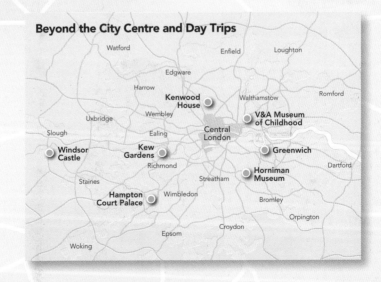

Beyond the City Centre and Day Trips

Watford
Enfield
Loughton
Edgware
Harrow
Kenwood House
Walthamstow
Romford
Uxbridge
Wembley
V&A Museum of Childhood
Slough
Ealing
Central London
Windsor Castle
Kew Gardens
Greenwich
Dartford
Richmond
Horniman Museum
Staines
Streatham
Hampton Court Palace
Wimbledon
Bromley
Orpington
Epsom
Croydon
Woking

EYEWITNESS TRAVEL
FAMILY GUIDE
LONDON

EYEWITNESS TRAVEL

FAMILY GUIDE
LONDON

DK

PUBLISHER
Vivien Antwi

LIST MANAGER
Christine Stroyan

MANAGING ART EDITOR
Mabel Chan

SENIOR EDITOR
Michelle Crane

EDITORS
Vicki Allen, Hugh Thompson,
Alexandra Whittleton

DESIGNERS
Louise Dick, Marisa Renzullo

PICTURE RESEARCH
Ellen Root

SENIOR DTP DESIGNER
Jason Little

SENIOR CARTOGRAPHIC MANAGER
Uma Bhattacharya

CARTOGRAPHER
Schchida Nand Pradhan

SENIOR CARTOGRAPHIC EDITOR
Casper Morris

PRODUCTION CONTROLLER
Rebecca Short

AUTHORS
Vincent Crump, Leonie Glass

PHOTOGRAPHY
Max Alexander

CARTOONS
Tom Morgan-Jones

OTHER ILLUSTRATIONS
Arun Pottirayil, Brian Delf, Trevor Hill,
Robbie Polley

DESIGN CONCEPT Keith Hagan at www.
greenwichdesign.co.uk

Printed and bound in China. First
published in the UK in 2012 by Dorling
Kindersley Limited, 80 Strand, London
WC2R 0RL.
A Penguin Random House Company

17 18 19 20 10 9 8 7 6 5 4 3 2 1

Reprinted with revisions 2016, 2018

Copyright 2012, 2018 © Dorling
Kindersley Limited, London

A CIP catalogue record is available from
the British Library.

ISBN 978-0-2413-0653-6

Contents

*Colourful soft toys in Eric Snook's toy
shop, Covent Garden*

Getting hands-on in a helicopter cockpit at the Royal Air Force Museum, Hendon

How to Use this Guide

This guide is designed to help families to get the most from a visit to London, providing expert recommendations for sightseeing with kids along with detailed practical information.

The opening section contains an introduction to London and its highlights, as well as all the essentials required to plan a family holiday (including how to get there, getting around, health, insurance, money and communications), a guide to family-friendly festivals and a brief historical overview.

The main sightseeing section is divided into areas. A "best of" feature is followed by the key sights and other attractions in the area, as well as options for where to eat, drink and play and have more fun. At the back of the book are detailed maps of London.

INTRODUCING THE AREA

Each area chapter is opened by a double-page spread setting it in context, with a short introduction, locator map and a selection of highlights.

Locator map locates the region.

Brief highlights give a flavour of what to see in the area.

THE BEST OF...

A planner to show at a glance the best things for families to see and do in each area, with themed suggestions ranging from history, art and culture to gardens and games.

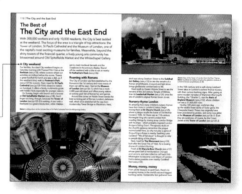

Themed suggestions for the best things to see and do with kids.

WHERE TO STAY

Our expert authors have compiled a wide range of recommendations for places to stay with families, from hotels and B&Bs that welcome children to self-catering apartments.

Easy-to-use symbols show the key family- friendly features of places to stay.

Price Guide box gives details of the price categories for a family of four.

SIGHTSEEING IN LONDON

Each area features a number of "hub" sights *(see below)*: pragmatic and enjoyable plans for a morning, afternoon or day's visit. These give adults and children a real insight into the destination, focusing on the key sights and what makes them interesting to kids. The sights are balanced by places to let off steam, "take cover" options for rainy days, suggestions for where to eat, drink and shop with kids, ideas for where to continue sightseeing, and all the practicalities, including transport.

Introductory text focuses on the practical aspects of the area, from the best time of day to visit to how to get around using public transport.

The hub map identifies the sights featured in the chapter, as well as restaurants, shops, places to stay, transport, and the nearest playgrounds, supermarkets and pharmacies.

The Lowdown gives all the practical information you need to visit the area. The key to the symbols is on the back jacket flap.

The hub sights are the best places to visit in each area, and use lively and informative text to engage and entertain both adults and children.

Key Features uses illustrated artworks to show the most interesting features of each sight, highlighting elements likely to appeal to children.

The Lowdown provides comprehensive practical information, including transport, opening times, costs, activities, age range suitability and how long to allow for a visit.

Kids' Corner is featured on all sightseeing pages *(see below)*.

Find out more gives suggestions for downloads, games, apps or films to enthuse children about a place and help them to learn more about it.

Eat and drink lists recommendations for family-friendly places to eat and drink, from picnic options and snacks to proper meals and gourmet dining.

Letting off steam suggests a place to take children to play freely following a cultural visit.

Next stop... suggests other places to visit, either near the key sight, thematically linked to the sight or a complete change of pace for the rest of the day.

Further sights around each hub, selected to appeal to both adults and children, are given on the following pages.

Places of interest are recommended, with an emphasis on the aspects most likely to attract children, and incorporating quirky stories and unusual facts. Each one includes a suggestion for letting off steam or taking cover.

Kids' Corners are designed to involve children with the sight, with things to look out for, games to play, cartoons and fun facts. Answers to quizzes are given at the bottom of the panel.

The Lowdown provides the usual comprehensive practical and transport information for each sight.

Colourful Union Jack balloons
floating in front of Big Ben

Introducing
LONDON

The Best of London

A city with a rich history, impressive architecture, world-class museums, lush parks, superb shops and incomparable theatre, London is a treasure chest for visitors and has a wide choice of family-friendly activities. Explore famous monuments, then relax on a river cruise or in a park. Attend an art workshop, take part in an exciting sport, then find time to witness the spectacle of one of London's traditional ceremonies, full of heritage, pomp and colour.

For culture vultures

Start the day at **Tate Britain** *(see pp68–9)* and try out the Art Trolley. Continue to **Westminster Abbey** *(see pp66–7)*, where you can follow the Children's Trail, and then dress up as monks in the museum. Spend the afternoon with exciting games, map-making and clue-matching in **Tate Modern** *(see p148)*.

Another day, take a family tour at the **National Portrait Gallery** *(see pp82–3)*. Break for lunch in Chinatown, near Leicester Square, then follow one of the children's audio tours or printed trails at the **National Gallery** *(see pp80–81)*.

Alternatively, climb up to the Whispering Gallery at **St Paul's Cathedral** *(see pp130–31)*, and then explore the fascinating **Museum of**

Right Toys from the past on display at the Museum of London
Below Soldiers taking part in the Changing the Guard

Children in colourful costumes taking part in the annual celebrations of the Notting Hill Carnival

London *(see pp136–7)*. Hop on the Tube to the **V&A Museum of Childhood** *(see pp208–9)* and spend the afternoon doing a gallery trail.

In three days

Take an open-top bus tour *(see p22)* and hop off at the Queen's London residence, **Buckingham Palace** *(see pp74–5)*, to watch the Changing the Guard. Spend the afternoon in the **Science** and **Natural History museums** *(see pp180–83)*, then let off steam in the **Diana Princess of Wales Memorial Playground** *(see p174)*.

Next day, arrive early for a morning at that castle of castles, the **Tower of London** *(see pp122–3)*, followed by lunch in picturesque St Katharine's Dock *(see pp126–7)*. Go by river bus to the South Bank for a trip on the **London Eye** *(see pp160–61)* and a 3D movie at the Imax.

On the last day, spend the morning at **Madame Tussauds** *(see pp114–15)*. Enjoy lunch in Marylebone High Street, then visit a classic attraction – **London Zoo** *(see pp110–11)* or the **British Museum** *(see pp102–3)*.

By season

In spring, visit **Kew Gardens** *(see pp228–9)* to see spectacular carpets of bluebells, yellow daffodils and stunning crocuses. Take part in free, fun activities, such as the chocolate workshop and Easter egg hunt.

Book tickets in advance for a summer concert at glorious **Kenwood House** *(see pp216–17)*; pack a rug and delicious picnic (or pre-order one). Dress up in something colourful for the lively, late August Notting Hill Carnival.

Go for an autumnal walk on **Hampstead Heath** *(see pp216–17)* to see the glorious leaf colours, and, if it's one of those clear, sunny, autumn days, take a trip on the London Eye.

Do some Christmas shopping in **Harrods** *(see p185)* and visit Santa's Grotto. Go skating on the large outdoor rink at Hyde Park's Winter Wonderland *(see p16)*, then warm up afterwards with traditional tea at Brown's Hotel *(see p248)*.

Outdoors

After a morning at **Battersea Park Children's Zoo** *(see pp188–9)*, hire bikes and cycle round the park. Take a train to Waterloo and have lunch in Gabriel's Wharf, before visiting **Shakespeare's Globe** *(see pp146–7)*.

Let the kids loose in **Coram's Fields** *(see p52)*, then explore the canals from Little Venice to **London Zoo** *(see pp110–11)*. After visiting the zoo, go for a row on the boating lake in **Regent's Park** *(see p112)* and finish with a play at Regent's Park Open Air Theatre.

Visit **Kew Gardens** *(see pp228–9)* to clamber inside a giant badger sett and along the Xstrata Treetop Walkway. Or take a river cruise to **Hampton Court Palace** *(see pp236–7)* and get lost in the 300-year-old maze.

Left *Costumed chefs rustle up historical delicacies in the Tudor kitchens at Hampton Court Palace*

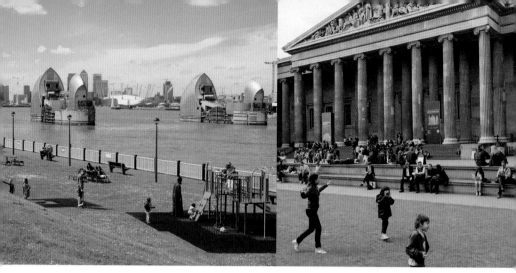

Above *Youngsters having fun in a playground by River Thames* **Above right** *Running around and letting off steam in the grounds outside the British Museum*

On a budget

Entry is free to the permanent collections of London's major museums and galleries. Many also offer complimentary or inexpensive children's tours, trails, storytelling and workshops. The capital's parks (see pp52–3) also provide plenty of free family entertainment, including some playgrounds. And the city's excellent urban farms, such as **Vauxhall** (www.vauxhallcityfarm. org) and **Mudchute** (www.mudchute.org), do not charge for admission – although a donation of some kind is appreciated.

A great way to get to know the city is on foot, as London and its fascinating, historic architecture is like a living walk-through museum. **Transport for London** (www.tfl.gov.uk/ gettingaround/walking/default.aspx) suggests routes, or simply follow the river and watch the boats as you walk. A stroll around **Covent Garden** (see pp88–9) guarantees hours of amusement from the street performers.

For discount theatre tickets, visit the **tkts** booth in Leicester Square (www.tkts.co.uk), or one of the internet sites: **www. discounttheatre.com** or **www.lastminute. com**. The cheapest places to eat (see pp36–9), apart from a do-it-yourself picnic in a park, are often local cafés or ethnic restaurants outside of the central touristy areas – sometimes only a few streets away from the main drag.

Stage and screen

A number of London theatres are dedicated to performances for children (see pp46–7). Other theatres stage plays for younger audiences,

particularly during school holidays, among them, the **Tricycle** (www.tricycle.co.uk), **Chickenshed** (www.chickenshed.org.uk), **Rose Theatre** (www.rosetheatrekingston.org), **New Wimbledon Studio Theatre** (www. ambassadortickets.com/Wimbledon) and **Hackney Empire** (www.hackneyempire.co.uk).

A pantomime is a Christmas holiday highlight – for adults as well as children: among the best are those at the **Old Vic** (www.oldvictheatre.com) and **Richmond Theatre** (www.atgtickets.com/venues/ richmond-theatre). Also at Christmas, there are ballets for children at the **Coliseum** (www.ballet.org.uk) and the **Royal Opera House** (see p90), and throughout the year at Sadler's Wells' **Peacock Theatre** and **Lilian Baylis Studio** (www.sadlerswells.com).

London's principal cinema chains are **Odeon** (www.odeon.co.uk), **Vue** (www.myvue.com) and **Cineworld** (www.cineworld.co.uk). These and the independent **Clapham Picture House** (www.picturehouses.co.uk/cinema/Clapham_ Picturehouse) and **Electric Cinema** (www. electriccinema.co.uk), have regular kids' clubs.

Active London

Sports-mad families will find plenty going on in London to keep their heart rates up, whether they want to be participants or spectators (see pp50–51). Other activities that should appeal to energetic kids are climbing, go-karting, bowling, inline skating and even dry skiing.

Westway Sports Centre has a terrific beginners' climbing wall and a junior programme that includes family sessions (www.westwaysportscentre.org.uk/climbing). The best places for budding racing drivers (aged 8+) to go karting are **Playscape** (www.playscape.co.uk) and **Daytona** (www.daytona.co.uk), while children's bowling is offered at **Hollywood Bowl** (www.hollywoodbowl.co.uk), with special lightweight bowls, and **Bloomsbury Bowling** (www.bloomsbury bowling.com). There are inline skating programmes for children in Kensington Gardens, run by **Kids Rollerblading Lessons** (www.kidsrollerbladinglessons.co.uk), **LondonSkaters** (www.londonskaters.com) and **Citiskate** (www.citiskate.co.uk), which also operates elsewhere. For dry skiing within the M25, try **Sandown Ski Centre** (www.sandown sports.co.uk) and **Bromley Ski & Snow Board Centre** (www.bromleyski.co.uk).

Above Children trying their hands at the arts and crafts on offer at Somerset House

Behind the scenes

London museums – big and small – often host highly imaginative workshops for families. Some of the best are at the **Geffrye Museum** (see p210), where the creative emphasis is on making or decorating objects. Workshops at the **Imperial War Museum** (see p166) can introduce children to storytelling through art and handle the difficult subject of war in a sensitive and involving way. At the small and slightly eccentric **Horniman Museum** (see pp222–3), children can find their imagination fired by being able to handle some of the extraordinary objects from the collection. As you would imagine, the **British Museum** (see pp102–3) puts on some excellent workshops, using technology to create fun, sometimes gruesome animations about mummification, fantastical creatures or the Aztec gods.

Going behind the scenes at a theatre can be fascinating for children, offering a glimpse into the hidden worlds of costumes, lighting, scenery shifting and even technical wizardry. Of all London's backstage tours, the most impressive are those organised by the **National Theatre** (see p162), **Royal Opera House** (see p90), **Shakespeare's Globe** (see pp144–7) and **Theatre Royal Drury Lane** (see p91).

Below Enjoying a rollerblading lesson from a member of the Kids Rollerblading Lessons team in leafy Kensington Gardens

London Through the Year

The best time for a trip to London depends on what your family likes to do. The late spring, summer and early autumn will appeal to families who like being outdoors, while those who are happiest visiting museums and galleries might prefer to come in the winter, when the city is quieter and activities are not so dependent on the weather. Regardless of the elements, every season in London has plenty to recommend it.

Spring

Springtime in London, when the blossom is out, can be wonderful for a visit. Although London is among the most temperate parts of the UK and spring is often pleasant, the weather can be unpredictable, chilly and wet, so warm clothes and waterproofs are sensible precautions. From March onwards, outdoor sporting (see pp50–51) and social events are fun for all the family and there is plenty in the calendar around Easter, especially for children.

A charming **Oranges and Lemons Service** is usually held on the third Thursday in March in St Clement Danes church. Pupils from the local primary school recite the well-known nursery rhyme, and each child is given an orange and a lemon after the service. On 21 March, the **Spring Equinox**, the first day of the solar New Year, is celebrated at Tower Hill in a historic pagan ceremony with contemporary druids dressed in long white robes.

On Good Friday, after an 11am service held at St Bartholomew the Great, Smithfield, hot-cross buns and coins are distributed to local children by the **Butterworth Charity**. Over the Easter weekend, there are **Easter egg hunts** at Battersea Park Zoo, Kenwood House, Fenton House, Handel House Museum and Kew Gardens. There is egg painting and rolling at Ham House, and, suitable for older children, the **London Bridge Experience** stages a gruesome treasure hunt for missing severed heads. There are traditional Easter **funfairs** on Hampstead Heath and the green opposite Hampton Court, and **London Friday Night Skate & Sunday Stroll** is a weekly family street-skating event in Hyde Park, aimed at skaters of all levels. Over the May Day bank holiday weekend, **Canalway Cavalcade** is a colourful occasion in Little Venice, featuring a boat rally, puppet shows and street entertainers. May is traditionally the month of fairs, and on the first Saturday in May, the **Punch and Judy Festival** is staged in Covent Garden Piazza, with shows from 10:30am–5:30pm. The **Covent Garden May Fayre and Puppet Festival** is celebrated on the Sunday nearest Punch's birthday on 9 May. A morning procession is followed by a service in St Paul's Church, and until 5:30pm there are performances of Punch and Judy shows on the site where, in 1662, Samuel Pepys watched the first ever show staged in England. Over four days at the end of May, gardeners can enjoy the gardens at the **Chelsea Flower Show** at the Royal Hospital Chelsea.

Below left Children taking part in the Easter egg hunt at Fenton House in Hampstead *Below right* A colourful and energetic performance of Crazy for You at Regent's Park Open Air Theatre

Summer

Although never entirely reliable, the weather in summer is usually fine and sunny, with long days and light evenings. People picnic in the parks; restaurants and cafés move their tables outside; and the city takes on an almost Mediterranean feel. There is always plenty to entertain families, from ceremonies (see pp18–19) and sporting events (see pp50–51) to open-air theatre and concerts. The downside is that London can be very hot and crowded during July and August.

Summer has arrived when the **Royal Academy Summer Exhibition** opens in early June. It continues until mid-August and has a reputation as the art world's most eclectic show. Also on throughout the summer is the **City of London Festival**, an extensive programme of music, art, films and talks all over the city, and there are open-air plays (some specifically for children) at the **Regent's Park Open Air Theatre** and **Shakespeare's Globe**, operas (some for children) in **Holland Park**, and picnic concerts at **Kenwood House**. One of the first outdoor events of the summer is the **London Green Fair** in Regent's Park, with eco-friendly attractions such as a mini farm, willow weaving, sewing classes and wigwam building. From

mid- to late June, the streets of East London are filled with classical, jazz and contemporary music at the **Spitalfields Festival**, which includes toddlers' concerts, guided walks and musical picnics. There is more lively outdoor music, plus dancing and processions at the week-long **Greenwich & Docklands International Festival**.

In early July, the five-day **Hampton Court Palace Flower Show** rivals Chelsea for its colour and variety, but is not as crowded. Mid-July sees the start of the ever-popular, eight-week-long **BBC Promenade Concerts** (the "Proms") at the Royal Albert Hall, founded to bring both classical and modern music to a wider audience. Also in mid-July, **Doggett's Coat and Badge Race** dates from 1714 and sees apprentice Watermen of the River Thames in bright costumes rowing single sculls from London Bridge to Chelsea Pier. The summer season culminates with the Caribbean **Notting Hill Carnival** over August bank-holiday weekend. Europe's largest carnival, it is musical, vibrant and colourful, with a procession of eye-catching floats and costumes, steel bands and food stalls. Sunday is children's day. Osterley Park, is the venue for **Big Camp**, on the first Saturday evening in September.

At this event, families pitch tents in the gardens of the manor house here, enjoy fun activities, roast marshmallows and spy bats at dusk.

Autumn

Once the summer crowds have gone, new shows open in the theatres, the shops restock and autumn days can still be blue-skied and sunny. In early September the **Mayor's Thames Festival** combines carnival, street art, music and river events between Westminster and Tower bridges. The highlight is **Sunday's Night Carnival**, when performers take to the streets, followed by fireworks on the river. The next Saturday, spectators return to the river to watch as some 300 boats, ranging from Hawaiian canoes to Viking longboats, row the **Great River Race**. Also in early September is **On Blackheath**, a family-friendly festival with music, arts and crafts and a village fête vibe.

In late September, the **Pearly Kings & Queens Harvest Festival** at St Martin-in-the-Fields church is the flagship event of the Pearly calendar, attended by Cockney pearly kings and queens.

Visit London between the end of October and the beginning of November for the festivals of Halloween and Bonfire Night.

Below left Vibrant costumes and floats take centre stage at the Notting Hill Carnival **Below right** Participants gearing up for the Great River Race, part of the Thames Festival

October Plenty, the autumn harvest festival held in Southwark, has a mix of fun-filled activities on its agenda, ranging from seasonal customs such as apple bobbing and conker fights to festive theatre and delicious food. For **Halloween**, there are always hair-raising shows at the London Dungeon and London Bridge Experience, and a spine-tingling tunnel ride on a narrowboat, courtesy of the London Canal Museum. Wrap up warm to watch the fireworks celebrating **Bonfire Night** on or near 5 November. Among the best are those in Bishop's Park, Ravenscourt Park, Battersea Park and on Blackheath.

If yours is a family of early birds, between sunrise and 8:30am on the first Sunday in November, a splendid collection of vintage, pre-1905 cars leaves Hyde Park on the **London to Brighton Veteran Car Run**. Sleepyheads might prefer to catch the cars as they parade down Regent's Street the day before, from 1–4pm.

As evidence that winter is on its way, mid-November sees the switching on of the **Regent Street Christmas Lights** and the arrival of **Winter Wonderland** in Hyde Park (until early Jan), with the city's largest outdoor ice rink, a circus, toboggan slide and a host of other rides.

Winter

From early December, Christmas lights twinkle in the streets, decorations transform shops and public places, and Santa mans his grottoes. Skaters flock to outdoor rinks (see pp50–51) and carol singing and the scent of roasting chestnuts spread through the streets. For families who enjoy culture, there are exhibitions, plays and ballets, and for those who prefer to shop, there are the sales. When it snows, children gather in the parks to toboggan and make snowmen. The downside is that transport tends to grind to a halt, and the snow quickly turns to slush.

If your children are aching for a glimpse of Father Christmas, take them to visit him in one of **Santa's Grottoes** in Harrods, Selfridges, Hamleys, Kew Gardens or Canary Wharf. On the first Thursday in December, there is a **Christmas Tree Lighting ceremony** to switch on the 500 lights that decorate the gigantic Norwegian spruce in Trafalgar Square. The event kicks off at 6pm with carol singing, and the lights are switched on at 6:30pm. Carols are sung beneath the tree most evenings in the run-up to Christmas, and there are also **carol concerts** at the Royal Albert Hall and the Horniman Museum and

carol services at many London churches. Magical candlelit services are held at St Mary-at-Hill, Southwark Cathedral and All Hallows-by-the-Tower.

A pre-Christmas treat for horse and dog lovers, the week-long **London International Horse Show** is held at Olympia in mid-December. Highlights include show jumping and dressage competitions, a Shetland pony race and dog agility and jumping events. Christmas Day is quiet in London, but there is a tremendous celebration on **New Year's Eve** with midnight fireworks at the London Eye (shown on giant screens in Trafalgar and Parliament Squares). The following day, more than 10,000 performers take part in the **New Year's Day Parade** from Piccadilly to Parliament Square from noon–3pm. There is a carnival atmosphere, with steel and marching bands, clowns, jugglers and classic cars and motorbikes.

Gasp at the impressive speed and skills of the sculptors at the **London Ice Sculpting Festival** in Canada Square Park in mid-January. In late January or early February, **Chinese New Year** is a wonderfully colourful and noisy Chinatown event, accompanied by dancing dragons, lanterns, flags, torches, food and firecrackers.

Below left A horse and rider taking part in an event at the Olympia London International Horse Show *Below right* One of the sculptors at work on his ice sculpture at the London Ice Sculpting Festival, held at Canary Wharf

The Lowdown

Spring

Battersea Park Zoo www.batterseaparkzoo.co.uk

Big Camp www.nationaltrust.org.uk/osterley-park-and-house/whats-on/big-camp-at-osterley

Butterworth Charity www.london-walking-tours.co.uk/butterworth-charity.htm

Canalway Cavalcade www.waterways.org.uk/events_festivals

Chelsea Flower Show www.rhs.org.uk

Covent Garden May Fayre & Puppet Festival www.alternativearts.co.uk

Fenton House www.nationaltrust.org.uk

Ham House www.nationaltrust.org.uk

Hampstead Heath funfair www.hampsteadheath.org.uk

Hampton Court funfair www.hamptoncourtfunfair.co.uk

Handel House Museum www.handelhouse.org

Kenwood House www.englishheritage.org.uk/daysout/properties/kenwood

Kew Gardens www.kew.org

London Bridge Experience www.thelondonbridgeexperience.com

London Friday Night Skate & Sunday Stroll www.lfns.co.uk

Oranges and Lemons Service www.calendarcustoms.com/articles/oranges-and-lemons-service

Punch & Judy Festival www.thepjf.com

Summer

BBC Promenade Concerts www.bbc.co.uk/proms

City of London Festival www.colf.org

Doggett's Coat and Badge Race www.watermenshall.org

Greenwich & Docklands International Festival www.festival.org

Hampton Court Palace Flower Show www.rhs.org.uk

Kenwood House www.english-heritage.org.uk/daysout/properties/kenwood-house

London Green Fair www.londongreenfair.org

Notting Hill Carnival www.thenottinghillcarnival.com

On Blackheath www.onblackheath.com

Regent's Park Open Air Theatre www.openairtheatre.org

Royal Academy Summer Exhibition www.royalacademy.org.uk

Shakespeare's Globe www.shakespearesglobe.com

Spitalfields Festival www.spitalfieldsfestival.org.uk

Autumn

Battersea Park www.wandsworth.gov.uk

Bishop's Park & Ravenscourt Park www.lbhf.gov.uk

Blackheath www.lewisham.gov.uk/NewsAndEvents/Events/Fireworks

Great River Race www.greatriverrace.co.uk

London Bridge Experience www.thelondonbridgeexperience.com

London Canal Museum www.canalmuseum.org.uk

London Dungeon www.thedungeons.com/london/en

London to Brighton Veteran Car Run www.veterancarruncom

Mayor's Thames Festival www.thamesfestival.org

October Plenty www.thelionspart.co.uk/octoberplenty

Pearly Kings & Queens Harvest Festival www.pearlysociety.co.uk

Regent's Street Christmas Lights www.regentstreetonline.com

Winter Wonderland www.hydeparkwinterwonderland.com

Winter

Carol services: All Hallows-by-the-Tower www.ahbtt.org.uk; **Horniman Museum** www.horniman.ac.uk; **Royal Albert Hall** www.royalalberthall.com; **St Mary-at-Hill** www.stmary-at-hill.org; **Southwark Cathedral** cathedral.southwark.anglican.org

Chinese New Year www.chinatownlondon.org

London Ice Sculpting Festival www.londonicesculptingfestival.co.uk

London International Horse Show www.olympiahorseshow.com

New Year's Day Parade www.londonparade.co.uk

Santa's Grottoes: Canary Wharf www.mycanarywharf.com; **Hamleys** www.hamleys.com; **Harrods** www.harrods.com; **Kew Gardens** www.kew.org; **Selfridges** www.selfridges.com; **Christmas Tree Lighting** www.london.gov.uk/priorities/art-culture/trafalgar-square/events

Public holidays

New Year's Day 1 Jan

Good Friday Mar/Apr

Easter Monday Mar/Apr

May Day first Mon in May

Spring Bank Holiday last Mon in May

August Bank Holiday last Mon in Aug

Christmas Day 25 Dec

Boxing Day 26 Dec

Below left Performers in lion costumes dance on podiums in Trafalgar Square to celebrate Chinese New Year *Below right* A young enthusiast inspects a display of vintage cars; part of the London to Brighton Veteran Car Run

London's Ceremonies

London has a full calendar of ceremonial events, occasions and customs, most of them connected with the royal family and many dating back to the Middle Ages or beyond. Not only are these colourful ceremonies historically important, but they are also bursting with spectacular costumes and pageantry, making them thrilling to watch for the whole family.

Trooping the Colour

Combining pageantry, military precision and music, this splendid ceremony in Horse Guards Parade honours the Queen's official birthday on a Saturday in mid-June. The Queen inspects a Guards' regiment from the Household Division, resplendent in their scarlet tunics and bearskins or plumed helmets and carrying the "colour" (their regimental flag). Afterwards, the Queen is escorted to Buckingham Palace to appear on the balcony.

Changing the Guard

Troops from the Household Division have been guarding the monarch since 1660, and a colourful ceremony marks the handover of duty from the old guard to a new one, usually with the Foot Guards in their full-dress uniform. Accompanied by a Guards' band, it takes place at Buckingham Palace daily from May–July and on alternate days throughout the rest of the year, starting soon after 11am. Children will enjoy the colour and spectacle.

State Opening of Parliament

The Queen opens the new session of Parliament each year, usually in November or December, with this historic ceremony. Although the actual ceremony – in which the Queen announces a programme of proposed legislation on behalf of her government – is closed to the public, it is televised and the royal procession from Buckingham Palace to Westminster can be seen along The Mall and Whitehall. The Queen travels in a state coach, while the Imperial State Crown has its own carriage.

Remembrance Day

Through this solemn ceremony in Whitehall on the second Sunday in November, the nation commemorates those who died in the two world wars and other more recent conflicts. The Queen and the royal family, political leaders and representatives of the armed forces observe a two-minute silence at 11am and, after the sounding of the Last Post, lay wreaths of poppies at the foot of the Cenotaph. Once the Queen has left, war veterans march past the Cenotaph to pay their respects.

Gun Salutes

The custom of firing a cannon was once a sign of respect or welcome, an unloaded gun indicating friendly intent. Today, gun salutes at the Tower of London and in Hyde Park mark royal occasions, such as

Below left The magnificent state coach taking part in the celebrations and pageantry of the Lord Mayor's Show
Below right Wreaths of poppies laid at the foot of the Cenotaph as part of the Remembrance Day ceremonies

birthdays or anniversaries, and in Green Park, state visits, the State Opening of Parliament and the Queen's birthday parade. The basic royal salute is 21 rounds, but 20 extra rounds are included if it is fired in a royal park, palace or fortress. Salutes usually take place at 11am or noon.

Ceremony of the Keys

Yeoman Warders, or "Beefeaters", have performed this ceremony, which is open to the public, to secure the Tower of London every night for 700 years. The gates are locked at exactly 9:53pm by the Chief Yeoman Warder, escorted by four armed guards. He is challenged by a sentry, who then allows him to pass, acknowledging that he is the bearer of the Queen's keys. The ceremony ends with the Chief Warder taking the keys to safety while a trumpeter sounds the Last Post.

Lord Mayor's Show

This procession occurs on the second Saturday in November, taking the newly elected Lord Mayor in a state coach from the Guildhall to the Royal Courts of Justice, where he/she pledges allegiance to the Crown, and then comes back again. The custom,

The Lowdown

Beating Retreat
www.royal.uk/
beating-retreat/
Beating the Bounds
www.allhallows
bythetower.org.uk/history/
beating-the-bounds
Ceremony of the Keys
www.hrp.org.uk/toweroflondon/
whatson/ceremonyofthekeys

Lord Mayor's Show
www.lordmayorsshow.org
Oak Apple Day
www.learnenglish.de/culture/
oakappleday.html
Royal Ceremonies (Trooping the Colour; Changing the Guard; State Opening of Parliament; Remembrance Day; Gun Salutes)
www.royal.uk/history-and-traditions

which is almost 800 years old, starts at 11am, includes floats, military bands and City guildsmen, and culminates in fireworks at 5pm.

Beating Retreat

In a spectacular show, the massed bands of the Household Division perform this ceremony on two consecutive mid-June evenings. It dates back to the time when a drum was used to communicate on the battlefield. Beating a retreat signalled the soldiers to stop fighting and return to camp. Rousing tunes are played by 300 musicians and the Queen usually takes the salute.

Oak Apple Day

Celebrated on 29 May, Oak Apple Day commemorates the lucky escape of the future Charles II from

Parliamentary forces by hiding in a hollow oak tree. The date was both Charles's birthday and the day in 1660 when he returned to London to claim the throne. Today, it is celebrated by Chelsea Pensioners, who decorate the statue of Charles II, their founder, at the Royal Hospital, and parade before royalty.

Beating the Bounds

Dating back to a time when there were few maps and boundaries were constantly in dispute, this custom involves walking around parish boundaries, whacking them with a stick and praying for protection. It is still observed on Ascension Day at All-Hallows-by-the-Tower, where the parish's southern boundary is in the middle of the Thames. Members of the party must board a boat to beat the boundary mark in the water.

Below left The Queen making her speech in the House of Lords during the State Opening of Parliament *Below right* Gun salute outside the Tower of London, marking a Royal occasion or celebration

Getting to London

London is a major European transport hub, and there are many ways to reach it. By air, there is a huge choice of carriers from all over the world, and competition and budget airlines have driven down prices. Eurostar links the UK to Europe, and ferries, jetfoils and catamarans cross the English Channel and North Sea. Coaches to London from Europe are often the cheapest option.

Arriving by air

Five airports serve London: Heathrow, Gatwick, Stansted, Luton and City.

FROM HEATHROW

Heathrow is 24 km (15 miles) west of Central London. The quickest way in is by the **Heathrow Express**, a 15–20-minute non-stop train to Paddington Station. Trains depart every 15 minutes 5am–11:40pm. **Heathrow Connect**'s 25–35-minute stopping trains to Paddington depart every 30 minutes 5am–11pm. Three stations link Heathrow to **London Underground**'s Piccadilly line, which takes around 50 minutes to reach the West End. At night, the N9 bus runs to Aldwych, Central London, leaving every 10–20 minutes.

National Express runs a coach service to Victoria from Heathrow's bus station from 5:20am–9:40pm. A shuttle bus service to various London hotels is run by **Heathrow Shuttle**

and **Skyshuttle**, a cheaper alternative to taxis, which cost £45–75. The journey into London by road takes around 1 hour. The high-speed Crossrail service on the Elizabeth line, scheduled to start in late 2018 or early 2019, will link Heathrow with Paddington, Bond Street, Farringdon, Liverpool Street and Whitechapel. This will reduce travel time considerably.

FROM GATWICK

London's second airport is 50 km (31 miles) south of the city and has two terminals. **Gatwick Express** trains leave the South Terminal every 15 minutes from 4:35am–1:35am and take 30–35 minutes to get to Victoria Station. Cheaper Southern services also run to Victoria and **Thameslink** connects Gatwick with St Pancras International and London Bridge. National Express coaches leave for Victoria every 30–60 minutes from 5:15am–9:45pm. Departing every 15 minutes round the

clock, **easyBus** runs coaches to Earl's Court/ West Brompton. There are coach pick-up points in both terminals and the journey takes 65 minutes. Taxis to central London cost £50–60.

FROM STANSTED

The quickest way to travel the 56 km (35 miles) southwest to London from Stansted is on the **Stansted Express**. Trains run to Liverpool Street every 15 minutes from 5:30–1am, and take about 45 minutes. National Express provides 24-hour coaches to Victoria (every 20–30 minutes) and Stratford (every 30 minutes). **Terravision** coaches leave every 30 minutes for Victoria (7am–1:40am) via Liverpool and Baker Street. The 24-hour easyBus runs coaches to Baker Street, King's Cross, Liverpool and Stratford every 30 minutes. Coaches to East London take 45–55 minutes and to the centre, 100–120 minutes. Taxis to the centre of town cost £70–80.

Below left Ferry leaving the port of Dover, heading for France *Below centre* The Docklands Light Railway station at London City Airport, from where the DLR takes passengers directly into Central London

FROM LUTON

From Luton, 50 km (31 miles) north of London, a 5–10-minute shuttle bus runs from 5am–midnight to Luton Airport Parkway station. From there, trains to St Pancras International are run by Thameslink (5am–midnight, every 15 minutes, taking 35–45 minutes) and **East Midlands Trains** (24-hour service, taking 40–50 minutes). **Green Line 757** and easyBus both have a 24-hour coach link to Victoria. The journey takes just over an hour. Green Line coaches leave every 20 minutes–1 hour; easyBus ones leave every 15–30 minutes.

FROM LONDON CITY

London City Airport is in Docklands, 14 km (9 miles) east from the centre. From the **Docklands Light Railway** (DLR) station, trains leave every 8–15 minutes to Canning Town, Tower Gateway and Bank, all near or on the Underground with connections to major rail stations. Taxis cost from £25 to the City and from £30 to the West End.

Arriving by train

St Pancras International is the London terminus for the **Eurostar**, the high-speed train linking the UK and Europe. From King's Cross

St Pancras Underground station, it is possible to travel almost anywhere in the city via six Underground lines. The city's other main stations and the areas they serve are **Liverpool Street**, East Anglia; **King's Cross**, the northeast; **Euston**, the northwest; **Paddington**, the west; **Waterloo**, the southwest; **Charing Cross** and **Victoria**, the southeast. Buy tickets in advance from **National Rail**.

Arriving by sea

The UK's ferry ports all have good rail links. Trains arrive at St Pancras International from **Dover**, which serves Calais and Ostend, and **Folkestone**, which is the terminus for the **Eurotunnel**, the drive-on-drive-off rail service for cars. From **Newhaven**, which serves Dieppe, trains arrive at Victoria. Trains from **Portsmouth**, which serve the northern French and northern Spain ports, arrive at Waterloo, and from **Harwich**, which serves the Hook of Holland, they stop at Liverpool Street.

Arriving by coach

Coaches from European and UK destinations arrive at **Victoria Coach Station**. The biggest operator within the UK is National Express, and **Eurolines** serves as its European arm.

The Lowdown

Airports
Heathrow www.heathrow airport.com
Gatwick www.gatwickairport.com
Luton www.london-luton.co.uk
London City www.londoncity airport.com
Stansted www.stanstedairport.com

Underground/Buses/DLR
Transport for London www.tfl.gov.uk

Buses/Shuttle buses
easyBus www.easybus.co.uk
Green Line 757 www.greenline.co.uk
Heathrow Shuttle www.heathrowshuttle.com
National Express www.nationalexpress.com
SkyShuttle www.skyshuttle.co.uk
Terravision www.terravision.eu

Trains/Stations
Charing Cross www.networkrail.co.uk
East Midlands Trains www.eastmidlandstrains.co.uk
Eurostar www.eurostar.com
Euston www.networkrail.co.uk
Gatwick Express www.gatwickexpress.com
Heathrow Connect www.heathrowconnect.com
Heathrow Express www.heathrowexpress.com
National Rail www.nationalrail.co.uk
Stansted Express www.stanstedexpress.com
St Pancras International www.stpancras.com
Thameslink www.thameslinkrailway.com

Ports
Dover www.doverport.co.uk
Eurotunnel www.eurotunnel.com
Harwich www.harwich.co.uk
Newhaven www.newhavenferryport.co.uk
Portsmouth www.portsmouth-port.co.uk

Coach
Eurolines www.eurolines.com
Victoria Coach Station www.tfl.gov.uk/modes/coaches/victoria-coach-station

Below left A British Airways plane on the tarmac at London City Airport Below right One of Eurolines' fleet of coaches, which serve the rest of the UK and much of Europe

Getting Around London

London has an excellent, comprehensive and busy public transport system. Transport for London (TfL) is responsible for buses, the Underground, Docklands Light Railway (DLR), London Overground, Santander Cycle Hire and River Buses. The worst times to travel are during the morning and afternoon rush hours, 8–9:30am and 4:30–6:30pm from Monday to Friday. Possibly the most pleasant way to travel in London is by river bus.

By bus

London buses generally run from 5am to 12:30am (7:30am–11:30pm Sun), with night buses, recognizable by the prefix N before the number, providing a less frequent service on many popular routes. Sometimes slow, particularly during rush hours, buses have dedicated lanes on most main roads and cover parts of the city that the Underground does not.

The traditional double-decker Routemaster, now only in service on two heritage routes, has been replaced by modern double-decker and single-decker buses. A line of eye-catching buses, known as the New Routemaster and conforming to the latest safety norms, has been introduced. More than 1000 of these buses have been plying across the capital. Routes are displayed at bus stops and on the **Transport for London** (TfL) website.

The destination is indicated on the front of the bus. Make sure you are heading in the right direction.

Although there are technically still two types of bus stop, compulsory and request, current TfL practice means you should always signal if you want to board a bus and, when on the bus, ring the bell if you want to disembark. Night buses only stop on request.

Routemaster heritage buses Nos 9 and 15 are great for sight seeing, but if the weather is fine, an even better way to see the city is from an open-topped double-decker. Guided bus tours are offer ed by **Big Bus Tours** and **Original London Sightseeing Tours**, which provide commentaries specially designed for children. Tickets are valid for 24 hours, the routes include most major landmarks, and the service is hop-on-hop-off. The London

Tramlink is a useful alternative to buses in some areas like Croydon. It is linked to Wimbledon Town Centre and connects the southernmost points of the Tube and London Overground as well.

By Underground, DLR and train

The London Underground (the "Tube") is the fastest and easiest way to get around the city. It operates daily, except for 25 December, from approximately 5am to 12:30am and from 7:30am to 11:30pm Sun. On Friday and Saturdays, an increasing number of lines (the "Night Tube") operate for 24 hours. Currently the service is offered on the Central, Victoria, Jubilee, Piccadilly and Northern lines, while expansion is planned for parts of the District, Circle, Metropolitan and Hammersmith and City lines in the

Below left An iconic red double-decker London bus travelling through Central London Below right London Underground sign showing where to pick up the different lines

near future. Trains can be very crowded during rush hours.

Stations are easily recognized by the TfL logo – a blue horizontal line across a red circle. There are 11 colour-coded lines, making it simple to plan journeys and changes. Maps are displayed in Tube stations and on trains. Some lines are straightforward single routes; others have branches.

Once you are through the ticket barrier *(see Tickets below)*, follow the signs to the platform for the line and direction you need. Check the front of the train and the platform's electronic indicator for the final destination to make sure it's not branching off or terminating early. On leaving the train, there are well-signed exits, as well as connections to other lines.

The **Docklands Light Railway** (DLR) is an automated, driver-less light rail system linking the City of London with the redeveloped Docklands area, including City Airport, and **London Overground**, a rail overground network serving suburban boroughs. The suburbs are also served by **National Rail** (visit its website). DLR trains run from 5:30am to 12:30am Mon–Sat and 6:30am to 11:30pm Sun. Overground train timetables are available on the TfL website.

With the exception of new stations, few Underground stations have a lift. In all, there are 66 stations with step-free access. The TfL website has a map marked with wheelchair symbols indicating Tube stations that have disabled access. Travelling on the Underground with a pram or pushchair can be awkward, particularly during the rush hours.

Tickets

TfL divides the city into six charging zones for Tube, DLR, London Overground and National Rail services, radiating out from the most central Zone 1 to Zone 6, which includes the outer suburbs. Zones 7–9 extend beyond Greater London. The most economical tickets that can be used on all forms of transport, including National Rail to Zone 9, are **Travelcards** – paper tickets available for one or seven days and in various combinations of zones – and **Visitor Oyster cards** – "smartcards" that store credit to pay for journeys. Both are available from the TfL website, Tube stations and **Travel Information Centres**. Oyster cards are also available from the many **Oyster Ticket Stops** across London and can be charged up here, at Travel Information Centres and at Tube stations A small

returnable deposit is charged for the card, but the card never expires so you can keep it for your next visit. Oyster cards are valid across all zones and automatically calculate the cheapest fare for the journeys you make in a day. To use your Oyster card, touch it on the yellow reader when you enter a bus and at the start and end of every Tube or train journey. Travelcards must be shown to the bus driver and placed into the ticket machine at the start and end of Tube or train journeys.

Children under 11 travel free on buses and up to four under-11s travel free on the Tube, DLR, London Overground and National Rail services when accompanied by an adult. Under-16s are also eligible for free bus and discounted Tube travel provided they have an 11–15 Oyster photocard, which must be ordered for a fee from the TfL website at least three weeks in advance. A simpler option, the child Travelcard gives 11–15-year-olds half-price travel on all Tube and rail networks.

Cash fares are not accepted on any buses in London. You must use a Travelcard, Oyster card or bank card to pay your fare. Contactless cards are touched on the yellow reader in the same way as Oyster cards are. They also calculate the discounted fare and daily price cap.

Below left The red, blue and white London Underground logo, which can be found at every Tube station throughout the city
Below right Platform in one of London's bustling overground stations

By taxi

London's distinctive "black" cabs (although some now sport different colours) have drivers who must pass a tough test to prove their familiarity with the city before being licensed. Cabs can be hailed in the street if their yellow "taxi" light is illuminated. They can also be found at ranks outside airports, stations and some major hotels and stores, as well as various other locations throughout the capital. Once they have stopped, taxis are obliged to take you to your destination, provided it is within 9.6 km (6 miles) of the pick-up point and inside the Metropolitan area. The fare is shown on the meter, which will start ticking as soon as the driver accepts your custom. There are three fare tariffs: between 6am and 8pm, and 8pm and 10pm on weekdays; and between 6am to 10pm on weekends. For public holidays, it is between 10pm and 6am. Tip the driver 10–15 per cent of the fare. Cabs can also be ordered online or by phone from **Radio Taxis** and **Dial-a-Cab**.

By mini-cab

Mini-cabs are not governed by the same strict regulations as black cabs and the drivers are not as well qualified, but they are quite professional. Order a mini-cab by phone, or email or by visiting a mini-cab office, and agree the fare in advance. Do not hail one in the street as it is illegal for mini-cab drivers to take customers without a booking. For names of local mini-cab firms, enter your location into **Cabwise** on the TfL website. **Lady Minicabs** only employs women drivers.

By car

Expensive parking and congestion charging are designed to deter people from driving in Central London, and traffic, particularly on arterial roads outside the congestion zone, can be very heavy during rush hours. The charge for driving in the congestion zone, which covers the area to the east of Park Lane, south of Marylebone/Euston Road, west of Tower Hamlets and north of Elephant and Castle, is £11.50 per day (7am–6pm, Mon–Fri), payable on the day, or £14 if paid by midnight the following day. It costs £10.50 if you register online for **Congestion Charging Auto Pay**. Payments can be made online, by phone, by text. If you fail to pay in time, you will be fined £130, reduced to £65 if you then pay within 14 days.

Parking in Central London, usually in pay-and-display bays with payment by mobile or text, can be scarce and restrictions need to be observed. Be careful not to park in a residents-only bay during the designated hours. There is also no parking on red routes or on double yellow lines. You can park on single yellow lines in the evenings and on Sundays. Parking illegally or overstaying the time limit in a pay-and-display bay can result in a fine and/or your car being wheel-clamped or towed away. A notice should be displayed informing drivers of where to go to pay their fine and collect their vehicle.

There are plenty of car-hire firms in London, including **Avis**, **Budget**, **Europcar**, **Hertz** and **Thrifty**, which have offices at airports and other locations throughout the city, but the best rates are through comparison websites such as **travelsupermarket. com**. For large families, **5th Gear** has 7- and 9-seaters, plus child and booster seats to rent. Most firms offer a car delivery and collection service. All drivers need to study the UK **Highway Code** and familiarize themselves with the traffic signs used in London.

By river

Regular river services are operated by TfL's **River Bus**, which operates

Below left A London "black" cab travelling through the streets of Central London *Below right* The many Santander Cycle Hire bikes at one of the ranks located throughout the city

four lines between Putney in the west and Woolwich Arsenal in the east. Timetables, which change according to the season, and maps are available on the TfL website. For river tours and cruises, see p28.

By bicycle

Santander Cycle Hire is a public bicycle-sharing scheme launched in 2010 and originally sponsored by Barclays. Its red-and-grey bikes are available from docking stations throughout London (shown on a map on the TfL website). Register online, or pay at the terminals, borrow a bike and drop it off at any docking station in the scheme. The bikes have three gears and adjustable seats. They are quite heavy though, so maybe not ideal for long rides. Bikes suitable for all the family can be rented from the **London Bicycle Tour Company**, which also arranges cycle tours, and **Go Pedal**, which offers child seats and trailers. If you are cycling with children, TfL promotes **Greenways** and **Quietways** – a network of safe, family-friendly routes running through parks, quiet streets and along waterways. It is always advisable to wear reflective clothing and a helmet when cycling and to use a lock to deter thieves.

The Lowdown

By bus
Big Bus Tours www.bigbustours.com
Original London Sightseeing Tours www.theoriginaltour.com
Transport for London www.tfl.gov.uk

By Underground, DLR & train
Docklands Light Railway www.tfl.gov.uk/dlr/timetable/dlr
Fares & Payment www.tfl.gov.uk/fares-and-payments
London Overground www.tfl.go.uk/modes/london-overground/
National Rail Enquiries www.nationalrail.co.uk
Oyster Ticket Stops ticketstoplocator.tfl.gov.uk

By taxi and mini-cab
Dial-a-Cab www.dialacab.co.uk
Cabwise https://tfl.gov.uk/modes/taxis-and-minicabs
Lady Minicabs http://ladyminicabs.lovemycab.co.uk
Radio Taxis www.radiotaxis.co.uk

By car
5th Gear www.5th-gear.net
Avis www.avis.co.uk
Budget www.budget.co.uk

Congestion Charging Auto Pay www.tfl.gov.uk/modes/driving/congestion-charge
Europcar www.europcar.co.uk
Hertz www.hertz.co.uk
Highway Code www.gov.uk/browse/driving/highway-code
Thrifty www.thrifty.co.uk
travelsupermarket.com www.travelsupermarket.com

By river
River Bus www.tfl.gov.uk/modes/river/about-river-bus

By bicycle
Go Pedal www.gopedal.co.uk
Greenways http://content.tfl.gov.uk/greenways-final-annual-monitoring-report.pdf
London Bicycle Tour Company www.londonbicycle.com
Quietways https://tfl.gov.uk/travel-information/improvements-and-projects/quietways
Santander Cycle Hire https://tfl.gov.uk/modes/cycling/santander-cycles

On foot
London Walks www.walks.com
Transport for London www.tfl.gov.uk/modes/walking

On foot

Although it is large, London is still a great city to explore on foot, whether it's a stroll around the back streets of Covent Garden or the City or a more serious ramble through the green spaces of Richmond Park or over Hampstead Heath. The TfL website has a walking route planner. A number of companies arrange themed walks, from Ghosts of the Old City to Harry Potter Film Locations. The most established operator is **London Walks**.

Below left A river bus cruising along the Thames, past Cleopatra's Needle on the Embankment *Below right* A family walking across Westminster Bridge, leaving the Houses of Parliament and Big Ben behind them

London by River
Westminster Bridge to Blackfriars Bridge

The Thames has always been at the heart of London life. Today, its banks are lined with important, historic buildings and monuments, from the medieval Tower to the Houses of Parliament. Although commercial ships no longer ply the Thames as they did until the 1950s, the river now has a role as an attraction. Whether you take a river cruise or a commuter shuttle, a boat trip is a fascinating way to see the city. For most cruises, children must be at least 5 years old.

**Westminster Bridge
to Blackfriars Bridge**

see next page

South Bank

① Big Ben (see p68) is the nickname of the huge bell inside the Palace of Westminster's clock tower, and is also used to describe the tower itself, one of the city's most recognizable symbols.

② Watch fish swim beneath your feet at the wonderful Sea Life London Aquarium (see p164), home to more than 500 different marine species, in the former seat of London's council.

③ Take a "flight" on the London Eye, a giant Ferris wheel (see pp160–61), for one of the capital's best views. The pods allow you to see for miles in every direction (as long as the weather is clear).

Temple

Waterloo Bridge

Savoy Pier

Charing Cross

Festival Pier

Embankment

Embankment Pier

Hungerford Railway and Golden Jubilee Footbridges

Waterloo Millennium Pier

Westminster Pier

Westminster

Westminster Bridge

④ Rejuvenated during the 1951 Festival of Britain, the South Bank boasts London's most important arts complex, as well as many other sights, including Shakespeare's Globe, Tate Modern and the BFI Southbank (see pp140–46).

⑤ Buried in the pedestal of Cleopatra's Needle *(see p81)*, the ancient Egyptian obelisk presented to Britain in 1819, is a Victorian "time capsule" containing such everyday items as hairpins, a baby's bottle, a railway guide and a map of London.

⑥ Britain's first luxury hotel, the Savoy, was built in 1881 by Richard D'Oyly Carte, who produced Gilbert and Sullivan operas at his adjacent theatre. The hotel reopened in 2010 after a three-year renovation, and though it is lovely to look at, it's more of an adult treat to visit.

⑪ Christopher Wren's masterwork, St Paul's *(see pp130–31)* once dominated the city skyline.

Blackfriars

Blackfriars Millennium Pier

Blackfriars Bridge

Millennium Bridge

⑦ In winter, head to 18th-century Somerset House *(see p93)* to skate on its central courtyard's open-air ice rink; in summer enjoy one of the concerts or outdoor movies held there. Inside is the superb Courtauld Gallery art collection.

⑧ A landmark building, the OXO Tower was owned by a company that makes beef stock. As advertisements were banned, the windows were designed to spell out the name of the famous brand. The top-floor restaurant and public gallery have terrific views.

⑨ The capital's showcase for significant international modern art, Tate Modern has 88 light and airy galleries in the former Bankside power station.

⑩ When the Millennium Bridge opened in 2000, pedestrians were unnerved to feel it swaying. The "Wobbly Bridge", closed for two years while the wobble was eliminated, connects Tate Modern *(see p148)* to St Paul's *(see pp130–31)*.

The Lowdown

Big Ben www.parliament.uk/ about/living-heritage/building/ palace/big-ben

London Eye www.londoneye. com

OXO Tower Barge House Street, SE1 9PH; www.harveynichols. com/oxo-tower-london

Savoy Hotel Strand, WC2R 0EU; www.fairmont.com/savoy-london/

Sea Life London Aquarium www.visitsealife.com/london/

Somerset House Strand, WC2R 1LA; www.somersethouse.org.uk

South Bank www. southbanklondon.com & www. southbankcentre.co.uk

Tate Modern Bankside, SE1 9TG; www.tate.org.uk/modern

London by River (continued)
Southwark Bridge to St Katharine's Dock

Southwark Bridge
to St Katharine's Dock

see previous   City
page

Southwark

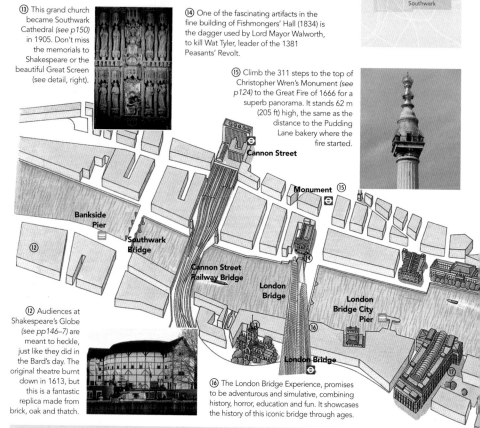

⑬ This grand church became Southwark Cathedral (see p150) in 1905. Don't miss the memorials to Shakespeare or the beautiful Great Screen (see detail, right).

⑭ One of the fascinating artifacts in the fine building of Fishmongers' Hall (1834) is the dagger used by Lord Mayor Walworth, to kill Wat Tyler, leader of the 1381 Peasants' Revolt.

⑮ Climb the 311 steps to the top of Christopher Wren's Monument (see p124) to the Great Fire of 1666 for a superb panorama. It stands 62 m (205 ft) high, the same as the distance to the Pudding Lane bakery where the fire started.

⑫ Audiences at Shakespeare's Globe (See pp146–7) are meant to heckle, just like they did in the Bard's day. The original theatre burnt down in 1613, but this is a fantastic replica made from brick, oak and thatch.

⑯ The London Bridge Experience, promises to be adventurous and simulative, combining history, horror, education and fun. It showcases the history of this iconic bridge through ages.

The Lowdown

 Fishmongers' Hall London Bridge, EC4R 9EL; www.fishhall.org.uk

Hay's Galleria London Bridge City, Tooley Street, SE1 2HD

HMS Belfast Morgan's Lane, Tooley Street, SE1 2JH; www. iwm.org.uk/visits/hms-belfast

The Monument www. themonument.info

St Katharine's Dock www. skdocks.co.uk

Shakespeare's Globe 21 New Globe Walk, Bankside, SE1 9DT; www.shakespearesglobe.com

Southwark Cathedral London Bridge, SE1 9DA; cathedral. southwark.anglican.org

Tower Bridge www.towerbridge. org.uk

Tower of London www.hrp.org. uk/toweroflondon

Thames Cruises, Taxi Services and River Buses Bateaux London 020 7695 1800; www.bateauxlondon.com

City Cruises (Westminster to Greenwich) 020 7740 0400; www.citycruises.com

Thames Clippers (London Eye to Greenwich) 0870 781 5049; www.thamesclippers. com

Thames Executive Private Charters & River Taxi 01342 820600

Thames River Services (Greenwich, Thames Barrier) 020 7930 4097; www. thamesriverservices.co.uk

Transport for London River Bus and River Tours Information www.tfl.gov.uk/river

Turks (Kingston, Richmond & Hampton Court) 020 8546 2434; www.turks.co.uk

Westminster Passenger Services Association (Westminster Kew, Richmond & Hampton Court) 020 7930 2062; www.wpsa.co.uk

⑱ Kids can clamber up ladders, duck through hatches and let their imagination run riot on the navigation deck of HMS *Belfast (see pp154–5)*, a World War II warship that played a crucial role in the Normandy landings of 1944.

⑲ Britain's most famous medieval fortress, the Tower of London *(see pp122–3)* is steeped in gory history. Prisoners were brought by boat through the notorious Traitors' Gate for execution. The Tower contains a superb collection of arms and armour as well as the priceless Crown Jewels.

Fishy fact: Jaws!

In February 2004, a recently dead red-bellied piranha, a native of the Amazon, was discovered on the deck of a boat in the Thames. The mystery was that this razor-toothed killer fish with short powerful jaws, which, in a group, can devour large prey in seconds, is unable to survive in cold temperatures. It appeared to have been dropped by a seagull onto the deck. But how had the seagull got hold of it? It is likely that it was a pet that grew too big and was set free by its owner. It died in the cold water and floated to the surface, where it was picked up by a gull, but the bird must have decided it had bitten off more than it could chew!

⑳ A London icon, Tower Bridge is still raised to let ships pass, but not as often as it was in the days of tall-masted cargo vessels. Visit the exhibition to see the hydraulic machinery that operated the bridge before electrification in the 1970s.

Tower
Millennium Pier

⑱ Tower Bridge ⑳

St Katharine's Pier

⑰ Known as the "Larder of London" in the 19th century, when it handled most of the city's imported dry goods, Hay's Galleria is a former wharf converted into a smart shopping arcade.

㉑ Now a lively marina, St Katharine's Dock *(see pp126–7)* was built on a site with over 1,000 years of history. This was London's first and most successful Docklands' redevelopment in the 1970s.

Practical Information

London has an impressive range of useful facilities for visitors, many of which are available 24 hours a day. Among them are cashpoint machines (ATM), bureaux de change, pharmacies and the health advice and information service, NHS Walk-In Centres. To make the most of a visit – and to ensure everything goes as smoothly as possible – it is essential to have some inside knowledge of the city.

Passports, visas and customs

Visitors from outside the European Economic Area (EEA) and Switzerland need a valid passport to enter the UK. Children (under the age of 18), travelling to the UK, like most other countries, must have their own invidual passport.

Visitors from European Union (EU) states do not need a visa. Neither do visitors from the USA, Canada, South Africa, Australia and New Zealand who intend to stay in the UK for less than six months. Visitors from other countries should visit the **Home Office UK Border Agency** website to check whether a visa is required and, if so, how to apply. Visitors from EU states can bring unlimited quantities of most goods into the UK for personal use without paying duty. For information about allowances from outside the EU, visit the **HM Revenue & Customs** website.

Travel Safety Advice

Visitors can get up-to-date travel safety information from the **Foreign and Commonwealth Office** in the UK (*www.gov.uk/foreign-travel-advice*), the **State Department** in the US (*www.travel.state.gov/*) and the **Department of Foreign Affairs and Trade** in Australia (*www.dfat.gov.au/smartraveller.gov.au/*).

Insurance

It is advisable to take out travel insurance to cover the cancellation or curtailment of your trip, the theft or loss of money and other personal property, and any necessary medical treatment. If you are planning to drive in London, take out fully comprehensive driving insurance and carry a valid driver's licence. Keep all car receipts and police reports in case of an insurance claim.

The UK has reciprocal health care agreements with all EEA states, Australia, New Zealand and a number of other countries listed on the **National Health Service** (NHS) website. Visitors from these countries are entitled to free treatment under the NHS. However, there are exceptions for certain kinds of treatment, which is why taking out medical insurance is always advisable. Ensure you bring all documentation with you, such as the **European Health Insurance Card** (EHIC).

Visitors from a country without a reciprocal health agreement, such as the US, are only covered for treatment received in a hospital Accident and Emergency (A&E)

Below left The twelve-sided pound coins currently in circulation in the UK *Below right* London police officers on duty in the busy area surrounding Piccadilly Circus

department, so insurance is particularly important.

Health

In a medical emergency, dial 999 for an ambulance. They are on call 24 hours a day. Many London hospitals have 24-hour A&E departments, but not all treat children. **Chelsea and Westminster**, the **Royal London** and **St Mary's** have specialist paediatric departments.

For minor injuries or ailments, head to the nearest **NHS walk-in centre** or consult a pharmacist. Most have the same opening hours as other shops, although some stay open later. **Zafash** is open 24 hours daily; pharmacies that open till midnight include **Pharmacentre, Bliss, Boots Victoria Station** (9pm Sun) and **Boots Piccadilly Circus** (6pm Sun). Although it is possible to buy many medicines over the counter, some are only available on prescription. Pack any prescription drugs your family is likely to need, including allergy medication. There is now a keen awareness of serious food allergies and intolerances and items in shops are usually clearly labelled. The UK sun can be surprisingly hot and burning, especially for young children, so it is wise to use a good sunscreen.

Personal safety

Crowded shopping areas such as Oxford Street, busy markets, and Tube stations and bus stops are popular with thieves, who sometimes work in teams. Carry a handbag that closes effectively and keep it near you. Don't carry large amounts of money, or valuables, around with you, and avoid badly lit areas at night.

Never leave a bag or suitcase unattended on the Tube, at a station or in any other public place. It may be treated as a suspect package and cause a security alert.

In an emergency, dial 999 or 112. Report serious crimes at a Police Station (the **Metropolitan Police** website lists station addresses). For non-emergency crimes you can complete a form (available on the website) or dial 101. If you lose something on public transport, report it via the TfL website or visit the **TfL Lost Property Office**.

When out, arrange a safe meeting place with your children in case you become separated. Make sure they know where you are staying and the best people to ask for help (a police officer or security guard) if they get lost. Remind your children that cars in the UK drive on the left, and to always use pedestrian crossings or underpasses to cross the road.

Money

The unit of currency in the UK is the pound sterling (£), divided into 100 pence (p). There are coins in circulation for 1p, 2p, 5p, 10p, 20p, 50p, £1 and £2, and notes for £5, £10, £20 and £50. There is no limit to the amount of cash you can bring into the UK, but a pre-paid cash passport, used like a debit card, or traveller's cheques are more secure alternatives. Keep a separate note of the cheques' serial numbers. Visa and MasterCard are the most widely accepted, followed by American Express, Diners Club and JCB.

High street banks, such as **HSBC, Barclays** and **NatWest**, and post offices will change money and traveller's cheques at better rates than bureaux de change, whose advantage is longer opening hours. **Thomas Cook** and **Chequepoint** have numerous London offices, and Chequepoint in Gloucester Road is open 24 hours. **Travelex** and **American Express** cash traveller's cheques (remember your passport). Cashpoint machines (ATMs) are also widely available, but beware of ATM crime. Only use an ATM where and when you feel comfortable. Never accept help from strangers while using the ATM, don't be distracted and always cover your hand when you enter your PIN.

Below left The Boots pharmacy in Piccadilly Circus *Below right* London police officers patrolling a busy platform in one of London's many Tube stations

Communications

The UK telephone country code is +44 and the area code for London is 020. To phone abroad, dial 00, followed by the country code. If you have problems with a number, call the operator on 100 or the international operator on 155. The main mobile phone network providers are **Three**, **O2**, **EE** and **Vodafone**. To save money, consider buying a UK SIM card. Most public phones are operated by coins, credit cards and **British Telecom Calling Cards**, available through the BT website. Some are Internet phones, from which you can send emails and texts.

Wi-Fi is available in most hotels, often for a fee, and for free in many cafés, parks and other public places. Public libraries offer free Internet access on their computers, although you might have to queue. **Visit London** features a list of Internet cafés.

Apart from numerous satellite and cable channels, UK television has a number of digital stations, of which two, BBC1 and BBC2, are public service; the rest, including ITV1, Channel 4 and Channel 5, are commercial. Check BBC News or Sky News for regular weather updates. London's radio stations, BBC London Live (94.9FM), Capital FM (95.8FM) and LBC (97.3FM), have regular news and travel bulletins. For news plus entertainment listings, the daily *Evening Standard* newspaper is free. The magazine *Time Out* is also excellent for listings. The *International Herald Tribune* is available on the day of issue, and European publications usually appear a day or so later. **Gray's Inn News** at 50 Theobald's Road stocks a range of foreign newspapers and magazines.

Opening hours

Shops are generally open 9:30am–6pm Mon–Sat and 11am–5pm Sun, with late-night shopping until 8pm on Wed or Thu in central areas. Official banking hours are 9:30am– 3:30pm Mon–Fri, although most banks stay open until 5pm and many are open 9:30am–noon Sat. In general, museums and galleries open daily 10am–5:30pm or 6pm; some stay open later one night a week, usually Friday. Tourist attractions often open at 9am or 9:30am; last admission is 30 minutes before closing time. Always check times before setting out.

Visitor information

The Visit London website provides information on popular attractions and places to stay and lists what's on.

The main Tourist Information Centre is **The City of London Information Centre**. Other information centres can be found at railway stations including **King's Cross St Pancras**.

Disabled facilities

Most of London's major sights are wheelchair accessible. Before a visit, phone to check that your needs can be met. Websites for accessible attractions are **Artsline** and Visit London (which also features hotels). For accessibility on public transport, visit the **TfL** website. There is an increasing number of adapted toilets; many are part of the National Key Scheme (NKS), unlocked by a key from the **Royal Association for Disability and Rehabilitation** (RADAR), which also produces a printed guide to their locations, as well as having a searchable guide for toilet locations.

Time

London operates on Greenwich Mean Time (GMT) in winter, 5 hours ahead of Eastern Standard Time, and from late March to late October, changes to British Summer Time, 1 hour ahead of GMT. You can check the exact time by phoning the BT Speaking Clock on 123.

Below left *The Internet café area of The Hoxton hotel* **Below right** *Child playing with a Nintendo DS – be sure to pack a variety of games and activities to keep youngsters occupied*

Electricity

UK voltage is 240V AC, and plugs have three square pins and take 3-, 5- or 13-amp fuses. Visitors will need an adaptor for appliances.

What to pack

If you forget something, don't worry unless it is your child's much-loved toy or blanket. You can buy almost anything else in London, but bring particular brands if your children have strong preferences. Let the children choose some of their favourite clothes and toys. Be super-organized and order nappies and wipes through **Amazon** to be delivered to your hotel or apartment.

Be prepared for changeable weather: raincoats and umbrellas are essential, even in summer, when you may also need sunscreen. In winter, bring warm clothes and shoes with non-slip soles. Always pack comfy shoes. For young children, a compact buggy might be handy.

Bring toys for the journey that will keep the kids occupied but won't disturb other passengers. If it's a long flight, buy a few new toys and hand them out at intervals. Include books, puzzles, crayons, paper, colouring and sticker books and cards.

The Lowdown

Visas and customs

Home Office UK Border Agency www.gov.uk/government/organisations/uk-visas-and-immigration

HM Revenue & Customs www.hmrc.gov.uk

Insurance

European Health Insurance Card www.gov.uk/european-health-insurance-card

NHS www.nhs.uk/NHSEngland/Healthcareabroad/Pages/Healthcareabroad.aspx

Health

Bliss 5–6 Marble Arch, W1H 7EL; 020 7723 6116; blisslife.co.uk

Boots Victoria Station; 44–6 Regent St, W1B 5RA; 020 7834 0676; www.boots.com

Chelsea and Westminster Hospital 369 Fulham Rd, SW10 9NH; 020 8746 8000; www.chelwest.nhs.uk

NHS Walk-In Centres www.nhs.uk/NHSEngland/AboutNHSservices/Emergencyandurgentcareservices/pages/Walk-incentresSummary.aspx

Pharmacentre 149 Edgware Rd, W2 2HU; 0207 7723 2336

Royal London Hospital Whitechapel Rd, E1 1BB; 020 7377 7000; www.bartshealth.nhs.uk/our-hospitals/the-royal-london-hospital/

St Mary's Hospital Praed St, W2 1NY; 020 3312 6666; www.imperial.nhs.uk/stmarys

Zafash 233–235 Old Brompton Rd, SW5 0EA; 020 7373 2798

Personal safety

Metropolitan Police 101

TfL Lost Property Office 200 Baker Street, NW1 5RZ; 0343 222 1234; www.tfl.gov.uk/corporate/useful-contacts/lost-property

Money

American Express www.americanexpress.com/uk

Barclays www.barclays.co.uk

Chequepoint www.chequepoint.com

HSBC www.hsbc.co.uk

NatWest www.natwest.com

Post Office www.postoffice.co.uk

Thomas Cook www.thomascookmoney.com

Travelex www.travelex.com

Communications

British Telecom Calling Cards bartshealth.nhs.uk/our-hospitals/the-royal-london-hospital/

EE www.ee.co.uk

Gray's Inn News graysinnnews.com

O2 www.o2.co.uk

Three www.three.co.uk

Vodafone www.vodafone.co.uk

Visitor information

King's Cross St Pancras Travel Information Centre Western Ticket Hall N1 9AL; www.visitlondon.com

The City of London Information Centre Guildhall, EC2P 2EJ; 020 7606 3030; www.cityoflondon.gov.uk

Disabled Facilities

Artsline www.artsline.org.uk

RADAR www.radar.org.uk

TfL www.tfl.gov.uk/gettingaround/transportaccessibility/1167.aspx

What to pack

Amazon www.amazon.com

Below left A woman browsing through a large collection of tourist brochures at a travel show Below right The main desk at the City of London Information Centre

Where to Stay

Staying in London is expensive, but there are plenty of family options among the hotels, B&Bs and apartments. Some hotels and B&Bs provide rooms for four, or suites of connected rooms. Some can provide camp beds or sofa beds, but typical rooms are not large and will be a squeeze for four. Apartments can be more flexible. The best family accommodation provides cots, high-chairs and even babysitting services. Check what is on offer before you book. For information on accommodation options, go to the Visit London website.

Hotels

London hotels once had a reputation for being unfriendly places for families, where children were rarely seen, and if they were, they should certainly not be heard. But times have changed and most welcome children now. Many have babysitting services, special children's rates or allow kids to stay free in their parents' room and provide them with complimentary or half-price breakfast. Some also have flexible meal times. Expensive West End hotels are now among the most child-friendly. Many employ kids' concierges, who can suggest fun outings and make reservations for shows and attractions. They also keep collections of story books, toys and suitable DVDs, arrange special meals, and provide a host of things to tempt tinies, from fun bed linen to cookery sessions. Hip designer hotels are not often so family-friendly, but in the same price bracket there is a core of charming, family-run establishments with genial staff prepared to go the extra mile for their younger guests.

Chain hotels can be an excellent choice for families. What they lack in character and location, they make up for in value for money and children's facilities. Among the family-friendliest chains are **Apex**, **Crowne Plaza**, **Marriott** and **Park Plaza** at the upper end of the market, and **Ibis Styles**, **Novotel** and **Premier Inn** at the budget end.

Bed & breakfast

There are two types of B&B: a simple hotel with no restaurant, and a private home where bedrooms are let out to guests. At their best clean, comfortable and friendly, the former offer a less expensive alternative to hotels and a base from which to explore the city (most have limited public areas and are not generally places in which to hang out). The breakfast is usually a full English and included in the price.

If the owners are welcoming and amenable, staying in a home can be remarkably successful, and you might even make friends for life. But success is not guaranteed: most private houses only have a few rooms to let and it can be tricky to find one with suitable family accommodation. Using a specialist homestay agency is advisable (see p242), or try the **Bed & Breakfast Association**, an affiliation of several reputable agencies whose properties are inspected regularly.

Below left Stylish bedroom at The Hoxton hotel in Shoreditch *Below right* The kitchen and living area of one of the self-catering SACO – Holborn apartments located in Central London

Self-catering

Staying in an apartment is probably the most relaxing option for families, especially if you are in London for more than a few days. Most apartments have a minimum stay of two nights to one week. Jet-lagged children, on the go from dawn, can have the run of the apartment without disturbing others. It also means you don't always have to eat out. You can cook your children's favourite meals (particularly useful for fussy eaters) and save money. Another alternative, is a home swap. This is best arranged through an established agency such as **Home Base Holidays**, **Home Link**, **Intervac** or the US-based **Home Exchange**.

The choice of apartments is between serviced and privately owned. Most London apartments are serviced, with a concierge and a cleaner. **BridgeStreet**, **Cheval Residences**, **Citadines**, **Fraser Place** and **SACO** all have several buildings in good locations for families. Other apartments are attached to a hotel, where guests can still have breakfast and use the facilities. Privately owned apartments are less expensive, but harder to find. Some agencies have them on their books (see p242). Most are in the suburbs.

The Lowdown

Apex www.apexhotels.co.uk
Bed & Breakfast Association www.bandbassociation.org
BridgeStreet www.bridgestreet.com
Cheval Residences www.chevalresidences.com
Citadines www.citadines.com
Crowne Plaza www.ihg.com/crowneplaza/hotels/gb/en/reservation
Expedia www.expedia.co.uk
Fraser Place www.frasershospitality.com
Home Base Holidays www.homebase-hols.com
Home Exchange www.homeexchange.com
Home Link www.homelink.org
Ibis Styles www.ibis.com
Intervac www.intervac-homeexchange.com/country/choose
lastminute.com www.lastminute.com
Late Rooms www.laterooms.com
Marriott www.marriott.co.uk
Novotel www.novotel.com
Park Plaza www.parkplaza.com
Premier Inn www.premierinn.com
SACO www.sacoapartments.com
Travelocity www.travelocity.com
Visit London www.visitlondon.com

Rates

London hotels usually quote room rates rather than prices per person and include VAT, but not always breakfast (double check before booking). Rates tend to remain high throughout the year, although it is possible to find reductions through special offers and weekend breaks, often on a minimum two-night stay. Generally, the longer you stay, the better the rate, and the best-value deals are available by booking in advance online. If they are not fully booked, some hotels offer last-minute discounts on their published "rack rates". Some of the best deals are available through websites such as **Late Rooms** and, for city breaks as well as accommodation, **Expedia**, **lastminute.com** and **Travelocity**.

Price categories

The three price categories in this guide are based on accommodation for a family of four for one night during high season, inclusive of service charges and any additional taxes. The inexpensive category is under £150; moderate is £150–250; and expensive is over £250. Inexpensive accommodation is extremely hard to find in London, where hotels are notoriously costly.

Below left The elegant exterior of the Arosfa B&B near Regent's Park *Below right* The smart lobby of the Grange City hotel, located minutes from the Tower of London

Where to Eat

Once Hushed and barely tolerant of children, London's restaurants have become more accommodating towards families, and dining has grown more informal. Noisy children will not be welcome in any restaurant, but even upmarket establishments will be happy to see well-behaved ones, and often provide high chairs, colouring books and crayons. The choice of cuisines is enormous, offering dishes from all over the world. Prices given in this guide allow for a two-course lunch for a family of four, excluding wine but including soft drinks.

Chinese

The obvious place to go for Chinese food is Chinatown in the West End. Its pulsing heart, pedestrian-only Gerrard Street, is lined with exotic aroma-filled supermarkets and restaurants that range from plain eateries with bare tables and rows of glazed ducks in the windows to elegant places with wide-ranging menus. Chinese families eat out regularly and the restaurants are all geared to cater for children. Many have high chairs, and all will provide small portions – try dim sum, which only comes in small servings. Most children love the delicate flavours, from rice, noodles and dim sum dumplings to spring rolls and crispy aromatic duck (a fun dish for children as they can construct their own pancake parcels).

Indian

Indian curries are among the UK's favourite dishes. For truly authentic dishes, head to the Indian communities of Southall in West London or Brick Lane and Bethnal Green in the east, where you will also find Bangladeshi and Pakistani restaurants. Although many dishes are likely to be too hot and spicy for young taste buds, there are many gentle versions that older children might relish, such as tandoori, tikka masala, korma and pasanda. Mild curries are often made with coconut milk. If the dish is too hot, a little yogurt will calm it down (water provides only temporary relief). Curries are served with rice or flat breads, such as naan or chapati, and crisp poppadoms. Vindaloo, madras and jalfrezi are among the spiciest. Two family-friendly Indian

restaurants with kids' menus are **Tamarind Kitchen**, which has its interiors designed by Russell Sage Studios, and the Covent Garden **Masala Zone**, with many Rajasthani puppets suspended from the ceiling.

Thai

Kensington and Fulham have a choice of Thai restaurants. There are also plenty of modest local restaurants and pubs and cafés that serve Thai food. Although some dishes are incredibly fiery (ask the waiter if unsure), Thai menus always contain milder ones, often inspired by Chinese cuisine. Satay (made with peanuts), noodle recipes such as pad Thai, sweet and sour dishes and spare ribs usually appeal to children.

Below left Indian restaurants and curry houses line Brick Lane in East London *Below right* The interior of a Chinese restaurant in Chinatown, in the heart of the West End

Greek and Turkish

The food is very similar to that of the Middle East, with meze (small bites and dips) being an integral part of the meal. Greek specialities include tzatziki (yogurt, garlic and cucumber dip), dolmadakia (vine leaves stuffed with rice, herbs and sometimes meat), spanakotyropita (filo pastry parcels filled with spinach and feta cheese), keftedes (meatballs with mint, garlic, breadcrumbs and eggs), moussaka (layers of potatoes, aubergines, courgettes and minced lamb topped with béchamel sauce and cheese), lamb and chicken kebabs and simply grilled meat and fish.

Similar Turkish dishes have slightly different names: for instance, cacik is a version of tzatziki and dolma of dolmadakia. It is traditional to start a meal with soup, and then children might enjoy kuzu tandir (oven cooked-lamb), eksili köfte (meatballs in a lemon sauce) or iskender (mixed grill with yogurt and tomato sauce served over pitta bread). In both cuisines, desserts such as baklava are very sweet and syrupy. Apart from Tas, with twenty branches across the city, these restaurants are concentrated in Central and North London, and dinner is often accompanied by music and dancing, and sometimes plate smashing in Greek restaurants. For Greek food, try the traditional tavernas **The Four Lanterns** and **Konaki**, while for Turkish, try **Sofra**.

Indonesian and Malaysian

If your children have adventurous tastes, seek out London's Indonesian and Malaysian restaurants: most are in the centre, including **Penang** and **Bali Bali**, which serve dishes from both countries. They don't have children's menus, but obliging staff will be happy to bring children's portions. Both cuisines have been influenced by Thailand, China, India and the Middle East. Rice and noodles are staples, and satay chicken and beef kebabs appear regularly on menus. Some dishes contain hot chilli peppers, but Indonesian specialities that might tempt children include gado-gado, (vegetable salad with peanut dressing) and nasi uduk (rice in coconut milk). Milder Malaysian dishes include Hainanese chicken and noodle dishes such as hokkien mee and konloh mee. Finish with fragrant purple mangosteen (fruit) or goreng pisang (banana fritters).

Below left The outside seating area of The Real Greek restaurant on the South Bank
Below right The beautiful decor at Masala Zone, Covent Garden

Middle Eastern

It is easy to overlook Middle Eastern food as a family option, but the selections of little hot and cold dishes – meze – particularly suit children. Most kids are familiar with hummus (a smooth, mild chickpea dip), but there are plenty of new dishes to try: samboussek (a pastry triangle filled with meat, cheese or vegetables), tabbouleh (a salad of bulgur wheat, chopped mint, parsley, tomato and spring onion, with lemon juice and olive oil) and fatoush (a lemon-flavoured salad with parsley, mint and thin, crisp pieces of toasted flatbread), as well as larger dishes of marinated chicken and lamb. At their best, these dishes are bursting with fragrant flavours without being too spicy. There is a cluster of Middle Eastern restaurants in and around Edgware Road, most of which specialize in Lebanese food, among them are several in the **Maroush** chain and, slightly further west, **Al Waha**.

British

Once burdened with a reputation for being tasteless and stodgy, British cuisine was unpopular with other nationalities. But times have changed and a clutch of high-profile chefs, such as Jamie Oliver, Heston Blumenthal and Gordon Ramsay, have transformed it, borrowing from other nations while never forgetting their roots.

Some British restaurants make a great effort to appeal to families: one such is **Roast** in the foodie paradise of Borough Market. Here, you will find high chairs, colouring books and a children's menu, as well as excellent traditional British cooking using locally sourced, free range and organic ingredients. Excellent food is also available in a number of the city's gastropubs – pub-restaurants that opened in the 1990s and serve good-quality food in pleasant surroundings, most of which welcome children.

Italian

Of all the world's cuisines, Italian food has to be the most child-friendly, at least in the form of pizza, pasta and ice cream. Children will also be welcomed and fussed over by the friendly staff in Italian restaurants, trattorie and pizzerias. The best places tend to be family-run and unpretentious, serving classic, reasonably priced dishes, with a special menu for children, perhaps including pasta with a simple sauce such as pesto (basil and cheese), pomodoro (tomato), bolognese (meat) or carbonara (eggs, cheese and ham or bacon), home-made pizza or simply cooked meat. There will usually be a choice of different flavoured ice creams to follow.

Spanish

The growing popularity of tapas restaurants and bars has raised the profile of Spanish cuisine in London. Like the Italians, the Spanish are well-disposed to children, and their tapas meals (small portions of different dishes) allow kids to try out new flavours and ingredients without having to order a whole course. The restaurants are usually informal and meals relaxed. Some have children's menus, but tapas such as jamón serrano and jamón ibérico (both dry-cured hams), calamares fritos (fried squid), gambas al ajillo (garlic prawns), tortilla (Spanish omelette) and croquetas (croquettes) are tasty without being too sophisticated.

French

The French, whose cuisine is considered one of the finest in the world, have been influencing British cooking ever since the Norman Conquest, and in London today

Below left A branch of the popular Italian chain Carluccio's *Below right* A serving of the classic British dish, fish and chips, best eaten straight from the paper wrapping it comes in

there are plenty of good French restaurants serving high-grade food. As people have become more health-conscious, the once typical rich cream- and butter-based sauces have been replaced by lighter, more delicate dishes. Brasseries and bistros are more likely to have children's menus than upmarket restaurants, and feature such favourites as steak or steak haché (burger) and frites (fries), chicken, omelettes and salade niçoise, with plenty of choice for dessert, from apple or lemon tart to chocolate mousse and ice cream.

North American

Londoners have had a love affair with North American food since the **Hard Rock Café** opened in 1971. With its juicy burgers and fries, hot dogs, barbecued chicken and ribs, creamy milkshakes, American-style decor and rock'n'roll music, the Hard Rock Café is a piece of the States transported to Old Park Lane. Other restaurants appeared in its wake, including the authentic and child-friendly **Chicago Rib Shack** in Knightsbridge, and a number of replica diners. The food is hearty, the setting is fun and children couldn't be better catered for.

Chain restaurants

They may not be the most imaginative choice, but chain restaurants are guaranteed to be a safe option for families, with high chairs, easy-wipe surfaces, suitable, good-value food, and no complicated dishes, pristine linen, snooty staff or exorbitant prices. For North American food, try **Ed's Easy Diner** and **The Diner**, replicas of a 1950s original; for good-quality burgers, try the **Gourmet Burger Kitchen**. Another popular chain, **Nando's**, specializes in chicken dishes with Portuguese flavours. For Chinese food, the **Ping Pong** chain serves up dim sum-style dumplings, and Pan-Asian dishes, mostly in soup forms, are staples at **Wagamama**. Although Japanese food is not usually popular with children, at **Benihana**, meals are theatre, with all the ingredients cooked sizzlingly before your eyes. **Maroush** and **Noura** are Lebanese chains; the **Real Greek** really is Greek; **Tas** is Turkish; **Wahaca** is Mexican and **Café Rouge** is French. Among the most family-friendly Italian chains are **Ask, Carluccio's, Pizza Express, Spaghetti House, Strada** and **Zizzi**. And for good-value international food that kids all love, there's **Giraffe** and restaurant chain **Leon**, with its delicious fast food.

Below left Tucking into a meal at Giraffe Below right A delicious selection of cakes and pastries on display at Paul

Shopping

Whether it's in a shiny modern mall, a famous traditional department store, a distinctive independent shop or a lively street market, shopping in London is an exciting experience. It is one of the world's great commercial cities, with thousands of stores selling everything anyone in the family could want. Although luxury items are expensive here, dedicated hunters can find bargains in year-round sales, street markets and cut-price shops.

Shopping streets

OXFORD STREET, W1

London's main shopping street is lined with more than 500 shops, from major department stores such as **Selfridges, John Lewis** (see Department stores and shopping malls for both) and **Debenhams** (Nos. 334–348), to the flagship stores of world-famous brands, including **Nike** (No. 236), **Topshop** (No. 216) and **Gap** (Nos. 223–225), along with a generous smattering of tacky tourist shops. At the western end, the Marble Arch **Marks & Spencer** (No. 458) is the company's largest and best-stocked store. Busy and brash, Oxford Street heaves with crowds at weekends, during the January and June sales and before Christmas, when it is decked with festive lights. When it's busy, using Oxford Street Tube station can be a disconcerting experience for anyone

with children. It's easier to use Bond Street Tube station, which is a little further west along Oxford Street, close to John Lewis and Selfridges.

KING'S ROAD, SW3

Chelsea's King's Road had its heyday in the "Swinging Sixties", when it was at the heart of bohemian London. Though not so trendsetting today, it remains popular for its upmarket High Street clothes, jewellery and accessories shops. On Sloane Square, **Peter Jones** is the department store West Londoners find indispensable. Other useful shops include **Trotters** (no. 34) and **Igloo** (no. 227) for children's clothes and a few toys; **Paperchase** (no. 289) for stationery, art supplies and gifts; and **Bluebird** (No. 350), a smart restaurant, chilled café with courtyard and food store rolled into one.

KENSINGTON HIGH STREET, W8

Favoured by fashion-conscious hippies in the 1960s and 1970s, "High Street Ken", as it is affectionately known, is not as crowded as Oxford Street and is possibly more functional than the King's Road. As for shops, it has all the usual suspects: **Trotters** (No. 127), **Topshop** (Nos. 42–44), for fashion-conscious children's clothes, **Russell & Bromley** (No. 151) for good-quality shoes, **Waterstone's** (No. 193) for books and magazines, and **TK Maxx** (Nos. 26–40), which sells designer clothes at knock-down prices. There is also a huge branch of the American organic grocery store, **Whole Foods Market** (Nos. 63–97). The best thing is that it's easy to escape to nearby Hyde Park or Kensington Gardens (see pp172–5) when the children start to droop and need an energizing runaround.

*Below left The children's clothing store Trotters, on the King's Road in Chelsea **Below right** Meeting a shop's mascot outside one of the many gift shops located on Oxford Street*

Department stores and shopping malls

HARRODS see p85
The UK's biggest shop will wow children and adults alike. It sells high-end clothes, beauty products, electronic goods, sports equipment, toys and has a fabulous food hall.

SELFRIDGES
One of London's most popular stores, Selfridges opened in 1909 in the Oxford Street building it still occupies today. It was founded by American magnate Harry Gordon Selfridge, who wanted to transform shopping from a chore into something fun. More recently it has become known for its bold window displays, which are almost as much of an attraction as the award-winning store itself. It has an excellent range of adult and kids' fashion, a superb food hall and a new toy department.

JOHN LEWIS
"Never knowingly undersold" is the motto of the John Lewis Partnership, which has a chain of practical, upmarket department stores in the UK, including Peter Jones. Its Oxford Street branch, opened in 1864 as a draper's shop, is the flagship store. It still has a particularly good range of fabrics, and holds a Royal Warrant as a supplier of haberdashery and household goods to the Queen. You'll also find everything you could possibly need for a baby, from rattles to a pushchair. Shoppers love the store's no-quibble returns policy and two-year guarantee on electrical goods.

WESTFIELD
This West London shopping mall, which opened in 2008, is so huge that it could comfortably hold 30 football pitches. It has plenty to occupy families who are happy to shop till they drop, with more than 250 shops over several levels, 50 restaurants and cafés, a "soft" play space and a multiplex cinema. Among the most child-oriented shops are the **Early Learning Centre**, **Mamas & Papas**, **LEGO**, **Build-A-Bear Workshop** and the **Disney Store**. "The Village" is an area devoted to the most sought-after designers, including **Versace**, **Miu Miu** and **Tiffany & Co**.

Clothing

RACHEL RILEY
Located in the heart of Marylebone, this stylishly decorated shop offers smart clothes for babies, children and ladies – all made in-house from beautiful fabrics. Launched in 1998, designer Rachel Riley's creations have become so popular that she has opened a store in New York. She designs custom-made outfits for special occasions on request. Also loved are her hand-made slippers, which are produced in France.

LA STUPENDERIA
If you're looking for something special for your children to wear, try the Italian label La Stupenderia, which has a swanky Knightsbridge store. The collection caters for boys and girls from newborn to 12 years old. The superb quality of the fabrics is typically Italian, and the look is classic and elegant: tweed jackets combined with shorts and waistcoats for boys; full skirts and dresses for girls. There are also plenty of well-cut casual styles, though even these come with a high price tag.

OH BABY LONDON
New Zealand-born designer Hannah McHalick was so uninspired by the choice of dull, pastel-coloured baby clothes on the market when she was pregnant, that she started creating her own fun, original designs. She sells her cool clothes online via the website, for kids aged 0–8, including T-shirts and playsuits with clever captions.

Below left Main concourse of the vast Westfield Centre in White City *Below right* Playtime in the Toy Kingdom area of the enormous Harrods department store in Knightsbridge

Books

TALES ON MOON LANE

This award-winning, independent children's bookshop is committed to making books and reading fun. The family-centred environment is the setting for regular public events, including book fairs and visits by popular children's authors, and the knowledgeable staff are always on hand to help identify a book that is right for your child.

CHILDREN'S BOOKSHOP

This family-run children's bookshop is one of the oldest in the UK and has delighted several generations of young customers. The shop stocks over 25,000 books, suitable for anyone from babies to teenagers, and hosts author signings as well as Thursday morning story time. The enthusiastic staff are always happy to offer guidance.

Toys and games

BENJAMIN POLLOCK'S TOYSHOP

If you think toys were better in the past than they are today, this is the place to confirm your belief. Pollock's sells all kinds of traditional toys, from spinning tops and music boxes to rag dolls and tiny tea sets. The original shop in Shoreditch was run by Benjamin Pollock, who

produced toy theatres. The Covent Garden shop still stocks a wonderful array of these, along with puppets – finger, glove and on strings.

DAVENPORT'S MAGIC SHOP

Tucked away in an arcade, this shop is a must for all aspiring members of the Magic Circle. It was established in 1898 by Lewis Davenport, a magician and music hall entertainer, and is the oldest family-run magic shop in the world. Whether you're a novice or a pro, it's a treasure trove of ingenious tricks and illusions, some simple, others sophisticated. There are cards, books, DVDs and accessories, including handkerchiefs, miracle rings, balls and beakers.

DISNEY STORE

For children besotted with Jack Sparrow or Hannah Montana, this US import will be a hit. The Oxford Street store is one of three in Central London. Kids might be tempted by a *Toy Story* Zurg's Blaster or 3-D puzzle, a pair of pink cowboy boots just like Hannah Montana's or an iconic Mickey Mouse T-shirt.

EARLY LEARNING CENTRE

A British chain specializing in toys for very young children, the Early Learning Centre has ten London franchises operating out of

Mothercare stores, with the most central in the giant Westfield mall. Colourful and well-made, the indoor and outdoor toys are designed not only for play, but also to encourage mental and physical development. Tough, hard-wearing materials range from wood to plastic, and toys include puzzles and activity centres. The stores are child-friendly, with toys to try out.

HAMLEYS *see p181*

This is the kind of shop that Santa Claus shops at – floor after floor of every type of toy and game.

MYSTICAL FAIRIES

A dream come true for little girls and boys alike, the Mystical Fairies, organise customised parties, for all events and occasions, at a location chosen by you. The entertainers are talented and experienced to recreate the magic of any fairytale. There are clothes, fancy-dress costumes, accessories, as well as craft kits, games, stationery and a host of other toys guaranteed to enchant your little ones. The fairy dust only completes the magical experience.

HONEYJAM

Honeyjam was inspired by childhood memories of toyshops bursting to the brim with the most

Below left A stall selling freshly baked bread, pastries and savoury treats at Borough Market *Below right* A member of staff welcoming customers to the jam-packed Hamleys toy shop

enchanting and desirable toys, hanging from ceilings and filling table tops. With seven children between them, the two owners are passionate about toys and cater to all tastes and budgets. The selection here is a glorious blend of traditional and modern, silly and educational. A delight for children and adults alike.

Markets

BOROUGH see p146

Open Monday to Saturday, Borough Market is foodie heaven, with top-quality (and top-dollar) global treats as well as the best of British produce.

CAMDEN LOCK MARKET

This rambling weekend market has a fun mix of junk and wonderful finds, including antiques, books, music, crafts and new and second-hand street fashion. It started in a small way in 1974, since when it has spread along Chalk Farm Road. With a hippie-punk vibe, the main market is down beside Regent's Canal and makes a great family outing on a Saturday; Sundays can be a crush.

PETTICOAT LANE

An East End institution, this Sunday street market spills over from Petticoat Lane (whose real location

The Lowdown

Benjamin Pollock's Toyshop 44 The Market, Covent Garden, WC2E 8RF; 020 7379 7866; www.pollockscoventgarden.co.uk

Camden Lock Market www.camdenmarket.com

Children's Bookshop 29 Fortis Green Road, Muswell Hill, N10 3HP; 020 8444 5500; www.childrensbookshoplondon.com

Davenport's Magic Shop 7 Charing Cross Underground Arcade, The Strand, WC2N 4HZ; 020 7836 0408; www.davenportsmagic.co.uk

Disney Store 350-352 Oxford Street, W1C 1JH; 020 7491 9136; www.disneystore.co.uk

Early Learning Centre (Mothercare) Unit 1082, Westfield Shopping Centre, W12 7GB; 020 8749 4924; www.elc.co.uk

Honeyjam 2 Blenheim Crescent, W11 1NN; 020 7243 0449; www.honeyjam.co.uk

John Lewis 300 Oxford Street, W1A 1EX; www.johnlewis.com

King's Road kingsroad.co.uk

Mystical Fairies 020 7431 1888; www.mysticalfairies.co.uk

Oh Baby London 07939 150974; www.ohbabylondon.com

Oxford Street www.oxfordstreet.co.uk

Portobello Road www.portobelloroad.co.uk

Rachel Riley 82 Marylebone High Street, W1U 4QW; 020 7935 8345; www.rachelriley.co.uk

Selfridges 400 Oxford Street, W1A 1AB; www.selfridges.com

La Stupenderia 16 Motcomb Street, SW1X 8LB; 020 7245 6656; www.lastupenderia.com

Tales on Moon Lane 25 Half Moon Lane Herne Hill, SE24 9JU; 020 7274 5759; www.talesonmoonlane.co.uk

Westfield uk.westfield.com/london

is Middlesex Street) into the maze of roads that surrounds it, and is where you might catch traders chatting in Cockney rhyming slang. If your children are extremely early risers, come with the serious bargain hunters at 4am. The more touristy part isn't in full swing till 9am, although it gets very crowded by 11am. Bargains are likely to be elusive, but there's an impressive range of leather goods, clothes, jewellery and toys, plus fast food.

PORTOBELLO ROAD

Follow the Friday or Saturday crowds from Notting Hill Gate Tube station swarming to this vibrant street, lined with stalls, arcades and funky shops. Several markets rolled into one, it has more than 1,000 stalls, from upmarket antiques, jewellery and silverware as it heads north, to bric-a-brac, crafts, food, clothes and music. Dodge into Portobello Green covered market, just north of the Westway, for original youth fashion.

Below left Storytime at one of London's popular children's bookshops **Below right** A second-hand stall at Camden Lock Market, bursting with collectibles – books, magazines, toys and much more

Entertainment

London's theatre *(see pp46–7)*, music and cinema scene is one of the very best in the world – and there's plenty for families to enjoy. There are children's festivals, most notably Imagine, on the South Bank in February. To find out what's coming up, register for a free bulletin at *www.officiallondontheatre.co.uk*, and check the listings on *www.timeout.com/london/kids* or *www.visitlondon. com/attractions/family*.

Music

London's smartest music venues are keen to woo families: the **Royal Opera House** *(see pp90–91)* puts on Christmas shows, Sounding Out workshops and a Summer Screens season, which beams live opera and ballet from Covent Garden onto big screens in Trafalgar Square and Canary Wharf. Nearby, at the London Coliseum, the **English National Opera's** kids' music-making sessions are pitched at ages six months and up – while the grown-ups get to sneak off and enjoy a matinee. There are Saturday afternoon classical concerts for families at **St Martin-in-the-Fields Church** on Trafalgar Square, and regular Discovery Concerts for ages 7–12 from the **London Symphony Orchestra**. There are also strong children's programmes at **Wigmore Hall** in the West End (mostly chamber music) and the **Southbank Centre's** *(see p164)* Royal Festival Hall (jazz, world and classical). Summer brings free outdoor music and theatre to **The Scoop**, beside Tower Bridge.

A popular outdoor concert venue is Hampstead's **Kenwood House** *(see pp216–17)*. London's grandest alfresco venue, however, must be **Somerset House** *(see p93)*, which invites pop stars to its courtyard in August.

Cinema

London's West End cinemas, such as the **Odeon Leicester Square**, show mostly mainstream Hollywood fare. For more eclectic movies, try the **Barbican Centre's** *(see p138)* Framed Film Club or its London Children's Film Festival week, in November, when kids get to make films as well as watch them. The Southbank Centre's **British Film Institute's (BFI)** *(see p162)* programme of children's film focuses on the BFI IMAX – book ahead for its Film Funday gatherings. Family clubs run at cinemas across the city, including **Clapham Picture House**, the **Electric Cinemas** in Portobello Road and Shoreditch and the **Renoir** in Bloomsbury; while summer heralds 12 days of screenings in the courtyard at Somerset House.

Arts and crafts

There is always something creative afoot for families at the city's art goliaths, such as the **National Gallery** *(see pp80–81)*, **Tate Modern** *(see p148)*, the **British Museum** *(see pp102–3)* and the **National**

Below left Children watching the interactive "bubbles bubbles bubbles" show at the Science Museum *Below right* A child learning how to knit with characters dressed in Tudor costume at Sutton House

Portrait Gallery *(see pp82–3).* Family days at **Sutton House** *(see p212)* offer fancy dress, activities and more.

The **Whitechapel Gallery** *(see p127)*, in the East End, boasts family workshops most weekends in its dedicated children's studio. At the distinctly more traditional **Dulwich Picture Gallery** *(see p224)* twice-monthly "Artplay" sessions spill out into the grounds on Wednesdays in summer: bring a picnic. Bloomsbury's **Cartoon Museum** has a permanent art room for kids, and monthly doodling drop-ins for families. In summer, don't miss the outdoor season at the **Serpentine Galleries** *(see pp176–7)*, set in its landmark pavilion on the lawns of Kensington Gardens. An art-themed "playscape" is in the offing at the Serpentine's new satellite gallery nearby.

The **V&A Museum** *(see p184)* offers "Drop-in Design" sessions on Sundays and Saturday workshops in applied arts for older children, and masterminds the **London Design Festival** every September.

The best of the rest

Little bookworms are well looked after in London, with free family storytelling events at nearly all the major museums across the city (covered in the sightseeing part of this guide). So, too, are budding scientists, with the plethora of live science demonstrations, shows and hands-on sessions that take place regularly: kids can get to grips with rocket-launching at the **Science Museum** *(see pp180–81)* and "speed surgery" at the **Old Operating Theatre**

(see p151). Entertaining "Nature Live" shows run more or less daily at the **Natural History Museum** *(pp182–3)*, while there are dedicated space shows for children at the **Royal Observatory's** *(see p201)* planetarium in Greenwich. Finally, no family should miss the world-class clowning, magic and pop-opera on the streets of Covent Garden.

The Lowdown

Cartoon Museum 35 Little Russell Street, WC1A 2HH; 020 7580 8155; www.cartoonmuseum.org

Clapham Picture House 76 Venn Street, SW4 0AT; 0871 902 5727; www.picturehouses.co.uk

Electric Cinemas 191 Portobello Road, W11 2ED; 020 7908 9696; 64-66 Redchurch Street, Shoreditch, E2 7DP; 020 3350 3490; www.electriccinema.co.uk

English National Opera London Coliseum, St. Martin's Lane, WC2N 4ES; 020 7845 9300; www.eno.org

Imagine Children's Festival Southbank Centre, Belvedere Road, London, SE1 8XX; 020 7960 4200; www.southbankcentre.co.uk/whats-on/festivals-series/imagine-childrens-festival

London Symphony Orchestra Barbican Centre, Silk Street, EC2Y 8DS; 020 7588 1116; www.lso.co.uk

London Design Festival 020 7242 6022; www.londondesignfestival.com

Odeon Leicester Square Covent Garden, Panton Street, Tottenham Court Road; 0871 224 4007; www.odeon.co.uk

Renoir Cinema Brunswick Square, WC1N 1AW; 033 0500 1331; www.curzoncinemas.com

Royal Observatory Blackheath Avenue, SE10 8XJ; www.rmg.co.uk

St Martin-in-the-Fields Church Trafalgar Square, WC2N 4JJ; 020 7766 1100; www.smitf.org

The Scoop 2a More London Riverside, SE1 2DB; 020 7403 4866; www.morelondon.com

Wigmore Hall 36 Wigmore Street, W1U 2BP; 020 7935 2141; www.wigmore-hall.org.uk

Below left Getting creative during the Framed Film Club at the Barbican Centre **Below right** *Enthralled children at a Sounding Out workshop at the Royal Opera House*

Best Theatres and Shows

One of the major centres of theatre in the world, London offers a remarkable range of superb, high-quality drama. Across the different categories of theatre – subsidized, West End and fringe – there is always a choice of plays to entertain and engage children of all ages, as well as their parents. Alongside new productions, there are also plenty of old favourites to choose from.

Best theatres

HALF MOON YOUNG PEOPLE'S THEATRE

Founded in the 1980s in East London, Half Moon produces theatre for and with young people. The company uses drama to teach, inspire and engage children from all backgrounds and with all abilities. Plays are often by promising new playwrights. The London season runs from October to April.

LITTLE ANGEL THEATRE

This 100-seat puppet theatre, in a former Temperance Hall in Islington, puts on plays and runs workshops, during which a production is developed and the puppets made. The Little Angel Theatre tours worldwide and showcases performances by visiting companies. Various cultures inspire productions, which include firm favourites *The Secret Garden* and *The Sleeping Beauty*.

The theatre also runs creative family Fun Days to coincide with shows.

LYRIC THEATRE HAMMERSMITH

It is not specifically a children's theatre, but the Lyric often puts on wonderful shows for children in its two superb performance spaces. The theatre also offers a lively pantomime at Christmas, as well as imaginative hands-on activities, usually geared to under-7s, such as "Messy Play" workshops.

NATIONAL THEATRE

Each year, London's main publicly funded theatre stages a number of productions for children, mostly during the holidays. It has three auditoriums, ranging from the grand Olivier, the Lyttelton and the more intimate Dorfman. The summer Watch this Space Festival, which celebrates outdoor theatre, offers children's performance classes.

POLKA THEATRE

More than 100,000 children visit this Wimbledon theatre every year. Its aim is to entertain, inspire and stimulate, both with brand-new plays and adaptations of much-loved classics. The plays, shown in two auditoriums, are chosen not only to spark kids' imaginations, but to be accessible and relevant. Its Early Years programme embraces simple, visual stories for children between ages 6 months and 6 years.

PUPPET BARGE

A unique concept, this floating puppet theatre makes a terrific family outing. The 55-seat barge has a regular mooring in Little Venice from April–July, but tours each summer, with a mooring in Richmond August–September. The company, Movingstage, is known for its inventive productions and traditional stories with a modern twist.

Below left A performance of The Tempest by puppets at the Puppet Barge, moored in Little Venice *Below right* Actors and puppets take to the stage in a vibrant performance of The Lion King

UNICORN THEATRE

From a mobile theatre operating out of an old truck, the Unicorn has grown into one of the UK's flagship children's companies, with an airy, purpose-built Borough district building. Here, it stages more than 600 performances a year. Family workshops complement the shows by exploring their various themes.

Best family shows

THE LION KING

Since 1999, this joyful screen-to-stage musical has been delighting audiences at the Lyceum Theatre with its magical evocation of the Serengeti Plain, re-created through movement and puppetry. Visually, it is spectacular: the stage is packed with dancers sporting fabulous costumes and masks, and there is rousing African-inspired music.

SHREK THE MUSICAL

The bad-tempered yet lovable green ogre, who won hearts in the hit DreamWorks movie, translates smoothly to the theatre. The lively show follows the improbable hero and his trusty donkey on a mission to rescue the beautiful but feisty Princess Fiona. **Shrek's Adventure**, a family-friendly attraction, with a 4-D movie and interactive fairytale

shows, is housed in the former London County Hall on South Bank.

WICKED

The stage prequel to *The Wizard of Oz*, *Wicked* delves into the past of two Oz witches reinvented as university students – the good Glinda and the Wicked Witch of the West, Elphaba. It premiered in London at the Apollo Victoria Theatre in 2006, and has been showing there ever since. It can be appreciated on by adults and children alike.

Tickets

London's West End theatreland is the place for blockbusting shows. Visit *www.thisistheatre.com* for the latest listings. Calls to a theatre box office will usually be redirected to ticketing giant **Ticketmaster**, which has an online 'Family Shows' section (*www.ticketmaster.co.uk*). For discounted seats, visit **Tkts** (Leicester Square; open 10am–7pm Mon–Fri, 11am–4pm Sun); the website lists bargains (*www.tkts.co.uk*), but does not sell tickets. Prime time for theatre-loving families is **Kids Week**, a fortnight of shows and workshops in August. Watch out for the Child's Play sessions at **Shakespeare's Globe** (*see pp146–7*). The **Theatre Royal Drury Lane** has

The Lowdown

Half Moon Young People's Theatre 43 White Horse Road, E1 0ND; 020 7709 8900; *www.halfmoon.org.uk*
Kids Week *www.kidsweek.co.uk*
Little Angel Theatre 14 Dagmar Passage, N1 2DN; 020 7226 1787; *www.littleangeltheatre.com*
Lyric Theatre Hammersmith Lyric Square, King Street, W6 0QL; 0871 221 1729; *www.lyric.co.uk*
National Theatre South Bank, SE1 9PX; 020 7452 3000; *www.nationaltheatre.org.uk*
Polka Theatre 240 The Broadway, SW19 1SB; 020 8543 4888; *www.polkatheatre.com*
Puppet Barge opposite 35 Blomfield Road, W9 2PF; 020 7249 6876; *www.puppetbarge.com*
Shrek's Adventure Westminstger Bridge Road, SE1 7PB; *www.shreksadventure.com/london*
Shrek The Musical *www.shrekthemusical.co.uk*
Theatre Royal Drury Lane Catherine Street, WC2B; 0844 412 4660; *www.reallyuseful.com/theatres*
The Lion King 0844 871 3000; *www.thelionking.co.uk*
Unicorn Theatre 147 Tooley Street, SE1 2HZ; 020 7645 0560; *www.unicorntheatre.com*
Wicked *www.wickedthemusical.co.uk/london*

London's child-friendliest backstage tour (book the costumed version) and those at the **National Theatre** and **Regent's Park Open-Air Theatre** (*see p112*) are fun, too.

Below left The interior of the Unicorn Theatre near London's South Bank Below right Actors performing in All Join in and Other Stories *at Wimbledon's renowned Polka Theatre*

London at Play

A visit to a theme park, playground or fun zone can be the highlight of a family holiday, but it's always best to plan ahead. Buy tickets in advance online and try to go on a weekday to avoid the biggest queues. Check with theme parks and fun zones for height restrictions – minimum and maximum – so if your children are too small or tall, they won't be disappointed. Fun zones can close to the public when hired for private parties, so check they're open before setting out.

Best theme parks

CHESSINGTON WORLD OF ADVENTURES
A mix of amusement park and zoo, Chessington and its themed lands will keep everyone entertained for the day. Older kids will be keen to try white-knuckle rides, such as Dragon's Fury, a spinning roller coaster, and Runaway Train, which careers along at speed, while the tamer Bubbleworks and Toytown rides are perfect for little ones. Take the Safari Skyway to spy the zoo's big cats, gorillas and sea lions.

THORPE PARK
Smaller than Chessington, Thorpe Park nevertheless features record-breaking rides including Stealth, Europe's fastest roller coaster and Tidal Wave, a terrifyingly high water ride, as well as the Colossus and Nemesis Inferno roller coasters. There are calmer alternatives exclusively for families with young children, such as the scenic Canada Creek Railway and the Wet Wet Wet water slide.

Best playgrounds

BATTERSEA PARK ADVENTURE PLAYGROUND
A host of fun things to climb up, slide down, swing on, scramble over and explore make this wooden adventure playground a great place for 5–16 year-olds. The nearby toddlers' playground is full of colourful structures to play on.

CORAM'S FIELDS
This Bloomsbury playground was built on the site of a children's hospital. There are grassy areas and equipment for all ages, including climbing frames, slides and a zip wire. The big draw for toddlers, apart from the sandpits and paddling pool, is pets' corner, with its sheep, goats, rabbits and other animals.

DIANA, PRINCESS OF WALES MEMORIAL PLAYGROUND see p174

HOLLAND PARK ADVENTURE PLAYGROUND
For any would-be Tarzan aged 5 plus, this playground is perfect. It contains swinging ropes, an aerial runway, a zip wire, climbing frames and a tower, as well as swings, a giant tyre and slides. Conveniently placed next door, is an enclosed play area for tots, with swings, slides and a seesaw.

Best fun zones

BRAMLEY'S BIG ADVENTURE
Kids up to age 11 play happily and safely in this indoor playground. It consists of a colourful three-level frame, a maze of slides, ball pools,

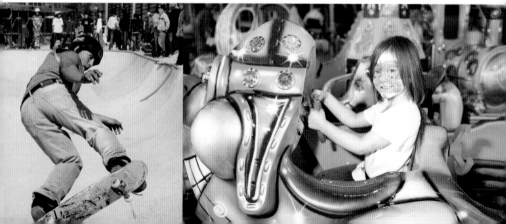

Below left Riding the excellent bowl at Camden's Cantelowe Skate Park *Below centre* All the fun of the fair on a carousel at Gambado Chelsea *Below right* Feeding time at the squirrel monkey enclosure, Chessington World of Adventures

Above *The exciting Colossus roller coaster at Thorpe Park* **Left** *Imaginative adventure park, Coram's Fields*

swings, ladders and a "spook den" complete with sound effects. It is all designed to build confidence by challenging children physically and intellectually as they work out their routes. There are separate areas for under-5s and babies, and a café for parents if the noise gets too much.

CLOWNTOWN

North London's version of Bramley's, ClownTown has a similar activity frame with slides, runways, rope climbs and "spook room" to keep young adventurers entertained. It has an area for crawlers and one for toddlers, with a ball pool, bouncy castle and climbing zone. On some weekdays, craft sessions are held and there is also an on-site café.

GAMBADO, CHELSEA

This large indoor adventure play centre holds dodgems, a "Tiger Pots" ride and a huge multi-level play frame. Kids will spend all day on the fairground rides, sliding, climbing and squeezing through tunnels, or having their faces painted. There's a junior climbing wall for budding mountaineers; a sensory play area for tots; and free Wi-Fi access for adults, while friendly staff are on hand. Birthday parties are

catered for, and there is another Gambado in Watford for those staying in north London.

Best BMX & skate parks

BAY SIXTY6

Tucked under the Westway in Notting Hill, this concrete street park is practical, well equipped and under cover if it rains. It has a bowl, jump and fun boxes, a handrail, transitions, ramps and pipes. The park suits beginners as well as experienced BMX riders and skate boarders. There are sessions for novice boarders on Saturday and Sunday mornings, and set times for BMXers.

CANTELOWES SKATEPARK

One of the best BMX/skateparks in London, this has a cradle, concrete bowl, mini and vertical ramps, skid rails, practice pavements, a fun box and performance platform. There are separate areas for beginners and experts. The park is supervised and floodlit after dark.

The Lowdown

Battersea Park Adventure Playground https://batterseapark.org/info/what-to-do/kids/playgrounds/
Bay Sixty6 66 Acklam Rd, W10 5YU; 020 8969 4669; www.baysixty6.com
Bramley's Big Adventure 136 Bramley Rd, W10 6TJ; 020 8960 1515; www.bramleysbigadventure.co.uk
Cantelowes Skatepark Cantelowes Gardens, 212 Camden Rd, NW1 9HG; www.skateparks.co.uk/london/cantelowes-skatepark/
Chessington World of Adventures Leatherhead Rd, Chessington, Surrey KT9 2NE; 0871 663 4477; www.chessington.com
ClownTown The Coppetts Centre, N12 0SH; 020 8361 6600; clowntown.co.uk
Coram's Fields www.coramsfields.org
Gambado, Chelsea 7 Station Court, Townmead Rd, SW6 2PY; 020 7384 1635; www.gambado.com/centres/chelsea/
Holland Park Adventure Playground www.dayoutwiththekids.co.uk/holland-park-adventure-playground
Thorpe Park Staines Rd, Chertsey, Surrey KT16 8PN; 0871 663 1673; www.thorpepark.com

Sporting London

London has an impressive variety of sports on offer, to be enjoyed both as a spectator and a player – below are some of the most popular. Enthusiastic young fans might enjoy a behind-the-scenes glimpse of their favourite sports stadium. Most of these, including Wembley (football), Twickenham (rugby) and Lord's (cricket), organize regular tours.

Athletics

Most major track and field events are held at **Crystal Palace National Sports Centre**, but one of the most fun events of the year is the **Virgin Money London Marathon**, with a course from Blackheath to the Mall through Central London. Runners will find tracks at **Battersea Park Millennium Arena** and **Linford Christie Sports Centre**. For more casual running, there's a track in **Regent's Park**.

Cricket

An integral part of an English summer, amateur cricket matches are played throughout London at the weekends. Among the more central are those in **Regent's Park** and on **Barnes Common**. Watch professional cricket, try **Lord's**, home of the famous MCC (Marylebone Cricket Club) and Middlesex, or Surrey's **Kia Oval**.

Football

Football (or soccer) is the UK's most popular spectator sport. The season runs from Aug–May, and fans flock to cup finals and international games at **Wembley Stadium**. London's top clubs are **Arsenal** and **Tottenham Hotspur** in north London and **Chelsea** in west London. However, it is easier to come by tickets to see less high-profile teams, such as west London's **Queens Park Rangers**, and **Crystal Palace** in south London.

Horse Riding

Stables are located near a number of London parks. **Ross Nye** and **Hyde Park Stables** are on Hyde Park's doorstep. **Stag Lodge Stables** are just outside Richmond Park's Robin Hood Gate, and **Ridgway** and **Wimbledon Village Stables** are both within easy reach of Richmond Park and Wimbledon Common.

Ice-skating

London's major permanent covered rinks are **Queens Club**, and **Streatham Ice Arena**. During winter months, outdoor temporary ice rinks crop up across the city. Popular ones are at **Broadgate, Hampton Court, Hyde Park,** the **Natural History Museum, Somerset House** and the **Tower of London**. All are floodlit, many run until 10pm.

Rowing

Of the regular races on the Thames, the highlight is the **Oxford and Cambridge Boat Race** from Putney to Mortlake. Supporters line the river to watch these rival universities compete on a Saturday in late March or in early April. Rowing is also a fun family activity, and there are boats for hire on the **Serpentine** (Easter–Oct) and the lakes in **Greenwich** (Feb–Oct) and **Regent's parks** (Apr–Sep).

Below left Skating on the outdoor ice rink at the Natural History Museum *Below centre* Enjoying a riding lesson at Hyde Park Stables *Below right* Fans celebrating in the stands at Wembley Stadium

Rugby

A 15-a-side sport, rugby union has certain similarities to American football. International and major matches are played at **Twickenham Stadium**, the sport's headquarters. London-based clubs include **Harlequins, London Welsh, London Scottish** and **Rosslyn Park**. Matches can be watched most Saturday afternoons (Sep–Apr).

Swimming

Although there are many pools in London, surprisingly few are geared towards children. For kid's pools, try **Brentford Fountain, Newham** and **Woolwich Waterfront Leisure Centres**, which all have water slides. **Finchley Lido Leisure Centre** has indoor and outdoor pools and is popular with families. **Chelsea Sports Centre** and **Oasis** are not so family-friendly, but are more central. For outdoor pools, try **Oasis** or the **Parliament Hill** or **Serpentine lidos**.

Tennis

There are quite a few municipal tennis courts around London, and these can usually be booked on the day. Bring your own tennis racket and balls. Good local courts include **Holland Park** and **Battersea Park**. When it comes to watching tennis, June–July brings the grass court **AEGON Championships** at Queens Club and, of course, **Wimbledon**, the home of the sport – a must for any tennis or strawberry enthusiast.

Water sports

Sailing, canoeing and kayaking courses and more are on offer for kids aged 8+ at **Thames Young Mariners, Docklands Sailing and Watersports Centre, Surrey Docks Watersports Centre** and **Royal Victoria Dock Watersports Centre**. For less complicated water sports, there is a children's pond in Regent's Park with mini pedal boats (over-5s).

The Lowdown

Athletics
Battersea Park Millennium Arena enablelc.org/bpma
Crystal Palace National Sports Centre www.bettervenues.org.uk/venues/crystal-palace
Linford Christie Sports Centre www.lbhf.gov.uk/sport/leisure-centres/linford-christie-outdoor-sports-centre
Regent's Park www.royalparks.org.uk/parks/the-regents-park
Virgin Money London Marathon www.virginmoneylondonmarathon.com

Cricket
Barnes Common Cricket Club www.barnescommoncc.com
Kia Oval www.kiaoval.com
Lord's www.lords.org
Regent's Park Cricket Club www.regentspark.play-cricket.com

Football
Arsenal www.arsenal.com
Chelsea www.chelseafc.com
Crystal Palace www.cpfc.co.uk
Queens Park Rangers www.qpr.co.uk
Tottenham Hotspur www.tottenhamhotspur.com
Wembley www.wembleystadium.com

Horse Riding
Hyde Park Stables www.hydeparkstables.com
Ross Nye Stables www.rossnyestables.co.uk
Ridgway Stables www.ridgwaystables.co.uk
Stag Lodge Stables www.ridinginlondon.com
Wimbledon Village Stables www.wvstables.com

Ice-skating
Broadgate www.broadgate.co.uk
Hampton Court www.hamptoncourtpalaceicerink.co.uk
Hyde Park www.hydeparkwinterwonderland.com
Natural History Museum www.nhm.ac.uk/visit/exhibitions/ice-rink.html
Queens Club www.queensiceandbowl.co.uk
Somerset House www.somersethouseicerink.org.uk
Streatham Ice Arena www.better.org.uk/leisure-centre/london/lambeth/streatham-ice-and-leisure-centre
Tower of London www.toweroflondonicerink.co.uk

Rowing
Greenwich www.parkboatslondon.co.uk/greenwich-park

Oxford and Cambridge Boat Race www.theboatrace.org
Regent's Park www.royalparks.org.uk/parks/the-regents-park/things-to-see-and-do/sports-and-leisure/boat-and-pedalo-hire
Serpentine www.royalparks.org.uk/parks/hyde-park/things-to-see-and-do/sports-and-leisure/boating-in-hyde-park

Rugby
Harlequins www.quins.co.uk
London Scottish www.londonscottish.com
London Welsh www.london-welsh.co.uk
Rosslyn Park www.rosslynpark.co.uk
Twickenham Stadium www.englandrugby.com/twickenham

Swimming
Brentford Fountain Leisure Centre www.fusion-lifestyle.com/centres/Brentford_Fountain_Leisure_Centre
Chelsea Sports Centre www.better.org.uk/leisure-centre/london/kensington-and-chelsea/chelsea-sports-centre
Finchley Lido Leisure Centre www.better.org.uk/leisure-centre/london/barnet/finchley-lido-leisure-centre
Newham Leisure Centre www.activenewham.org.uk/newham
Oasis www.better.org.uk/leisure-centre/london/camden/oasis-sports-centre
Parliament Hill Lido www.cityoflondon.gov.uk/things-to-do/green-spaces/hampstead-heath/swimming/Pages/default.aspx
Serpentine Lido www.serpentinelido.com
Woolwich Waterfront Leisure Centre www.better.org.uk/leisure-centre/london/greenwich/waterfront-leisure-centre

Tennis
AEGON Championships www.lta.org.uk/major-events/aegon-championships/
Battersea Park www.batterseapark.org/info/what-to-do/sports/tennis/
Holland Park www.rbkc.gov.uk/leisure-and-culture/sports/tennis
Wimbledon www.wimbledon.com

Water sports
Docklands Sailing and Watersports Centre www.dswc.org
Royal Victoria Dock Watersports Centre www.royaldockstrust.org.uk/summerwatersports.htm
Surrey Docks Watersports Centre www.everyoneactive.com/centre/surrey-docks-water-sports-centre
Thames Young Mariners www.surreyoutdoorlearning.uk/facilities/thames-young-mariners

Outdoor London

Celebrated for its many beautiful parks, London even manages to cram green spaces into its bustling centre. Most of these larger expanses – and some of the small ones – date from the Middle Ages: some were always common land, others were preserved for the exclusive use of royalty as hunting grounds, and only later opened to the public. As a result, wherever you are in London, you are only minutes away from historic open spaces.

Battersea Park

With a boating lake, a small zoo and an adventure playground, this is an all-action destination (see pp186–9).

Blackheath

Once covered by thick gorse, which made it popular with highwaymen, Blackheath has long been a rallying point, from Wat Tyler's rebellious peasants in 1381 to suffragette marches in the early 20th century. It also has a sporting heritage: James I introduced the Scottish game of golf to England here, and it is the start of the London Marathon (see p50). The most popular pastime here is kite-flying.

Enjoying a pedalo session in the glorious surroundings of Regent's Park boating lake

Coram's Fields

This space has enough to keep kids happy: a paddling pool, a farmyard, a playground, sports pitches and play sessions (see p48 and p106).

Green Park

With mature trees and grassy lawns, Green Park (see p73) is perfect for walks and picnics. In early spring, carpets of daffodils turn the grass yellow. A royal hunting ground until Charles II enclosed it in 1668, it was turned into a pleasure garden in the early 18th century, with temples and pools (now long gone). Later, it became a favourite spot for duels.

Greenwich Park

You can see most of London on a clear day from this park. On its eastern side, excavations have unearthed evidence of a Roman temple. On one of the hills that crown it, stands the Royal Observatory, where east meets west at the Meridian Line (see p196).

Hampstead Heath

"The Heath", as locals call it, is a stunning area of hills, ponds, woods and glades. There is plenty for families, from outdoor swimming, model boating or the adventure playground. Nearby, Golders Hill Park has a children's zoo and putting green, and there's a great view from Parliament Hill (see p214).

Holland Park

Although bombs destroyed most of the Jacobean Holland House in 1941, its glorious park survived, with paths that wind through woods, and a wildlife enclosure that is home to peacocks and other exotic birds. A peaceful Japanese and formal flower garden, an adventure playground and play area, and space to kick a football, make it a park for all ages.

Hyde Park and Kensington Gardens

One of the finest royal parks in London, this is also close to many must-see sights (see pp174–5).

Primrose Hill

A good place to come when it snows, this 78-m (256-ft) hill (see p113), just north of Regent's Park, is perfect for tobogganing. In the 16th century, Henry VIII appropriated it for hunting, and it was not until 1841

Above Panoramic view over London from Primrose Hill *Below* A fine 12-pointer red deer stag and small female in Richmond Park

that the public were allowed in. It can be very windy at the top, which makes it popular with kite-flyers. From here, the view includes the O2 Arena and the Post Office Tower.

Regent's Park

Run around in open spaces to the sound of lions from nearby London Zoo, walk along the canal or enjoy the boating lake (see p112).

Richmond Park

Charles I's personal hunting ground, Richmond (see p232) is the largest and most wild of the royal parks. Its heath and woods are home to a large variety of native plants, birds and animals, including herds of red and fallow deer that roam freely.

Royal Botanic Gardens, Kew

No longer a stuffy Victorian botany collection, there are lots of exciting things for kids at the Royal Botanic Gardens (see pp228–9).

St James's Park

The oldest of the royal parks, this is close to Buckingham Palace (see p72).

Wimbledon and Putney Commons

Once popular for duels, these commons form London's largest expanse of heath and woodland. They are used for activities ranging from golf and horse riding to model boating and blackberry picking. Don't

miss the 1817 windmill, now the Windmill Museum (open Apr–Oct: 2–5pm Sat, 11am–5pm Sun & public hols; www.wimbledonwindmill.org. uk), with displays of models, and machinery, and a nearby Nature Trail.

WWT London Wetland Centre

More than 180 species of birds and animals shelter in this lovely nature reserve (see p230).

The Lowdown

Blackheath www.lewisham.gov.uk/inmyarea/openspaces/parks/blackheath/pages/default.aspx
Green Park www.royalparks.org.uk/parks/green-park
Greenwich Park www.royalparks.org.uk/parks/greenwich-park
Hampstead Heath www.cityoflondon.gov.uk/things-to-do/green-spaces/hampstead-heath/pages/default.aspx
Holland Park www.rbkc.gov.uk/leisure-and-culture/parks/holland-park
Primrose Hill www.royalparks.org.uk/parks/the-regents-park/things-to-see-and-do/primrose-hill
Richmond Park www.royalparks.org.uk/parks/richmond-park
St James's Park www.royalparks.org.uk/parks/st-jamess-park
Wimbledon and Putney Commons www.wpcc.org.uk
Windmill Museum www.wimbledonwindmill.org.uk

The History of London

Although there was only a small collection of huts beside the River Thames at the time of the first Roman invasion in 55 BC, some 100 years later, a small port and trading community had been established, which the Romans called "Londinium". Growing rapidly, London was the obvious choice for the capital by the time of the Norman Conquest in 1066. Over the next 1,000 years, the city grew in size and importance, becoming one of the major cities of the world.

The Romans

In AD 43, rampaging Romans under the Emperor Claudius defeated the unruly Celtic tribes of southeastern Britain and, in AD 50, founded "Londinium", building a bridge across the River Thames close to the site of the later London Bridge.

Early Roman London became a flourishing port and settlement at the centre of the network of straight roads that the Romans were so fond of building. In AD 60–61, a revolt by the Iceni tribe from Norfolk, led by the fierce warrior Queen Boudicca, ended with London being burnt to the ground. Like a phoenix, the city rose from the ashes to become capital of England, a prosperous financial and trading centre, and headquarters of Britain's Roman governor, with a market and its own mint. By AD 200, the Romans had fortified the city with a defensive wall, but the Roman Empire was already in decline. At the end of the 3rd century, the Romans had to use ferocious Germanic mercenaries to help them repel Saxon raiders. Roman rule ended in AD 410.

The Anglo-Saxons

The Romans' fine houses were left to decline, and the city remained mostly uninhabited for some 400 years. When the Anglo-Saxon warrior kings eventually arrived, they settled an area just to the west of the old Roman city. Anglo-Saxon London was not as developed as Roman London had been, becoming instead a simple farming town. During the early 9th century, however, London's importance as a market town increased. England reunited under the Kings of Wessex from Winchester (including King Alfred), Christianity was reintroduced and with it came education.

The Vikings

In 836 London was sacked by the Vikings, who continued their attacks throughout the 9th century. After Alfred the Great's victory over the Vikings in 878, London was returned to the Anglo-Saxons and there was a brief period of calm, during which the inhabitants moved east, back to the more secure area within the

A 10th-century vellum depicting Vikings arriving in England

rebuilt Roman walls. The raids started again in 994, until a final battle in 1014. Legend has it that in a fine strategic move, Olaf, an ally of the Anglo-Saxons, tied his boats to London Bridge and pulled it down – possibly the basis for the song, *London Bridge is Falling Down.*

The Normans

The year 1066 saw the Norman invasion of England. After the death of the Anglo-Saxon king, Edward

Timeline

Roman invaders build a bridge across the Thames and found "Londinium", fortifying it with a defensive wall

London sacked by Vikings; later the Anglo-Saxons regain control under Alfred the Great

First stone London Bridge constructed. Lined with houses and shops, it survives for more than 600 years

The Black Dea ravages the ci killing half of a Londoners

| AD 200 | 410 | 836 | 1070 | 1176–1209 | 1259 | 134 |

The Romans withdraw from Britain. London declines, becoming an Anglo-Saxon market town

Tower of London begun by William I to consolidate power after the Norman Conquest

"Provisions of Westminster" signed by Henry III, laying foundations for parliament

the Confessor, his war-like cousin, William of Normandy, claimed the throne, but found that Edward's brother-in-law Harold had been crowned in his place. William defeated Harold at Hastings, but didn't want to attack well-fortified London. Instead, he razed the fields around it and the city swiftly accepted William the Conqueror as king. He was crowned in Westminster Abbey on Christmas Day 1066.

Under the Normans, London thrived and in 1070 William started work on the Tower of London, where he lived until he moved to the Palace of Westminster, built alongside Westminster Abbey by Edward the Confessor in the mid-11th century.

The Middle Ages

In 1215, angered by heavy taxes, London supported the barons in drafting Magna Carta to limit the powers of King John. The 13th century saw a building boom in the city, with the construction of Henry III's abbey at Westminster (1245–1269) and the first St Paul's Cathedral (1280) – half as tall as the current version.

In 1338, Edward III made Westminster the place for regular Parliamentary sessions, but there was trouble ahead. In 1348, the Black Death struck the city, killing half its 60,000 inhabitants. In 1381, the peasants revolted: an army of serfs led by Wat Tyler took over London for two days, but the revolt ended when Tyler was killed by the

mayor. The early 15th century saw the rise of a wealthy class of former soldiers and tradesmen, threatening the feudal aristocracy. By 1461 London's support was crucial to Edward IV, who won the Wars of the Roses, to restore stability to England.

The Tudors

During the 16th-century rule of the Tudors, England was transformed from a minor state into a major world power, London's economy boomed and its population quadrupled. The downside was that slums developed on its outskirts. In Henry VIII's Reformation of 1533, the new gentry acquired the land freed by the dissolution of the monasteries (half of the city was occupied by religious buildings). After Henry's death, "Bloody Mary" reinstated Catholicism and martyred hundreds of Protestants at Smithfield from 1553–8. On Mary's death, Protestant Elizabeth I came to the throne. She was supported by the people of London for her 45-year reign, during which the city flourished as a centre of European trade, exploration and discovery.

A painting of Henry VIII with his third wife, Jane Seymour, and their son, Prince Edward, circa 1545

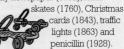
The "Princes in the Tower", 12-year-old Edward V and his brother Richard, disappear. Their uncle becomes King Richard III

Globe Theatre built by William Shakespeare's theatre company, the Chamberlain's Men

1381	1483	1533	1597

Rebels storm the Tower of London to demand an end to serfdom, in the failed Peasants' Revolt

Henry VIII breaks with the Vatican and forms the Church of England

The Stuarts

In the 17th century a new generation of moneyed gentry expanded the city's boundaries westwards by building on land in Piccadilly and Leicester Square. Puritanism increased as a reaction against the high-handed Stuart kings, James I and Charles I, and in the ensuing English Civil War (1642–9), London merchants put their finances behind Parliament. The war ended when Charles I was beheaded in London in 1649 and England became a Commonwealth republic under Oliver Cromwell. After Cromwell's death, there were numerous quick-fire changes of government and, fed up with the Puritan restrictions on simple pleasures such as dancing and theatre, Londoners vigorously supported the restoration of Charles II to the throne in 1660.

Illustration showing residents fleeing the Great Fire of London in 1666

Plague and fire

The Black Death broke out in 1665. Although there had been earlier outbreaks, this was the last and the worst, in which nearly 100,000 people died. Pits were dug and cartloads of bodies thrown into them. The following year, the Great Fire of London swept through the medieval city, after a blaze that started in a bakery in Pudding Lane spread to the surrounding streets. The fire destroyed 60 per cent of London, including St Paul's Cathedral. Reconstruction in the late 17th century saw stone buildings replace wooden ones and narrow streets swapped for broad ones. Sir Christopher Wren built 52 churches, including his masterpiece, the new St Paul's. The fire also cleansed the city of rats – the carriers of plague – and led to the dispersal of the population over a wider area.

Georgian London

In the early 18th century, the population exploded again, with an increase in the poor as well as the rich. By 1750 London had 675,000 inhabitants. The villages of Kensington, Knightsbridge and Marylebone were incorporated into the city, building started in Greenwich, and stylish St James's and Mayfair were developed for the elite. There were also slums to the east and south, where the poor drank too much gin and only one child in four lived beyond the age of five. In 1750 Westminster Bridge was opened – only the second over the Thames. The 1780 Gordon Riots, a violent Protestant uprising against Roman Catholic freedoms, led eventually to the establishment of the Metropolitan Police force in 1829. The policemen were known as "Bobbies" or "Peelers" after their founder, Robert Peel. Between 1820 and 1838, the foppish Prince Regent (later George IV) and architect John Nash developed Regent Street, Regent's Park, Buckingham Palace and The Mall.

The Victorian era

During the 19th century, London the rich, powerful capital of the British Empire. But as its wealth increased, so did its poverty. The overcrowding and foul, insanitary conditions of London's slums preoccupied Charles Dickens and other writers. In 1832–66 cholera killed thousands, and in the summer of 1858, the

Timeline

Guy Fawkes and his Catholic conspirators make an abortive attempt to blow up Parliament in the Gunpowder Plot

The Great Fire destroys the city, clearing the way for Sir Christopher Wren's city of stone, including St Paul's

Queen Victoria ascends the throne, and Buckingham Palace becomes the monarch's official residence

Canary Wharf, spearhea the regeneration of the Docklands as a busines quarter

| 1605 | 1649 | 1666 | 1721 | 1837 | 1863 | 199 |

Charles I beheaded at the Banqueting House, as Oliver Cromwell's Parliamentarians triumph in the English Civil War

Robert Walpole is named First Lord of the Treasury, effectively Britain's first prime minister

The first line opens on th London Underground; a comprehensive sewerag network follows later

smell of sewage in Thames grew so bad that it was called the "Great Stink" and Parliament had to stop work. But not everything was bad, Victorian successes included the 1851 Great Exhibition, celebrating British dominance in trade, science and industry; Charles Barry's Gothic Palace of Westminster (1840); the UK's railway network; London's first Underground line (1863); and Joseph Bazalgette's sewage system (1865–75). The quality of life improved with more mobility and progress in public health and education. In 1897, the normally rather reserved Victorians joyfully celebrated Queen Victoria's Diamond Jubilee with street parties.

Model Twiggy on the King's Road during the "Swinging" 1960s

The 20th century

In the early years of the 20th century, public transport expanded and so did the sprawling suburbs. During World War I (1914–18), women took over many of London's public services, and in 1918 the suffragettes won the vote for some women. In 1920–30, immigration increased, reaching an all-time population peak in 1939. In World War II, London was bombed heavily during the 1940–41 Blitz. The post-war years saw the Olympics at

Wembley in 1948, the Festival of Britain (1951) and a property boom from 1955–65. After the Great Smog of 1952, the 1956 Clean Air Act put a stop to London's famous "pea-soupers" and marked the end of using coal for heating.

In the 1960s, the city became known as "Swinging London", a centre of fashionable youth culture. There was conflict in the 1970s, when "The Troubles" in Northern Ireland made London a target of terrorist attacks by the Provisional IRA, and again in the mid-1980s when racial tension surfaced in the Brixton Riots. A boom in the 1980s was followed by bust in the 1990s.

The 21st century...

In 2000, Tony Blair's government created the Greater London Authority, led by an elected mayor. On 6 July 2005 London won the bid for the 2012 Olympics, but celebrations were short lived; terrorists bombed the London Underground and a bus the next day. Amid economic crisis, the first coalition government since World War II was formed in May 2010. In April 2011, London celebrated the wedding of Prince William and Kate Middleton and in 2012 it celebrated the Queen's Diamond Jubilee, followed by the Olympics. Theresa May took charge of the UK at one of the most volatile phases in its political history as UK voted to leave the EU. The referendum passed on 23 June, 2016 is commonly known as Brexit.

HEROES & VILLAINS

Boudicca
She burnt London to the ground in AD 60, but this warrior queen is a heroine to many because she almost beat the Roman invaders. Look for her on Westminster Bridge *(see p69)* and at All Hallows by the Tower *(see p125)*.

Dick Whittington
This 14th-century merchant became Lord Mayor of London four times. He was much loved – but nobody knows if he really owned a cat! Look for him at Westminster Abbey *(see pp66–7)* and The Guildhall *(see p133)*.

Guy Fawkes
In 1605 Fawkes tried to wipe out King James I by stacking gunpowder under the Houses of Parliament. He is remembered on Bonfire Night (5 Nov). Look for him at the Museum of London *(see pp136–7)*.

Christopher Wren
London's greatest architect helped the city rise from the ashes after the Great Fire of 1666, building 51 churches and St Paul's Cathedral. Look for him there *(see pp130–31)*, and at The Monument *(see p124)*.

Colonel Thomas Blood
This Irishman is famous for plotting to steal the Crown Jewels in 1671, disguised as a priest. His gang stuffed some of the gems down their trousers – but were captured while fleeing. Look for him at the Tower of London *(see pp122–3)*.

Charles Dickens
This famous writer created Oliver Twist and Mr Scrooge, and campaigned against the cruel treatment of poor children and orphans in London. Look for him at the Charles Dickens Museum *(see pp106–7)*.

	The Shard, the tallest building in the city opens	A terror attack in Westminster near the Houses of Parliament	
2012	**2013**	**2016**	**2017**
The Olympic Games come to London for the third time		Theresa May, becomes the second female prime minister. Sadiq Khan becomes London mayor. UK votes to leave the European Union	

The Queen's Household Cavalry
Mounted Regiment outside
Buckingham Palace

Exploring
LONDON

Westminster
and the West End

Only two things stand still in the thumping heart of Central London: the "living statues" in their fabulous costumes in Covent Garden, and the stony-faced sentries standing like toy soldiers outside Buckingham Palace. Everything else seems in perpetual motion, and there is enough to keep families fulfilled for weeks, including 40 theatres, a dozen cinemas and some of the world's greatest museums and galleries.

Bloomsbury and
Regent's Park

The City and
the East End

**Westminster
and the
West End**
Southwark and
the South Bank

Kensington,
Chelsea and
Battersea

Highlights

Guards Museum
Watch the Foot Guards leave Wellington Barracks, then don a bearskin in the museum and take home a soldier or two from the shop (see p76).

St James's Park
Say hello to squirrels and see the famous pelicans near Duck Island in this lush green wedge between Westminster and the West End. It's picnic paradise (see p74).

London Transport Museum
Step back in time in this giant "play barn" full of classic buses to board and vintage trains to ride. All aboard! (see p92).

Royal Opera House
Peeking into a rehearsal on a backstage tour of the opera house feels like a great privilege, while the family Christmas shows are amazing spectacles (see pp90–91).

Somerset House
Pack your beachwear and brave the water jets in the Neo-Classical Fountain Court. In winter, it hosts one of the most glamorous ice rinks in London (see p93).

The National Gallery
This place cleverly brings painting alive with "Teach Your Grown-ups About Art" trails, where the kids lead the tour (see pp80–81).

Left *Panoramic view of Westminster showing part of the London Eye, Big Ben and Westminster Abbey*
Above *The Young Dancer (1988), by Enzo Plazzotta, is a fitting statue for the theatrical area of Covent Garden*

The Best of
Westminster & the West End

From Big Ben to Buckingham Palace, Nelson's Column to the National Gallery, this is picture-postcard London, squeezing scores of museums and monuments into 5 square kilometres (2 square miles) on the north bank of the Thames. Visiting families can be in the House of Commons one minute, pretending to be the prime minister, and wander through the Queen's throne room the next – but please don't sit on Her Majesty's chair!

Pomp and circumstance

Soaking up the full majesty of royal London takes careful planning. The State Rooms at **Buckingham Palace** *(see pp74–5)* are open in summer only: book ahead online for the first tour of the day at 9:45am. There's just enough time to tour the palace and get to Wellington Barracks by 11am, when the troops line up for the **Changing the Guard** *(see p76)* – it gets less crowded here than on the Palace forecourt.

Visit the tombs of former monarchs at **Westminster Abbey** *(see pp66–7)* – resting place of 16 kings and queens – and be sure to follow the engaging children's trail. Admire, too, Big Ben and the impressive **Houses of Parliament** *(see p68)*. After lunch by the lake in **St James's Park** *(see p74)*, watch the pelicans get theirs – the daily feed takes place at 2:30pm. Finish the day with a horsey treat: either a tour of The Royal Mews (Mar–Dec – *see p76)* or a close-up look at the sentries at **Horse Guards Parade** *(see p70)*, where kids can dress up as guardsmen at the museum.

Seasonal festivities

Spring makes a colourful splash here, from the St Patrick's Day Parade that musters in Green Park in March to the London Marathon on The Mall in April. Children will love the twirling ribbons and dancing strings of the Covent Garden May Fayre & Puppet Festival (May).

In summer, Trooping the Colour at **Horse Guards Parade** celebrates the Queen's official birthday in June. It's a great time to take a riverboat cruise along the Thames. In the West End meanwhile, children can get free theatre tickets to a host of shows during Kids' Week *(see p46)*, which runs for a fortnight in August.

London puts on a good Christmas, too. Enjoy carols round the Norwegian Christmas tree in

Above right Covent Garden May Fayre & Puppet Festival
Right Spectacular New Year's Eve fireworks display

Above *Crowds gathered outside Buckingham Palace on The Mall, the finishing line for the London Marathon*

Trafalgar Square *(see p82)*, the bright lights of **Hamleys** toy shop in Regent Street *(see p85)*, or the fairy-tale ice rink at **Somerset House** *(see p93)*. There are two New Year celebrations to choose from: the fireworks show along the Thames on 31 December, or the dragons dancing through Chinatown for Chinese New Year about a month later.

Backstage West End

Begin a starry day out in Theatreland at the **Royal Opera House** *(see p90)* in Covent Garden. If it's Monday, be at the box office for 10am to get tickets for the free lunchtime recital. Failing that, sign up for the 10:30am backstage tour – a glimpse behind the scenes at the Royal Ballet, to see where the principal dancers practise their *pas de deux*. Next, explore the smart boutiques and busy lunch spots around **Covent Garden** *(see pp88–9)*, where there's always a mix of performers to see on the streets.

If it's Wednesday or Saturday, take in a matinée of a musical at Britain's oldest working playhouse, the **Theatre Royal Drury Lane** *(see p91)*. For star-struck youngsters, the stage door is in Russell Street. This theatre, too, offers family-friendly daily tours. As night falls, head for **Leicester Square** *(see p84)* and hunt for film-star handprints in the pavement, grab cut-price tickets for a show, or choose from dozens of films at the cinemas on every corner.

Art versus Science

It may be best known for shows and shopping, but the West End offers plenty to stimulate young minds, too. The galleries beside Trafalgar Square are the perfect introduction to fine art: the **National Gallery** *(see pp80–81)* has three audio-trails just for families, plus drawing and daubing workshops. Next door, the **National Portrait Gallery** *(see p82)* has artist-led "tour and draw" events. Tiny geniuses may prefer **Tate Britain** *(see pp68–9)*, which dispenses free build-it-yourself art boxes to children.

For children unmoved by Van Gogh and Van Eyck, how about the fascinating Faraday and Franklin? Both men have museums dedicated to them here. **The Royal Institution** *(see p77)* has restored the lab where Michael Faraday tamed electricity, and kids get to explore using a cool console packed with puzzles and games. The **Benjamin Franklin House** *(see p83)* uses a sound and light show to tell the great statesman's story.

Right *Buckingham Palace guards in traditional red tunics and bearskin hats during the Changing the Guard*

Westminster Abbey and around

Ever since Christmas Day 1066, when William the Conqueror was crowned here, Westminster Abbey has been the coronation site of monarchs – and the resting place of many too, including Henry V and Elizabeth I. Outside, the pomp of Parliament Square is dented a little by traffic, so save the surrounding sights for a Sunday, when it's quieter. St James's Park and the attractions along Whitehall can be comfortably tackled on foot, but hop on a bus (number 87 or 88) to visit the Tate Britain gallery.

Westminster and the West End

National Gallery *p78*

Covent Garden *p86*

Buckingham Palace *p72*

Westminster Abbey

River bus – a fun way to see many of the sights of Central London

The Lowdown

🚗 **Train** Charing Cross. **Tube** Westminster or St James's Park; Pimlico for Tate Britain. **Bus** Parliament Square: route numbers 3, 11, 12, 24, 53, 87, 88, 148, 159, 211 or 453; Tate Britain: 87, 88, C10, 185, 360, 436. **River bus** Westminster Pier to St Katharine's Dock daily, May–Sep; to Bankside on weekends and public holidays in winter. Seasonal services to Hampton Court, Kew Gardens to the west; Tower of London, Greenwich to the east

ℹ️ **Visitor information** Victoria Railway station, SW1E 5NE

🍽️ **Supermarkets** Tesco Express, 8 Bridge St, SW1A 2JR (opposite Big Ben). Costcutter, 31 Horseferry Rd, SW1P 2AY **Markets** Strutton Ground (St James's Park tube), 8am–6pm Mon–Fri; and Tachbrook St (Pimlico tube) 8am–6pm Mon–Sat

🎊 **Festivals** New Year's Day Parade (1 Jan); Trooping the Colour, Horse Guards Parade (Jun); Mayor's Thames Festival (Sep); Festival of Remembrance, Whitehall (11 Nov); State Opening of Parliament (Nov); Christmas Carol Service, Westminster Abbey (23 & 24 Dec)

➕ **Pharmacies** Boots, 11 Bridge St, SW1A 2JR (across from Big Ben), open daily. Or search at www.nhs.uk/servicedirectories

🛝 **Nearest playgrounds** Victoria Tower Gardens (Lambeth Bridge end); Causton St playground; and playground in St James's Park

Lancaster House

GREEN PARK

Buckingham Palace

BRESSENDEN PLACE

Cardinal Place

Victoria

Westminster Cathedral

Victoria

Queen Mother Sports Centre

BELGRAVE

WARWICK

The Houses of Parliament, seen from across the River Thames

Trying on a uniform at the Household Cavalry Museum on Horse Guards Parade

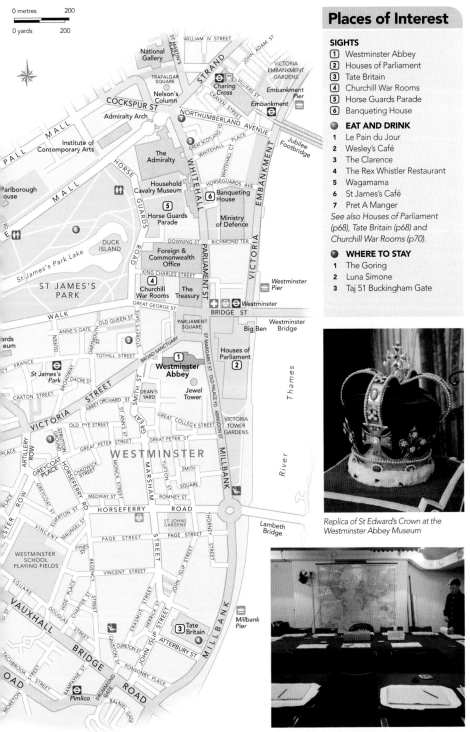

0 metres 200

0 yards 200

Places of Interest

SIGHTS

1. Westminster Abbey
2. Houses of Parliament
3. Tate Britain
4. Churchill War Rooms
5. Horse Guards Parade
6. Banqueting House

EAT AND DRINK

1. Le Pain du Jour
2. Wesley's Café
3. The Clarence
4. The Rex Whistler Restaurant
5. Wagamama
6. St James's Café
7. Pret A Manger

See also Houses of Parliament (p68), Tate Britain (p68) and Churchill War Rooms (p70).

WHERE TO STAY

1. The Goring
2. Luna Simone
3. Taj 51 Buckingham Gate

Replica of St Edward's Crown at the Westminster Abbey Museum

The shelter in the Churchill War Rooms, from where the prime minister conducted Britain's World War II campaign

① Westminster Abbey
Poets, princes and some rather smelly monks

Henry VIII ejected the Benedictine monks in 1540 when he dissolved the monasteries and founded the Church of England, but Westminster Abbey has retained its importance down the centuries. As well as witnessing the coronations of 39 kings and queens, the atmospheric building is also the final resting place of many world-famous writers, musicians and scientists. It is packed full of spooky tombs, sleeping knights and secret gardens, and there is even a creepy wax museum.

Gargoyle over the door of Westminster Abbey

Key Features

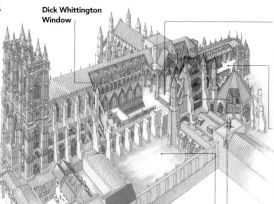

Dick Whittington Window

Dick Whittington Window This shows London's most famous lord mayor – his cat is hiding at his feet in the stained glass.

High Altar Queen Elizabeth II was crowned here in 1953, in front of 8,251 packed-in people. The gilded Coronation Chair is 700 years old – and has been carved with graffiti by naughty Westminster schoolboys.

Lady Chapel This 16th-century chapel has a stone ceiling as delicate as a cobweb, and there are cheeky carvings under the choir stalls. Look for a wife thrashing her husband's bottom with a birch rod!

Poets' Corner The first great writer buried here was Geoffrey Chaucer in 1556. The novelist Thomas Hardy's ashes are here, but not his heart, which is buried alongside his first wife in his beloved Dorset.

Cloisters These contain the earliest parts of the abbey, including the Pyx Chamber, a strong room where kings kept some of their treasure. The monks lived around the cloisters, and they even bathed here – though only four times a year.

Queen Elizabeth I's Tomb (above) is shared with Queen Mary Tudor. **Grave of the Unknown Warrior (left)** This tribute to all who have lost their lives in war was unveiled in 1920.

The Lowdown

🌐 **Map reference** 16 G1
Address 20 Dean's Yard, SW1P 3PA; 020 7222 5152; www.westminster-abbey.org

🚗 **Tube** Westminster. **Bus stop** Westminster Abbey or Victoria. St. **River bus** Westminster Pier

🕐 **Open** 9:30am–3:30pm Mon–Fri (11am–6pm Wed); 9:30am–1:30pm Sat. Last admission 1 hour before closing. On Sun and religious holidays, the abbey is open for worship only – all are welcome

💲 **Price** £45; under-5s free

🧑 **Skipping the queue** Tickets can't be pre-booked. Attending church services is free: the choir sings Evensong daily except Wed (5pm weekdays; 3pm weekends)

🎧 **Guided tours** Free audio tour; there are verger-led guided tours up to five times daily (£5)

🧑‍🧒 **Age range** 5 plus

🧑‍🧒 **Activities** Children's trail (ages 5–12) in English, French, German, Spanish, Italian; kids aged 5–12 can dress up as a monk in the museum (free). Art, dancing and drama workshops

on summer afternoons in College Garden (ages 5 plus, free)

⏱ **Allow** Up to 2 hours

♿ **Wheelchair access** Yes, via North Door; some areas inaccessible

☕ **Café** Cellarium Café in the cloisters offers afternoon tea

🛍 **Shop** Outside the West Door

🚻 **Toilets** Near Poets' Corner

Good family value?
Plenty to dazzle here, though adult admission is expensive.

Prices given are for a family of four

College Garden, Westminster Abbey, once used by monks for growing herbs

Letting off steam

The tidy lawns and paths of **College Garden**, in the grounds of Westminster Abbey, are open certain days only: concerts and children's events are held here in July and August. However, for a proper run-around, head for **St James's Park** with its lake and playground, at the Buckingham Palace end (see p74). If it rains, get even wetter at the **Queen Mother Sports Centre** (223 Vauxhall Bridge Road, SW1V 1EL; open daily), where the children's swimming pool has a great flume.

Eat and drink

Picnic: under £22; Snacks: £23; Real meal: £44; Family treat: £60 or more (based on a family of four)

PICNIC Le Pain du Jour (10 Strutton Ground, SW1P 2HP; 020 7222 3722; 7:30am–4pm Mon–Fri) is the pick of a parade of sandwich places along Strutton Ground, near St James's Park tube. Eat by the lake in St James's Park.
SNACKS Wesley's Café (Central Hall Westminster, Storey's Gate, SW1H 9NH; 020 7654 3834; 8am–4pm Mon–Fri, 9am–4pm Sat & Sun) is located downstairs at the Methodist Central Hall and serves hot and cold meals, as well as paninis, salads and sandwiches. It also offers a wide range of cakes, scones and biscuits in the afternoon.

Enjoying lunch at Wesley's Café, Methodist Central Hall

REAL MEAL There are limited options near Parliament Square so try **The Clarence** (53 Whitehall, SW1A 2HP; 020 7930 4808; noon–11pm Mon–Sat; noon–10:30pm Sun), a scrubbed-up gastropub with half-price children's dishes, including beef stew and gammon and eggs.
FAMILY TREAT The Rex Whistler Restaurant at Tate Britain (020 7887 8825; noon–3pm daily) is a posh pillared dining room with food to match. One child under 13 can lunch for free with an adult eating a main and a dessert à la carte (£30–36). The murals, painted by Whistler in 1927, when he was still a student, make a jolly talking point.

Find out more

DIGITAL Create your own colourful coat of arms like those of the knights of Westminster Abbey at www.makeyourcoatofarms.com. Test your knowledge about Guy Fawkes and the Gunpowder Plot – and answer as quick as you can, to stop the fizzing fuse, at: www.bbc.co.uk/history/british/civil_war_revolution/launch_gms_gunpowder_plot.shtml.

The famous front door at No. 10 Downing Street

Next stop...

NO. 10 DOWNING STREET Stroll along Whitehall to peek through the railings into Downing Street, home of prime ministers since 1730. Until 1982 tourists could walk up and take photos of No. 10.
WESTMINSTER CATHEDRAL Near Victoria station is this impressive cathedral, which is the Catholic Church's headquarters in Britain (42 Francis Street, SW1P 1QW; www.westminstercathedral.org.uk; 8am–7pm Mon–Fri; 10am–1pm Sat & Sun). The viewing gallery at the 83-m (272-ft) tower is open daily.

The Neo-Gothic Houses of Parliament, rebuilt in the 19th century after a massive fire

② Houses of Parliament

Home of UK democracy and those famous bongs

Officially called the Palace of Westminster, the Houses of Parliament began with Westminster Hall, built in 1097 by the son of William the Conqueror and little changed since. Guy Fawkes was tried here after attempting to blow the building up in 1605, Sir Winston Churchill lay in state in 1965, and Henry VIII's tennis ball was found in the rafters, nearly 400 years after it got stuck there. Today, the hall is a pretty grand visitors' lobby – with its lofty timber roof, it feels like being inside an upturned Viking longship.

Free guided tours begin here and run all year for British residents, plus every Saturday and on weekdays in summer for paying visitors. When MPs are in session, or "sitting", it's also possible to attend a debate by queuing down the ramp on Cromwell Green. The tour passes through Westminster Hall and the shop, set inside St Stephen's Hall, where Spencer Perceval was shot dead in 1812 – Britain's only assassinated prime minister.

Where Guy Fawkes failed, a cleaner succeeded, accidentally burning down Parliament in 1834. Most of the building visible today was designed by Charles Barry in Victorian Gothic style and built in 1840–60 with sumptuous interiors by Augustus Pugin. The 75-minute tour is unstuffy and full of anecdotes

and follows the same route as the Queen when she attends the State Opening of Parliament each November. The tour reveals why Her Majesty arrives on a blue carpet, the location of her secret toilet, and why the statues of past prime ministers have shiny shoes. It doesn't visit Big Ben, though – that tour is only available to British residents (age 11 plus) who apply to their MP. The tower's iconic clock first ticked on 31 May 1859 and its famous "bongs" have heralded BBC radio news bulletins since 1923.

The standard tour climaxes in the Commons Chamber, a surprisingly snug space just 20 m (66 ft) long – it can seat only 427 of Britain's 650 MPs. Visitors are able to stand where the prime minister does, but

sitting down on any of the seats is not allowed – only MPs can do that. Parliament Square, just outside, is home to several large statues of leaders and politicians.

Letting off steam

Victoria Tower Gardens (*Abingdon Street, SW1P 3*) has a grassy riverside, plus a small swing park.

③ Tate Britain

A masterpiece in every room

This site once stored prisoners, not paintings: in Victorian times the Millbank Penitentiary held convicts about to be shipped off to Australia as punishment. In 1897 Henry Tate, the sugar tycoon, paid for a national gallery, and it became the world's biggest collection of British art.

The Lowdown

🌐 **Map reference** 16 G1
Address St Margaret's Street, SW1A; 020 7219 3000; *www.parliament.uk*

🚗 **Tube** Westminster. **Bus stop** Bridge Street, Parliament St, Millbank. **River bus** Westminster Pier

🕐 **Open** 8am–11pm Mon–Thu; 8am–8pm Fri; 9am–6pm Sat

💲 **Price** Attending debates is free

🧍 **Skipping the queue** UK residents can arrange a free tour through their MP (six-month waiting list). Arrive early for tour

🎫 **Guided tours** Paid tours Tue & Sat Aug–Sep, plus Sat all year round: £50–70 (0333 321 9999; *www.ticketmaster.co.uk/ housesofparliament*)

👫 **Age range** 7 plus; visitors attending debates must be silent

🏃 **Activities** Good children's brochures are usually available at the Westminster Hall reception

🕐 **Allow** 2 hours

♿ **Wheelchair access** Yes, all tours

🍴 **Eat and drink** Snacks Jubilee Café, off Westminster Hall (*10am–5:30pm Mon–Fri, till 6pm Sat*), is lovely, but open only to tour and debate goers *Real Meal* Wagamama, (*76–98 Victoria Street, SW1E 5JE; 020 7828 0561*) in Cardinal Place shopping centre, has a kids' menu and outdoor seating

🛍 **Shops** In St Stephen's Hall

🚻 **Toilets** In Westminster Hall

Prices given are for a family of four

The Lowdown

- **Map reference** 16 G3
- **Address** Millbank, SW1P; 020 7887 8888; www.tate.org.uk/visit/tate-britain
- **Tube** Pimlico, Vauxhall **Bus stop** Millbank, Vauxhall Bridge Road, John Islip Street **River bus** Tate Boat (www.tate.org.uk/visit/tate-boat) shuttles every 40 minutes to Tate Modern (see p148) during opening hours
- **Open** 10am–6pm (last admission 5:15pm); till 10pm Fri
- **Price** Free; special temporary exhibitions individually priced
- **Skipping the queue** Tickets for temporary exhibitions can be booked ahead online
- **Guided tours** Free tours four times daily, plus multimedia guide £4
- **Age range** 3 plus
- **Activities** Children's activity packs; Art Trolley on weekends and school holidays (free); occasional family workshops
- **Allow** 1–2 hours
- **Wheelchair access** Yes, Manton entrance, Atterbury Street
- **Eat and drink** Snacks The Café has a kids' menu. Family treat The Rex Whistler Restaurant offers a free meal for one child under 13 when an adult orders two courses à la carte
- **Shops** Millbank and Manton entrances
- **Toilets** Manton entrance

The 30-room collection spans 500 years and includes everything from Hogarth to Hockney, Gainsborough to Gilbert and George. What's actually on display varies, but there are always plenty of works to capture young imaginations: story pictures (perhaps *The Lady of Shalott* by John Waterhouse); scary pictures (try Bacon's *Figures at the Base of a Crucifixion*); pictures of animals (Stubbs's *Horse Devoured by a Lion*) and of children (Sargent's *Carnation, Lily, Lily, Rose*). The Pre-Raphaelites, with their fairytale lushness, go down especially well, and in the Modern and Contemporary galleries, children will be heartened to learn that bold stripes of colour (Bridget Riley) or splodges of paint (Gillian Ayres) can also qualify as genius. Beware, though: Damien Hirst's pickled sheep is lurking.

The gallery also encourages kids to scribble their way around. Begin at the Manton entrance and ask for a themed activity pack. Give your age to ensure you get the right one. At weekends, the Tate, in partnership with a regularly changing programme of artists, runs a session called Liminal, in which younger visitors are invited to physically and socially interact with sculpture. The dedicated Tate Kids website (http://kids.tate.org.uk) is brimming with craft ideas and interactive games.

Letting off steam

Tucked away in a back street 5 minutes from the Tate, the terrific **Causton Street Playground** has two separate play areas for ages 3–7 and older children.

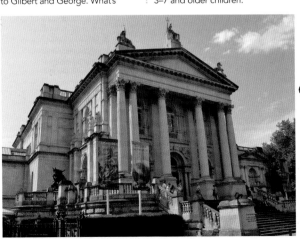

The façade of Tate Britain

④ Churchill War Rooms

Hidden passages, secret messages

Everyone loves a secret labyrinth, and here's one right under the heart of London. The Churchill War Rooms are where Winston Churchill ran Britain's campaign against the Axis powers during World War II. This warren of chambers was designed to resist enemy bombs – just as well, as the House of Commons took a direct hit during the Blitz. The rooms became the nerve centre for picking up secret messages from the front, with some staff living like moles almost full time, even using sun-lamps to prevent Vitamin D deficiency.

What is enthralling is that along with a few shop-dummy typists and military men poised over maps, the rooms remain frozen in time, filled with original clutter and musty smells. Churchill's bedroom looks like he's just popped out for a quick cigar – which he liked to do, often climbing to the roof during Luftwaffe raids to watch.

The children's audio tour extends into the adjoining Churchill Museum,

Plotting the course of World War II in Churchill's Cabinet War Rooms

a 21st-century space that uses audio, film and touch-screen wizardry to canter through Churchill's career. Despite all the gizmos, this area will mainly interest older children.

Letting off steam

Cross the road into **St James's Park** *(see p74)*, which has refreshment kiosks and plump ducks to feed.

⑤ Horse Guards Parade

A polished performance

In Tudor times, the royal palace was at Whitehall, and Horse Guards Parade started life as Henry VIII's jousting yard. That's why Her Majesty's Life Guard stand sentry on the pavement here to this day. Every morning, the new guard trots in on horseback along The Mall from Hyde Park Barracks, silver helmets glinting, heading for the

changing ceremony – a 15-minute silent stand-off followed by lots of bellowing as the old guard departs. Beside the parade ground is the Household Cavalry Museum, displaying historic regimental memorabilia. The main attraction, though, is the cobbled stables – a glass wall in the museum looks right in on the troops as they groom their horses and prepare their kit. Most of the action happens at the guard-change time, and at 4pm, when the troops dismount. The smells are authentic, too! There is real armour

Filling in a quiz-sheet kit inspection at the Household Cavalry Museum

Mounted sentries on Horse Guards Parade

for kids to try on, quiz sheets to complete and touch-screen TVs with footage of the guards talking about their work. Young recruits spend up to 12 hours a day buffing their uniforms, and each morning the smartest one gets to be a mounted "boxman" or sentry, while the least polished is saddled with foot duty. So, is it acceptable for visitors to pull faces and make them smile? Permission denied!

Letting off steam

The spacious and well-tended lawns and lakes of **St James's Park** (see p74) are right opposite.

⑥ Banqueting House

Where a king lost his head

Four hundred years ago, English kings believed they were agents of God. James I threw dazzling courtly entertainments, or masques, in which actors cavorted as devils and beasts with the monarch restoring order at the end. Banqueting House was built in 1622 to stage them and designed by Inigo Jones, who excited London with the Neo-Classical architecture he had brought back from Italy.

Today, a visit begins with a film history in the Undercroft, moodily lit by candelabras. Then, head upstairs into the white-and-gold hall with its double-decker columns and painted ceiling. This was commissioned from Baroque master Peter Paul Rubens by Charles I and shows his father, King James I, rising gloriously into Heaven. Children are encouraged to lie on their backs and ogle the closest thing in the UK to the Sistine Chapel in Rome. The lively audio guide tells the building's stories, such as the "touching the king's evil" ceremony, where sufferers of the hideous skin disease scrofula gathered to be "cured" by the monarch's touch.

Charles I inherited his father's belief in the superiority of kings over the common man. However, in 1649, just 11 years after his ceiling was finished, Charles was marched out of Banqueting House and had his head chopped off for treason.

Letting off steam

St James's Park (see p74) is across the road, via Horse Guards Parade, with activities for kids of all ages.

The Lowdown

🌐 **Map reference** 10 G6
Address Whitehall, SW1A; 020 3166 6154; www.hrp.org.uk/banquetinghouse

🚇 **Tube** Westminster, Charing Cross, Embankment **Bus stop** Whitehall **River bus** Westminster Pier

🕙 **Open** 10am–5pm daily (last admission till 5pm, call in advance as can close ahead of functions)

💷 **Price** £6, under-16s free. Free audio guide

🚶 **Skipping the queue** Rarely busy

Guided tour No

👫 **Age range** 9 plus

⏱ **Allow** Up to 1 hour

♿ **Wheelchair access** Limited. Call 020 3166 6155/6152 for details

🍴 **Eat and drink** *Picnic* Pret A Manger (1 Whitehall, SW1A 2DD; 020 7932 5216) offers eat in or out sandwiches and salads *Snacks* The Portrait Café serves light meals (see p82)

🛍 **Shop** On the main stairwell

🚻 **Toilets** In the Undercroft

Buckingham Palace and around

Each year, thousands press their noses to the gilded railings of Buckingham Palace, the headquarters of the royal family since 1837. The Palace has been open for pre-booked tours (late July and through September only) since 1993, but check the calendar to ensure your visit coincides with the Changing the Guard ceremony. Approach along Birdcage Walk from St James's Park Tube Station, and explore the children's playground en route. Then while away the afternoon around the lake in St James's Park, or wander across Green Park to window shop in the swish arcades along Piccadilly. It's all within walking distance.

Westminster and the West End

Covent Garden *p86*

National Gallery *p78*

Buckingham Palace

Westminster Abbey *p64*

0 metres 200

0 yards 200

The small but compelling Guards Museum, filled with military kit from historic battles to modern-day wars

One of the Queen's garden parties at Buckingham Palace

The Lowdown

Train Victoria (five-minute walk) or Charing Cross (10–15 minutes) **Tube** Victoria, St James's Park or Green Park **Bus** Grosvenor Place: route numbers 2, 16, 36, 38, 52, 73, 82, 148, 436 or C2; or Buckingham Palace Rd: 11, 211, C1 or C10

i **Visitor information** Victoria Railway Station (opposite platform 8) or Piccadilly Circus Underground Station, W1D 7DH

Supermarkets Sainsbury's, 150 Victoria St, SW1E 5LB; Marks & Spencer, 78 Piccadilly, W1J 8AQ **Markets** Arts & crafts market, St James's Churchyard, Piccadilly W1J 9LL; 10am–6pm Wed–Sat

Festivals St Patrick's Day Parade, Green Park (Sun nearest Mar 17); Trooping the Colour, Horse Guards Parade (any Sat in Jun); Virgin London Marathon, ends in The Mall (Apr); Royal Academy Summer Exhibition (Jun–Aug)

Pharmacies Boots, 13 Cathedral Walk (8:30am–7pm Mon–Sat, 9am–4pm Sun). For 24-hour pharmacies, search at www.nhs.org.uk/Service-Search

Nearest playground St James's Park (Buckingham Palace end of Birdcage Walk)

Places of Interest

SIGHTS

1. Buckingham Palace
2. The Royal Mews
3. Guards Museum
4. Royal Institution

EAT AND DRINK

1. St James's Café
2. The Parlour at Fortnum & Mason
3. The Café at the Institute of Contemporary Arts
4. Benihana
5. Crumpets
6. Le Signore
7. Picnic Kiosk
8. Caffe Grana
9. Laduree

See also Royal Institution (p77) and Shopping (below)

SHOPPING

1. Prestat
2. Burlington Arcade
3. Fortnum & Mason

WHERE TO STAY

1. 44 Curzon Street Apartments
2. Athenaeum Apartments
3. Brown's
4. Duke's
5. Flemings Apartments
6. The Goring
7. Taj 51 Buckingham Gate

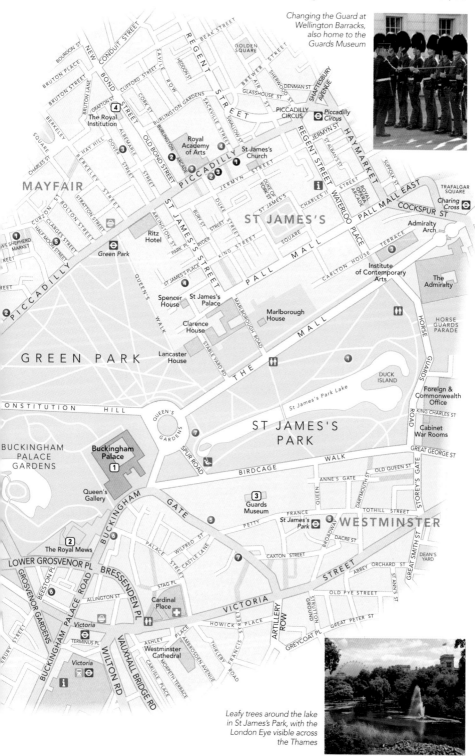

Changing the Guard at Wellington Barracks, also home to the Guards Museum

MAYFAIR

The Royal Institution

Royal Academy of Arts

St James's Church

Ritz Hotel

Green Park

ST JAMES'S

Spencer House

St James's Palace

Clarence House

Lancaster House

Marlborough House

GREEN PARK

BUCKINGHAM PALACE GARDENS

Buckingham Palace

Queen's Gallery

The Royal Mews

LOWER GROSVENOR PL

Cardinal Place

Victoria

Westminster Cathedral

ST JAMES'S PARK

St James's Park Lake

DUCK ISLAND

Institute of Contemporary Arts

The Admiralty

Admiralty Arch

HORSE GUARDS PARADE

Foreign & Commonwealth Office

Cabinet War Rooms

Guards Museum

St James's Park

WESTMINSTER

Leafy trees around the lake in St James's Park, with the London Eye visible across the Thames

① Buckingham Palace

When the Queen's away, there are visits to pay

Full of priceless porcelain, jewelled cabinets and gold leaf, Buckingham Palace owes its splendour to George IV, who came to the throne in 1820 and lavished a fortune on it – but never lived here. Queen Elizabeth II first moved in as a 10-year-old princess, and now shares the palace with 350 staff, from cleaners to courtiers. Visitor tours operate in summer, when Her Majesty is at her holiday home, Balmoral Castle in Scotland. Only 19 state rooms are open to the public – just as well, as there are 775 rooms in all.

Sentry guard

Key Features

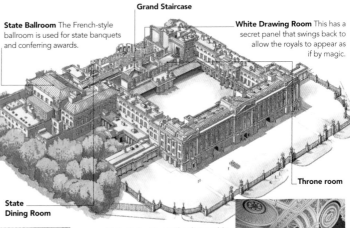

Grand Staircase

State Ballroom The French-style ballroom is used for state banquets and conferring awards.

White Drawing Room This has a secret panel that swings back to allow the royals to appear as if by magic.

Grand Staircase This was the centrepiece of George IV's extravagant conversion of the old "Buckingham House". The ornate bronze cast balustrade alone cost £200,000 in today's money.

State Dining Room

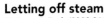

Throne room

State Dining Room The dining table seats 46 guests, and the footmen carry special rulers to make sure cutlery and glassware are positioned correctly. The Queen always makes a final check!

Throne Room The two thrones here are embroidered with "ER" and "P" and were used by Elizabeth II and the Duke of Edinburgh at the Coronation in 1953.

Letting off steam

St James's Park (0300 061 2350; www.royalparks.org.uk /parks/ st-jamess-park) is nearby, with a great playground for children aged up to 11 at the Palace end – it has kids-only toilets, a refreshment kiosk and picnic tables. Admire the geese and swans as they glide across the lake, but the kings of the park are the pelicans, fed at 2:30pm near Duck Island. The first pelicans were a gift from the Russian ambassador in 1664. There's a smart conservatory restaurant nearby (see right) and deck chairs for hire, band concerts on summer weekends, guided walks… and no "keep off the grass" signs.

Prices given are for a family of four

Eat and drink

Picnic: under £20–40; Snacks: £28–40; Real meal: £25–40; Family treat: £45–60 (based on a family of four)

PICNIC St James's Café (St James's Park; 020 7925 2985; www.benugo. com/public-spaces/st-james-s-park; 8am–6pm Mon–Sat, 9am–5pm Sun) is a lakeside eatery in the park, which excels at traditional English breakfast menu and the French toast is quite popular with kids. It serves mid-day platters and even has a range of vegetarian options. The wooden terrace offers views to the Eye and Horse Guards Parade.
SNACKS The Parlour at Fortnum & Mason (181 Piccadilly, W1A

Clambering over boulders in St James's Park sandpit

1ER; 020 7734 8040; www.fortnum andmason.com; 10am–7pm Mon–Sat; 11:30am–5pm Sun) does superb ice-cream sundaes and hot chocolate, and has a handy toasted sandwich menu for under-8s.

The Lowdown

Map reference 15 D1
Address Buckingham Palace Road, SW1A; 020 7766 7300; *www.royalcollection.org.uk*

Tube Victoria, St James's Park.
Bus stop Buckingham Palace Rd

Open State Rooms Aug: 9:30am–7:30pm (last admission 3:45pm). Changing the Guard May–Jul: 11:30am daily; Aug–Apr: alternate days; cancelled in heavy rain

Price £39.50 adult, £100 family

Skipping the queue Book tickets in advance online. The palace forecourt gets squeezed during the Changing the Guard – children will get a better view on nearby Friary Court, outside St James's Palace. Aim to be there before 11am

Guided tours Free audio guide in eight languages

Age range 5 plus

Activities Children's audio guide (ages 7–11), plus garden nature trail on request (or downloadable online). Family room with free activities during summer holiday: design a hat for a garden party

Allow 2 hours

Wheelchair access Yes, but must be booked in advance: 020 7766 7324

Café On the garden terrace

Shop Large shop at the end of the Palace gardens, at the end of the visit

Toilets In the garden at the end of visit

Good family value?
The palace tour is far from cheap, though the children's audio guide and sparky summer activities make it just about worth the money.

REAL MEAL The Café at the Institute of Contemporary Arts *(020 7930 8619; 11am–11pm Tue–Sun)*, on The Mall, is a cool alternative to the chain restaurants on nearby Haymarket. No children's menu, but smaller portions of pasta and burgers on request. High chairs and baby-changing facilities, too.
FAMILY TREAT Benihana *(37 Sackville Street, W1S 3EH; 020 7494 2525; www.benihana.co.uk; noon–3pm daily; 5:30–10:30pm Mon–Sat; 5–10pm Sun)* is cooking as theatre: the Japanese dishes sizzle up spectacularly on a teppan hot-plate at your table.

Shopping

After visiting the Queen, head for the aristocratic shops of St James's. **Prestat** *(14 Princes Arcade, SW1Y 6DS; www.prestat.co.uk)* purveys deluxe chocolates and truffles, while in the exclusive **Burlington Arcade** *(Mayfair, W1; www.burlington-arcade. co.uk)*, which claims to be the world's first mall, the top-hatted security guards – Beadles – have been keeping the peace since 1819. **Fortnum & Mason** *(181 Piccadilly, W1A 1ER; www.fortnumandmason. com/stores)* has elegant frock-coated assistants who look like escaped palace footmen. See if the kids will try the chocolate-covered scorpions.

The confectionery counter inside Fortnum & Mason, Piccadilly

Find out more

DIGITAL Take one of Buckingham Palace's most famous inhabitants, Queen Victoria, to the seaside, then help her to write a postcard, at *www.museumnetworkuk.org/ portraits/activities/activities.html.*
FILM At the start of the 1996 film *101 Dalmatians*, Anita and Roger fall into the lake (and in love) in St James's Park thanks to their dogs.

Next stop...

QUEEN'S GALLERY Just around the corner on Buckingham Gate, the Queen's Gallery *(www.royal collection.org.uk/collection)* shows off art, jewels and family heirlooms from the royal collections. There's also a good children's trail.

② The Royal Mews
A coach fit for Cinderella

This must be the most picturesque garage in London: a 200-year-old Georgian stable yard, complete with an ornate clock tower and surrounded by the cottage-like quarters of the Queen's coachmen and their families. It looks enchanting at Christmas, when Santa slides in on his regal sleigh to the Queen's annual children's party.

Up to 30 horses are stabled here – they go to school for two years before they are qualified to pull a coach. The trainers wave flags, blow trumpets and play the sound of cannon fire to prepare them for the London crowds. The horses even learn to stop at red traffic lights.

As well as Santa's sleigh, a visit takes in the Glass Coach that Lady Diana Spencer rode in to her wedding to Prince Charles in 1981, and the little donkey carriage (or barouche) once driven by Queen Victoria's children. Apparently, the latter came in handy to get to the bathrooms in the vast royal palaces. The biggest gasp of all is reserved for the Gold State Coach used for coronation parades, presented in full harness and looking every bit like it's been borrowed from Cinderella. It is so big they have to remove a wall to get it out of the building.

The magic of the Mews for most children, though, springs from being among the sounds and smells of a working stable in the heart of London – and, if they're lucky, there might be a horse or two to meet and greet at the exit.

Helping a guardsman with his job (and getting a photo) at Horse Guards Parade

Letting off steam

A few minutes along Buckingham Gate lies **St James's Park** (see p74), with its excellent children's playground, just off Birdcage Walk.

③ Guards Museum
Royal sentries and toy soldiers

Part of Wellington Barracks, this modest museum fills a handful of basement rooms with the bloody exploits of the five British Guards regiments (and Household Cavalry). Learn the stories behind Charles II's musketeers, Wellington's overcoat and Florence Nightingale's medicine cup. Most compelling, perhaps, is the display of kit and mementos from the conflict in Afghanistan.

A quiz sheet for youngsters is usually available, and the kids can don a guard's tunic and bearskin for a photo, though there's an extra charge. If short of time, head for the toy soldier shop on the forecourt, which has shelf after shelf of brilliant thumb-sized battle scenes.

Outside, on the parade ground, troops line up at 11am ready to march to Buckingham Palace for the Changing the Guard ceremony (see p75), and viewpoints here are usually less congested than the more famous observation points at the Palace. There are often drills at other times too: listen out for the military drum beat booming out across St James's Park.

Letting off steam

The excellent **St James's Park** playground, complete with sandpit, is just across the road (see p74).

Toy soldiers at the Guards Museum – perfect for children of all ages

Exploring the elements, Royal Institution

④ Royal Institution

A genius introduction to ground-breaking science

Smash glass, electrocute a frog and blow up a laboratory assistant. That's the irresistible promise of a visit to the "Science in the Making" exhibition at the Royal Institution. Luckily, the glass-smashing and frog-frazzling are achieved virtually, using the museum's ingenious eGuide – a hand-held console which plays interactive cartoons of historic experiments at regular points around the museum. Even so, it's a great way to get budding geniuses interested in the mysteries of science.

Fourteen Nobel Prize winners have worked at the Royal Institution,

so there are fascinating artifacts to see – Alessandro Volta's prototype battery, James Dewar's first vacuum flask and Michael Faraday's original transformer. The laboratory where Faraday first harnessed electricity survives just as it was in the 1850s. In a clever touch, the Institution has a laboratory right opposite, where scientists can sometimes be seen working on special projects, such as developing tiny nanomagnets that can find and zap cancer cells.

Most children will be more engaged by the eGuide and its amusing clips and games. The handy device also brings to life some of the most popular bits of the Royal Institution's celebrated Christmas lectures, which have been enthralling children since 1825. For example, learn how a toy kangaroo can unlock the secrets of gravity, and how to turn a bicycle wheel into a gyroscope.

Letting off steam

A 10-minute walk away along Piccadilly lie the grassy expanses of **Green Park** *(see p73)*, perfect for a run around, with deck-chair hire and refreshment kiosks.

The Lowdown

- 🌐 **Map reference** 9 D4
  Address 21 Albemarle St, W1S 4BS; 020 7409 2992; *www.rigb.org*
- 🚗 **Tube** Green Park or Piccadilly Circus. **Bus stop** Berkeley St or Piccadilly
- 🕐 **Open** 9am–6pm Mon–Fri
- 💲 **Price** Free
- 🎫 **Guided tours** No; free eGuide
- 🚶 **Age range** 7 plus
- 🤾 **Activities** Hands-on science sessions six times a year (ages 5–12): £16–20
- ⏱ **Allow** Up to 2 hours
- ♿ **Wheelchair access** Yes
- 🍽 **Eat and drink** *Snacks* Laduree (71 Burlington Arcade, W1J 0QX; www.laduree.com/en_gb/) was established in Paris in 1862 and is a temple to French macaroons *Family treat* The Atrium Café offers lunch (noon–3pm) as well as coffee, tea, wine and beer till 5pm.
- 🚻 **Toilets** In the lobby

Michael Faraday glass egg, used to test theories about electricity

National Gallery and around

In one room, St George spears the dragon straight through the eye. In another, a teenaged queen is led blindfolded to the chopping block. Who said art galleries are boring? The National unlocks the stories behind every canvas, with kids' trails and workshops. Its Sainsbury Wing is the best way in for families – aim left when approaching across Trafalgar Square. The cinemas and street life of the West End are a short stroll up Charing Cross Road – and best explored by day. To see Piccadilly Circus and Hamleys toy shop, take the Bakerloo Line from Charing Cross.

Westminster and the West End

Covent Garden *p86*

National Gallery

Buckingham Palace *p72*

Westminster Abbey *p64*

Above The grand porticoed entrance of the National Gallery, completed in 1838
Below Holbein's The Ambassadors (1533) shows two stately men with symbols of power

Below The metal in the brass lions in Trafalgar Square reputedly came from French guns captured at the Battle of Trafalgar (1805)

Inside the National Portrait Gallery

The Lowdown

🚗 **Train** Charing Cross **Tube** Charing Cross, Embankment or Leicester Square **Bus** Trafalgar Square: routes 3, 6, 9, 11, 12, 13, 15, 23, 24, 29, 53, 87, 88, 91, 139, 159, 176, 453; Piccadilly Circus: 3, 6, 9, 12, 13, 15, 22, 23, 88, 94, 139, 159, 453; Shaftesbury Avenue: 14, 19, 38 **River bus** Embankment Pier, services to Westminster and St Katharine's Dock (Crown River Cruises: 020 7936 2033; www.crownriver.com)

ℹ️ **Visitor information** Leicester Square; Britain & London Visitor Centre, 1 Regent St; or at Piccadilly Circus Tube Station

🍲 **Supermarkets** New Loon Moon Chinese supermarket, 9a Gerrard St, W1D 5PL; Tesco Metro, 17–25 Regent St, SW1Y 4LR **Markets** Berwick Street (food, fish, flowers) and Rupert Street (books, jewellery, hot food), both

in Soho: 9am–6pm Mon–Sat

Festivals New Year's Day Parade, Trafalgar Square (1 Jan); Chinese New Year, Soho (Feb); St George's Day, Trafalgar Square (Apr); Kids' Week Theatre Festival, West End theatres (Aug); Regent Street Festival (Sep); Trafalgar Day Parade (Oct); London Film Festival, Leicester Square cinemas (Oct); Christmas Lights, Regent Street (Nov–Dec)

➕ **Pharmacies** Boots, 5–7 Strand, WC2N 5HR (7:30am–9pm Mon–Fri, 9am–8pm Sat, 11am–5pm Sun). For 24-hour pharmacies search at www.nhs.uk/servicedirectories

Nearest playgrounds Phoenix Garden in St Giles-in-the-Fields churchyard, or in St James's Park (see p73)

0 metres 200
0 yards 200

Places of Interest

SIGHTS

1. National Gallery
2. Trafalgar Square
3. National Portrait Gallery
4. Benjamin Franklin House
5. Leicester Square
6. Piccadilly Circus
7. Hamleys

EAT AND DRINK

1. Tesco Metro
2. The Café in the Crypt
3. Ed's Easy Diner
4. Portrait Restaurant
5. Leon
6. Patisserie Pompidou
7. Lupita
8. Häagen-Dazs Café
9. Little Lamb
10. Millie's
11. The Rainforest Café
12. Refectory

See also Trafalgar Square (p82), National Portrait Gallery (pp82–3) and Hamleys (p85)

SHOPPING

1. Marchpane
2. TokyoToys

William Hamley's toy shop has been bewitching children since 1760 and is now a major tourist attraction

① National Gallery
Heroes and angels, monsters and murderers

Britain's richest art collection began life in 1824 with just 38 paintings. Now it has 2,300, from the vivid saints and serpents in the medieval galleries, to the iconic sunflowers and waterlilies in the 19th-century rooms. With school groups sitting cross-legged in front of assorted canvases, there is plenty of happy hubbub throughout. Start at the audio guide desk, where family trails include Teach Your Grown-Ups About Art, a genius idea that turns children into instant experts.

National Gallery
main entrance

Key Features

Main Gallery Building
Paintings from 1500 to 1900 are displayed here.

Sainsbury Wing This houses the early Renaissance Collection of paintings from 1250 to1500.

③ **Perseus Turning Phineas and his Followers to Stone (1680s)** An attacking army is petrified by the face of the snake-haired Medusa, a mythological event brilliantly captured by Luca Giordano. (Room 32)

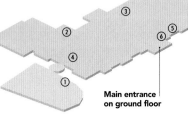

Main entrance on ground floor

② **Peepshow (1655–60)** A mind-boggling "perspective box" by Samuel Von Hoogstraten. Through the main window it all looks skewed, but have a look through the eyeholes for a surprise. (Room 25)

① **St George and the Dragon (1470)** Paolo Uccello illustrates two episodes from the story of St George in one picture: the knight's victory, and the rescued princess bringing the fearsome prey to heel. (Room 54)

⑥ **Sunflowers (1888)** Vincent van Gogh sold only one painting, for about £50, during his lifetime. His famous *Sunflowers* is now worth a million times that sum. The flowers symbolized happiness for him. (Room 45)

④ **The Execution of Lady Jane Grey (1833)** Paul Delaroche's painting shows the doomed, blindfolded 17-year-old queen groping towards the chopping block. Gallery-goers wept when it was first exhibited in 1834. (Gallery D)

⑤ **Bathers at Asnières (1884)** Georges Seurat used his new technique – tiny dots of contrasting colour called pointillism – to make his paintings glow. (Room 41)

The Lowdown

Map ref 10 F4
Address Trafalgar Square, WC2N 5DN; 020 7747 2885; www.nationalgallery.org.uk

Train Charing Cross
Tube Charing Cross or Leicester Square.
Bus stop Trafalgar Square **River bus** Embankment Pier

Open 10am–6pm daily; until 9pm Fri. Closed 1 Jan, 24–26 Dec

Price Permanent collection free; temporary exhibitions individually priced

Skipping the queue The Sainsbury Wing entrance (corner of Trafalgar Square) is less busy. Arrive early for kids' workshops

Guided tours "Taster tours" of the collection twice daily, plus Fridays at 7pm

Age range 5 plus

Activities Family audio tours (under-12s free), plus themed workbook trails: download these at www.nationalgallery.org.uk/families. Family Sunday sessions for under-5s and for 5–11s (2 hours; free). There are school holiday workshops, too

Allow Up to 3 hours

Wheelchair access Yes

Café National Café (Level 0) for brunch, lunch and afternoon tea; National Dining Rooms (Level 1) for more formal dining (lunch only)

Shop Sainsbury Wing and main building, selling art-themed books, cards, prints, jewellery and gifts

Toilets All floors main building; Level 1, Sainsbury Wing

Good family value?
Excellent, thanks to the inventive kids' stuff. Visit the Art Start room (Sainsbury Wing) to find out what's happening on the day.

Prices given are for a family of four

Letting off steam

Outside the gallery, in **Trafalgar Square** (see p82), there is fun to be had chasing pigeons, dodging spray from the fountains and scampering around Nelson's Column – though riding his famous lions is fraught with slippery danger. For softer landings, stroll 2 minutes through Admiralty Arch onto the well-kept lawns of **St James's Park** (see p74).

Chasing pigeons outside The National Gallery on Trafalgar Square

Eat and drink

Picnic: under £20; Snacks: £20–40; Real meal: £40–60; Family treat: £60 or more (based on a family of four)

PICNIC Buy supplies from the **Tesco Metro** supermarket behind St Martin's Lane (22–25 Bedford Street, WC2E 9EQ; 0845 677 9173; 7am–10pm Mon–Sat, noon–6pm Sun) and walk down to Victoria Embankment Gardens for a picnic.
SNACKS The Café in the Crypt (Trafalgar Square, WC2N 4JJ; 020 7766 1158; www.stmartin-in-the-fields.org/cafe-in-the-crypt/; 8am–8pm Mon–Tues; 8am–10.30pm Wed (jazz night ticket holders only after 6:30pm); 8am–9pm Thu–Sat; 11am–6pm Sun) serves super-fresh canteen-style dishes in the crypt of St Martin-in-the-Fields church.
REAL MEAL Ed's Easy Diner (12 Moor Street, off Old Compton Street, W1D 5NG; 020 7287 1951; www.edseasydiner.com; 9am–11pm Mon–Wed, 9am–11:30pm Thu, 9am–11:30pm Fri & Sat, 9am–10pm Sun) is a temple to 1950s Americana, with hot dogs, shakes and retro jukeboxes at every table.
FAMILY TREAT Portrait Restaurant (National Portrait Gallery; 020 7312

The magnificent Cleopatra's Needle, situated on the Embankment

2490; www.npg.org.uk; 10am–6pm daily; till 8pm Thu, Fri & Sat) offers half-size portions of its dishes for kids, with fantastic views of Admiral Nelson in Trafalgar Square, Big Ben, and the London Eye. Book well in advance for Saturday night dining.

Shopping

West End shopping heaven is close by, dominated by the seven storeys of hyperactive play and a range of toys at **Hamleys** (see p85). For vintage children's and illustrated books, there is **Marchpane** (16 Cecil Court, WC2N 4HE). Teenage anime fiends will love **TokyoToys**, in the Trocadero Centre (13 Coventry Street, W1D 7DH).

Find out more

DIGITAL Make 3D designs akin to Barbara Hepworth's sculptures at http://kids.tate.org.uk/create/3d_designer.shtm.

Next stop...

ROYAL ACADEMY OF ARTS On nearby Piccadilly, the **Royal Academy** (www.royalacademy.org.uk) is another treasure house of British painting, with Art Detective family trails, downloadable guides and occasional free workshops for families. In summer, its café spills into the courtyard, and kids are even able to frolic in the fountains.
CLEOPATRA'S NEEDLE Stroll down to the Embankment and investigate this 3,500-year-old Egyptian obelisk, raised beside the river in 1878. Its guardian (19th-century) sphinxes are at child-friendly height for a photo.

The entrance courtyard of the Royal Academy of Arts, Piccadilly

② Trafalgar Square

Lions and fountains

As monumental playgrounds go, Trafalgar Square, with its splashing mermaids and watchful lions, is as grand as it gets. This has been the official centre of London for 800 years – ever since Edward I erected the original "Charing Cross" here to remember his queen, Eleanor. The square was completed by Nelson's Column in 1843, and Britain's most famous naval commander gazes off towards Portsmouth, home of his flagship HMS *Victory*, from a 46-m (151-ft) plinth above the crowds.

At times of national celebration or mourning, people gather here: the square has seen anti-apartheid rallies, World Cup victory parades and a record-breaking performance by "the world's largest coconut orchestra". A big talking point has been the Fourth Plinth, vacant for decades because nobody could agree on what to erect there. It is now a yearly changing showcase for contemporary art, including (in 2009) Antony Gormley's *One and Other*, which invited 2,400 ordinary people to occupy the podium for 1 hour each – with eccentric results.

Visitors have always flocked here, but today more do so than ever before, thanks to a 2003 redevelopment, which pedestrianized the National Gallery side of the square, installed a café

Nelson's 5.5-m (18-ft) statue atop his column made of Dartmoor granite

and toilets, and drove out most of the 35,000 pigeons with falcons. Uniformed "heritage wardens" are now on 24-hour duty to help visitors.

Take cover

St Martin-in-the-Fields Church (*020 7766 1100; www.smitf.org*), beside the square, is home to the London Brass Rubbing Centre, where indoor fun can be had waxing William Shakespeare or King Arthur. Prices vary, instruction given. There's a good café and Saturday afternoon concerts most months (ages 5 plus). The church itself is worth a look, too.

③ National Portrait Gallery

Famous faces and much more

"The world's biggest collection of faces" numbers a jaw-dropping 160,000 portraits in all, and crams 1,000 of them onto the walls of its three gallery levels, from King Henry

Exterior of the National Portrait Gallery

VII (Room 1) to actor Ian McKellen, perhaps recognisable to youngsters as "Gandalf the Grey" (Room 37).

Begin with those schoolbook favourites, the Tudors, on Floor 2, where there are plenty of extravagantly dressed children to catch the eye: the future King Charles II, for example, painted by Anthony Van Dyck in full armour at the age of eight. It's an exaggeration of history, though: Charles didn't fight seriously until the Battle of Edgehill (1642)… when he was 12!

Floor 1 spans the Victorians to the 20th century, showcasing many names that kids may know: Beatrix Potter, LS Lowry, Paul McCartney, Princess Diana and Winston Churchill. A multimedia guide just for children reveals historical nuggets along the way: find out the grisly truth about Walter Raleigh's head, and meet the strange pet that Florence Nightingale kept in her pocket.

For celeb-spotting, though, the ground floor galleries win every time: the contemporary cast here might include JK Rowling, Lily Allen or

The Lowdown

- 🌐 **Map reference** 10 F4
  Address St Martin's Place, WC2H; 020 7306 0055; www.npg.org.uk
- 🚆 **Train** Charing Cross **Tube** Charing Cross, Leicester Square or Embankment **Bus stop** Trafalgar Square
- 🕑 **Open** 10am–6pm Sun–Wed; 10am–9pm Thu–Fri
- 💷 **Price** Permanent collection free; temporary exhibitions individually priced
- 👫 **Skipping the queue** Tickets for the free family art workshops are put on sale 1hr before the event
- 🚻 **Guided tours** No. Audio guide £3
- 👫 **Age range** 6 plus
- 👫 **Activities** Free storytelling sessions (age 3 plus) at 10:30am & 1:30pm and art workshops (age 5 plus) at 11:30am & 2:30pm on 3rd Sat of every month; artist-led sessions in school holidays. Activity cards and audio tours for kids from front desk.
- 🕑 **Allow** 2 hours
- ♿ **Wheelchair access** Yes
- ☕ **Eat and drink** *Snacks* Portrait Café (*Floor 3*) offers light snacks and meals. *Real meal* Portrait Restaurant (*Floor 3*) is a great option for à la carte with a view.
- 🛍 **Shop** Ground floor
- 🚻 **Toilets** On Floor 0 and Floor 3

The Lowdown

- 🌐 **Map reference** 10 F5
  Address WC2H; www.london. gov.uk/priorities/arts-culture/ trafalgar-square
- 🚆 **Train** Charing Cross **Tube** Charing Cross, Embankment or Leicester Square **Bus stop** Trafalgar Square
- 👫 **Activities** Annual events include St Patrick's Day (Mar), St George's Day (Apr), Eid (varies), the Diwali Festival (Oct or Nov), and Christmas carols in Dec; check website.
- 🕑 **Allow** 1 hour
- ☕ **Eat and drink** *Snacks* The Café on the Square (*10am–6pm daily*), under the central staircase, is a good lunch option. *Real meal* Leon (*73–76 Strand*), part of a chain of burgeoning "healthy fast food" restaurants, is in striking range.
- 🚻 **Toilets** Under the central staircase

A peaceful promenade with pretty flower displays in Victoria Embankment Gardens

David Beckham – though it pays to check online beforehand, because the faces change regularly. Kids can search for favourites using the computers in the mezzanine lounge.

Letting off steam
The fountains and lions – perfect for running around – are mere strides away in **Trafalgar Square**.

④ Benjamin Franklin House
Lightning flashes of inspiration and voices from the past

The tall-windowed townhouse at 36 Craven Street looks unremarkable at first, but its walls once contained a human whirlwind. Benjamin Franklin, American Founding Father, inventor, diplomat, and all-round Enlightenment hero, lived here for 16 years, working as deputy postmaster to the Colonies, inventing the lightning rod, measuring the Gulf Stream and calming unrest between England and America. The latter was unsuccessful – and by 1775, as the War of Independence loomed, Franklin had to flee to avoid arrest.

The house itself is an experiment in "museum as theatre" – visitors are whisked through its apartments by "Polly Hewson", Franklin's surrogate daughter, while being assailed by the smells of a Georgian kitchen, flashes of lightning from the laboratory, and the echoing voices of Franklin and his landlady. It's a

state-of-the-art effects show that older kids will find especially engaging. Franklin, ever the innovator, would have approved.

Letting off steam
It's a 2-minute walk to **Victoria Embankment Gardens**, which offers lunchtime concerts (May to August), and the Embankment Café (*020 7930 1471*).

The Lowdown

🌐 **Map reference** 10 G5
🏠 **Address** 36 Craven St, WC2N; 020 7925 1405; www.benjaminfranklinhouse.org
🚆 **Train** Charing Cross **Tube** Charing Cross or Embankment **Bus stop** Trafalgar Square or Strand
🕐 **Open** noon–5pm Wed–Mon. The Historical Experience runs at noon, 1pm, 2pm, 3:15pm, 4:15pm Wed–Sun
💲 **Price** £8, under-16s free
🔫 **Guided tours** Yes. Mon only (times as above): adults £6, under-16s free
👫 **Age range** 8 plus
👪 **Activities** School holiday art and science workshops; period-dress Christmas party for kids
⏱ **Allow** 1 hour
♿ **Wheelchair access** No
🍴 **Eat and drink** *Snacks* Patisserie Pompidou (*35 Villiers St, WC2N 6ND; 020 7839 6010*), sells salads and sandwiches. *Real meal* Lupita (*13 Villiers St, WC2N 6ND; 020 7930 5355*) dishes up Mexican fare in kid-friendly tasting portions.
🚻 **Toilets** In the basement

⑤ Leicester Square

Blockbusters and buzz

Every autumn a gaudy funfair sets up in Leicester Square Gardens – which seems like overkill. This is already London's most garish entertainment zone, ringed by blockbuster cinemas (often host to starry premieres), fast-food palaces and souvenir stores manned by giant bears in guards' uniforms. There is also a squad of street artists scribbling caricatures of passers-by and usually a choice of buskers.

The square once had more illustrious residents, among them scientist Isaac Newton (1643–1727) and artists Joshua Reynolds (1723–92) and William Hogarth (1697–1764) – look for their statues here.

Although the atmosphere can be a bit grown-up at night, by day it's a buzzy place for all; traffic-free and with benches for lunch, it's a good spot to check out the evening's theatre bargains. The best ticket booth is TKTS on the south side of Leicester Square Gardens (10am–7pm Mon–Sat, 11am–4:30pm Sun).

A 2-minute walk away, around Gerrard Street, lies the lively and aromatic Chinatown (www.chinatown.co.uk), with its colourful pagoda gateways and authentic Chinese grocery stores, barbers and beauty parlours. Again, it's perhaps best explored by day.

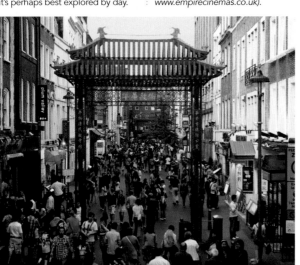

The main thoroughfare in bustling Chinatown

The Lowdown

- 🌐 **Map reference** 10 F4
- 🚇 **Tube** Leicester Square or Piccadilly Circus **Bus stop** Shaftesbury Avenue or Charing Cross Road
- 🧗 **Activities** There are about 50 film premieres annually, mostly at the Odeon Leicester Square (0871 224 4007; www.odeon.co.uk). There's also a Christmas fair, occasional funfairs and music events. For Chinese New Year (late Jan or early Feb; www.chinatown.co.uk), Chinatown comes alive with lion dances, acrobatics and music
- ⏱ **Allow** 1 hour
- ☕ **Eat and drink** Snacks Häagen-Dazs Café (14 Leicester Square WC2H 7NG; 020 7287 9577) has sumptuous ice cream Real meal Little Lamb (72 Shaftesbury Ave, W1D 6NA; 020 7287 8078) offers the chance to cook your own meal – dip titbits into communal hot and spicy broth (messy fun, best for older kids)
- 🚻 **Toilets** Underground on the north side, with changing facilities

Take cover

With 20 screens and more than 6,000 seats to choose from, it has to be the cinema if it rains. Check which of the latest films are showing at Odeon Leicester Square (0871 224 4007; www.odeon.co.uk), Vue (0871 224 0240; www.myvue.com) and the Empire (0871 471 4714; www.empirecinemas.co.uk).

Bustling with people and traffic, colourful Piccadilly Circus

⑥ Piccadilly Circus

Bright lights and amusement arcades

Piccadilly Circus is often used in books, film and television to signify London – children might know it as the scene of a horseback chase in Anthony Horowitz's *Alex Rider* novels, for example; it also starred as Dr Evil's lair in the first Austin Powers movie. Basically a traffic intersection, thanks to its power as a geographical signifier (and the Trocadero Centre), it's a focal point for visitors. Sit on the steps of the famous fountain (installed to honour philanthropist Lord Shaftesbury in 1893, and one of the first statues cast in aluminium) and take in the famous giant neon billboards, first erected in 1923.

The tube station is a good starting point for exploring London's Theatreland district – it has a Visitor Information desk and toilets. Right on the junction stands the **Ripley's Believe It Or Not** attraction (1 Piccadilly Circus, W1J 0DA;

The Lowdown

- 🌐 **Map reference** 10 E4
- 🚇 **Tube** Piccadilly Circus. **Bus stop** Piccadilly Circus
- ⏱ **Allow** 1 hour
- ☕ **Eat and drink** Picnic Millie's (Trocadero Centre, W1D 7DH; www.milliescookies.com) sells freshly baked cookies Real meal The Rainforest Café (20 Shaftesbury Ave, W1D 7EU) is an extraordinary themed restaurant, set in an animatronic jungle with monsoon soundtrack. Queues at weekends
- 🚻 **Toilets** In the subway to Piccadilly Circus tube station

Enjoying a freaky exhibit at Ripley's Believe It or Not

- **Map reference** 9 D3
  Address 188–196 Regent St, W1B; www.hamleys.com
- **Tube** Piccadilly Circus or Oxford Circus. **Bus stop** Regent Street
- **Open** 10am–8pm Mon–Wed; 10am–9pm Thu & Fri; 9:30am–9pm Sat; noon–6pm Sun
- **Activities** Lots of hands-on play tables in store, plus storytime sessions and costumed events, often linked to promotions. Real reindeer visit at Christmas.
- **Allow** Up to 1 hour
- **Eat and drink** Snacks Crumbs and Doilies (1 Kingly Court, W1B; 11am–7pm Mon–Sat, noon–6pm Sun) has great cupcakes and other sweet delights.
- **Toilets** Top floor

Star spotting

Look for the handprints of film stars who have walked the red carpet to their film premieres, set in the pavement around Leicester Square. Can you find the actors who played these roles (there's an anagram of their names to help)?

1 Nanny McPhee (Phantom memos)
2 The Grinch (I cry, Marje)
3 Gandalf (Kneel, criminals)
4 Professor McGonagall (Made hammiest gig)

Answers at the bottom of the page.

www.ripleyslondon.com), part fun-park, part freak-show. It brings together bizarre curiosities from across the globe, from Maori cannibal forks to cars coated in crystals. Beware, though: it's implausibly expensive, unless you book two weeks in advance.

Take cover

Located inside the former Foyles Bookstore building, **Star Command** (3–10pm Mon–Fri, 11am–10pm Sat & Sun) is the latest in laser tag combat. Surreal lighting and full surround sound help players immerse themselves in the game. Pricey for just 20 minutes play; discounts can be found online (www.londontrocadero.com).

⑦ Hamleys

Toys, toys, toys

This emporium is considered by some to be "the world's finest toy shop". Kids certainly think so, and entering the seven-storey store on Regent Street feels like plunging headlong into a children's play heaven. Wandering jesters blow bubbles, conjurors make things magically disappear and tots gather, giggling, around the puppet theatre, while remote-control planes whizz overhead: it's undeniably fun.

And that's just the ground floor. Other levels are themed: working up from the basement, they feature computer games and Lego; then board games and jigsaws; pre-school books and toys; dolls and dressing-up; hobbies, train sets and remote-control cars; and finally action figures. If it all gets a little too

manic, head to the princess-themed café on the top floor.

The equivalent of Hamleys for grown-ups is close by. **Carnaby Street** (www.carnaby.co.uk), somewhat changed since its 1960s heyday as the epicentre of Swinging London, is a pedestrianized precinct of mostly chain boutiques of casual wear, along with gift shops and cafés. Shop for baby and toddler gear at **Carry Me Home** (Kingly Court; carrymehome.co.uk).

Letting off steam

It is only 5 minutes around the corner to grassy **Hanover Square** (Mayfair, W1): stop off along the way at **Sunflower Café** (3 Pollen Street, W1S 1NA) for picnic supplies.

Absorbed in a doll's house at Hamleys toy shop

RAT, PIG OR SNAKE?

Each Chinese Year is represented by one of 12 animals. Which year were you born in? 1998: Tiger. 1999: Rabbit. 2000: Dragon. 2001: Snake. 2002: Horse. 2003: Ram. 2004: Monkey. 2005: Rooster. 2006: Dog. 2007: Pig. 2008: Rat. 2009: Ox. And then the cycle starts again.

Circus trick

Where are the clowns at Piccadilly Circus? In Latin, circus means "circle" – like the roundabout at Piccadilly. Here's how some other London streets got their names …
- Birdcage Walk: King Charles II had an aviary here, and even kept a crane with a wooden leg!
- Pall Mall: The French game of "paille maille", similar to croquet, was played here in the 1600s.
- Bear Gardens: In Tudor times, bears were fought against dogs here.

Bamboozle an adult!

Ask if they can name the statue at Piccadilly Circus. Did they say Eros? Wrong! The sculptor Alfred Gilbert modelled his cherub on Anteros, a different Greek love god.

Answers: 1 Emma Thompson **2** Jim Carrey **3** Sir Ian McKellen **4** Dame Maggie Smith

Covent Garden and around

From the high art at the Royal Opera House to the low comedy of the street-corner clowns, children love the buzz of London's original public square. The pedestrianized piazza is safe for kids, and surrounded by the city's oldest theatre, its quirkiest church and the London Transport Museum. On summer weekends, the sheer volume of the crowds can overwhelm Covent Garden's charms: instead, consider visiting on a Monday, when the markets are quieter and the opera company stages free lunchtime recitals at the Swiss Church.

Westminster and the West End

Covent Garden

National Gallery *p78*

Buckingham Palace *p72*

Westminster Abbey *p64*

Places of Interest

0 metres 100
0 yards 100

SIGHTS

1. Covent Garden
2. St Paul's Church
3. Royal Opera House
4. Theatre Royal Drury Lane
5. London Transport Museum
6. Somerset House
7. Sir John Soane's Museum
8. Hunterian Museum
9. St Clement Danes

EAT AND DRINK

1. Kastner and Ovens
2. Lola's
3. Masala Zone
4. Wahaca
5. Paul (29 Bedford Street, WC2E 9ED)
6. Gourmet Burger Kitchen
7. Zizzi
8. Hope and Greenwood
9. Benito's Hat
10. Rules
11. Paul (296–98 High Holborn, WC1V 7JH)
12. Strada
13. Caffè Nero (Kingsway)
14. Fleet River Bakery
15. Caffè Nero (Strand)
See also Royal Opera House (p90), London Transport Museum (p92) and Somerset House (p93)

SHOPPING

1. Tintin Shop
2. Eric Snook's
3. Benjamin Pollock's Toyshop

WHERE TO STAY

1. Citadines Prestige Holborn-Covent Garden
2. Rosewood London Hotel
3. Strand Palace Hotel

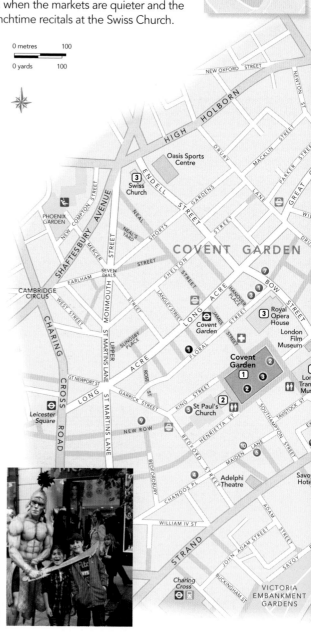

A personal perfomance, given in the streets around Covent Garden

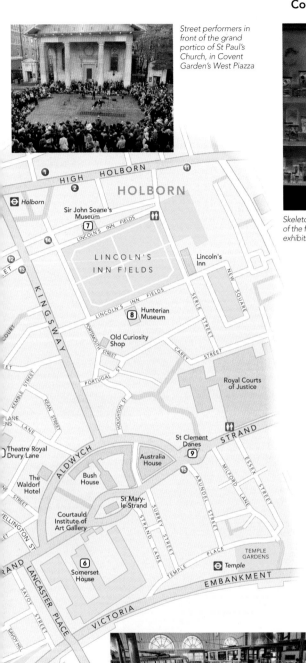

Street performers in front of the grand portico of St Paul's Church, in Covent Garden's West Piazza

Skeleton of a "giant" at the Hunterian Museum, one of the fascinating, varied and sometimes a little gory exhibits at the Royal College of Surgeons

The Lowdown

🚗 **Train** Charing Cross (5-minute walk away)
Tube Covent Garden, Leicester Square or Holborn
Bus Nearest stops at Aldwych, route numbers RV1, 9, 13, 15, 23, 139 or 153; Strand: 6, 9, 11, 13, 15, 23, 87, 91, 139, 176 **River bus** Embankment Pier, beside Charing Cross – services to Westminster and St Katharine's Dock *(Crown River Cruises: 020 7936 2033; www.crownriver.com)*

🛒 **Supermarkets** Supersave Express, 158 Drury Lane, WC2B 5QG; Tesco Metro, 22–25 Bedford St, WC2 5RF; Marks & Spencer, 107–111 Long Acre, WC2 3RG.
Markets Antiques market, Mon; craft markets daily plus "Real Food" market on the East Piazza, Apr–Dec, 11am–7pm Thu (becomes Christmas market in Dec)

🎪 **Festivals** Covent Garden May Fayre and Puppet Festival, St Paul's Church Gardens (2nd Sun in May)

➕ **Pharmacies** Boots, 4 James St, WC2E 8BH: 8:30am–9pm Mon–Fri; 9am–9pm Sat; 10am–7pm Sun. For 24-hour pharmacies, visit www.nhs.ukservicedirectories.

🛝 **Nearest playground** Drury Lane Gardens, WC2N 5TH, 8am–dusk *(see p91)* and Phoenix Garden, 21 Stacey St, WC2H 8DG *(www.thephoenixgarden.org)*

Wonderful taxis, buses and trains from a bygone era at the London Transport Museum

① Covent Garden
Fire-eaters, opera singers and lots and lots of cupcakes

From the Apple Market to the Apple Store, Covent Garden is London's best location for shopping as entertainment and an irresistible visitor attraction. It is scary to think it was almost bulldozed in the 1970s – locals fought to save it. The square was built by Inigo Jones in 1632, based on a Palladian piazza he had seen in Livorno, Italy. Today, it's full of child-pleasing fun, from the "living statues" along James Street to the street performers who dice with death daily outside St Paul's Church.

London Transport Museum poster

Key Sights

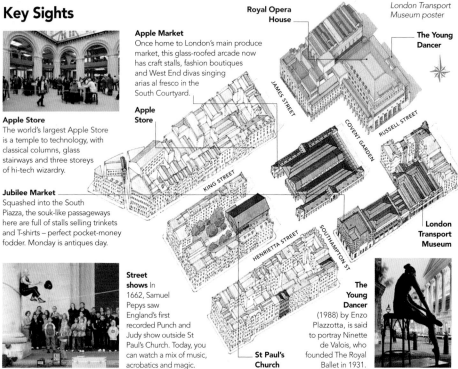

Apple Market
Once home to London's main produce market, this glass-roofed arcade now has craft stalls, fashion boutiques and West End divas singing arias al fresco in the South Courtyard.

Apple Store
The world's largest Apple Store is a temple to technology, with classical columns, glass stairways and three storeys of hi-tech wizardry.

Jubilee Market
Squashed into the South Piazza, the souk-like passageways here are full of stalls selling trinkets and T-shirts – perfect pocket-money fodder. Monday is antiques day.

Royal Opera House

The Young Dancer

Apple Store

JAMES STREET

COVENT GARDEN

RUSSELL STREET

KING STREET

London Transport Museum

HENRIETTA STREET

SOUTHAMPTON ST

Street shows In 1662, Samuel Pepys saw England's first recorded Punch and Judy show outside St Paul's Church. Today, you can watch a mix of music, acrobatics and magic.

St Paul's Church

The Young Dancer (1988) by Enzo Plazzotta, is said to portray Ninette de Valois, who founded The Royal Ballet in 1931.

Letting off steam

The piazza is cobbled and car-free, but for more room to race about, head for **Somerset House** (see p93). For a weatherproof option, walk north along Endell Street to the **Oasis Sports Centre** (020 7831 1804; www.better.org.uk/leisure-centre/london/camden/oasis-sports-centre), with pools, a sun deck and towel hire.

Eat and drink

Picnic: under £20; Snacks: £20–40; Real meal: £40–60; Family treat: £60 or more (based on a family of four)

Prices given are for a family of four

PICNIC Kastner & Ovens *(52 Floral St, WC2E 9DA; 8am–5pm weekdays)* does fabulous quiches, pies, salads and mouth-watering cakes to take away. Pick up some treats for a picnic on the jaunty benches in **Neal's Yard** *(see opposite)*.
SNACKS The classic choice for Covent garden's best cupcakes is **Lola's** *(14–18 Neal Street, WC2H 9LY; 8am–8pm Mon–Wed, 8am–9pm Thu & Fri;9am–9pm Sat, 11am–7:30pm Sun)*, with its display cabinet filled with delicious sugary treats. Two types of cupcake frostings are available – butter cream and cream cheese.

REAL MEAL Masala Zone *(48 Floral St, WC2E 9DA; 020 7379 0101; noon–3pm & 5–11pm Mon–Fri; 12:30–11pm Sun)* is a great option for Indian fare. The restaurant is super-friendly, its ceiling all a-dangle with Rajasthani puppets, and serves an authentic thali platter for kids.
FAMILY TREAT Wahaca *(66 Chandos Place, WC2N 4HG; 020 7240 1883; noon–11pm Mon–Sat; noon–10:30pm Sun)* offers a zingy take on Mexican cuisine, serving up authentic street food. There are child-size portions, high chairs and baby-changing facilities.

The Lowdown

🌐 **Map ref** 10 G3
Address Covent Garden Piazza,
WC2E 8HD; 0870 780 5001;
www.coventgarden.londonuk.com

🚗 **Tube** Covent Garden
Bus stop Aldwych **River bus**
Embankment Pier

🕐 **Open** Apple Market: 10:30am–
6pm daily (till 7:30pm Thu).
Jubilee Market: 10:30am–7pm
Tue–Fri; 10am–6pm Sat & Sun.
Apple Store (1 The Piazza,
WC2E 8HA): 10am–8pm
Mon–Sat; noon–6pm Sun

👥 **Skipping the queue** Covent
Garden tube can be a scrum
at rush hour and lunchtime;
consider walking from
Holborn, Temple, Leicester

Square or Charing Cross
(10–15 mins)

👫 **Age range** All

Activities Check website for
family street events – circus
workshops in summer holidays;
reindeer-petting at Christmas

🕐 **Allow** 2 hours for shopping and
street entertainment

🚻 **Toilets** West Piazza, beside St
Paul's Church; Tavistock Place
(with baby-changing facilities),
right of the Transport Museum

Good family value?
Hours of free fun just window-
shopping and busker-watching –
but do put a pound in the hat
if the show is any good!

Benjamin Pollock's Toyshop, a jewel of a place selling creative and theatrical toys

Shopping

Many shops have closed in
the recent years owing to online
competition and spiralling rents,
but some such as **Tintin Shop**
(34 Floral Street, WC2E 9DJ),
having reinvented themselves
still survive. Best of all are the
area's historic toy emporia:
Eric Snook (32 The Market, WC2E
8RE) – open since 1980 – and
Benjamin Pollock's Toyshop
(44 The Market, WC2E 8RF),
selling paper theatres, puppets
and shadow boxes since 1880.

Find out more

DIGITAL Download a 19th-century
toy theatre to build and colour, at
the Victoria & Albert Museum site:
www.vam.ac.uk/content/articles/m/
make-your-own-toy-theatre/
FILM The movie musical *My Fair
Lady* begins at the Royal Opera
House, where Henry Higgins sees
flower-seller Eliza Dolittle and vows
to turn her into "a proper lady".

Take cover

The **London Transport Museum**
(see p92) is a strong wet-weather
standby: its shop and café alone
should while away an hour.

Next stop...

NEAL'S YARD It's a short stroll
north to this cluster of healthfood
shops and New Age cafés painted
in bright colours. There is picnic
space, a magic mirror, and infinite
I-spy potential.
ENGLISH NATIONAL OPERA
Kids who enjoyed their blast of
street opera can book a workshop
here *(St Martin's Lane, WC2N 4ES;
020 7632 8484; www.eno.org)*.
Scheduled so that parents can take
in a matinée, Opera Tots is for ages
6 months to 4 years, and Opera
Stars ages for 7–12.

*The shop and café in the fascinating
London Transport Museum*

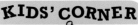

That's the way to do it!

Three things you never knew
about Punch and Judy shows ...
1 They arrived in Covent
Garden from Italy nearly
400 years ago. At first, the
performances were for adults.
2 Some early shows used a real
dog to play the part of Toby.
Good job they didn't use a real
baby – Mr Punch usually throws
him out of the window!
3 Punch and Judy men are
always called "Professor". They
make the squawky voice using
a mouthpiece called a swazzle.
Can you do a Mr Punch voice?
One way to do it is to pinch
your nostrils shut!

FESTIVE FACT

The craziest Covent Garden
event is the Great Christmas
Pudding Race held in December.
People dress up as Santas, elves
or reindeer and dash
over a series of
obstacles
carrying plum
puddings.
You can watch
a typical race at *www.
xmaspuddingrace.org.uk.*

3-minute wonders

Covent Garden's amazing
entertainers have to audition
to win a chance to perform here,
and just like singers on a TV
talent show, they
only get 3
minutes to
impress! What
act would you
do to entertain
the judges?

The Lowdown

- 🌐 **Map reference** 10 G4
  Address Bedford St, WC2E; 020
  7836 5221; www.actorschurch.org
- 🚇 **Tube** Covent Garden or Leicester
  Square **Bus stop** Aldwych
- 🕐 **Open** 8:30am–5pm Mon–Fri;
  times vary Sat; 9am–1pm Sun
- 💲 **Price** Donations
- 🎭 **Activities** Services Tue, Wed
  & Sun; plus regular concerts
- ⏱ **Allow** 30 minutes
- 🍴 **Eat and drink** Snacks Paul (29
  Bedford Street, WC2E 9ED)
  offers sumptuous pastries and
  cakes Real meal Gourmet Burger
  Kitchen (13–14 Maiden Lane,
  WC2E 7NE) has fine tasty burgers
- 🚻 **Toilets** Next door, on the West
  Piazza

② St Paul's Church

The actors' church

Where's the door? That's the
mystery of St Paul's portico, with
its soaring marble columns. The
answer is: around the back. After
Inigo Jones designed the church
as the centrepiece of his new piazza
in 1631, the Bishop of London
insisted the altar must be at the
eastern end, so that worshippers
faced Jerusalem – which means this
grand gateway was never used.

Today, it makes a perfect stage
for Covent Garden's acrobats and
clowns, which is fitting, since St Paul's
has long been the "actors' church",
and inside there are inscriptions
remembering Charlie Chaplin,

Vivien Leigh and more. Children
can hunt for the actor who first
played Frankenstein's monster,
Boris Karloff, and Percy Press,
"King of Punch and Judy", whose
memorial depicts the puppet pair.

Look out, too, for the church's
vintage model theatre, which was
once shown off in village halls to
raise money for a London hostel
where actors could lodge their
children while they went on tour.

The first victim of the Great
Plague of 1665–66, Margaret
Porteous, is buried here. It went
on to claim one in five Londoners.

Letting off steam

Escape the Covent Garden crowds
in the church garden – but get there
early to bag a bench for lunchtime.

*Drury Lane Gardens, a small playground
for little ones in the backstreets*

③ Royal Opera House

Tenors, sopranos and pirouetting ballerinas

Home to both the Royal Opera
and Royal Ballet companies, this
showpiece theatre was begun in
1732 by John Rich, a famous
harlequin who staged Britain's first
pantomime. George Frideric Handel
(1685–1759) was its musical director:
he gave his *Messiah* its UK premiere
here and also introduced the risqué
dancing of Marie Sallé.

Following a makeover in the
1990s, the theatre has endeavoured
to lessen opera's elitist image. Ticket
prices have been reduced, there's a
free recital most Mondays and

guided backstage tours daily. Tours
start in the jaw-dropping auditorium,
built in 1858, with its 15-m- (50-ft-)
high stage and balconies dripping
with gilt. Tours usually visit the
Model Room, too, where doll's-
house-size sets are delicately

The Lowdown

- 🌐 **Map reference** 10 G3
  Address Covent Garden, WC2E;
  020 7304 4000; www.roh.org.uk
- 🚇 **Tube** Covent Garden
  Bus stop Aldwych
- 🕐 **Open** 10am–3:30pm Mon–Sat
  and for performances
- 💲 **Price** Show tickets start
  from £40
- 🎫 **Skipping the queue** Tickets for
  free Monday recitals are released
  online nine days ahead, but most
  are held back till the day – 10am
  at the box office
- **Guided tours** Mon–Sat (£39–42)
- 🎭 **Activities** A free children's activity
  trail explores the public areas;
  creative workshops in May
  half-term; Christmas productions
  suit kids aged 6 and up
- 👫 **Age range** 8 plus (guided tours);
  7 plus (workshops)
- ⏱ **Allow** 75 minutes for the tour
- ♿ **Wheelchair access** Yes, lifts give
  access to most of the auditoria
- 🍴 **Eat and drink** Snacks The
  rooftop terrace at the
  Amphitheatre Bar serves light
  lunches 10am–3pm Real meal
  Zizzi (20 Bow St, WC2E 7AW)
  serves up scrumptious pizzas
- 🛍 **Shop** Covent Garden entrance and
  in Amphitheatre Bar before a show
- 🚻 **Toilets** In the lobby

The green spaces of St Paul's Church garden, an oasis of calm in Covent Garden

Royal Ballet dancers performing Swan Lake at the Royal Opera House

constructed for every new show. But the highlight is peering into a Royal Ballet rehearsal studio, where the dancers might be pirouetting away.

Letting off steam
The tiny playground in **Drury Lane Gardens** (along Broad Court, then right on Drury Lane) used to be a graveyard! Today it has swings and slides for ages 3–7.

④ Theatre Royal Drury Lane
Theatrical magic and spooks

London's oldest working playhouse started life in 1663, when Charles II lifted the 11-year theatre ban imposed by Oliver Cromwell. The entire building would fit on the stage today: it was roofless and featured Britain's first ever female actors and the first proscenium arch or "picture box stage".

Today, the oak-lined lobby is worth a peek, or take a backstage tour run by actors in costume. Nell

An entertaining backstage tour at the historic Theatre Royal Drury Lane

Gwynne, actress and mistress of Charles II, reveals the royal retiring room where George V knighted the actor Frank Benson with his own prop sword, then it's down under the stage to see the trap doors.

Shows at "the Lane" have been famous for their spectacular special effects, including an earthquake and a horse race with 12 real horses running on a treadmill. *Miss Saigon*, which ran for 10 years and 4,263 performances, "landed" a real helicopter on the stage every time!

Letting off steam
To reach **Drury Lane Gardens** playground (*see left*), head along Russell Street and turn left.

The Lowdown

- 🌐 **Map reference** 10 H3
  Address Catherine St, WC2B; *www.reallyuseful.co.uk*
- 🚇 **Tube** Covent Garden or Holborn. **Bus stop** Aldwych
- 🕐 **Open** Box office 10am–8pm
- 🎫 **Price** Show tickets from £80
- 🎭 **Guided tours** Twice daily, Mon–Sat (£32–6)
- 🚻 **Age range** Tours suit ages 6 plus
- ⏱ **Allow** 1 hour for the tour
- ♿ **Wheelchair access** Limited. Call 0844 412 4648 for information
- 🍴 **Eat and drink** *Picnic* Hope and Greenwood (*1 Russell St, WC2B 5JD*) sells old-fashioned sweets. *Real meal* Boswell's (*8 Russell St, WC2B 5HZ*) offers sandwiches, salads, pastries and more.
- 🚻 **Toilets** On request

⑤ London Transport Museum

This really is travelling back in time

Don't be put off by the subject matter – this is one of the most hooting, tooting museums in London. It crams 20 vintage buses, trams and trains into a steel-and-glass cavern once occupied by the Covent Garden flower market, and visitors get to climb aboard many of them to "take a drive". It's a hands-on experience, so hold tight!

Start on Level 2, up in the rafters, with its full-size sedan chair and London's earliest horse-drawn omnibus. Jump in and sit beside a top-hatted gent as he reels off the rules of the road, 1829-style. There are sound clips of crossing-sweepers (who cleared a path through the horse muck) and bus conductors, and cartoon quizzes to answer.

Level 1 has the first underground steam train from the 1860s, occupied by lifelike passengers, while vintage posters recall how the expansion of the tube sent London sprawling out into the suburbs. On a balcony is the Interchange, a push-button zone for children (age 7–11), where they can dress up as engine drivers and try their hand at driving the latest eco-friendly bus.

Younger kids will want to sprint straight to the open-plan and neon-lit ground floor (Level 0), with

Above One of the many vintage trains at the London Transport Museum
Below right Enjoying a hands-on experience – driving a bus

a dozen or so vehicles to explore, plus sit-in simulators where they can manoeuvre the "dead man's handle" that drives a modern-day tube train (once the adults get out of the way). There is a themed play corner for under-7s, with picnic tables alongside. Finally, it's out into the shop and café, with retro-cool posters for parents, die-cast models for kids, and Circle Line smoothies for all.

Letting off steam

The museum is comfortable about kids careering around. For outdoor frolics, head along Russell Street to **Drury Lane Gardens**, with slides and seesaws for ages 3–7; or across Strand into Somerset House (see opposite).

The Lowdown

🌐 **Map ref** 10 H3
Address Covent Garden Piazza, WC2E 7BB; 020 7565 7299; *www.ltmuseum.co.uk*

🚗 **Tube** Covent Garden
Bus stop Aldwych

🕐 **Open** 10am–6pm Sat–Thu; 11am–6pm Fri (last adm 5:15pm)

💷 **Price** £18.50, under-18s free

🎟 **Skipping the queue** Tickets give free entry for a whole year

🚩 **Guided tours** No

👪 **Age range** 3 plus

🎨 **Activities** Collect cards from the ticket desk for kids to stamp as they go around the museum. Download trails from the website beforehand. There are free drop-in activities in school holidays

⏱ **Allow** Up to 3 hours

♿ **Wheelchair access** Yes, but some vehicles are inaccessible

🍴 **Eat and drink** *Snacks* Upper Deck café-bar in lobby serves quick bites *Family treat* Rules (35 Maiden Lane, WC2E 7LB; 020 7836 5314) serves classic British dishes

🛍 **Shop** Gifts and memorabilia

🚻 **Toilets** Ground floor gallery

On board a horse-drawn double-decker "London Omnibus", phased out in 1911

Prices given are for a family of four

Splashing around in the Fountain Court, Somerset House

⑥ Somerset House

Enjoy a great day at the office

Somerset House looks like a palace, and originally there was one here, the scene of 17th-century royal masques *(see p71)*. But the Palladian quadrangle we see today was actually the first ever purpose-built office block, for decades the home of tax inspectors and the register of births, deaths and marriages.

It is now open to the public, and the Embankment Galleries, by the riverside, house temporary shows on 20th-century fashion, design and photography, usually incorporating lots of interactive gizmos and family workshops. The Courtauld Gallery, by Strand, is a modest collection

with several paintings that even little ones might know: Van Gogh with his ear bandaged, Manet's staring barmaid at the Folies-Bergère and Degas's graceful ballet dancers.

The big draw for families, though, is the spectacular Fountain Court in the centre, now a pleasure space where 55 water jets dance from Easter till October, just begging for youngsters to chase and splash. There are big-name pop concerts and family film matinées here in summer, while from November to January it becomes London's most glamorous ice rink, with cocktails, DJs and a giant Christmas tree.

Letting off steam

Fountain Court takes on a seaside feel in summer, with café tables at the edges and families spreading out towels and donning swimsuits.

The Lowdown

🌐 **Map ref** 10 H4
Address Strand, WC2R 1LA; 020 7845 4600; www.somersethouse. org.uk; 020 7848 2777; www. courtauld.ac.uk

🚇 **Tube** Temple **Bus stop** Strand **River bus** Embankment pier

🕐 **Open** Embankment Galleries and Courtauld Gallery 10am–6pm daily; Fountain Court 7:30am–11pm

💲 **Price** Embankment Galleries Adult admission fee varies, under 12s free; Courtauld Gallery £14–19, under-18s free

👥 **Skipping the queue** Tickets for Saturday workshops are released at 1pm sharp. Book ahead for the popular ice rink (www.somerset house.org.uk/ice-rink)

🚩 **Guided tours** Thu and Sat (free)

👫 **Age range** All

🎨 **Activities** Family fact-finding sheets for most temporary shows. Free art and fashion workshops on school-holiday weekends, plus every Sat for ages 6–12, and 1st Sun of the month for under-5s. There are studio days for teens in the school holidays

🕐 **Allow** 1 hour

♿ **Wheelchair access** Yes

🍴 **Eat and drink** *Snacks* The Café at the Courtauld is cosy, with a patio garden, funky teapots and yummy cakes *Real Meal* Tom's Kitchen, in the Embankment wing, serves brasserie food in a refectory-style area, run by Michelin-starred chef Tom Aikens

🛍 **Shop** Rizzoli Bookshop sells art books; Courtauld Shop offers items inspired by the artworks

🚻 **Toilets** Downstairs, on the Embankment side

⑦ Sir John Soane's Museum

3,000 years of history packed into one house

This townhouse museum comprises a warren of poky passages filled with wonders: a magic picture gallery, a monk's cell, even a real mummy's coffin from ancient Egypt.

Sir John Soane was a bricklayer's son who became a top architect: he designed the Bank of England in 1788. He brought his young family to the house in 1792, and spent the next 45 years filling every nook and cranny with his bizarre collection of gargoyles, statues, busts and bric-à-brac from the ancient world. Luckily, before he died Soane insisted everything was left exactly as it was, for visitors to enjoy.

This means the house is one big time capsule. Audio guides lead the way, but watch out for Soane's tricks: mirrors where you can't see your feet; secret panels that reveal hidden paintings; even a writing desk hidden inside a statue. Best of all is the

Inside the fascinating Sir John Soane's Museum

mummy's sarcophagus down in "the Crypt", which belonged to Pharaoh Seti I. It is 3,300 years old and covered in hieroglyphics. Soane paid £2,000 for it, and threw a three-night candlelit party to celebrate.

Letting off steam

Lincoln's Inn Fields, opposite, was laid out in the 17th century by Inigo Jones. The lawns, once popular for duels, are green and wide. There are tennis courts (*£11.65 per hour, seniors and under-16s £4.45; 07525 278647*).

The Lowdown

🌐 **Map reference** 10 H2
Address 13 Lincoln's Inn Fields, WC2A 3BP; 020 7405 2107; *www.soane.org*

🚇 **Tube** Holborn **Bus stop** High Holborn, Aldwych or Kingsway

🕐 **Open** 10am–5pm Tue–Sat (last entry 4:30pm). Candlelit opening 6–9pm 1st Tue of each month

💷 **Price** Free

Skipping the queue No pre-booking, so there are often large queues. Get there by 10am

Guided tours 11:30am Tue–Fri (also 3:30pm Wed & Thu); 11am Sat (£10 per person)

Age range 7 plus

Activities Children's audio tour must be downloaded before visiting. Imaginative holiday workshops for ages 7 plus (£20 full day, £12 half day)

⏱ **Allow** 1–2 hours

♿ **Wheelchair access** Limited, due to stairs. Contact 020 7405 2107

🍴 **Eat and drink** *Snacks* Paul (296–298 High Holborn, WC1V 7JH) offers filled baguettes and patisserie *Real Meal* Strada (6 Great Queen Street, WC2B 5DH) does pizzas and classic Italian food

Toilets In the basement

The Lowdown

🌐 **Map reference** 10 H2
Address 35–43 Lincoln's Inn Fields, WC2A 3PE; 020 7869 6560; *www.hunterianmuseum.org*

🚇 **Tube** Holborn or Temple
Bus stop High Holborn, Aldwych or Kingsway

🕐 **Open** Closed till 2020

💷 **Price** Free

Skipping the queue Download the audio guide from the website for free before visiting; at the museum it costs £4

Guided tours Wed, 1pm (free)

Age range 6 plus, though parental guidance advisable

Activities Half-term holiday sessions for families

⏱ **Allow** 1–2 hours

♿ **Wheelchair access** Yes, via Nuffield College entrance

🍴 **Eat and drink** *Picnic* Caffè Nero (77d Kingsway, WC2B 6ST) serves sandwiches and snacks *Snacks* Fleet River Bakery (71 Lincoln's Inn Fields, WC2A 3JF) does sandwiches, salads and soup

Toilets In the basement

⑧ Hunterian Museum

Bones and body parts

The Hunterian might be the most stomach-turning museum in London but most children are gripped by its sparkling cut-glass receptacles full of bits and pieces of bodies, wildlife and gruesome gadgets, all collected in the 18th century by John Hunter, the pioneer of modern surgery.

Hunter is not very well-known these days, but he's the man who insisted surgery should be based on evidence – which meant cutting things up to show what they look like inside. He performed public dissections for his students at a time when only the bodies of hanged criminals could be used for medical science: don't miss the display about the notorious bodysnatchers who raided local graveyards to supply Hunter with

Lincoln's Inn Fields, London's largest public square, a great place to stretch the legs

Items from the early days of anatomical discovery at the Hunterian Museum

corpses. These were bumped upstairs at his grand house in Leicester Square – a house big enough to hold his stuffed giraffe, the first ever seen in England.

The museum has an audio guide suitable for older children and adults, plus quiz sheets for ages 5–7 and 8–11. The upstairs gallery has gory TV clips of modern operations and there are art materials, moveable skeletons and tunics stuck with Velcro organs in a side room, which is usually open for kids (phone ahead to check). Much might change and there could be new additions post refurbishment.

Letting off steam
The well-tended lawns of **Lincoln's Inn Fields** are right opposite *(see left)*, perfect for running around.

⑨ St Clement Danes

Home of a nursery rhyme?
The strange name of this church is said to come from the Vikings, who murdered and pillaged their way along what is now the River Thames in the 9th century. Finally defeated by King Alfred the Great, those with English wives were allowed to settle in this part of London.

St Clement's has been rebuilt twice: by Christopher Wren after the Great Fire of London (1666) and again after being blasted by German bombers in the Blitz (1941) – which is why it became the central church of the Royal Air Force. Aim to visit at 9am, noon, 3pm or 6pm, when

the church bells peal out the tune to the nursery rhyme *Oranges and Lemons*. First written down in 1744, some say it refers to local children who helped smugglers unload their cargo from the Thames, and were given fruit as a reward. Oranges and lemons are still handed out to children here today, as part of a service in March.

The church's creepiest treasure is in the crypt: a chain that was used to clamp shut coffins to protect the recently deceased from the bodysnatchers who raided graveyards to steal corpses for medical research.

Letting off steam
Temple Gardens, at the bottom of Arundel Street, has slivers of grass, but for more space, head along the Strand to **Somerset House** *(see p93)*.

The Lowdown

🌐 **Map reference** 11 A3
Address Strand, WC2 1DH; 020 7242 8282; *www.raf.mod.uk/stclementdanes/*

🚇 **Tube** Temple **Bus stop** Strand

🕐 **Open** 9am–4pm (except bank holidays); services Wed, Fri & Sun

💷 **Price** Donations

⏱ **Allow** 30 minutes

🍴 **Eat and drink** *Snacks* Caffè Nero (181 Strand, WC2R 1EA), opposite, serves sandwiches and snacks *Real Meal* The Courtauld Gallery Café (150 Somerset House, WC2R 0NR; daily 10am-5:30pm) is cooler, with quirky crockery and big cakes

🚻 **Toilets** No

Bloomsbury
and Regent's Park

It's hard to beat this part of London for sheer
spectacle: it has mummies and movie stars, lions
and labyrinths. It's possible to go a full weekend
without setting foot outside Regent's Park, thanks
to its zoo, open-air theatre, canals and lakes,
while the busy Madame Tussauds is nearby. If
the vast treasures of the British Museum don't
attract, then fascinating smaller museums cover
canal boats, toys, medicine and more.

**Bloomsbury and
Regent's Park**

The City and
the East End

Westminster
and the
West End   Southwark and
the South Bank

Kensington,
Chelsea and
Battersea

Highlights

British Museum
Among this museum's many
marvels, the mummy galleries
will always be the star attraction.
Plan ahead and kids can even
have a sleepover (see pp102–3).

Coram's Fields
Possibly London's top playground,
Coram's Fields has an adventure
play area, zipwire and sandpits,
plus a farmyard (see p106).

Wellcome Collection
Children get a cardboard
moustache to wear during their
visit here. Why? Who knows! It is
part of the zaniest – and best –
children's museum pack in
London (see p104).

ZSL London Zoo
Yes, there are lions and tigers,
gorillas and giraffes, but George
the scarlet macaw upstages
them all in the daily Animals in
Action live show (see pp110–11).

Puppet Theatre Barge
This red-and-yellow narrowboat at
Little Venice is home to London's
most delightful family theatre
experience. Glide there along the
canal from Camden (see p111).

Camden Market
It's about as close as London
gets to a souk. Older children
especially love exploring the
market's labyrinth of exotic stalls
and shops (see pp112–13).

Left The London Canal Museum on the Regent's Canal
Above Getting up close to a tarantula at London Zoo

The Best of
Bloomsbury & Regent's Park

This well-to-do part of London divides neatly in two – one half cerebral, the other sensory. Both are walkable for even the littlest legs and filled with literary and artistic connections. To the east, stately Bloomsbury offers a day or two of family-friendly brainwork, its mix of unusual museums providing all manner of kids' activities. For more active fun or some relaxation, head west to the great green playground of Regent's Park.

A Year in Regent's Park

With or without a trip to London Zoo, little ones will adore **Regent's Park** (see p112). In spring, guided walks show off the blooms of the wildlife garden near York Bridge; or venture out on the boating pond. June is prime time for the roses in Queen Mary's Gardens, where the rock garden is perfect for hide-and-seek. The school summer holiday heralds playground sessions and sports coaching at The Hub, and there are matinée performances at the Open Air Theatre.

Come autumn, the tree-lined towpath along Regent's Canal is very colourful, and October's Frieze Art Fair dots eye-catching artworks around the park. By November, over-wintering wildfowl are swooping onto the lake from colder climes: Long Bridge is the best viewing spot. If it really freezes, warm up in the indoor rainforest pavilion at **ZSL London Zoo** (see pp110–11), or take in the Christmas show at the **Puppet Theatre Barge** (see p111). Whatever the season, the friendly Garden Café has a menu to match (see p111).

Storybook London

Pooh and Potter, Peter Pan and Paddington – many favourites from children's literature have links with this part of London. The original Winnie the Pooh lived at London Zoo (see pp110–11) in the 1920s: author AA Milne and his son Christopher Robin loved visiting the bear, and a statue now remembers Winnie in the zoo's Animal Adventure zone. Just across the fence in Regent's Park stood the home of Pongo and Missis, heroes of *The Hundred and One Dalmatians*; while over in Bloomsbury, a statue of Peter Pan and Tinkerbell stands outside Great Ormond Street children's hospital; Peter's creator JM Barrie donated the royalties from his play to hospital funds.

Above right *Playing on the forecourt of the British Museum*
Below right *Gorillas lounging at ZSL London Zoo*

Above *Admiring the spring flowers in Regent's Park, one of London's most beautiful green spaces*

It's a short walk from there to the **Charles Dickens Museum** *(see pp106–7)*, where the great Victorian novelist wrote *Oliver Twist* – see the window that Oliver scrambled through on his burgling mission with Bill Sikes. Wander up to the **British Library** *(see p105)* and flick through a digital version of Lewis Carroll's original manuscript for *Alice in Wonderland*, before heading home – preferably via platform 9¾ at King's Cross Station, Harry Potter's departure point for Hogwarts School of Witchcraft and Wizardry.

A Bloomsbury sketch

There's nowhere better in London for families to travel armed with sketchbook and pencils. An inspiring place to start is the **Cartoon Museum** *(see p103)*, with its art room and monthly family workshops. Just up the road, **Pollock's Toy Museum** *(see p104)* devotes a gallery to the exquisite paper theatres stencilled and coloured by Benjamin Pollock and his family in Victorian times, and sells kits to

construct at home. The **Wellcome Collection** *(see pp104–5)* also encourages budding artists – its children's pack includes modelling clay and a mask-making kit – while the nearby **Foundling Museum** *(see p104)* invites young visitors to design a postcard inspired by its exhibition, and hosts family craft sessions each month.

Running out of paper? Never fear: the **British Museum** *(see pp102–3)* has the mother of all children's activity programmes – and hands out free art materials to every junior visitor.

A fun-filled weekend

There is always something afoot for families at the British Museum *(see pp102–3)*, but especially on Saturdays. Arrive by 10am, check out the day's programme, then head for the Paul Hamlyn Library, which hands out children's packs and trails. Organized kids' activities get going at around 11am, usually in the magnificent Great Court. For lunch, escape to nearby Russell Square for a splash in the fountain, and pizza and ice cream from the terrace café. Just around the corner is **Coram's Fields** *(see p106)*, one of London's very best playgrounds.

Sunday is all about **Camden Market** *(see pp112–13)*, a maze of stalls selling everything from musky smelling patchouli oil to vintage clothing. Younger children will especially like Camden Lock, with its jaunty narrowboat rides, and Yumchaa teashop is nice for elevenses. Escape before 1pm, when busy Camden Town tube station becomes exit-only, and hop two tube stops south to Euston, where the weird and wonderful **Wellcome Collection** *(see pp104–5)* will amaze young and old alike with its array of curiosities. Don't miss the free tour at 2:30pm.

Left *People enjoying at the various eateries in Stables Market, Camden Lock, a great place to browse, with 700 stalls and shops*

British Museum and around

With Sir Norman Foster's splendid Great Court, a cavernous igloo of white space, the British Museum has one of the grandest entrance lobbies in the world. All-action art workshops take place here every weekend, and there is a dedicated children's shop and two cafés. The museum is free to visit and picnicking is permitted: throw in the marvellous playground at nearby Coram's Fields, and this must be London's best budget day out for families. Bloomsbury has a clutch of smaller museums too, devoted to toys, cartoons, canal boats and more.

Bloomsbury and Regent's Park

ZSL London Zoo p108

British Museum

The British Museum, packed with interesting and exotic exhibits from around the world

Exploring Pollock's Toy Museum, filled to bursting with toys, both past and present

Places of Interest

SIGHTS
1. British Museum
2. Pollock's Toy Museum
3. Wellcome Collection
4. British Library
5. Foundling Museum
6. Charles Dickens Museum
7. London Canal Museum

EAT AND DRINK
1. Little Waitrose
2. My Old Dutch
3. Heal's Café
4. Hakkasan
5. Planet Organic
6. Patisserie Valerie
7. Giraffe
8. Simmons
9. Café Oz

See also British Museum (pp102–3), Wellcome Collection (p104), British Library (p105), Foundling Museum (p106) and Charles Dickens Museum (p106)

WHERE TO STAY
1. Alhambra
2. Arosfa
3. Bedford
4. Euro
5. Jesmond
6. Jesmond Dene
7. SACO-Holborn

0 metres 200

0 yards 200

Bronze statue of Sir Isaac Newton outside the British Library

London Canal Museum ⑦

④ British Library

Exploring the fascinating Wellcome Collection

Foundling Museum ⑤

Charles Dickens Museum ⑥

British Museum ①

Cartoon Museum ②

The Lowdown

🚇 **Tube** Tottenham Court Road or Holborn **Bus** New Oxford Street: 8, 25, 55, 98; Great Russell Street: 8, 10, 14, 24, 25, 29, 55, 73, 98, 134, 390

ℹ️ **Visitor information** Holborn Information Kiosk, Kingsway, WC2B 6BG; Euston Travel Information Centre, Euston Rail Centre, NW1 2HS

🛒 **Supermarkets** Hannells Food & Wine, 52–56 New Oxford Street, WC1A 1ES; Sainsbury's Central, 129 Kingsway, WC2B 6NH; Waitrose, 23–39 The Brunswick Centre, WC1N 1AF **Markets** Chapel Market (food and household goods) Penton Street, N1 9PX, 9am–5pm Tue–Sat; 10am–4pm Sun (including farmers' market); Camden Passage antiques market, N1 8EA, 9am–5:30pm Wed & Sat. Both are near Angel tube. Covent Garden's markets are also within (30-min) walking range (see pp86–7)

🎭 **Festivals** Bloomsbury Festival, music and arts (Oct)

➕ **Pharmacies** Clockwork Pharmacy, 150 Southampton Row, WC1B 5AN (9am–7pm Mon–Fri; 9am–6pm Sat). For 24-hour pharmacies, search at www.nhs.uk/servicedirectories

🛝 **Nearest playgrounds** Alf Barrett Playground (see p102), Coram's Fields (see p106) and Crabtree Fields (see p104).

Enjoying one of the many attractions at the popular Coram's Fields playground and park

The Lowdown

🌐 **Map ref** 10 G1
Address British Museum, Great Russell Street, WC1B 3DG; 020 7323 8000; www.britishmuseum.org

🚇 **Tube** Tottenham Court Road or Holborn **Bus stop** New Oxford Street, Great Russell Street

🕐 **Open** Galleries 10am–5:30pm daily; selected rooms till 8:30pm Fri. Great Court 9am–6pm Sun–Thu; till 8:30pm Fri

💲 **Price** Free. Special exhibitions charge entrance fees

🎫 **Guided tours** Free 30-min tours daily in selected galleries; multimedia guide £17

👫 **Age range** 3 plus

🤸 **Activities** Children's audio tour with a choice of themes. Family workbook trails (ages 3–5 and 6–11) plus activity backpacks available until 3pm at weekends and daily during school holidays from the Great Court. Object-handling in galleries 1, 2, 24, 33, 49 and 68 (11am–4pm). Free family activities and workshops on weekends and school holidays. Free digital workshops every Wed (age 7 plus). Young Friends club (annual membership £20) arranges six sleepovers a year; www.britishmuseum.org/membership/young_friends.aspx

⏱ **Allow** At least 3 hours

♿ **Wheelchair access** Yes

☕ **Café** Court Cafés (Great Court, Ground Floor) serve snacks and sandwiches. Gallery Café (Ground Floor) has family-friendly hot dishes. Court Restaurant (Great Court, Upper Floor) serves an à la carte menu. Ford Centre for Young Visitors (Lower Floor) has a baby-feeding room and allows picnicking

🛍 **Shops** Several – in the foyer and the Great Court

🚻 **Toilets** On all floors

Good family value?
Unbeatable, with lots of free stuff to hold children's interest, from activity backpacks to object-handling tables and weekend workshops. It's even permissible to bring your own sandwiches.

① British Museum
Heaps of human history under one roof

Pirate gold, a crystal skull, fanged demons – the British Museum is jammed full of wonders. Three floors of galleries chart two million years of human civilization across the globe, so it pays to be choosy. The Egyptian Collection (Rooms 61–66) and Living and Dying (Room 24) are impressive, with their mummies and skulls. Start in the Families Centre in the Great Court, for free kids' trails and backpacks.

Key Features

◾ **Levels 4 & 5** Special exhibitions and Asia: China and Korea

◾ **Level 3** Ancient Egypt, Greece and Rome; Middle East and Europe

◾ **Levels 1 & 2** Asia: China, India, Japan, Southeast Asia

◾ **Ground floor** America: North America and Mexico; Ancient Greece and Rome, Middle East and Egypt

◾ **Level –1** Africa, Greek and Roman architecture

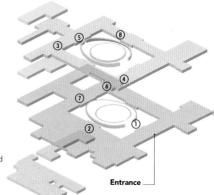

Entrance

Letting off steam

Alf Barrett Playground (Old Gloucester Street, WC1B 4DA), 10 minutes east of the museum on the corner of Old Gloucester Street and Gage Street, caters for kids up to age 13. Behind the museum, **Russell Square**, remodelled to its original 200-year-old Humphry Repton design, has the perfect fountain for splashing through, plus ice creams to enjoy from the terrace café.

Eat and drink
Picnic: under £20; Snacks: £20–40; Real meal: £40–60; Family treat: £60 or more (based on a family of four)

PICNIC Little Waitrose (227–233 Tottenham Court Road W1T 7QF; 0800 184 884) is a smaller version of the high-quality British supermarket chain. Pick up a picnic here and eat in nearby Bloomsbury Square.
SNACKS My Old Dutch (131 High Holborn, WC1V 6PS; 020 7242 5200; www.myolddutch.com) lets kids build their own crêpes – anyone for a pineapple and red

Taking a break in the comfortable surroundings of Meals at Heals

chilli pancake? It also does good smoothies and shakes.
REAL MEAL Heal's Café (196 Tottenham Court Road, W1T 7LQ; 020 7636 1666; www.heals.co.uk), on the first floor of Heals, has child-friendly fare.
FAMILY TREAT Hakkasan (8 Hanway Place, W1T 1HD; 020 7927 7000; www.hakkasan.com) is at the forefront of contemporary Chinese cuisine and has a Michelin star. The "small eat" dishes are ideal for kids.

① **Great Court** Once an outside courtyard, this is now the largest covered public space in Europe.

② **Rosetta Stone** Carved with a pharaoh's decree from 196 BC, this is the museum's most visited treasure. It is written in three languages, which enabled experts to decode Egyptian hieroglyphs for the first time. (Room 4)

③ **Abydos cat mummy** The ancient Egyptians worshipped cats, mummifying thousands as offerings to the cat-goddess Bastet. (Room 62)

④ **Pirate treasure** Long John Silver's parrot squawked "pieces of eight" – and here they are. In Tudor times (c.1500–1600), these Spanish coins were worth about £50. (Room 68)

⑤ **The Royal Game of Ur** This Ludo-like dice game was played 4,500 years ago in Mesopotamia. Players raced across the board, trying to land on the lucky rosettes. (Room 56)

⑥ **Ball game belt** This toad-shaped belt featured in the world's oldest team sport, a type of volleyball played in ancient Mexico. Defeat could be dangerous – the losers were sacrificed to the gods! (Room 27)

⑦ **Camera coffin** The Ga people of Ghana have been fashioning these fantastical coffins since the 1950s to represent the dead person's interests – such as photography, eagles or planes. (Room 24)

⑧ **Mold Cape** Discovered in a Welsh burial mound, this Bronze Age cape was a pile of gold fragments, leaving curators with a giant jigsaw puzzle to tackle. (Room 51)

Find out more

DIGITAL The museum's website has a great zone just for children: browse through the informative project, "Teaching History with 100 Objects" at http://www.teaching history100.org/, that promotes kids' interest in history.

Make your own mummy at www. bbc.co.uk/history/ancient/egyptians/launch_gms_mummy_maker.shtml.

In the BBC Radio 4 series *A History of the World in 100 Objects*, British Museum director Neil MacGregor chose his world-changing artifacts. Download the series at www.bbc.co.uk/ahistoryoftheworld/.

Next stop...

THE PETRIE MUSEUM Part of the University College of London, this museum (*Malet Place, WC1E 6BT; Tue–Sat 1–5pm; www.ucl.ac.uk/culture/petrie-museum*) is stacked high with Egyptian items – and has an art table and Roman togas for children to model.

THE CARTOON MUSEUM This fun place (*35 Little Russell Street, WC1A 2HH; 020 7580 8155; 10:30am–5:30pm Tue–Sun; www.cartoonmuseum.org*) has an art room where kids can doodle their own masterpiece. British cartoons and comic art from the 18th century to the present day are on display. It also offers drop-in family cartooning on the second Saturday of the month and terrific school-holiday workshops for ages 8 plus.

Aspiring young cartoonists getting instruction at the Cartoon Museum

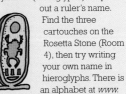

② Pollock's Toy Museum

Playtimes from the past

Winding your way around the snaking stairways and attic rooms of this rickety old house feels like going back in time – which is appropriate, since they are filled with a treasure trove of toys spanning two centuries. Don't tell the children, but it's an irresistible nostalgia trip for parents, too.

The charming, idiosyncratic collection includes Schoenhut's Humpty Dumpty Circus from 1903, and a reconstructed early 20th-century boy's den, complete with dangerous-looking chemistry set and blow football. One room is devoted to the delicate but magical paper theatres of the Pollock family, whose renowned Victorian toy emporium spawned the museum in 1956. Other rooms concentrate on early teddy bears, toy soldiers and slightly spooky wax dolls.

The labels are yellowing and there's little to touch or play with, so give thanks for the toyshop at the end of the visit, stacked with superannuated treats – spinning tops, kaleidoscopes and classic card games such as Happy Families. Pollock's Toy Shop in Covent Garden (see p89) also sells great toys.

Letting off steam

One minute's walk south, **Crabtree Fields** (Whitfield Street, W1T 2BJ) has a fun-filled playground and an attractive pergola walkway.

Browsing among the exciting toys in the toyshop of Pollock's Toy Museum

The Lowdown

- 🌐 **Map ref** 10 E1
  Address 1 Scala Street, W1T 2HL; 020 7636 3452; www. pollockstoys.com
- 🚇 **Tube** Goodge Street
  Bus stop Tottenham Court Road
- 🕐 **Open** 10am–5pm Mon–Sat (last admission 4:30pm)
- 💲 **Price** £18
- 🚩 **Guided tours** No
- 🎭 **Activities** Occasional toy theatre or puppet shows during school holidays (call to check)
- 👫 **Age range** 5 plus
- ⏱ **Allow** 1 hour
- ♿ **Wheelchair access** Only to ground floor shop due to stairs
- 🍴 **Eat and drink** Picnic Planet Organic (22 Torrington Place, WC1E 7HJ) is a healthy grocery-cum-café – picnic on Bedford Square Snacks Patisserie Valerie (24 Torrington Place, WC1E 7HJ) sells less virtuous, delicious cakes
- 🛍 **Shop** Toys and gifts
- 🚻 **Toilets** Ground floor

③ Wellcome Collection

Shrunken heads and massive moustaches

On a par with Ripley's Believe It or Not (see p84) is the Wellcome Collection. This giant store of curiosities was collected by an eccentric adventurer called Henry Wellcome, who made his fortune as a medicine salesman, grew Victorian England's bushiest moustache, then travelled the world hunting for medical marvels. He returned with

Examining the curious medical exhibits in the Wellcome Collection

some very bizarre booty indeed: prepare to be amazed by a torturer's mask, a Peruvian mummy (minus bandages) and a peculiar device for blowing tobacco smoke up a drowning person's bottom.

The historical gallery is beautifully arranged: slide open drawers to hear sound clips about key objects or to reveal artifacts to touch. The curators are oddly ambivalent about younger visitors: they stress that some of the material has adult themes, yet the museum has produced one of the best children's explorer kits in London, with modelling clay, a false moustache and a guide to making a shrunken head. Parental discretion is needed – steer sensitive souls away from the birth and death cabinets, and focus instead on the exotic masks, votive amulets and celebrity ephemera (Napoleon's toothbrush, George III's hair).

The Wellcome's second gallery, Medicine Now, feels very different:

The Lowdown

- 🌐 **Map ref** 4 E6
  Address 183 Euston Road, NW1 2BE; 020 7611 2222; www. wellcomecollection.org
- 🚆 **Train** Euston, King's Cross or St Pancras **Tube** Euston Square; Warren Street **Bus stop** Euston Road, Euston Bus Station, Upper Woburn Place
- 🕐 **Open** 10am–6pm Tue–Sat, 11am–6pm Sun; 10am–10pm Thu
- 💲 **Price** Free
- 🚩 **Guided tours** Free 30-min tours of the Medicine Now and Medicine Man galleries; timings vary, book in advance
- 👫 **Age range** 6 plus, though parental guidance advisable
- 🎭 **Activities** Young Explorers Pack for under-14s. Events programme tends to be adult-focused
- ⏱ **Allow** 2 hours
- ♿ **Wheelchair access** Yes
- 🍴 **Eat and drink** Snacks Wellcome Café offers light lunches, muffins and pies Real meal The Wellcome Kitchen (Level 2) offers a full lunch, dinner and drinks menu
- 🛍 **Shop** Books, gifts and collection-based souvenirs
- 🚻 **Toilets** On all floors

The spacious courtyard of the British Library

starkly lit and stylish, and devoted to modern wonders such as Dolly the cloned sheep and the human genome. Downstairs in the lobby there are temporary exhibitions on health and well being, plus a cool café with free Wi-Fi and screens for browsing the museum's collection.

Letting off steam
Nearby **Gordon Square Garden** *(Gordon Square, WC1H 0AR)* has a full 100-m (330-ft) lawn, and there's a toddler play-park in adjacent **Woburn Square** *(WC1H 0AB).*

④ British Library
Sshhh! – a temple for books and the printed word

Fourteen million books, three million sound recordings, almost a million journals and newspapers and just one permanent public gallery. For such a vast institution, the British Library offers thin pickings for the general visitor, especially for families – guided tours are pitched at adults and under-18s are barred from accessing the sound archives.

However, the Treasures Gallery offers a changing collection of important tomes, from England's first printed book, the *Gutenberg Bible* (c.1455), to Leonardo's da Vinci's notebooks, a draft score of Handel's *Messiah*, and Captain Scott's South Pole diaries. For children, the displays are saved from dryness by sound stations where they can listen to bursts of Brahms or the Beatles, and especially by the Turning the Pages interactive displays with touch-screen browsing. Flick through Lewis Carroll's original *Alice's Adventures Under Ground,*

with the author's own pictures; or novelist Jane Austen's *History of England*, written when she was 15 – she had very neat handwriting, too.

Letting off steam
There is a small swing park along Judd Street, across the Euston Road, or walk south for about 15 mintues to **Coram's Fields** *(see p106).*

The Lowdown

🌐 **Map ref** 4 F4
   Address 96 Euston Road, NW1 2DB; 0843 208 1144; www.bl.uk

🚗 **Train** King's Cross or St Pancras
   Tube King's Cross St Pancras
   Bus stop Euston Road

🕐 **Open** 9:30am–8pm Mon, Thu; 9:30am–5pm Fri–Sat; 11am–5pm Sun

💷 **Price** Free

🎫 **Guided Tours** Free Viewing Gallery tours at 1am & 3pm Mon–Sat, 11:30am & 3pm Sun & Public Holidays; Library Tour (£29; call 01937 546546 to book) 3pm Mon–Sat, plus 10:30am Sat. Free conservation tour 2pm first Thu of month (over-12s); audio tours are downloadable online

👫 **Age range** 7 plus

🎨 **Activities** Occasional free family workshops during school holidays, linked to temporary exhibitions

⏱ **Allow** 1 hour

♿ **Wheelchair access** Yes, via lifts and ramps

🍴 **Eat and drink** *Snacks* Café Oz (53 Caledonian Road, N1 9BU), does good sandwiches and pasta; *Real meal* The British Library Restaurant & Terrace (9:30am–5pm Mon–Fri; 9:30am–4pm Sat) offers stir-fries and salads

🛍 **Shop** Ground floor near the entrance

🚻 **Toilets** On all levels

⑤ Foundling Museum

A poignant tale of children lost and found

No single room in any London museum tells a more moving story than the main gallery here. In the early 18th century, before orphanages were established, a thousand babies were abandoned in London's backstreets each year – most of them reluctantly – by their destitute mothers. Pioneering shipwright Thomas Coram (1668–1751) led a heroic 20-year campaign to launch a Foundling Hospital to take them in.

The story has all the ingredients of a blockbuster, from the hospital's celebrity patrons (George Frideric Handel performed his *Messiah* to raise funds; William Hogarth donated paintings, which still hang upstairs) to anguished mothers drawing lots to discover whether their tiny bundles would be saved by the orphanage. Today, visitors get to experience the lottery too – if

Dressing up in a rich child's costume at the Foundling Museum

they draw out a black ball, their "baby" is rejected. There are recordings of interviews with former foundlings (the hospital finally closed in 1953), and most heart-rending of all, a collection of tokens left behind by mothers who hoped one day to reclaim their child.

Themed activity packs help to focus young minds on the story, while in the immaculate Georgian picture gallery, kids can dress up, or browse in the reading corner – which includes *Hetty Feather*, a tale about a Victorian inmate by Jacqueline Wilson. Better still, the book is a perfect way to whet the appetite before a visit.

Letting off steam

Just across the square, **Coram's Fields** *(93 Guildford Street, WC1N 1CN; www.coramsfields.org)* is not so much a playground as a kids' kingdom, with its Olympic-sized paddling pool, mini-farmyard, toddler play sessions, zipwire and sports pitches.

The Lowdown

- 🌐 **Map ref** 4 G6
  Address 40 Brunswick Square, WC1N 1AZ; 020 7841 3600; www.foundlingmuseum.org.uk
- 🚗 **Train** King's Cross, St Pancras **Tube** Russell Square **Bus stop** Russell Square, Gray's Inn Road
- 🕐 **Open** 10am–5pm Tue–Sat; 11am–5pm Sun
- 💲 **Price** £16.50–33, under-16s free
- **Guided tours** Yes. Download group booking form
- 👫 **Age range** 3 plus
- **Activities** Free treasure-hunt trails (ages 3–12) and activity backpacks (ages 3–5 and 5–8). Drop-in family workshops 1st Sat of each month, plus Thu–Fri in school holidays
- ⏱ **Allow** Up to two hours
- ♿ **Wheelchair access** Yes
- 🍴 **Eat and drink** *Snacks* The Foundling Museum Café does light lunches and cream teas and has a children's menu *Real meal* Giraffe *(19–21 Brunswick Centre, WC1N 1AF; 020 7812 1336)* serves burgers, sausages and pizzas and has a kids' menu
- 🛍 **Shop** In reception, selling toys and collection-inspired gifts
- 🚻 **Toilets** Lower ground, ground and first floor

⑥ Charles Dickens Museum

Oliver Twist's birthplace

The creator of Oliver, Tiny Tim and Little Nell loved children – he had 10 of his own after all. A leading proponent of child welfare in poverty-stricken Victorian London, Dickens lived at this smart Holborn townhouse from 1837–1839, and wrote *Oliver Twist* and *Nicholas Nickleby* here.

The building has been preserved as Dickens knew it, and original furniture, manuscripts and interesting memorabilia such as the

The Lowdown

- 🌐 **Map ref** 4 H6
  Address 48 Doughty Street, WC1N 2LX; 020 7405 2127; www.dickensmuseum.com
- 🚗 **Tube** Russell Square, Chancery Lane or Holborn **Bus stop** Gray's Inn Place Theobald's Road
- 🕐 **Open** 10am–5pm Tue–Sun (last admission 4pm)
- 💲 **Price** £26, under-6s free
- **Guided tours** Group bookings
- 👫 **Age range** 8 plus
- **Activities** Free children's trail; occasional family activities
- ⏱ **Allow** 1 hour
- ♿ **Wheelchair access** Yes, via ramp but some limitations due to age of building
- 🍴 **Eat and drink** *Snacks* The onsite garden café, with a lovely ambience, offers light lunches, cakes, drinks and even mulled cider in winter
- 🛍 **Shop** Sells memorabilia
- 🚻 **Toilets** Basement floor

The Dining Room at the Charles Dickens Museum

quills he used are on display. There are Victorian cookery demonstrations and the house is animated by sound clips of Dickens' words. After a major refurbishment, the museum is more child-friendly, with regular family activities and a kids' trail.

Letting off steam
Coram's Fields, with its playground, pool and other exciting attractions, is just around the corner.

⑦ London Canal Museum

Horse dung and ice cream

Britain's canal age endured for longer than one might imagine – barges carrying cargo were still moving through Battlebridge Basin on the Regent's Canal in the 1960s. That's good news for the museum that now sits here, because lots of fascinating oral history survives – pick up the antique-style telephones and listen to William Tarbit describe what it was like to live and work on the canals: how he had to crawl into his narrowboat's coal box to clean it – aged three! – and how he snared rabbits and pheasants for his mother's poacher's pie.

The museum has a traditional feel, with an authentic 1850s warehouse setting. It is half filled by the vintage barge *Coronis*, on which younger children can play. The cramped cabin might once have accommodated a family of six. Step out onto the wharf for a look at some modern narrowboats, and

visit the re-created blacksmith's workshop and stable upstairs.

The museum's other theme is guaranteed to get kids' taste buds tingling: the Victorian ice cream trade. The underground chasm in the downstairs gallery once stored vast blocks of ice, imported on barges from Norway by the pioneering pudding-maker Carlo Gatti in the days before refrigeration. And never fear – there is ice cream for sale at the museum shop.

Letting off steam
A 10-minute walk via York Way and Goods Way leads to **Camley Street Natural Park** (*12 Camley Street, NW1 0PW; www.wildlondon.org.uk reserves/camley-street-natural-park*), a canalside wildlife oasis set in a former coalyard amid the bustle of King's Cross. The visitor centre offers activities from 10am–5pm daily (to 4pm in winter). April to August is the best time to visit.

Interactive display showing how a lock's mitre gate works

The Lowdown

🌐 **Map ref** 4 H3
Address 12–13 New Wharf Road, N1 9RT; 020 7713 0836; www.canalmuseum.org.uk

🚗 **Train** King's Cross, St Pancras. **Tube** King's Cross **Bus stop** Caledonian Road, Pentonville

🕐 **Open** 10am–4:30pm Tue–Sun (last admission 4pm); till 7:30pm on 1st Thu of the month

💷 **Price** £10, under-4s free

🚩 **Guided tours** There is an audio tour, which must be downloaded beforehand from the website to an MP3 player

👫 **Age range** 6 plus

🏃 **Activities** Small play corner with books and building blocks; family trails, guided boat trips on some

summer Sun, plus children's activity days every Tue in Aug.

⏱ **Allow** 1–2 hours

♿ **Wheelchair access** Yes

🍴 **Eat and drink** *Snacks* Simmons (32 Caledonian Road, N1 9DT) is a tiny, trendy teahouse. Drop in for a pot of tea and a cupcake in the afternoon, or a fruit beer in the evening *Real meal* Oz Café (53 Caledonian Road, N1 9BU) is a cheery lunchtime diner serving pasta and paninis

🛍 **Shop** Sells books, pottery, soft toy ducks and model barges

🚻 **Toilets** Ground floor

ZSL London Zoo and around

There are gorillas and tigers to see of course, but these days London Zoo gives centre stage to its smaller creatures, devoting walk-through enclosures to monkeys and meerkats, penguins and sloths. Wait for some sunshine, and dedicate a full day to get the best value for the entrance fee. The nearest Tube station is Camden Town, but it gets congested on Sundays, when the area's manic markets are in full swing. Consider travelling to Baker Street or Regent's Park station, and walking across Regent's Park, with a game of hide-and-seek along the way. Another great option is a canal tour from Camden Lock.

Bloomsbury and Regent's Park

ZSL London Zoo

British Museum p100

PRIMROS▶

An "Animals in Action" demonstration at ZSL London Zoo

Far left
Youngsters enjoying a costumed talk at the Wallace Collection
Left Elegant bandstand in Regent's Park

Places of Interest

SIGHTS
1. ZSL London Zoo
2. Regent's Park
3. Camden Market
4. Jewish Museum
5. Madame Tussauds
6. Sherlock Holmes Museum
7. The Wallace Collection

● **EAT AND DRINK**
1. Whole Foods Market
2. Gelato Mio

3. Strada
4. The Regent's Bar & Kitchen
5. The Cow and Coffee Bean
6. Smokehouse
7. Yumchaa
8. The Ice Wharf
9. Caffè Nero
10. The Boathouse Cafe
11. Caffè Saporito
12. Nando's
13. Caffè Fratelli

See also Jewish Museum (p113) and Wallace Collection (p115)

● **WHERE TO STAY**
1. 23 Greengarden House
2. Blandford
3. Hart House
4. The Landmark
5. Lincoln House
6. New Inn

Below Browsing at Camden Lock Crafts Market

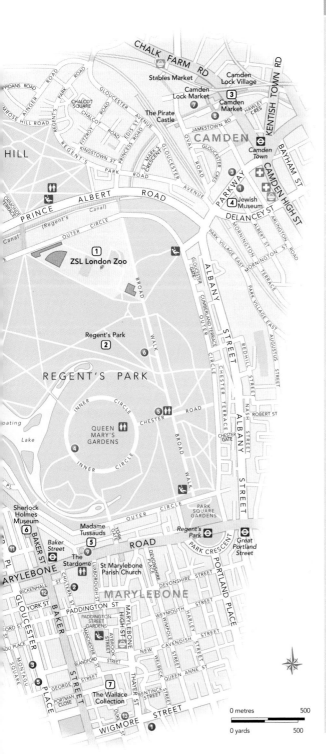

The Lowdown

🚃 **Train** Camden Road or Marylebone **Tube** Camden Town, St John's Wood **Bus** Prince Albert Road: route number 274; Parkway: C2 **Canal** Services from Camden Lock to Little Venice, daily in summer, weekends in winter (www.londonwaterbus.com; www.jasons.co.uk)

ℹ️ **Visitor information** See pp100–101

🛒 **Supermarkets** Somerfield, 131–133 Camden High Street, NW1 7JR; Morrisons, Chalk Farm Road, NW1 8AA; Waitrose, 98–101 Marylebone High Street, W1U 4SD **Markets** Camden Markets (fashion, crafts, antiques, gifts) 10am–6pm daily. Marylebone Farmers' Market (mainly produce, Cramer Street Car Park, W1U 4EW) 10am–2pm Sun. Cabbages & Frocks Market (food, fashion, crafts), St Marylebone Parish Church, NW1 5LT, 11am–5pm Sat. Church Street Market (food, clothes, bric-a-brac), 13–25 Church Street, NW8 8DT, 8:30am–4pm Mon–Thu (to 5pm Fri & Sat). Alfies Antique Market, 13–25 Church St NW8 8DT, 10am–6pm Tue–Sat

〰️ **Festivals** Taste of London (food/restaurant festival), Regent's Park (Jun); London Green Fair, Regent's Park (Jun); Pride London (diversity and equality festival) – parade begins Baker Street (Jun–Jul); Frieze Art Fair, Regent's Park (Oct)

➕ **Pharmacies** JP Pharmacy, 139 Camden High Street, NW1 7JR (9am–6:30pm Mon–Fri, 9am–6pm Sat, 10am–4pm Sun). Boots, 173–175 Camden High Street, NW1 7JY (8:30am–8pm Mon–Fri, 9am–7pm Sat, noon–6pm Sun). For 24-hour pharmacies, visit www.nhs.uk/servicedirectories

🚸 **Nearest playgrounds** Regent's Park, NW1 4NR: Marylebone Green, Gloucester Gate, Hanover Gate; Primrose Hill, Prince Albert Road, NW1 4NR; Paddington Street Gardens W1U

The Lowdown

🌐 **Map reference** 3 B3
Address Regent's Park, NW1 4RY; 020 7722 3333 and 0344 225 1826; www.zsl.org

🚗 **Train** Camden Road Station **Tube** Camden Town, St John's Wood **Bus stop** Prince Albert Road; Parkway **Canal** Scheduled service along Regent's Canal between Camden Lock and Little Venice, Apr–Sep: daily; Oct: Thu–Sun, plus winter weekends (www.londonwaterbus.com)

🕐 **Open** 10am–4pm daily (check website for longer summer opening hours); animal houses close 30 minutes earlier

💲 **Price** £75.80, under-3s free (optional 10% surcharge supports conservation work); online saver offers 10% reduction for families (2+2 or 1+3)

👫 **Skipping the queue** Online tickets allow fast-track admission. Head straight for Gorilla Kingdom, before the queues build

🚩 **Guided tours** No

👫 **Age range** All

👫 **Activities** Daily programme might include watching the otters being fed, seeing the llamas on their daily walk and watching penguins waddle on the Penguin Beach. Plus storytelling in the Animal Adventure teepee and brass-rubbing in the Activity Den

⏱ **Allow** At least half a day

♿ **Wheelchair access** Yes – however, there are two steep ramps that need caution

☕ **Eat and drink** The Terrace Restaurant offers hot lunches, including children's portions, baby food and a pick-and-mix picnic counter. Also Animal Adventure Café, seasonal pancake and hot dog stands, and picnic lawns

🏷 **Shops** Near entrance and in Barclay Court

🚻 **Toilets** Near entrance, in Oasis Restaurant and around zoo

Good family value?

It's wildly expensive, though cut-price deals can sometimes be found online. To get value for money, arrive early, pick up the "Dayplanner" events leaflet, and plot the day carefully.

① ZSL London Zoo
Face to fang with the world's wildlife

An architectural oddity, ZSL London Zoo is full of strange 1930s buildings, but it also has a gorilla compound, an interactive children's zoo, a tiger territory and a "penguin beach". Kids will be kept busy tiptoeing along the balancing bars in the monkey enclosure, crawling into an aardvark's burrow, or smiling at sloths in the walk-through rainforest. The zoo's watchword is "immersive", and it brings visitors closer to the animals than ever before.

Key Features

① **Butterfly Paradise** A walk-through butterfly house set in a giant inflatable caterpillar. The fluttering insects sometimes mistake brightly dressed visitors for flowers, so watch out for hitchhikers!

② **Blackburn Pavilion** Home to jewel-coloured hummingbirds and splendid sunbirds, this steamy tropical bird-house is themed on Victorian explorers. Get ready to take flight!

③ **Rainforest Life** This hothouse takes visitors right in among snoozing sloths and scurrying tamarin monkeys, which chase along the creepers overhead.

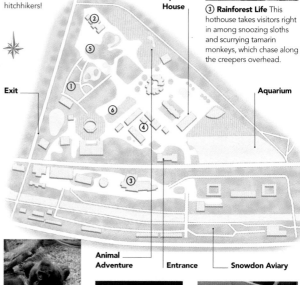

Reptile House

Exit

Aquarium

Animal Adventure

Entrance

Snowdon Aviary

④ **Gorilla Kingdom** This luxury island enclosure is home to a troop of western lowland gorillas. Watch these impressive apes show off their skills on a climbing wall and swing ropes.

⑤ **B.U.G.S!** There are handling sessions here and views of bird-eating spiders, naked mole rats and the zoo's bug experts in their laboratory.

⑥ **Animals in Action** The zoo's captivating live show runs daily in the amphitheatre. Kids watch wide-eyed as George the Macaw and Archie the Owl swoop on the stage.

Letting off steam

If crawling among porcupines and knuckle-walking with gorillas doesn't tire out your flock, there is formal play equipment at the zoo, next to Butterfly Paradise and in the Animal Adventure zone. Beyond the zoo, head for the Gloucester Gate entrance to **Regent's Park**, which has a spacious playground and (just south of its enclosure) an exciting tangle of tree trunks arranged for scrambling, where children really can make like monkeys.

Climbing in the Animal Adventure zone playground

Eat and drink

Picnic: under £20; Snacks: £20–40; Real meal: £40–60; Family treat: £60 or more (based on a family of four)

PICNIC Whole Foods Market *(49 Parkway, NW1 7PN; 020 7428 7575; www.wholefoods market. com/stores/camden; 8am–9pm Mon–Sat; 9am–9pm Sun)* is on the way from Camden Town Tube station to the zoo, with healthy, high-class picnic food. Throw a rug down in Regent's Park to eat it.

SNACKS Gelato Mio *(138 St John's Wood High Street, NW8 7SE; 020 0011 3889; www.gelatomio.co.uk; 9am–10pm Mon–Thu (to 11pm Fri); 10am–11pm Sat & Sun)* serves possibly the tastiest authentic Italian ice creams and sorbets in London. Choose from a wide range of classic flavours.

REAL MEAL Part of a chain, the Italian restaurant **Strada** *(40–42 Parkway, NW1 7AH; 020 7428 9653;*

www.strada.co.uk; 11:30am–11pm Mon–Sat; to 10:30pm Sun) is a welcoming spot for lunch, with a kids' menu and activity pack.

FAMILY TREAT The Regent's Bar & Kitchen *(Inner Circle, Regent's Park, NW1 4NU; 020 7935 5729; 8am–5pm daily)*, is set in an idyllic location in Regent's Park and offers pizzas and fusion dishes – including 'Little Hedgehog's' menu for children.

Find out more

DIGITAL ZSL London Zoo's interactive website has exciting updates for kids such as the arrival of new baby animals and announces events and activities, that would especially be of interest to kids, such as the 'Vets in Action' week.

Dramatic performance for children on the Puppet Theatre Barge

Next stop...

TOWPATH TRAIL Regent's Canal runs right past the zoo. Escape the excitement with a tranquil walk along the towpath to Camden, with its chaotic, exotic markets *(see pp112–13)*. Head west, perhaps by waterbus, and you'll reach Little Venice, a genteel canal quarter with flower-festooned narrowboats and the delightful **Puppet Theatre Barge**, which puts on seasonal shows for children (nearest tube station Warwick Avenue; 020 7249 6876, www.puppetbarge.com).

Choosing between the many mouthwatering flavours of ice cream at Gelato Mio

② Regent's Park
Playgrounds and playhouses

On a sunny day, few stretches of ground in London lift the spirits quite like Regent's Park. There is just so much to do here: hide-and-seek and ducks to feed for toddlers; football coaching and adventure playgrounds for older children; an open-air theatre and smart dining for mum and dad; even rose gardens and band concerts for granny and grandad.

The park looks wonderful, too: first laid out in 1811 by John Nash, the Buckingham Palace architect, for his great patron the Prince Regent, it was opened to the public 30 years later. There are four excellent playgrounds here (each with attendants and toilets), which often stage activities during school holidays. The elegant Inner Circle has a labyrinthine tangle of snaking pathways, Chinese bridges and cascades, plus the celebrated open-air theatre, which usually includes a family-friendly Shakespeare play in its summer season.

To the west, the pretty boating lake attracts grey herons and has rowing boats and pedalos for hire. Nearby, the Holme Green bandstand stages sedate jazz on Sunday evenings from June to August, when deckchairs can be

Messing about on the water, always a fun option for children in Regent's Park

rented too. There are a number of wildlife walks and allotment workshops in season, including Get Growing family sessions; while to the north of the park, what looks like a crashed flying saucer among the football pitches is actually The Hub *(0300 061 2323; open daily)*, offering a wide range of sports for all ages and holiday sports camps for kids.

Take cover

If it rains, it's a short stroll to the Odeon Camden *(14 Parkway, NW1 7AA; 0871 224 4007; www.odeon. co.uk)*, which offers several film screenings every afternoon.

③ Camden Market
London's most bizarre bazaar

For a first-time visitor, plunging into Camden's maelstrom of markets can feel a little like tumbling down Alice in Wonderland's rabbit hole. It is a passport to an incense-scented alternative universe where the tattooed and pierced buy and sell jewellery, clothes, music, novelties, furniture and food from right across London's vivid cultural spectrum. Take a deep breath, hold on tight to little hands, and go with the flow.

The gentlest introduction is Camden Lock, a cute courtyard right beside Regent's Canal, where prettily painted narrowboats chug out to Little Venice past ZSL London Zoo. The market hall next door majors in sparkly crafts and accessories, from earrings and scarves to candles and carvings, and there's a tasty parade of multi-ethnic food stands. Behind here, things get more chaotic: the labyrinthine Stables Market occupies the site of the stables, horse hospital, warehouses and vaults connected with the canal trade in Victorian times – hence the bronze carthorses that spring out from assorted corners. Teenagers love the groovy goth-punk vibe, while the characterful Horse Tunnel area has more grown-up bric-à-brac.

Just across Chalk Farm Road is Camden Lock Village, another zone of mostly street-fashion stalls set in wooden cabins – look out for the food stands with motor-scooters as seating.

The Lowdown

🌐 **Map ref** 3 B4
Address London NW1 4NR; 030 0061 2300; www.royalparks. org.uk/parks/the-regents-park

🚆 **Train** Marylebone, Euston
Tube Regent's Park, Baker Street, Great Portland Street, Camden Town, St John's Wood **Bus stop** Prince Albert Road, Parkway, Marylebone Road, Baker Street

🕐 **Open** 5am–dusk daily (closing time varies from 4:30 pm (Dec) to 9:30 pm (Jul); park office 8:30am–4pm)

💲 **Price** Free

🚩 **Guided tours** Free wildlife walks from spring to autumn (check website)

👫 **Age range** All

🧗 **Activities** Four playgrounds, with summer holiday activity programme (check website); bandstand and open-air theatre (mid-May–mid-Sep, 0844 826 4242; www.openairtheatre.org;

admission to the theatre is not permitted for under 4s); boating lakes (boat hire £25, Apr–Sep, daily from 10:30am; 020 7724 4069);
holiday sports camps (020 7935 2458); pay-and-play tennis (020 7486 4216)

⏱ **Allow** Up to a full day

♿ **Wheelchair access** Yes, the park has level access and there are specially adapted toilets

🍴 **Eat and drink** *Picnic* The Cow and Coffee Bean *(St Mary's Gate, Chester Road; 020 7224 3872; 9am–8pm in summer, 10am–3pm in winter)* serves a selection of sandwiches, alongside milkshakes, ice cream and delicious cakes. *Snacks* Smokehouse *(The Broadwalk on NW side of park; 020 7224 3872; 8am–9pm daily)* offers a simple BBQ menu of ribs, burgers & sausages. Vegetarian options too

🚻 **Toilets** Throughout the park, including all playgrounds

Prices given are for a family of four

The Lowdown

🌐 **Map ref** 3 C1

Address Camden High Street, NW1; 020 7284 2084; www.camdenmarket.com

🚇 **Tube** Camden Town, Chalk Farm
Bus stop Chalk Farm Road, Camden Town Station **Canal** London Waterbus (www.londonwaterbus.com) and Jason's Trip (www.jasons.co.uk) run daily in spring and summer; London Waterbus runs winter weekends

🕐 **Open** 10am–6pm daily

💲 **Price** Free

👪 **Skipping the queue** The market heaves at weekends: 1–5:30pm Sun, Camden Town tube station is exit only. Weekdays are quieter.

👫 **Age range** 7 plus

🎯 **Activities** Canal trips (see above)

⏱️ **Allow** Up to 2 hours

♿ **Wheelchair access** Yes, via lifts (disabled toilet in Unit 23 on the Stables street level).

🍽️ **Eat and drink** Snacks Yumchaa (91–92 Camden Lock Place, NW1 8AF; www.yumchaa.com) offers a huge variety of teas and cakes. Real meal The Ice Wharf (28 Jamestown Road, NW1 7BY; www.jdwetherspoon.co.uk/home/pubs/the-ice-wharf) overlooks the lock and has a good kids' menu

🚻 **Toilets** Various; basement of Stable Market, bridge of Middle Yard

Letting off steam

Primrose Hill, a 10-minute walk via the canal towpath, is a lofty northern satellite of Regent's Park popular with kite fliers. The Pirate Castle (020 7267 6605; www.thepiratecastle.org), a canalside youth club offering kayaking or canoeing sessions for ages 8–16 on Tue, Thu and Sat, plus most weekdays in summer holidays, is on the way.

Exploring the bustling Camden Lock crafts market

④ Jewish Museum

A poignant 1,000-year immigrant odyssey

From the life of the Victorian prime minister Benjamin Disraeli to that of Auschwitz survivor Leon Greenman, the Jewish Museum puts an emphasis on personal stories. You can get a free taste of the museum from the ground-floor gallery, but the history hall is the highlight, tracing the 1,000-year story of Britain's Jewish community, from their arrival with William the Conqueror in 1066. The senses are engaged: smell the chicken soup in a re-created East End street, play a board game based on the Jewish diaspora or try Yiddish karaoke. Especially poignant for kids are the keepsakes from the Kindertransport, carried by the 10,000 Jewish children who fled Nazi Germany in 1939.

Letting off steam

It's a 5-minute walk along Parkway to Gloucester Gate playground, in **Regent's Park**.

The Lowdown

🌐 **Map ref** 3 D2

Address 129–131 Albert Street, NW1 7NB; 020 7284 7384; www.jewishmuseum.org.uk

🚇 **Tube** Camden Town, Mornington Crescent
Bus stop Delancey Street, Camden High Street **Canal** Camden Lock (www.londonwaterbus.com; www.jasons.co.uk)

🕐 **Open** 10am–5pm Sun–Thu; 10am–2pm Fri (last admission 30 minutes earlier)

💲 **Price** £22 (family, up to 4 kids)

🗣️ **Guided tours** No

👫 **Age range** 7 plus

🎯 **Activities** Family workshops on occasional Sundays and in school holidays, include glass-painting, candle-making and drumming

⏱️ **Allow** 1–2 hours

♿ **Wheelchair access** Yes

🍽️ **Eat and drink** Snack Banner's (21 Park Road, N8 8TE; 020 8348 2930) serves breakfast apart from other meals. Children's menu features unprocessed food. Real meal The museum's Kosher Café (10am–4pm Sun–Thu; till 2pm Fri) has salt beef, bagels and a kids' menu

🛍️ **Shop** Ground floor

🚻 **Toilets** All floors

Iconic red telephone boxes outside the world-famous Madame Tussauds

⑤ Madame Tussauds

Schmooze with the stars

No attraction in the capital divides opinion quite like Marie Tussaud's waxwork show founded in 1835. Despite the pricey admission, visitors queue around the block – and that's really the problem. The galleries can get crowded, defeating the main purpose of a visit – to have your photograph taken with Lady Gaga, Rihanna or Johnny Depp. Small children may even struggle to see

The Lowdown

- 🌐 **Map ref** 3 B6
- 📍 **Address** Marylebone Road, NW1 5LR; 0871 894 3000; www.madametussauds.com/london
- 🚇 **Train** Marylebone **Tube** Baker Street **Bus stop** Marylebone Road, Baker Street
- 🕐 **Open** 9:30am–5:30pm Mon–Fri; 9am–6pm Sat–Sun
- 💲 **Price** £106–200. Half-price tickets after 5pm, online only
- 🎫 **Skipping the queue** Book online for fast-track entry; online tickets are about 10 per cent cheaper.
- 👫 **Age range** 5 plus
- 🏃 **Activities** Visit the interactive zones and kids can pose with their favourite heroes at the Star Wars Legends Experience.
- ⏱ **Allow** 2 hours
- ♿ **Wheelchair access** Yes, apart from the Spirit of London moving ride. No prams allowed in attractions
- 🍴 **Eat and drink** *Snacks* Caffè Nero (*Marylebone Road, NW1 5LR; 8am–6:30pm Mon–Fri, 8:30am–7:30pm Sat–Sun*) serves small eats. *Real meal* The Boathouse Cafe (*Boating Lake, Hanover Gate, Regent's Park, NW1 4NR; 020 7724 4069*) sells pizzas, pastas and salads.
- 🛍 **Shop** In the exit lobby
- 🚻 **Toilet** A-list Party and Sports zones

Waxwork of British Olympic diving medal winner Tom Daley

their heroes in the melee. But go when it's quieter, ideally on a weekday morning, and there's no denying the glamour of walking into the first hall – a celebrity party where the likes of Kate Winslet, Robert Pattinson and Emma Watson are waiting for their close-up. Most of the models are spookily lifelike, and there are no ropes to segregate visitors from "VIPs", so you really can rub shoulders with the stars. Younger children may prefer the Hollywood hall, with its rampaging dinosaur and giant Shrek, while downstairs they can play simulated tennis and football (queues permitting), as Nadal and Beckham look on.

In the basement, the Scream horror attraction has live serial killers jumping out of shadowy corners – not for the under-13s. Younger kids can head straight for the two attractions at the end; a ride through London's history in a black cab and a 4D film in which Spider Man, the Hulk and Wolverine battle baddies in modern London.

Letting off steam

Regent's Park is very close – from York Gate, turn right to find the Marylebone Green playground.

⑥ Sherlock Holmes Museum

Home of the world's most famous detective

It's hard to think of many museums devoted to fictional characters – and indeed, some fans refuse to believe that Sir Arthur Conan Doyle's great detective didn't exist. There is a file of genuine letters

The Lowdown

- 🌐 **Map ref** 3 A6
- 📍 **Address** 221b Baker Street, NW1 6XE; 020 7224 3688; www.sherlock-holmes.co.uk
- 🚇 **Train** Marylebone **Tube** Baker Street **Bus stop** Baker Street, Marylebone Road
- 🕐 **Open** 9:30am–6pm daily
- 💲 **Price** £15–50
- 🚩 **Guided tours** None
- 👫 **Age range** 8 plus
- ⏱ **Allow** Up to 1 hour
- ♿ **Wheelchair access** No
- 🍴 **Eat and drink** *Snacks* Caffè Saporito (*14 Melcombe Street, NW1 6AH*) is great for breakfasts, pizza or dessert. *Real meal* Nando's (*113 Baker Street, W1U 6RS*) serves Afro-Portuguese flame-grilled chicken, plus a Nandino's menu for under 10s.
- 🛍 **Shop** Next door
- 🚻 **Toilet** In basement

here, from people around the world, asking for Sherlock Holmes's help with solving their own personal mysteries.

Holmes the sleuth, repeatedly revived by Hollywood, lives on in this moody Victorian townhouse, though kids unfamiliar with the tales will feel a little clueless. The first mystery is the address: why is 221b Baker Street between numbers 237 and 241? Inside, staircases creak, gas-lamps splutter and Dr Watson lurks on the landing, ushering visitors into Holmes's study to sit in his chair, or even puff on his pipe.

Youngsters in period hats, outside the front door of 221b Baker Street

The other five rooms are filled with clues and murder weapons from his famous cases. It is atmospheric, if rather kitschy, and there's not much on more recent screen adaptations. One puzzle remains: why isn't the cleaner dressed up as Mrs Hudson?

Letting off steam

Regent's Park is 2 minutes away, with pedaloes and a playground at nearby Hanover Gate.

⑦ The Wallace Collection

No Gromit, but lots of armour and The Laughing Cavalier

First impressions can be deceptive. The Wallace Collection looks like a typical hushed and highbrow museum of old, a marbled mansion dripping with weighty chandeliers and gilt-framed Old Masters. Even its splendid restaurant has bibbed waiters and pricey food.

However, the Wallace is very keen to woo families: it has teamed up with pupils from a nearby school to create a children's "acoustiguide" and I-Spy trails, and has published a kids' art book based on key exhibits, for sale in the shop.

The collection was mostly put together by the Francophile Fourth Marquess of Hertford in the 1800s and is especially strong on French furniture and Sèvres porcelain – look out for Catherine the Great's tea set. Children will be most excited by the rooms full of gleaming armour displays, which include Rajput warrior regalia and medieval knights on horseback. Upstairs, a series of stuccoed salons are lined with fine art, including Titians, Rembrandts, 22 Canalettos and a certain very famous jovial horseman.

Letting off steam

There is an excellent playground at **Paddington Street Gardens** (Paddington Street, W1U 4EF; ages 3–11), just north of the museum.

A "Meet Marie Antoinette" costumed talk at the Wallace Collection

The City
and the East End

Now synonymous with global money markets and the Bank of England, the City of London (or Square Mile) is also where London began – the Romans built a wall around it in AD 200, parts of which still survive. The area is brimful of brilliant buildings and history. The vibrant East End has undergone a radical transformation since Jack the Ripper's time and is now filled with a host of stylish galleries and fun Sunday markets.

Bloomsbury and Regent's Park

The City and the East End

Westminster and the West End

Kensington, Chelsea and Battersea

Southwark and the South Bank

Highlights

The Monument
Climbing this memorial comes with a deep sense of occasion – 311 steps to the top, then out onto a blustery balcony 50 m (164 ft) above the City (see p124).

Tower of London
The Tower's famous Beefeaters deliver the most entertaining tour in London. Ask them what happened to the luckless Duke of Monmouth (see pp122–3).

St Paul's Cathedral
It is polite to whisper in church – but high inside the dome here, a whisper travels further than most. The curious acoustics are captivating for kids (see pp130–31).

Postman's Park
This picnic-friendly spot houses a most touching memorial – hand-painted tiles recall people who gave their lives to save others. Bring a hankie (see p136).

Bank of England Museum
This museum is surprisingly welcoming to families – no sign of a pinstripe suit – and where else can you lift up a gold ingot worth more than a house (see p132)?

Here be dragons
Dragons are the City's legendary guardians, and there's great fun to be had tracking them down on statues and street signs. Start hunting at the Guildhall (see p133).

Left Stately and magnificent, St Paul's Cathedral is one of London's most famous landmarks **Above** The fascinating engine room at Tower Bridge

The Best of
The City and the East End

With 300,000 workers and only 10,000 residents, the City is best tackled at the weekend. The focus of the area is a triangle of top attractions: the Tower of London, St Paul's Cathedral and the Museum of London, one of the capital's most exciting museums for families. Meanwhile, beyond the shiny towers of the financial quarter, a lively young arts community has blossomed around Old Spitalfields Market and the Whitechapel Gallery.

A City weekend

For families, the ideal City weekend begins on Saturday morning with Framed Film Club at the **Barbican** (see p138), where curators wheel out activities on trolleys before the movie. There's a great foodhall for lunch and also a deli, so if the weather's kind, walk to **Postman's Park** (see p137) for a picnic. Next, head for **St Paul's Cathedral** (see pp128–9) (it's closed to visitors on Sundays). It offers a family multimedia guide with hidden facts especially for younger visitors.

On Sunday, begin with brunch and a browse at **Old Spitalfields Market** (see p138). Don't linger too long, though, because the **Tower of London** (see pp122–3) is waiting. A tour with a Beefeater is a great introduction, while children

get to meet medieval damsels and fire crossbows in the armoury display. Round off the weekend with a bite to eat at nearby **St Katharine's Dock** (see p126).

Roaming with Romans

The City of London was first established by the Romans in the 1st century and many traces of them can still be seen. Start at the **Museum of London** (see pp136–7), which has a mock 2,000-year-old street and offers young visitors an activity pack full of Roman fun and games.

Around the corner on Noble Street stands the best surviving part of Roman London's defensive wall, which once stretched all the way from modern-day Tower Bridge to Blackfriars. Next,

Below Looking down at the intricate floor of St Paul's Cathedral from the Whispering Gallery

stroll east along Gresham Street to the **Guildhall Art Gallery** (see p133) to see the remains of a Roman amphitheatre. A sound and light show brings gladiatorial combat back to life.

Head south to Queen Victoria Street to see the remains of the 3rd-century Temple of Mithras, then hit **Leadenhall Market** (see p124), once the site of London's original Roman forum, to eat.

Nursery-rhyme London

It's amazing how many children's nursery rhymes have their roots in London's history. Begin tracing them at **St Olave's Church** (see p125), where a plaque recalls the burial of Old Mother Goose in 1586. St Olave was an 11th-century Norwegian king who saved London from invading Vikings by towing away London Bridge with his ships – which probably inspired London Bridge is Falling Down. The spooky skulls on the church's gateway remember the plague victims buried here, so why not play a game of Ring-a-Ring-o-Roses in nearby Seething Lane Gardens? "We all fall down" is thought to refer to people dying of the plague.

Next, head for **The Monument** (see p124), built after the Great Fire of 1666, for a rousing chorus of London's Burning.

Finish at **St Mary-le-Bow Church** (see p131) whose great bell is mentioned in Oranges and Lemons, and also tolled to call back Dick Whittington to become Lord Mayor of London: Dick's statue presides over nearby Guildhall Yard (see p133).

Money, money, money

From pirate treasure to gold bars, there's no escaping money in the world's second-biggest banking centre. Goldsmiths first gathered here

Above The Tower of London, as seen from the River Thames
Below Guildhall Art Gallery bringing the gladiator combat of London's Roman amphitheatre to life

in the 15th century and a walk along Lombard Street takes in London's earliest finance houses, with their curious banking signs. After gazing at some modern temples of Mammon (the Lloyd's Building, the "Gherkin"), visit the **Bank of England Museum** (see p132), where children can see a £1,000,000 note.

Nearby, 100 years ago, workmen dug up the world's finest cache of Tudor gems: the Cheapside Hoard. These may have originally have been plundered by pirates, and some now glitter at the **Museum of London** (see pp136–7). Even they are outshone, of course, by the Crown Jewels at the **Tower of London** (see pp122–3).

Tower of London and around

Begun in 1078 by William the Conqueror to subdue his new Anglo-Saxon citizens, the Tower of London has extended its special brand of hospitality to the likes of Anne Boleyn, Guy Fawkes and Captain Blood. There's a full day of family fun here, so book online to skip the queues, and try to avoid weekends. The Tower, the Monument and St Katharine's Dock all have an outdoor dimension, so this area is good to visit on a sunny day.

The City and the East End

Museum of London p134

St Paul's Cathedral p128

Tower of London

Places of Interest

SIGHTS
1. Tower of London
2. The Monument
3. Leadenhall Market
4. All Hallows by the Tower
5. Tower Bridge
6. St Katharine's Dock
7. Whitechapel Gallery

EAT AND DRINK
1. Apostrophe
2. Ebb
3. Bodean's
4. The Perkin Reveller
5. Temples
6. Pod
7. Pret A Manger
8. Pizza Express
9. Eat
10. Café Rouge
11. Kilikya's
12. Ping Pong

See also Tower of London (p122), Leadenhall Market (p124) and Whitechapel Gallery (p127)

WHERE TO STAY
1. Apex City of London
2. Grange City
3. Hamlet (UK)

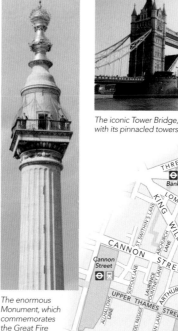

The iconic Tower Bridge, with its pinnacled towers

The enormous Monument, which commemorates the Great Fire of London

Far left The magnificent Tower of London, seen from across the River Thames
Left The attractive and vibrant marina at St Katharine's Dock

Enjoying an arts and crafts workshop at the cutting-edge Whitechapel Gallery

The Lowdown

🚗 **Train** Fenchurch Street, Cannon Street or Tower Gateway (Docklands Light Railway) **Tube** Tower Hill, Monument, Aldgate or Aldgate East **Bus** Tower Bridge Approach: route numbers 42, 78, RV1; Tower Hill: 15, 25, 100; Gracechurch Street (for the Monument): 35, 40, 47, 48, 149, 344 **River bus** Tower Pier, to Embankment and Woolwich Arsenal via London Eye, Greenwich (0870 781 5049, *www.thamesclippers.com*); to Greenwich and Westminster via London Eye (020 7740 0400; *www.citycruises.com*). St Katharine's Pier, circular to Westminster via Embankment, Festival Pier, Bankside Pier (020 7936 2033; *www.crownriver.com*); to Westminster and Thames Barrier via Greenwich (020 7930 4097; *www. thamesriverservices.co.uk*)

ℹ️ **Visitor information** See pp128–9

🧺 **Supermarkets** Tesco Metro, 6 Eastcheap, EC3M 1AE; or (much larger) Waitrose at 41 Thomas More Street, St Katharine's Dock, E1W 1YY **Markets** St Katharine's Dock (food), 11am–2pm Fri. Leadenhall Market (general), 11am–4pm Mon–Fri. Petticoat Lane Market (clothing), Middlesex Street, E1 10am–2:30pm Mon–Fri; 9am–2pm Sun

🎋 **Festivals** City of London Festival, music and arts (Jun–Jul); Thames Festival, Tower Bridge (Sep); City Life Family Festival, Leadenhall Market (Sep); Leadenhall Market Winter Festival and Christmas lights (from mid-Nov)

➕ **Pharmacies** Boots, 54 King William St, EC4R 9AA (7:30am–7:30pm Mon–Fri, 10am–4pm Sat). For 24-hour pharmacies, visit *www.nhs.uk/ servicedirectories*

🛝 **Nearest playground** Tower Hill Gardens, corner of Tower Hill and Minories Hill

① Tower of London
A pop-up-book castle in modern London

With its stories of beheadings, child-slayings and torture, the Tower has a gory appeal for kids. There are ramparts to patrol, spiralling staircases, execution sites and chambers full of treasure. The interiors are interactive, too: meet a minstrel in Henry III's medieval palace, try on a helmet in the Peasants' Revolt exhibit and fire a crossbow in the White Tower. Touching the Crown Jewels is still banned, however – the last time the guards allowed that, in 1671, Colonel Blood tried to stuff them down his breeches.

A Beefeater standing guard

Key Features

Jewel House The Crown Jewels, including the royal sceptre, which holds one of the largest diamonds in the world, are stored here.

White Tower This houses Henry VIII's armoury – visitors can handle the replica weapons.

Wakefield Tower This has a rack for stretching, manacles for dangling and the "scavenger's daughter", for crushing people to a pulp.

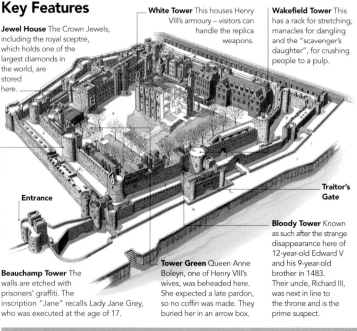

Traitors' Gate Prisoners, many on their way to die, entered the Tower by boat through these gates.

Entrance

Traitor's Gate

Bloody Tower Known as such after the strange disappearance here of 12-year-old Edward V and his 9-year-old brother in 1483. Their uncle, Richard III, was next in line to the throne and is the prime suspect.

Beauchamp Tower The walls are etched with prisoners' graffiti. The inscription "Jane" recalls Lady Jane Grey, who was executed at the age of 17.

Tower Green Queen Anne Boleyn, one of Henry VIII's wives, was beheaded here. She expected a late pardon, so no coffin was made. They buried her in an arrow box.

The ravens Housed at night, the six ravens are now the only prisoners here. Legend says that if they ever leave, the tower and the kingdom will fall.

The Lowdown

🌐 **Map ref** 12 G4
Address Tower of London, EC3N 4AB; 0844 482 7777; www.hrp.org.uk/toweroflondon

🚗 **Train** London Bridge, Fenchurch Street, Tower Gateway (Docklands Light Railway – DLR) **Tube** Tower Hill. **Bus stop** Tower Bridge Approach, Tower Hill **River bus** Tower Pier and St Katharine's Pier

🕐 **Open** Mar–Oct: 9am–5:30pm Tue–Sat; 10am–5:30pm Sun–Mon; Nov–Feb: till 4:30pm (last admission 30 minutes earlier)

💲 **Price** £45–63

👪 **Skipping the queue** Book online beforehand (prices are lower,

too); or the day before your visit from ticket office on Tower Hill

🚩 **Guided tours** Free 45-minute tours every 30 minutes; themed audio tours (extra charge)

👫 **Age range** 5 plus, although torture exhibition and Yeoman Warder tour can be scary

👫 **Activities** Activity books available free from the Welcome Centre. Downloadable family trails, and an Explore Kit that also covers HMS *Belfast* and Tower Bridge. Costumed interpreters daily in St Thomas's Tower, plus free family fun days on 1st Sat of the month and regular school-holiday children's events.

Tower Moat ice rink, Nov–Jan (extra charge; www.toweroflondonicerink.com)

🕐 **Allow** At least half a day

♿ **Wheelchair access** Limited – there's a downloadable map of accessible areas on the website

☕ **Café** The Armouries Café offers children's meal deals, high-chairs and a microwave for baby food

🛍 **Shops** Five shops selling play armour, books and sweets

🚻 **Toilets** Behind Waterloo Block

Good family value?
London's most popular visitor attraction – and it deserves to be.

Enjoying a picnic in the sunshine in the Tower of London's grounds

Letting off steam

There's plenty of running-about room inside the Tower, along the ramparts and on the grass, while riverside **Tower Wharf** is traffic-free, and boasts picnic benches and cannons for youngsters to clamber over. Alternatively, cross Tower Hill to the corner of **Minories Hill**, where you'll find a new playground with swings and slides.

Eat and drink

Picnic: under £20; Snacks: £20–40; Real meal: £40–60; Family treat: £60 or more (based on a family of four)

PICNIC Picnicking is encouraged at the Tower. Try the moat (in summers), the benches around the White Tower, or the riverside at Tower Wharf, where award-winning café **Apostrophe** (8am–6pm Mon–Fri, from 9am Sat & Sun) sells super sandwiches.

SNACKS Head for St Katharine's Dock, and **Ebb** (Ivory House, E1W 1AT; 020 7702 9792), a cute coffee house by the water that sells good milkshakes and boasts comfortable seats and a vibrant atmosphere.
REAL MEAL Bodean's (16 Byward Street, EC3R 5BA; 020 7488 3883; www.bodeansbbq.com; noon–11pm; till 10:30pm Sun) offers sizzling barbecue dishes, as well as delicious salads and vegetarian options. One child eats free with an adult between noon and 5pm daily.
FAMILY TREAT The Perkin Reveller (The Wharf, EC3N 4AB; 020 3166 6949; www.perkinreveller. co.uk; 10am–9pm Mon–Sat, till 4pm Sun), a modern-day dining hall with views across the Thames, serves delicious meals using seasonal British ingredients.

Find out more

DIGITAL See if you have what it takes to don some armour, grab a weapon and challenge King Henry VIII, at henryviiidressedtokill. viral-game.co.uk/. For more kid-friendly information with fun trivia, games and photos, visit www.hrp.org.uk/palace-kids.

Next stop...
TRINITY SQUARE GARDENS

Across Tower Hill in this park (Tower Hill, EC3N), a plaque marks the site of the Scaffold, where 125 churchmen and nobles were publicly beheaded while jugglers and acrobats entertained the crowd. Their heads were placed on spikes along London Bridge.

KIDS' CORNER

Trick a grown-up!
Try this riddle on an unsuspecting adult. Thirteen towers on the inner wall, six towers on the outer wall... How many towers does the Tower of London have in total? Answer: 20. Bet they forgot to count the White Tower in the middle!

Sticky ends
Search the Tower and try to match these prisoners with their fates: beheaded; tortured; pardoned; and escaped...
1 Guy Fawkes Plotter who tried to blow up Parliament
2 Colonel Blood Daring adventurer who tried to steal the Crown Jewels
3 Sir Walter Raleigh Explorer who wrote a history of the world while imprisoned
4 The Earl of Nithsdale Rebel who wanted to overthrow King George I

Answers at the bottom of the page.

Stair puzzle
The Tower's spiral staircases all twist clockwise on the way up. Can you work out why?

Answers at the bottom of the page.

THE ROYAL ZOO
Kings often kept exotic animals at the Tower. These included a grizzly bear named Martin, an elephant that drank wine and a polar bear that liked to fish for salmon in the River Thames.

Answers: Sticky ends 1 Stretched on the rack **2** Freed, after charming the king **3** Sent to find gold in South America – but beheaded on his return **4** Fled dressed in his wife's clothes – despite having a beard! **Stair puzzle** It makes them easier to defend – attackers coming up the stairs can't use their sword arm (right hand) easily

Youngsters sword-fighting against the impressive backdrop of the Tower

② The Monument

Climb up among the rooftops for views over London

Three centuries before the London Eye, it was possible to admire the city's skyline from 50 m (164 ft) aloft. The view is hard earned: there are 311 corkscrewing steps to reach the caged platform atop The Monument, erected by Sir Christopher Wren in the 1670s to remember the Great Fire of London.

The fire broke out in September 1666, in a bakery in nearby Pudding Lane, and within three days it had reduced 13,000 homes, 87 churches and St Paul's Cathedral to ashes. The good news: it also saw off the Great Plague, which had wiped out 100,000 people the year before.

The Monument is still the world's tallest free-standing column and must have been a marvel in its day. Wren built a laboratory in the basement for conducting his experiments, but soon it was open for visitors. The climb is a challenge for little legs, but well worth it to emerge among the spires and skyscrapers of modern London. The telescope commentaries are hardly worth bothering with; instead, just savour the fabulous views. There is a certificate for everyone who makes it down again intact.

Letting off steam

Still got some puff left after the big climb? A few minutes east, via Lower Thames Street, is the bombed-out shell of the church of St Dunstan in the East (Dunstan's Hill, EC3R), now a garden and perfect for a picnic.

The viewing deck at the top of Wren's grand Monument

The Lowdown

- **Map ref** 12 F4
  Address Monument Street, EC3R 8AH; 020 7626 2717; www.themonument.info
- **Train** London Bridge or Fenchurch Street **Tube** Monument **Bus stop** Gracechurch Street
- **Open** 9:30am–6pm daily (to 5:30pm Oct–Mar); last admission 30 mins before closing
- **Price** £13.60; combined ticket with Tower Bridge Exhibition £26.50
- **Skipping the queue** At weekends, arrive before 11am to avoid waiting
- **Age range** 5 plus
- **Allow** 30 minutes
- **Wheelchair access** No
- **Eat and drink** Picnic Temples (17 Cullum St, EC3M 7JJ), sells excellent salt beef sandwiches Snacks Pod (75 King William St, EC4N 7BE; 020 7283 7460) serves good salads, Korean and Lebanese snacks
- **Toilets** In nearby Monument Street

③ Leadenhall Market

From Dick Whittington to Harry Potter

This area has a fascinating 600-year history – and it really looks the part. The warren of cobbled arcades is encased in fancy ironwork and lit by quaint lanterns, while pillars gleam in bold carousel colours – cream, claret and green. Snarling dragons guard every corner and there are topsy-turvy taverns and streetwise shoeshine stands. It's like looking into a Victorian kaleidoscope.

The centre of Roman London was here – the ruins of its 1st-century basilica, the same length as St Paul's Cathedral, lie buried beneath the Lamb Tavern. In 1411, the merchant Richard (Dick) Whittington, of pantomime fame, donated Leadenhall to the City of London, and by 1800 it was Europe's best-supplied market, specialising in beef and game.

The arcades were designed in 1881, and now host gourmet butchers and cheesemongers, slick brasseries and bars, plus Pandora's Box and Ben's Cookies for sweet treats. As a family lunch spot, Leadenhall has genuine wow factor – especially when you reveal the Harry

The interior of historic Leadenhall Market, with its bustling cafés

Potter connection. Bull's Head Passage was transformed into Diagon Alley, where our hero buys his wand in Harry Potter and the Philosopher's Stone.

Letting off steam

Head towards the Tower of London, to the excellent playground on the corner of Minories (see p123).

The Lowdown

- **Map ref** 12 F3
  Address Gracechurch Street, EC3V 1LR; www.leadenhallmarket.co.uk
- **Train** Fenchurch Street, Bank (DLR) **Tube** Bank or Monument. **Bus stop** Gracechurch Street
- **Open** 10am–6pm Mon–Fri; market stalls 11am–4pm
- **Price** Free
- **Skipping the queue** Aim to be there before 1pm, when the eateries fill up with City workers
- **Activities** Winter Festival with lunchtime concerts (mid-Nov); City Lights Family Festival, Sep
- **Wheelchair access** Yes
- **Eat and drink** Snacks Chop'd (1 Leadenhall Mkt, EC3V 1LR), serves hearty but healthy stews, broths and sandwiches Real meal La Tasca (27 Leadenhall Mkt, EC3R 5AS) gets busy at lunchtime but the tapas are good
- **Toilets** In Monument Street

Grim skull and bone reliefs above the entrance to St Olave's church

④ All Hallows by the Tower

Boudicca, beheadings… and brass-rubbing

London's oldest church is packed to the tower-top with quirky history, from the battles of Boudicca to beheaded bodies and the glowing embers of the Great Fire of 1666.

Begin in the crypt, where a pristine chunk of 2nd-century pavement was uncovered in 1926, along with a layer of ash dating from Queen Boudicca's burning of the city in AD 60. There's also an intricate model of Roman London to look at and scraps of salvaged pottery from imperial days.

Fast forward to Saxon times – an archway survives from the original 7th-century church, revealed suddenly when a bomb blasted the building during World War II. In the 16th century, All Hallows took in the headless corpses from Henry VIII's execution scaffold (see p123), including that of Sir Thomas More. The church survived the Great Fire of London thanks to the quick wits of Admiral William Penn (father of Penn of Pennsylvania fame), who blew up nearby buildings to create a fire-break. Meanwhile, Penn's next-door neighbour, Samuel Pepys, climbed the steeple to watch the blaze – having first buried his prized truckle of Parmesan in his garden.

If that doesn't impress the kids, they can take home their very own medieval knight – the church's visitor centre offers brass-rubbing sessions most weekday afternoons.

Letting off steam

Cross Byward Street into Seething Lane Gardens to St Olave's Church – worth a peek for its spooky skulls and crowded plague graves. The woman thought to be responsible for bringing the plague to London is buried here, along with nursery-rhyme character Mother Goose.

Above The Saxon archway from the original 7th-century All Hallows
Below Exposed Roman pavement inside All Hallows

The Lowdown

🌐 **Map ref** 12 G4
Address Byward Street, EC3R 5BJ; 020 7481 2928; www.ahbtt.org.uk

🚗 **Train** Fenchurch Street, Tower Gateway (DLR) **Tube** Tower Hill, Monument **Bus stop** Tower Hill

🕐 **Open** 8am–5pm Mon–Fri; 10am–5pm Sat & Sun; Sung Eucharist service takes place at 11am on Sundays

💲 **Price** Free

🧑‍🤝‍🧑 **Activities** Free guided tours are available most weekdays from 2–4pm Apr–Oct. Occasional themed walking tours in the City (£8 per person) take between 90 minutes to 2 hrs. Check website for dates and times

♿ **Wheelchair access** Yes

🍽 **Eat and drink** *Picnic* Pret A Manger (12 Byward Street, EC3R 5AS; 6am–7pm Mon–Fri, 8:30am–5:30pm Sat–Sun; www.pret.com) offers sandwiches and salads *Real meal* Pizza Express (1 Byward Street, EC3R 7QN; 11:30am–11pm Mon–Sat, 11:30am–10pm Sun; 020 7626 5025; www.pizzaexpress.com) is a perennial favourite with families

🚻 **Toilets** In Tower Place, next door

The impressive Tower Bridge with breathtaking views

⑤ Tower Bridge
The legend of the flying bus driver

"Tawdry … pretentious … absurd". When Tower Bridge opened in 1894, the architecture critics didn't think much of Horace Jones's flamboyant Gothic design. Today, it is London's number-one icon, and its drawbridge-style bascules (the "see-saw" parts) are still raised 1,000 times a year to allow ships to pass. The patriotic paint scheme, first added in 1977 to mark the 25th anniversary of the accession of Queen Elizabeth II, used 22,000 litres (4,840 gallons) of red, white and blue paint.

The bridge's high walkways were designed for pedestrians – but nobody wanted to climb the 300 stairs to use them. Today, an elevator whisks visitors 42 m (138 ft) up onto the twin gantries, for breathtaking views along the river. Little ones may need lifting up to get the full impact, though there's an Explore Kit to keep them occupied, and stickers to collect en route.

Displays focus on bridge trivia, including stories about straying whales, cheeky fighter pilots and Albert Gunter, the "flying bus-driver", who found himself airborne in 1952 when the bascules opened while his No. 78 bus was still crossing the bridge.

The exhibition continues in the Victorian engine rooms, showing off the shiny steam turbines that powered the bridge until 1976, when oil, electricity and hydraulics took over. Here, kids can get to grips with interactive models: for example, sit an unsuspecting sibling in a chair, turn a handle, and watch them suddenly lurch skywards.

Letting off steam

At the southern end of the bridge, on the right as you cross north to south, lies **Potters Fields** (*www. pottersfields.co.uk*). It is possibly the most panoramic picnic spot in London.

⑥ St Katharine's Dock
London's floating treasure trove

Hidden behind a phalanx of high buildings, St Katharine's Dock is one of London's loveliest backwaters, where a powerhouse of the Industrial Revolution has been transformed into a jaunty marina lined with yachts and waterside cafés. It's a great place to kick back after tramping around the Tower of London.

The dock's roots as a shipping hub date back to the 10th century, when King Edgar granted 5 ha (13 acres) to 13 knights, with permission to trade. It grew into a prosperous and important mercantile area over the centuries. In the 1820s, the great civil engineer Thomas Telford built the basins we see today, and their warehouses were stacked high with treasure from across the British Empire – marble, ivory, wine, spices and perfume. As late as the 1930s, St Katharine's was reckoned to hold the world's largest concentration of portable wealth.

These days, the warehouses have been turned into office blocks and the money is not in the cargoes, it's in the boats themselves. For children, a wander among the yachts and pleasure cruisers is a glorious glimpse into life afloat.

Boats in the pretty marina at St Katharine's Dock

The Lowdown

- 🌐 **Map ref** 12 H5
  Address Tower Bridge Road, SE1; 020 7407 9191; *www.towerbridge.org.uk*
- 🚗 **Train** Fenchurch Street, London Bridge, Tower Gateway (DLR) **Tube** Tower Hill **Bus stop** Tower Bridge Approach **River bus** Tower Pier, St Katharine's Pier
- 🕐 **Open** Apr–Sep: 10am–5:30pm; Oct–Mar: 9:30am–5pm (last admission one hour earlier)
- 💰 **Price** £20.30–22.50, under-5s free; combined ticket with The Monument £26.50–30.90
- 👥 **Skipping the queue** Buy tickets online to avoid queuing and get discounted prices
- 🚩 **Guided tours** Available for groups of 10 or more only (extra charge)
- 👫 **Age range** 5 plus
- 👪 **Activities** A kids' passport, from the ticket desk, has stickers to collect.

- Separate Family trail app and Explore Kit must be downloaded beforehand. School-holiday activities might include Victorian games and storytelling
- ⏱ **Allow** 1 hour
- ♿ **Wheelchair access** Yes, via lifts and an alternative ramped route
- 🍽 **Eat and drink** *Picnic* EAT (2 Tower Hill Terrace, EC3N 4EE; 020 7488 1526) is a chain of sandwich bars selling freshly prepared wraps, salads, sandwiches and juices. *Real meal* Café Rouge (Unit 4, Quayside Road, St Katharine's Dock, E1W 1AN; 020 7702 0195; www.caferouge.com/locations/st-katharine-dock) is a chain French bistro set in a pretty spot beside St Katharine's Dock
- 🛍 **Shop** At end of visit
- 🚻 **Toilets** In South Tower and Engine Rooms

The Lowdown

- **Map ref** 12 H5
  Address St Katharine's Way, E1W
  1LA; 020 7488 0555; www.
  skdocks.co.uk/marina
- **Train** Fenchurch Street, Tower
  Gateway (DLR) **Tube** Tower Hill.
  Bus stop Tower Hill Approach,
  East Smithfield **River bus** St
  Katharine's Pier, Tower Pier
- **Activities** Fine food market on Fri
  outside Dickens Inn (11am–3pm).
  Check website for lock opening
  times – a good time to see boats
  enter and exit the marina
- **Age range** All
- **Allow** Up to 1 hour
- **Wheelchair access** Yes
- **Eat and drink** Picnic Kilikya's
  (St Katharine's Dock, E1W 12 AT)
  serves excellent Turkish cuisine,
  wine and soft drinks **Real meal**
  Ping Pong (Tower Bridge House,
  E1W 1BA) sells tasty, reliable
  Chinese dim sum
- **Toilets** Near Starbucks coffee
  shop (Cloister Walk, E1W 1LA)

Letting off steam

The Tower Hill/Minories playground
(see p123) is reached via the
underpass to Tower Hill tube station.

⑦ Whitechapel Gallery

Art on the edge

Little Miss Muffet is menaced by
a malevolent tarantula. A cute
teddy bear suffers an extremely
grisly disembowelling. When
commissioning artists to
mastermind a new exhibition for
children, Jake and Dinos Chapman
may not seem like an obvious

Creating a masterpiece in one of the Whitechapel Gallery's workshops

choice. But the Whitechapel
Gallery likes to push boundaries.

The gallery has been at the
cutting edge of contemporary art
since 1901, introducing the likes
of Frida Kahlo, Jackson Pollock and
Gilbert & George to British
audiences. In 2009 a £13 million
revamp doubled the exhibition
space and added a dedicated
children's studio on the top floor.
The Chapman Brothers' 2010
summer show typified the
Whitechapel's thought-provoking
approach to art for kids.

The gallery offers free workshops
and family days most weekends, and
1–2 day courses (cost varies), inspired
and often led by artists. Available all
the time is the Make It Yours art
detective kit, loaded with scrapbook,
stickers and drawing materials.

Letting off steam

Head past Aldgate tube station to
find the playground overlooking
the Tower of London (see p123).

The Lowdown

- **Map ref** 12 H2
  Address 77–82 Whitechapel High
  Street, E1 7QX; 020 7522 7888;
  www.whitechapelgallery.org
- **Train** Liverpool Street, Tower
  Gateway (DLR) **Tube** Aldgate
  East. **Bus stop** Whitechapel
  High Street, route numbers 15,
  25, 115, 135
- **Open** 11am–6pm Tue–Sun;
  till 9pm Thu
- **Price** Free; charge for special
  temporary exhibitions
- **Age range** 4 plus
- **Activities** Free children's trail suits
  ages 4–12; weekend and school-
  holiday children's workshops
  (check website)
- **Allow** 1 hour
- **Wheelchair access** Yes
- **Eat and drink** Snacks The gallery's
  café-bar claims to make London's
  best brownies **Family treat** For
  something more upscale, try the
  Gallery Dining Room
- **Shop** Selling art books and cards
- **Toilets** Ground, basement and
  2nd floor

KIDS' CORNER

Which bridge?

1 Which of London's bridges,
opened in 2000, was nicknamed
the "Wobbly Bridge" because it
swayed when people first
walked across it?
2 Which famous bridge over the
Thames was sold to an American
businessman and rebuilt stone
by stone in Arizona?
3 Which bridge is nicknamed
"Ladies Bridge", because it
was built by women while the
men were away fighting in World
War II?

Answers at the bottom of the page.

Flying high

The most spectacular Tower
Bridge crossing ever was by
Robbie Maddison, who did a
back-flip as he flew across the
open drawbridge on his
motorbike, 30 m (98 ft) above
the river, in 2009. Watch a film of
the feat at the Tower exhibition.
But that's nothing. Robbie holds
the world record for the longest
motorbike jump, at 106.9 m
(351 ft) – longer than ten buses!

Sculpture trail

The sculptures scattered around
St Katharine's Dock hark back to
some of the riches that were once
traded there. See if you can find
a pair of elephants, a peacock
and a turtle. Which precious
goods do you think these
creatures provided?

Answers: **Bridges 1** Millennium
Bridge **2** London Bridge **3** Waterloo
Bridge **Sculpture trail** Elephants for
ivory; peacocks for hat and fan
feathers; turtles for tortoiseshell
jewellery

St Paul's Cathedral and around

Left smouldering by the Great Fire of London in 1666, London's grandest church owes its modern-day magnificence to the great Renaissance architect Christopher Wren, who worked for more than 40 years on his masterpiece. Best visited at the weekend, its most dramatic approach with children is on foot via the pedestrianized promenade from Millennium Bridge. Join a guided walk (free for under-12s) from the nearby City of London Information Centre, then climb the cathedral's famous dome and enjoy the fantastic views of the city's skyline.

The City and the East End

Museum of London *p134*

St Paul's Cathedral

Tower of London *p120*

The Millennium Bridge, linking the Tate Modern on Bankside with St Paul's Cathedral and the City

Places of Interest

SIGHTS
1. St Paul's Cathedral
2. Bank of England Museum
3. Dr Johnson's House
4. Guildhall Art Gallery

● EAT AND DRINK
1. Starbucks
2. The Café at St Paul's
3. Byron
4. Barbecoa
5. Chop'd
6. Tortilla
7. The Natural Kitchen
8. Ye Olde Cheshire Cheese
9. Hummus Bros
10. The Café Below

● WHERE TO STAY
1. Cheval Calico House

Mosaic of a crocodile at Nelson's tomb in St Paul's Cathedral, made by women prisoners at Woking Gaol in the 19th century

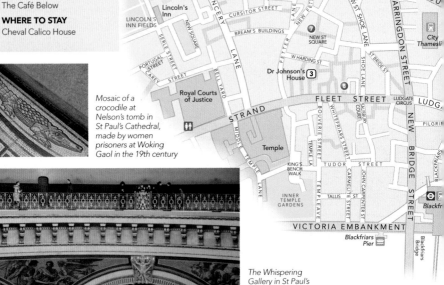

The Whispering Gallery in St Paul's Cathedral – a whisper against its walls is audible on the opposite side

The Lowdown

🚗 **Train** Blackfriars, Cannon Street, City Thameslink
Tube St Paul's, Mansion House
Bus Fleet Street/Cannon Street: route numbers 4, 11, 15, 23, 26, 76, 172; Threadneedle Street (for Bank of England): 8, 11, 23, 26, 242, 388; Cheapside (for Guildhall): 8 and 25 **River bus** Blackfriars Pier, weekday-only services between London Eye and Woolwich or Blackfriars Pier to Putney via Chelsea (www.thamesclippers.com).

ℹ️ **Visitor information** City of London Information Centre, St Paul's Churchyard, EC4M 8BX;

www.cityoflondon.gov.uk/things-to-do/visiting-the-city/pages/default.aspx

🛒 **Supermarkets** M&S Simply Food, 3a One New Change, EC4M 9AF; Sainsbury's Local, 10 Paternoster Square, EC4M 7DX; Tesco Metro, 80b Cheapside, EC2V 6EE
Markets Leadenhall Market (mostly fine food), 11am–4pm Mon–Fri; Leather Lane Market (North of Holborn Circus; mixed stalls), 10:30am–3pm Mon–Fri

🎎 **Festivals** London Maze history festival, Guildhall (Apr); City of London Festival, music and arts

(Jun–Jul); Pearly Kings and Queens Harvest Festival, St Mary-le-Bow (Sep); The Lord Mayor's Show, procession from Mansion House and fireworks (2nd Sat in Nov); Christmas at St Paul's, carols and services (Dec)

✚ **Pharmacies** Boots, 104 Cheapside, EC2V 6DN (7am–7pm weekdays; 9am–6pm Sat; closed Sun). For 24-hour pharmacies, visit www.nhs.uk/servicedirectories

✂️ **Nearest playground** Fortune Street Park, Fortune Street, EC1 0RY (north of the Barbican)

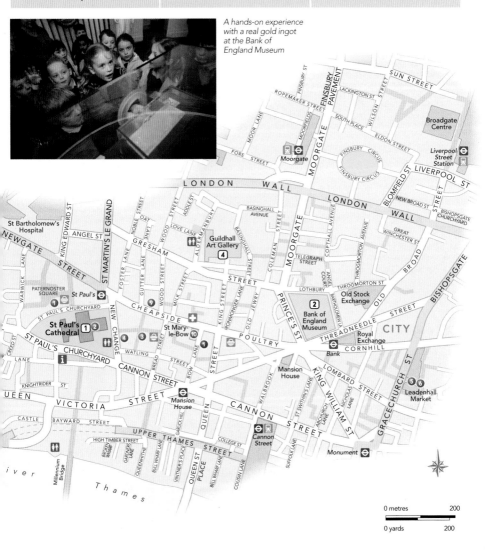

A hands-on experience with a real gold ingot at the Bank of England Museum

① St Paul's Cathedral
Possibly the most spectacular church in Christendom

Boasting Britain's biggest bell, Europe's largest crypt and a dome weighing 64,000 tonnes, St Paul's is a superlative building. Its shadowy crypt is full of famous memorials, including those of the Duke of Wellington, Florence Nightingale and Admiral Nelson, but what children will adore is counting the steps to the Whispering Gallery, and the magical sound effects they can create there. The family audio guide keeps things fun, with cartoons, quizzes and nuggets of trivia designed to dazzle even grown-ups.

Wellington Monument

The Lowdown

- 🌐 **Map ref** 11 D3
  Address The Chapter House, St Paul's Churchyard, EC4M 8AD; 020 7246 8350 or 020 7246 8357; www.stpauls.co.uk

- 🚗 **Train** Cannon Street, Blackfriars
  Tube St Paul's, Mansion House
  Bus stop St Paul's Churchyard
  River bus Blackfriars Pier

- 🕐 **Open** 8:30am–4:30pm Mon–Sat (last admission 4pm); cathedral galleries 9:30am–4:15pm. Attending services is free, including Evensong, 5pm Tue–Sat and 3:15pm Sun

- 💷 **Price** £39–44, under-6s free

- 👫 **Skipping the queue** Buy tickets online beforehand to get the cheaper family price and use the fast-track entrance

- 🚩 **Guided tours** Free 90-minute tours four times daily, plus multimedia guide

- 👫 **Age range** 6 plus

- 🧒 **Activities** Family multimedia guide (English only); or download various materials before visiting

- ⏱️ **Allow** Up to 2 hours

- ♿ **Wheelchair access** Yes, except for the Whispering, Stone and Golden galleries, and the Triforium, which are reached via many steps

- ☕ **Café** The café in the crypt (see opposite), plus the more formal restaurant alongside

- 🛍️ **Shop** In the crypt, selling books and souvenirs

- 🚻 **Toilets** Beside the café

Good family value?
Cheaper than Westminster Abbey – and a visit includes a free workout to reach one of the most spectacular views in London.

Key Features

The Dome It's as heavy as 50,000 elephants, so Wren cleverly designed a dome within a dome, to bear the weight. As it was built, he was hauled up in a basket twice a week to inspect it.

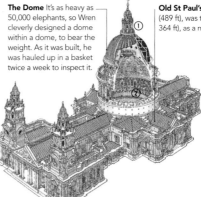

Old St Paul's The old cathedral, at 149 m (489 ft), was taller than the new one (111 m/364 ft), as a model in the crypt shows.

① **Golden Gallery** Lying at the highest point of the dome, it's a pull up all those steps. It's worth the effort – visitors are rewarded with a spellbinding view across London at the top.

② **Whispering Gallery** The quirky acoustics inside the spectacular dome throw a whisper all the way around the walkway, making this an atmospheric echo chamber kids will love.

Oculus This exciting multimedia show, in the former Treasury in the crypt, brings the cathedral's 1,400 years of history to life.

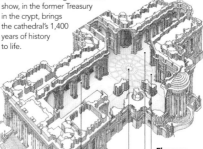

Florence Nightingale's Memorial

Oculus

Wellington Monument
This tribute to one of Britain's most famous soldiers is in the North Aisle. He died in 1852 – his tomb is in the crypt.

Florence Nightingale's Memorial The hospital reformer first came to prominence as a nurse during the Crimean War (1853–6). She was the first woman to receive the Order of Merit.

Nelson's Tomb Buried in a coffin hollowed out of the mast of a defeated French flagship, Horatio Nelson gets star billing in the centre of the crypt. Look for seafaring symbols in the mosaic floor.

A quiet spot under the shade of the trees in the gardens at St Paul's Cathedral

Letting off steam

The cathedral's churchyard has small lawns to loll on, or there are the **Festival Gardens** right next door, with a sunken lawn, cooling wall fountain and a great view back to the Dome. Alternatively, how about a romp on the panoramic rooftop of **One New Change** (www.onenewchange.com), the sleek shopping centre just east of the cathedral? Six floors high, it claims to be London's loftiest public terrace, and there's a café, too.

Eat and drink

Picnic: under £20; Snacks: £20–40; Real meal: £40–60; Family treat: £60 or more (based on a family of four)

PICNIC Starbucks (*1 Paternoster House, Unit 7, EC4M 7DX; 010 7236 3014*) serves teas, coffees, sandwiches, salads and pastries to eat in or take away – perhaps into neighbouring Paternoster Square, whose stone benches are broad enough for a full family picnic.
SNACKS Located in the crypt of the cathedral, **The Café at St Paul's** (*9am–5pm Mon–Sat, 10am–4pm Sun*), is open to all and specializes in classic British food. Pick a ploughman's lunch from the "Barrow in the Crypt", with ingredients sourced from Borough Market (*see p146*).
REAL MEAL Lots of options in the One New Change centre, including **Byron** (*17 Upper Cheapside Passage, EC2V 6AG; 020 7236 1855; www.byronhamburgers.com*). Serving classy burgers (and knickerbocker glories!), Byron has a dedicated children's menu that includes all the usual favourites.
FAMILY TREAT Barbecoa (*20 New Change Passage, EC4M 9AG; 020 3005 8555; www.barbecoa. com; 11:30am–11pm Mon–Sat, noon–10pm Sun*) is the hot ticket here, co-owned by celebrity chef Jamie Oliver and majoring in chargrilled meats. There's a selection of seafood starters as well as fish of the day. There is no children's menu but the chef will happily adapt dishes to suit children's tastes.

Find out more

DIGITAL Family trails are available to download from *www.stpauls.co.uk/learning-faith/schools-families/families*
FILM The children's classic *Mary Poppins* has lovely dreamlike sequences featuring St Paul's, including the "Feed the Birds" scene on the cathedral's steps.

Next stop. . .

ST MARY-LE-BOW CHURCH
Walk along to St Mary-le-Bow church (*Cheapside, EC2V 6AU*), another Christopher Wren gem, with an extravagant tower and a golden dragon atop its steeple. It's said you must be born within the sound of Bow Bells to be a true Cockney. There's a very cosy café in the crypt (*see p133*).
GUIDED WALKS AND TOURS Opposite St Paul's, the City Information Centre (*Cannon Street, EC4M 8BX*) is the starting point for walks exploring the oldest part of London: discover more Wren churches or learn about Samuel Pepys every Wed & Sun at 2pm (adults £7, under-12s free).

The "feed the birds" scene from the 1964 film Mary Poppins, set outside St Paul's

② Bank of England Museum

Crack a safe, grab some gold

Walking into the grand hall of this museum is one of the more surprising experiences in London. There are kids everywhere: piloting hot-air balloons, designing bank notes, cracking safes. This playroom approach strives to make simple economics palatable to young minds – never an easy task.

The hot-air balloon works as an effective metaphor for the nation's finances and kids can get their hands on the controls. Nearby, there's a safe to unlock with the help of quiz answers gathered from around the room.

The rest of the museum is more sober and includes a £1 million note and a gold ingot worth more than £300,000, which children can try their hand at lifting. Look out for the showcase featuring Ratty and

The Sir John Soane-designed building housing the Bank of England Museum

Mole, creations of *Wind in the Willows* author Kenneth Grahame (1859–1932), who was secretary to the bank from 1879 to 1908.

Letting off steam

The skyscrapers of the **Broadgate Centre** (*Eldon Street, EC2M 2QT*) enclose traffic-free squares, including grassy **Exchange Square**, with its train-set view into Liverpool Street Station, and **Broadgate Circle**, whose ice rink is open daily mid-Nov–early Feb (*www.broadgateicerink.co.uk*).

③ Dr Johnson's House

The home of an English eccentric

He collected orange peel, wore the same clothes for weeks, and liked to start every journey with the same foot. But the eccentric Samuel Johnson was a London legend, and

Dressing up in period costume in Dr Johnson's House

The Lowdown

- 🌐 **Map ref** 12 E3
  Address Bartholomew Lane, EC2R 8AH; 020 7601 5545; *www.bankofengland.co.uk/museum*
- 🚗 **Train** Cannon Street or Bank (DLR) **Tube** Bank **Bus stop** Threadneedle Street
- 🕐 **Open** Weekdays only 10am–5pm (last admission 4:30pm)
- 💷 **Price** Free
- **Skipping the queue** Queues rare
- **Guided tours** None, but free audio tour
- 👫 **Age range** 5 plus
- **Activities** Five different children's trails, graded from pre-school to ages 15–17. School holiday events
- ⏱ **Allow** 1 hour
- ♿ **Wheelchair access** Yes, via ramps, please call in advance
- ☕ **Eat and drink** *Snacks* Chop'd (*1 Leadenhall Market, EC3V 1LR; 020 7626 3706; www.chopd.co.uk; 7am–3pm Mon–Fri*) offers all-natural healthy food *Real meal* Tortilla (*28 Leadenhall Market, EC3V 1LR; 020 7929 7837; www.tortilla.co.uk; 11am–7pm Mon–Fri*) does California-style burritos and soft tacos
- 🛍 **Shop** Souvenirs and gifts
- 🚻 **Toilets** At the rear of museum

The Lowdown

- 🌐 **Map ref** 11 B3
  Address 17 Gough Square, EC4A 3DE; 020 7353 3745; *www.drjohnsonshouse.org*
- 🚇 **Tube** Chancery Lane **Bus stop** Fleet Street
- 🕐 **Open** Mon–Sat 11am–5:30pm; Oct–Apr till 5pm
- 💷 **Price** £12.50, under-5s free
- **Skipping the queue** Queues rare
- **Guided tours** None; Johnson's London walks, 1st Wed of the month, 3pm (*see website*)
- 👫 **Age range** 9 plus
- **Activities** Free kids' guide. Occasional concerts and jazz evenings. Activities and trails are organised during school holidays
- ⏱ **Allow** Up to 1 hour
- ♿ **Wheelchair access** No, there are some unavoidable steps
- ☕ **Eat and drink** *Picnic* The Natural Kitchen (*15–17 New Street Square, Fetter Lane, EC4A 3AP; 020 7353 5787; www.thenaturalkitchen.com; 7am–5pm Mon–Fri*) has a fresh feel to its take-away food. *Real meal* Ye Olde Cheshire Cheese (*145 Fleet Street, EC4A 2BU; 020 7353 6170; 11am–11pm daily*) is a 17th-century pub.
- 🛍 **Shop** Selling books, booklets, posters and souvenirs
- 🚻 **Toilets** Basement

the great and the good gathered at his house off Fleet Street to enjoy his witty conversation. Today, Dr Johnson is remembered mainly for his English dictionary, compiled here in the 1750s, with a team of scribes who copied literary snippets to illustrate 42,000 definitions. It took nine years to write, during which the debt-ridden Johnson once had to barricade the door with his bed to fend off bailiffs.

Johnson's jokes will fly over the heads of most children, but there is a film telling his story and a dressing-up rack of Georgian frockcoats to try on. Point out the spiked window above the door, to deter burglars from smuggling boy accomplices inside; and challenge kids to track down Hodge, Johnson's spoilt cat. Clue: he's out on the tiles.

Letting off steam

Head west across Fetter Lane to **Lincoln's Inn Fields** (WC2A) with its picnic-perfect lawns and public tennis courts (*see p94*).

④ Guildhall Art Gallery

Where gladiators fought

Dragons, Dick Whittington, Britain's biggest painting and a ruined Roman amphitheatre – these are just some of the unlikely attractions at the Guildhall Gallery. It stands beside the 15th-century Guildhall, seat of City government since medieval times, whose courtyard has a statue of Dick Whittington, every child's favourite Lord Mayor. The yard is menaced on all sides by dragons, the City's armorial emblem – ideal for a game of I-Spy.

The gallery itself is dominated by John Singleton Copley's eye-popping painting *The Siege of Gibraltar* (1791) – so big that it occupies two floors. Youngsters may prefer the Undercroft Galleries downstairs, lined with sentimental Victorian pictures of children, including John Everett Millais' funny portraits of his daughter dozing off in church.

The main reason to come here, though, lurks in a dark cavern in the basement – the ruins of London's 2,000-year-old Roman amphitheatre, stumbled upon by archaeologists in 1988. In Roman times, up to 6,000 people sat here to watch bloody animal fights, public executions and gladiatorial combat – to the death. Scant foundations survive, but children won't notice that, because spotlights and sound effects do a brilliant job of bringing the arena to life. Stride in through the eastern entrance, as gladiators once did long ago, past the pens used to hold wild beasts, and listen to the deafening roar of the crowd.

The Lowdown

🌐 **Map ref** 12 E2
Address Guildhall Yard, Gresham Street, EC2V 5AE; 020 7332 3700; www.cityoflondon.gov.uk/things-to-do/visiting-the-city/attractions-museums-and-galleries/

🚇 **Tube** St Paul's, Bank, Moorgate **Bus stop** Cheapside

🕙 **Open** 10am–5pm Mon–Sat; noon–4pm Sun (last admission 30 minutes earlier)

💷 **Price** Free (fee charged for some exhibitions); under-16s free

🚻 **Skipping the queue** Queues rare; go after 3:30pm (or any time Fri) for free admission

Guided tours Fri pm only (free)

🚶 **Age range** 5 plus

Activities Sketching tables in the Undercroft Galleries

⏱ **Allow** Up to 1 hour

♿ **Wheelchair access** Yes

🍽 **Eat and drink** *Snacks* Hummus Bros (128 Cheapside, EC2V 6BT; 020 7726 8011; 7:30am–9pm Mon–Thu, 7:30am–5pm Fri, 11am–5pm Sat) offers hummus and pitta breads and salads *Real meal* The Café Below (Cheapside, EC2V 6AU; 020 7329 0789; 7:30am–2:30pm Mon & Tue, to 9:15pm Wed–Fri) serves rustic European dishes in the crypt of St Mary-le-Bow Church

🏷 **Shop** Near reception

🚻 **Toilets** Floor C by cloakroom

Letting off steam

St Mary Aldermanbury Garden (EC2 2EJ), behind the Guildhall, has picnic benches and a majestic bust of William Shakespeare. The master playwright's contemporaries, John Hemynge and Henry Condell, are commemorated in the gardens; it is to them that we owe the printing of Shakespeare's *First Folio* of work.

The Siege of Gibraltar, *one of the UK's biggest paintings at the Guildhall Art Gallery*

Picnic under £20; **Snacks** £20–40; **Real meal** £40–60; **Family treat** £60 or more (based on a family of four)

Museum of London and around

A £20 million revamp has made the Museum of London a supremely welcoming place for families, from the pink-shirted "hosts" to the hands-on exhibits that animate London's story. Arrive on foot along Aldersgate Street from St Paul's tube station, and take the escalator on the right-hand pavement. Weekends are the prime time to visit, when there are fewer school parties, free family events on Sundays and children's films every Saturday at the nearby Barbican. To combine the museum with Old Spitalfields Market, take the Hammersmith & City line from Barbican to Aldgate East.

The City and the East End

Museum of London

St Paul's Cathedral p128

Tower of London p120

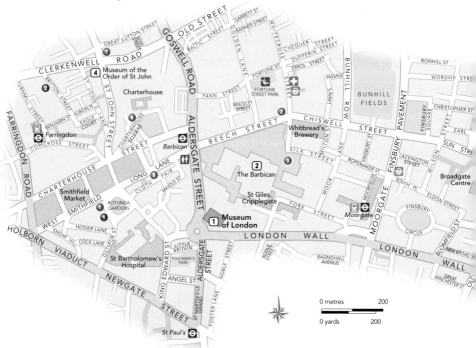

0 metres 200

0 yards 200

Prisoners' elegant graffiti in an 18th-century cell at the Museum of London

Built in 1757, the Lord Mayor's state coach in the Museum of London is beautifully crafted and still used for the Lord Mayor's Parade

Places of Interest

SIGHTS

1 Museum of London
2 The Barbican
3 Old Spitalfields Market
4 Museum of the Order of
 St John

● EAT AND DRINK

1 Carluccio's
2 Benugo Café Barbican
3 Barbican Kitchen

4 Malmaison Brasserie
5 Patisserie Valerie
6 The Breakfast Club
7 Benugo
8 Dose
*See also The Museum of London
(p137) and the Barbican (p138)*

● WHERE TO STAY

1 Market View by Bridge Street
2 MiNC Eagle Court Apartments

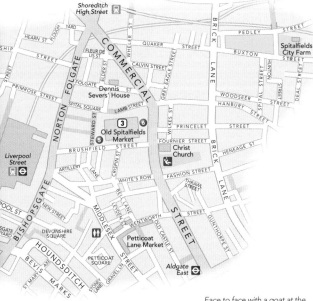

*Face to face with a goat at the
popular Spitalfields City Farm*

The Lowdown

 Train Moorgate (5-minute walk), Liverpool Street, Farringdon (10-minute walk); Shoreditch High Street (for Spitalfields Market) **Tube** Barbican, Moorgate, St Paul's **Bus** Moorgate; route numbers 4, 56; London Wall: 100; Barbican tube station: 153; King Edward Street: 8, 25, 242, 521

i Visitor information *See pp128-9*

Supermarkets Waitrose, 6L Cherry Tree Walk, EC1Y 8NX. Marks & Spencer, 70 Finsbury Pavement, EC2A 1SA
Markets Leather Lane Market (mixed stalls), 10am–3pm Mon–Fri. Petticoat Lane Market (clothing), Middlesex Street, E1, 10am–2:30pm Mon–Fri; 9am–2pm Sun. Spitalfields Market (antiques, fashion and art), 10am–5pm Mon–Wed; 9am–5pm Thu & Sun; 11am–5pm Sat

Festivals East London Comics and Arts Festival, arts (Jun; *www.elcaf.co.uk*). London Children's Film Festival, Barbican Centre and other venues (Nov); Spitalfields Music Festivals (Jun–Jul; Dec–Jan; *www.spitalfieldsmusic.org*)

✛ Pharmacies Portman's Pharmacy, Cherry Tree Walk, 5 Whitecross Street, EC1Y 8NX (9am–8:30pm Mon; 9am–6:30 Tue–Fri; 9am–5pm Sat). For 24-hour pharmacies, visit *www.nhs.uk/servicedirectories*

Nearest playgrounds Christ Church play area (Commercial Street, E1 6LY); Fortune Street Park (Fortune Street, EC1Y 8)

① Museum of London
Don't touch? Don't be so old-fashioned!

It's not easy to bring 450,000 years of history to life for children, but the Museum of London does just that, using a mix of interactive gadgetry and eye-catching presentation. The upstairs rooms are arranged chronologically and are packed with prehistoric skulls and Roman treasures, while the Galleries of Modern London resemble a series of spectacular stage sets – including a shadowy Georgian prison cell and a Victorian high street. The excellent activity trails and backpacks encourage kids to explore.

Battersea Shield c.350–50 BC

Key Features

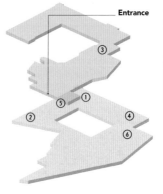

Entrance

① **Victorian Walk** Window-shop along a lively Victorian high street, complete with toy shop, pub, bank and barber's shop. The fixtures and fittings are all original.

② **Wellclose Prison Cell** Enter the dark, claustrophobic cell from a 1750 debtors' prison, its walls scratched with the names of desperate inmates and echoing with their pleas for mercy.

③ **Archaeology in Action** Get to grips with ancient pottery and other precious booty found in London at the artifact-handling sessions.

▓ **Entrance level** History of London from 450,000 BC to the 1660s: Roman London; Medieval London; War, Plague and Fire

▓ **Lower Galleries** History of London from 1670s to Today: Expanding City; Victorian Walk; People's City; Modern London

④ **Evacuees' Trunks** Lift the lids to read real-life letters from schoolchildren on the eve of World War II – and discover what they packed for their flight from London.

⑤ **Georgian Pleasure Gardens** Explore this re-creation of an 18th-century park, with its harlequins, acrobats and elegant ladies in fancy hats. Children were expected to behave like miniature adults.

⑥ **Bill and Ben** Find out what children's TV was like in the 1950s, by exploring the wall of toys and TV screens in the museum's Playtime Zone.

The Lowdown

Map ref 11 D2
Address 150 London Wall, EC2Y 5HN; 020 7001 9844; www.museumoflondon.org.uk

Tube Barbican, Moorgate, St Paul's **Bus stop** Moorgate Street, Barbican Station, London Wall

Open 10am–6pm daily

Price Free

Skipping the queue Grab a ticket on arrival for the guided tours – they are free, but numbers are limited

Guided tours Free tours of specific galleries four times a day; plus guided walks around the City monthly

Age range 4 plus

Activities Free activity sheets and packs from the welcome desk for ages 4–7 and 7–11. Interactive quizzes and costumes to try on throughout the galleries. There are also regular free family events at the weekends and in school holidays that are constantly updated, and for under-5s there is a rolling programme (www.museumoflondon.org.uk/families/visit-museum-london)

Allow At least 2 hours

Wheelchair access Yes

Cafés The museum's Benugo

entrance hall café has a snacks fare for eating in or takeaway, while the London Wall Bar & Kitchen offers a more elaborate menu, including a kids' eat free offer. Plus, there's an indoor picnic area in the Clore Learning Centre, across the forecourt

Shop In the entrance lobby, selling books, cards and posters related to the exhibitions

Toilets Behind lobby area

Good family value?
Absolutely crawling with children, and with all the hands-on activities and trails, it's easy to see why.

Nursery Garden at the Museum of London – one of two small gardens

Letting off steam

The nearest playground is 10 to 15 minutes away, at Rotunda Gardens (5-minute walk) and Fortune Street (10–15 minute walk). **Postman's Park** is much closer, just across Aldersgate Street beside St Botolph's church. It doesn't have climbing apparatus, but there is a small spread of lawns and benches, plus the moving George Frederic Watts Memorial, which honours ordinary folk who sacrificed their lives saving others. Each is remembered on a painted tile, and there are several poignant tales of childhood bravery to discover.

Eat and drink

Picnic: under £20; Snacks: £20–40; Real meal: £40–60; Family treat: £60 or more (based on a family of four)

PICNIC Carluccio's *(12 West Smithfield, EC1A 9JR; 020 7329 5904; www.carluccios.com/caffes/ smithfield; 8am–11pm Mon–Fri, 9am–11pm Sat, to 10:30pm Sun)*, just up the road, beside the splendid Victorian halls of Smithfield meat market, offers deli-style delights. Opposite, the shady benches of West Smithfield Park make ideal picnic territory. Postman's Park (see above) is also a good picnic spot.

The manicured green lawns at the Postman's Park

SNACKS The **Benugo Café** in the Barbican Centre *(Cinemas 2 & 3, Beech Street, EC2Y 8AE; 8am–10pm Mon–Fri, 10am–10pm Sat & Sun)* offers a range of healthy salads, wraps, tasty sandwiches and desserts at reasonable prices. In the evening, the bar opens to serve small bites and drinks.
REAL MEAL The **Barbican Kitchen** *(Barbican Centre, Silk Street, EC2Y 8DS; 020 7638 4141; www.benugo. com/restaurants/barbican-kitchen; 9am–8pm Mon–Sat, 11am–8pm Sun)* on Level G serves more elaborate meals, including home-made pizzas, complemented by the lakeside views. For every adult ordering a main meal, one child eats free.
FAMILY TREAT The plush burgundy-and-black **Malmaison Brasserie** *(18–21 Charterhouse Square, EC1M 6AH; 020 3750 9402; www.malmaison.com/locations/ london/; 7am–10pm Mon–Fri; 8am–11pm Sat & Sun)* has a serious commitment to sourcing seasonal and local ingredients. It is also a very family-friendly place, offering smaller portions for children on request. It also offers an attractively priced two-course menu.

Find out more

DIGITAL The museum's website has activities and stimulating online games; *www.museumoflondon.org. uk/families/visit-museum-london*. Kids can also play and learn from home via *www.museumoflondon. org.uk/families/fun-home*. Play "Roman snakes and ladders", and discover more about historic artifacts on the way, at *http://romans.tullie house. co.uk/flash/snakes/index.htm*.

Next stop...

DENNIS SEVERS' HOUSE After breezing through London's entire history in half a day, try a different kind of museum: Dennis Severs' House *(noon–2pm & 5–9pm Mon, Wed, Fri; noon–4pm Sun; bookings required for most sessions; 18 Folgate St, E1 6BX; 020 7257 4013; www.dennissevershouse.co.uk)* is a unique time capsule created by a Canadian designer. He furnished his home as a series of still-life tableaux spanning two centuries, as though the occupants have just stepped outside. It's not for younger children, though.

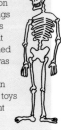

② The Barbican
Cartoons and crazy art

If you're looking for somewhere to lose the children, the Barbican might just be it. With its innumerable entrances and tangles of stairways and courtyards, Europe's biggest multi-arts complex is a little difficult to navigate. Never fear – head for the main entrance round the back on Silk Street, which curves down into the heart of things.

Inside is a vast black-and-orange bunker packing in two theatres, two art galleries, a music and dance space, a library, three restaurants and three cinemas.

Ensconced in the Saturday Film Club at the Barbican

Bustling Old Spitalfields Market filled with a variety of stalls

There is always something happening and it's often for kids, from the Family Film Club every Saturday morning to a fistful of annual festivals, including the London Children's Film Festival in November and Animate the World in May. The Curve Gallery on Level 0 showcases the kind of conceptual art that's guaranteed to excite the imagination of children, and the library on Level 2 also has a great children's section.

Check the website to find out what's on, or just drop in and enjoy a meal at one of the half-dozen places to eat and drink.

Letting off steam

Walk north along Whitecross Street to **Fortune Street Park** (see p136), where swings and scrambling nets will keep the kids happy.

③ Old Spitalfields Market
London's liveliest and coolest marketplace

The first market at "Spittle Fields" was licensed to sell flesh, fowl and roots by King Charles I in 1638, but the area's wholesale green-grocers outgrew the site in 1991, paving the way for an inventive community of craftspeople and designers to move in.

Today, Spitalfields Market is cutting-edge cool and on a busy Sunday up to 1,000 traders specializing in vintage fashion, bespoke jewellery and gifts set up stalls. The vibe is youthful and positive – a winner with fashion-conscious kids. Stalls operate from Thursday to Sunday, offering a variety of items.

Don't miss a browse among the offbeat boutiques that have popped up in adjoining streets, too – including Wood 'n' Things (57 Brushfield Street, E1 6AA), for high-quality toys and dolls, traditional wooden toys, well-crafted doll's houses, train sets, as well as sit-and-ride toys. The market's "food village" serves aromatic dishes from the world over, while a fine foods market runs on Thursday, Friday and Sunday in nearby Crispin Place.

Just south of Old Spitalfields Market, along Middlesex Street, lies the historic Petticoat Lane Market, a more down-to-earth affair where traders have been shouting their wares since the 1750s – mostly street clothing, leather goods and shoes.

The Lowdown

🌐 **Map ref** 11 D1
Address Silk Street, EC2Y 8DS; 020 7638 4141, Box Office 020 7638 8891; www.barbican.org.uk

🚍 **Train** Liverpool Street, Farringdon, Blackfriars **Tube** Barbican **Bus stop** Barbican tube station, London Wall

🕐 **Open** 9am–11pm Mon–Sat; noon–11pm Sun

💲 **Price** Shows and exhibitions individually priced. Access to Curve Gallery, library, restaurants and courtyard is free

🏃 **Skipping the queue** Online booking available for most events

👣 **Guided tours** Architecture tours Thu–Sun afternoon; £45

👫 **Age range** All

👫 **Activities** Framed Film Club (11am Sat) lays on art activities before the

film on the last Saturday of each month. Special teenager tickets for London Symphony Orchestra concerts and talks are also available. Do Something Different weekends (Mar & Jul) offer activities for all. Check website for full programme

♿ **Wheelchair access** Yes, via Silk Street entrance

🍴 **Eat and drink** *Snacks* Bonfire (Level 1) and Benugo Café near the cinemas are fine for light bites. *Family treat* The Osteria (Level 2) and the Barbican Kitchen (Level G) are more formal but affordable

🏷 **Shops** The ground-floor foyer shop has a good stock of toys and kids' books; Art Gallery Shop (Level 3) sells souvenir books, postcards and posters

👫 **Toilets** On most levels

The Lowdown

🌐 **Map ref** 12 G1
Address 105a Commercial Street, E1 6BG; 020 7247 8556; www.oldspitalfieldsmarket.com

🚂 **Train** Liverpool Street **Tube** Liverpool Street, Aldgate East **Bus stop** Commercial Street, Bishopsgate

🕐 **Open** Spitalfields: Thu (antiques); Fri (records); Sat & Sun (mixed). Petticoat Lane: 10am–2:30pm Mon–Fri; 9am–2pm Sun

💲 **Price** Free

👫 **Age range** All

🤸 **Activities** Spitalfields Music Festival, biannually in Jun–Jul and Dec–Jan (www. spitalfieldsmusic.org.uk)

♿ **Wheelchair access** Yes, the market is accessible but may be difficult to navigate if busy

🍽 **Eat and drink** *Snacks* Patisserie Valerie (37 Brushfield Street, E1 6AA) offers salads, wraps and gorgeous homemade Italian ice cream. *Real meal* The Breakfast Club (12–16 Artillery Lane, E1 7LS) serves brilliant brunches (till 5pm)

🚻 **Toilets** In the market and surrounding restaurants and cafés

Letting off steam

There is a small play area beside Christ Church, opposite the market on Commercial Street. Alternatively, head east to Buxton Street, where kids can commune with Bayleaf the donkey, Bentley the goat and friends at **Spitalfields City Farm** (closed Mon; admission free; Buxton Street, E1 5AR; www.spitalfieldscityfarm.org).

The Lowdown

🌐 **Map ref** 11 C1
Address St John's Gate, St John's Lane, EC1M 4DA; 0207 324 4005; www.museumstjohn.org.uk

🚂 **Train** Farringdon **Tube** Farringdon **Bus stop** Farringdon Road, Clerkenwell Road

🕐 **Open** 10am–5pm Mon–Sat; closed 22 Dec–1 Jan

💲 **Price** Free (optional donation £5)

Guided tours 11am and 2:30pm (free) Tue, Fri and Sat

👫 **Age range** 8 plus

🤸 **Activities** Challenge Trail (ages 6–11) plus sticker trail for younger kids (free); actor-led interpretation sessions; drop-in craft activities,

Costumed guide at the Museum of the Order of St John

④ Museum of the Order of St John

From nurses to knights

There's something distinctly magical about visiting the historic home of real knights in the heart of London. The building certainly looks the part – built in 1504, it is a remnant of the priory of the Knights Hospitallers, the medieval crusaders who went from helping sick pilgrims in Jerusalem to fighting Saladin.

The museum uses TV screens, armour and artifacts to relay its stirring story of chivalric sacrifice. A separate gallery is devoted to the St John's Ambulance movement, the 20th-century reincarnation of the order, still based here. It may be fairly conventional, but the museum succeeds in bringing history to life.

Letting off steam

The peaceful lawns at **Rotunda Gardens** (West Smithfield, EC1A 9BD) belie its grisly past as an execution site. Those executed include the Scottish knight William Wallace (1305) and Wat Tyler (1381); today there is a jolly playground.

3rd Sat of the month, plus school-holiday workshops

♿ **Wheelchair access** Main galleries are accessible, but crypt and upper floor are reached via stairs

🍽 **Eat and drink** *Picnic* Benugo (116 St John Street, EC1V 4JS; 020 7253 3499; www.benugo.com) does made-to-order sandwiches and salads for eating in or taking out *Snacks* Dose (70 Long Lane, EC1A 9EJ; 020 7600 0382) serves up great salads, homemade bread and cakes

🛍 **Shop** A small gift shop

🚻 **Toilets** Ground floor

Southwark
and the South Bank

The South Bank first blossomed as an arts district in 1951, when it was chosen as the focal point for the Festival of Britain. However, it took another 50 years, and the opening of the London Eye, for the area to finally become a prime visitor destination. Today, it offers an irresistible array of family-friendly attractions, from Shakespeare's Globe and Tate Modern to the National Theatre and IMAX Cinema.

Bloomsbury and
Regent's Park

The City and
the East End

Westminster
and the
West End

**Southwark and
the South Bank**

Kensington,
Chelsea and
Battersea

Highlights

The *Golden Hinde*
Every child loves a pirate fancy-dress party – and there's no more authentic place to enjoy one than aboard Sir Francis Drake's gorgeous treasure galleon. Ahoy, matey *(see p150)*!

Borough Market
The stalls of this bustling market allow brave gastronomes to explore many of the world's cuisines. Pick up a picnic, then head for the tables outside Southwark Cathedral *(see p150)*.

Imperial War Museum
Despite the planes, tanks and guns, what kids will remember most about this museum are the personal stories, and the mud and madness of its World War I Trench Experience *(see p166)*.

River Thames RIB-tour
When sightseeing starts to feel a little sedate, jump aboard this speedboat for a spray-drenched blast past the London Eye and other riverside sights *(see p161)*.

The Old Operating Theatre
On Saturday afternoons, limbs are swiftly lopped off in a bloodcurdling demonstration of Victorian surgery at this museum. Needless to say, most children love it *(see p151)*.

Left *Fun and frolics on the Golden Hinde – youngsters come face to face with a buccaneer during a "Pirate Days" activity session* **Above** *Marine life at the Sea Life London Aquarium*

The Best of
Southwark & the South Bank

For all its imposing parks and squares, London never really had one long, traffic-free promenade – until the 21st-century transformation of the South Bank. A walkway now stretches virtually unbroken along the Thames from Tower Bridge to the London Eye, offering a terrific pleasure trail for families. Runners rush, seagulls soar, speedboats skim… and when the tide goes out, there's even a beach.

A South Bank stroll

Start at Tower Hill Tube station, and cross Tower Bridge to pick up The Queen's Walk past the imposing bulk of **HMS Belfast** (see pp152–3). From here, the City's skyline is visible across the water. At London Bridge, turn left and take the stairs down beside **Southwark Cathedral** (see p150), where Borough Market (see p146) may be in full swing (Thu–Sat) – a great place to gather a picnic for later.

Return to the river, where you'll soon pass a pair of brilliant attractions, **Shakespeare's Globe** (see pp146–7) and **Tate Modern** (see p148), both very welcoming for families. Beyond Blackfriars Bridge, break out your lunch among the craft studios and cafés of **Gabriel's**

Wharf (see p163), then press on past the **Southbank Centre** (see pp164–5) to the **London Eye** (see pp160–61), its glass capsules guaranteed to elicit gasps from all. Cross Westminster Bridge to the Tube station and Big Ben – a fitting finale to a River Thames walk.

Dressing-up time

Who do you want to be today? A sea captain or a pirate? Perhaps a fighter pilot or a star of the Elizabethan stage? A clutch of museums along the South Bank offer children the chance to act the part. **Shakespeare's Globe** (see pp146–7) has sound booths where kids can play Juliet or King Lear, and there are occasional drama workshops during matinee performances.

Below The naval gunship HMS Belfast on the Thames

Younger kids may prefer the **Golden Hinde** (see p150), a replica of Sir Francis Drake's globetrotting Tudor galleon, which holds regular pirate sleepovers for families. Nearby, **HMS Belfast** (see pp154–5) is perhaps the most atmospheric of all, evoking life on a battleship with the help of a lively children's audioguide and the chance to be a pint-sized admiral.

Further along, the **Fashion and Textile Museum** (see pp156–7) will appeal to the more creative youngster interested in fashion, while the **London Bridge Experience** (see p157) promises to be exhilarating fun.

The world's a stage

At the southern end of Waterloo Bridge is a true village for the arts, from classical music to comedy, cinema to circus. There is always plenty going on, and families are well catered for, especially during the summer festival season. The **National Theatre** (see p162) hosts every kind of production from large, extravagant works to small, one-man shows. The complex is a lively social centre and worth a visit, even if not for a play but only for a backstage tour.

Virtually next door, the **Southbank Centre's** (see p164) summer celebration focuses on the Udderbelly pop-up theatre, housed in an upside-down purple cow. The London Film Festival follows in October, at the nearby **BFI** (see pp162–3) – and at any time of year, it offers free film and TV in its Mediatheque suite, plus monthly film-making workshops for kids at the BFI IMAX, Britain's largest cinema screen.

In a weekend

The essential Southwark weekend begins on Saturday morning, gathering cosmopolitan edibles from Borough Market (see p146). Kids love soaking up the sounds, smells and free samples, and Monmouth coffee shop (2 Park Street, SE1 9AB) does all-you-can-eat bread and jam for £3. Afterwards, sign up for a story-filled tour at **Shakespeare's Globe** (see pp146–7) – family fundays are on the second weekend of every month. Picnic by the river, then head off to **Tate Modern** (see p148) for the art trails.

On Sunday, head for the dark side, getting up early to beat the queue at the **London Dungeon** (see p164). Afterwards, if you can stomach it, the nearby George Inn (see p147), an atmospheric old coaching tavern, serves Sunday roast. Then it's off to view the spooky potions and pickled parts at the **Old Operating Theatre** (see p151), which has a herb-handling session at 2pm.

Shakespeare's Globe and around

The Globe is a genuine time-travel experience for children, set in a thatched theatre straight from a picture book. River bus services dock at Bankside Pier, opposite the gates. The theatre is just one of several attractions on the South Bank, so book ahead for the auditorium tour, then build the day around it. Families can happily spend a full day on museum-going, pavement-dining and people-watching – while barely encountering a single car.

Southwark and the South Bank

Shakespeare's Globe

London Eye *p158*

HMS *Belfast* *p152*

Southwark Cathedral, the oldest cathedral in London, dating from the 7th century

The open-roofed Shakespeare's Globe theatre – a lively experience for all

The Lowdown

🚗 **Train** Blackfriars and London Bridge stations are about a 10-minute walk away; Cannon Street, about 15 minutes away
Tube London Bridge, Mansion House, Cannon Street
Bus Southwark Bridge Road: route number 344; Southwark Street; London Bridge: 17, 21, 35, 40, 43, 47, 133, 141, 149, 343, 521
River bus Bankside Pier, en route from Westminster to St Katherine's Dock (020 7936 2033; *www.crownrivercruise. co.uk*); and from London Eye to Greenwich (0870 781 5049; *www.thamesclippers.com*). The Tate to Tate Boat (020 7887 8888; *www.tate.org.uk/visit/ tate-boat*) shuttles between Tate Britain and Tate Modern during gallery opening hours.

ℹ️ **Visitor information** City of London Information Centre *(see pp128–9)*

🛒 **Supermarket** Marks & Spencer Simply Food, Bankside, 90 Southwark St, SE1 0HX; open daily
Market Borough Market, 8 Southwark St, SE1 1TL, *www. boroughmarket.org.uk* (fine foods), 10am–5pm Mon–Thu, 10am–6pm Fri, 8am–5pm Sat

🎏 **Festivals** Shakespeare's Birthday, the Globe (Apr); Coin Street Festival, Bernie Spain Gardens (Jun–Jul); Thames Festival (Sep); Bankside Winter Festival (Dec)

➕ **Pharmacies** Boots, 8–11 Hays Galleria, SE1 2HD; 020 7407 4276 (7:30am–7pm Mon–Fri, 10am–6pm Sat, 11am–5pm Sun). For 24-hour pharmacies, visit *www.nhs.uk/servicedirectories*

🐾 **Nearest playground** Little Dorrit Park *(www.london-se1.co.uk/places/ little-dorrit-park)*; Mint Street Adventure Playground *(see p146)*

0 metres 100
0 yards 100

Testing the torture equipment at
the Clink Prison Museum

Tasting delicious Spanish food at
Brindisa, Borough Market

Places of Interest

SIGHTS

1. Shakespeare's Globe
2. Tate Modern
3. Clink Prison Museum
4. The *Golden Hinde*
5. Southwark Cathedral
6. The Old Operating Theatre

● EAT AND DRINK

1. Borough Market
2. Tate Café
3. Swan at the Globe
4. OXO Tower Brasserie
5. The Rooftop Cafe
6. Gourmet Burger Kitchen
7. Caffè Nero
8. Fish!
9. Frank's Cafe
10. The George Inn

*See also Shakespeare's Globe
(p147), Tate Modern (p148) and
Southwark Cathedral (p151)*

● WHERE TO STAY

1. Ibis Styles London
   Southwark Rose
2. London Bridge

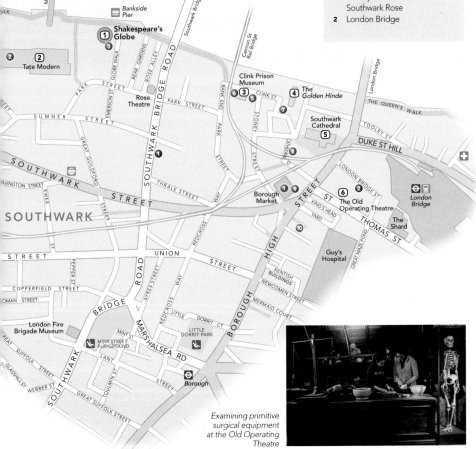

Examining primitive
surgical equipment
at the Old Operating
Theatre

① Shakespeare's Globe

The roar of the crowd, the smell of the greasepaint

In Shakespeare's time, going to the theatre was not the genteel experience it is today. Rival acting troupes competed to attract an audience – who would drink and shout at the actors during plays packed with murder, magic and comedy. The original Globe was built nearby in 1599, after Shakespeare and his company, the Lord Chamberlain's Men, transported a playhouse, timber by timber, across the Thames from Shoreditch. Today's open-air theatre, a near replica, opened in 1997.

Detail from the Globe's gates

Key Features

THE GLOBE IN 1600

The actors Until 1661, boys as young as 13 performed the female roles. It is believed that many died early, poisoned by the lead in their make-up.

The plays *Hamlet, Macbeth* and *Julius Caesar* all had their premieres at the original Globe Theatre. Shakespeare often performed minor roles in his own plays.

The audience 3,000 people would cram inside for a play. It cost a penny to watch from the yard – in summer, it got so smelly, these spectators were called "penny stinkards".

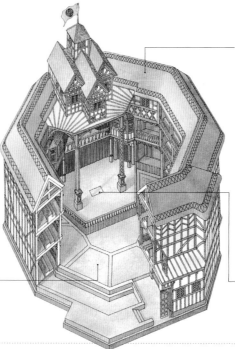

THE GLOBE TODAY

The building It uses 16th-century materials, such as hand-made bricks and wooden pegs, not nails. The thatched roof was the first in the city since the Great Fire of London.

The theatre season runs from April to October. After the monthly Child's Play workshops, kids get to sneak in to watch the end of the Saturday matinee.

The stage Look out for trapdoors (above and below), which allow surprise entrances by devils or ghosts in puffs of smoke, or angels and fairies flying down on ropes.

Letting off steam

When the tide is out, get down to the riverside in front of **Gabriel's Wharf** for a bit of beach time (check the tides at *www.pla.co.uk*). There is a stretch of grass in front of nearby Tate Modern, but for swings and slides, head south to **Mint Street**

At Gabriel's Wharf, kids can play on the beach in the centre of the city

Prices given are for a family of four

Adventure Playground (*Lant St, SE1 1QP*), or to **Nelson Square Garden** (*Nelson Square, SE1*), near Southwark Tube station.

Eat and drink

Picnic: under £20; Snacks: £20–40; Real meal: £40–60; Family treat: £60 or more (based on a family of four)

PICNIC Borough Market (*8 Southwark St, Borough, SE1 1TL; www.boroughmarket.org.uk; 10am–5pm Mon–Thu, 10am–6pm Fri, 8am–5pm Sat*) makes foraging for food a gastronomic, globetrotting adventure, though it's not cheap: its classy picnic offerings include Spanish hams and cheeses at Brindisa (*www.brindisa.com*) and rye bread from the Karaway Bakery.

SNACKS Tate Café (*Tate Modern, Bankside, SE1 9TG; 020 7401 5014; www.tate.org.uk/modern; open daily*) allows one child to eat for free at lunchtime when an adult chooses a main course. The café serves soup, many other savoury dishes, cakes and homemade smoothies.

REAL MEAL Swan at the Globe (*21 New Globe Walk, SE1 9DT; 020 7928 9444; www.swanlondon.com; open daily – check website for times*) is located right next to the theatre with a great view of the river Thames, and specializes in upmarket pub food.

The Lowdown

🌐 **Map ref** 11 D4
Address 21 New Globe Walk, Bankside, SE1 9DT; 020 7401 9919; www.shakespearesglobe.com

🚗 **Train** Blackfriars, Cannon Street, London Bridge **Tube** London Bridge, Cannon Street
Bus stop Southwark Bridge Road, Southwark Street
River bus Bankside Pier

🕐 **Open** Exhibitions: 9am–5:30pm daily; Box Office: 10am–6pm daily

💲 **Price** Museum: visit £50, under-5s free. Theatre tickets from £20–£45

👫 **Skipping the queue** During the theatre season (late Apr–Oct), auditorium tours are mornings only; afternoon tours focus on the remains of the Rose Theatre, contemporary with the Globe

🚩 **Guided tours** 40-minute tour included in the museum visit

👫 **Age range** 6 plus

🎭 **Activities** Live demonstrations of stage combat, Elizabethan stage costumes or printing most days in the museum (phone to check). Family activity weekends (2nd weekend of month) and school holiday workshops, free with museum admission

🕐 **Allow** Up to 2 hours

♿ **Wheelchair access** Yes, via lifts and ramps

☕ **Café** In the theatre lobby; plus the Swan at the Globe (see below left)

🛍️ **Shop** Selling theatre merchandise and souvenirs

🚻 **Toilets** Inside exhibition space

Good family value?
The exhibition is pricey, but there's plenty happening for children.

Fresh artisan bread sold at The Flour Station, Borough Market

FAMILY TREAT OXO Tower Brasserie (Barge House St, SE1 9PH; 020 7803 3888; www.harveynichols.com/restaurant/the-oxo-tower; open daily), eight storeys above the river, feels like dining in the sky: European cooking for grown-ups, spaghetti bolognese or sausages for kids.

Find out more

DIGITAL Watch the BBC's Shakespeare: the Animated Tales, collected together at www.ovguide.com/tv/shakespeare_the_animated_tales.htm. For more Shakespeare activities, including themed word searches, jigsaws and mazes, visit www.folger.edu/shakespeare-kids

Next stop. . .

THE GEORGE INN Head across Southwark to the George Inn (77 Borough High St, SE1 1NH; www.nationaltrust.org.uk/george-inn/) to see London's last surviving galleried coaching tavern. In the days before formal playhouses, actors performed in the cobbled courtyards of inns like this one (note: children are admitted only when accompanied by an adult).
UNICORN THEATRE The Unicorn Theatre (147 Tooley St, SE1 2HZ; 020 7645 0560; www.unicorntheatre.com) is London's dedicated children's playhouse, with family shows plus kids' workshops on Sundays.

The purpose-built Unicorn Theatre, close to Tower Bridge

② Tate Modern

Shattering, splattering, exploding… art

There's no need to worry whether children will enjoy Tate Modern. Whether it's a Jackson Pollock splatter painting, Henri Matisse's colourful collages, or Claes Oldenburg's make-believe hamburgers, chances are they have already created something along the same lines at school or in their bedroom. If not, they soon will, after a wander around London's most mind-expanding art gallery. Copying Niki de Saint Phalle, who created her paintings by shooting at them, should probably be discouraged, however.

Housed in the tall-chimneyed former Bankside Power Station, Tate Modern was a smash hit from the moment it opened in 2000, and a £215 million redevelopment has doubled the exhibition space to help soak up its five million annual visitors. The gallery offers masses for children. A dedicated team occupies the family concourse on Level 3 every weekend afternoon, suggesting art trails and challenges for kids aged five and above. The "Interactive Zone" on Level 5 is available full time, with touch-screen consoles and video clips that illuminate and explain the collection. The children's audio tour is strong on quizzes and puzzles, and there's even a "Tate Trumps" game to download as an app for iPhone – collect seven favourite works

then pit them against art chosen by friends. Exploring the gallery is less daunting than it first appears: while there are seven storeys in all, the permanent collection is only on levels 2 and 4, and is grouped by theme into four wings. A great approach is to let kids lead the way, wandering the 20 or so rooms on each floor in search of appealing pieces. Rewarding stops include Room 2 of the "Poetry and Dream" wing, for Dali; Room 1 of "Structure and Clarity" on Level 4, for Matisse; and Room 1 of "Energy and Process" for Malevich. Also look

for Cy Twombly in "Energy and Process" on Level 4. Note that the Tate often loans out or removes work for restoration so works may not always be on display. Don't leave without a visit to the Turbine Hall, right at the bottom, housing a single, huge installation.

Letting off steam

Tate Modern's extension opens up into a piazza to the south and west of the gallery. The **Millennium Bridge** is a great spot for watching the Thames water traffic.

The Lowdown

- 🌐 **Map ref** 11 C5
  Address Bankside, SE1 9TG; 020 7887 8888; www.tate.org.uk
- 🚐 **Train** Blackfriars, Cannon Street, London Bridge **Tube** Southwark, London Bridge, Cannon Street **Bus stop** Southwark Bridge Road, Southwark Street **River bus** Bankside Pier
- 🕐 **Open** 10am–6pm Sun–Thu; 10am–10pm Fri–Sat (last admission to exhibitions: 45 mins before closing)
- 💲 **Price** Turbine Hall and permanent collection free; temporary shows charge
- 🧍 **Skipping the queue** The extension should ease weekend congestion
- 🚩 **Guided tours** Free 45-minute tours daily at 11am, noon, 2pm and 3pm, each covering one of the four wings of the permanent collection. There are one-hour tours of temporary shows – times and prices vary

- 👫 **Age range** All
- 🧑‍🤝‍🧑 **Activities** Free guided kids' activities (age 5 plus) every Sat & Sun noon–4pm, also Thu & Fri in school holidays. Family zone with art books and materials on Level 0; free art trails (age 5 plus) from information desks on Levels 1 and 2. Kids' multimedia guide from Levels 2 and 3 (£3.50)
- ⏱️ **Allow** At least 2 hours
- ♿ **Wheelchair access** Yes
- 🍽️ **Eat and drink** *Snacks* Tate Café (Level 1) has good-value lunch deals for under-12s, also sandwiches and pastries. *Real meal* Tate Modern Restaurant (Level 9) has river views and a more ambitious menu; also open for dinner Fri–Sat
- 🛍️ **Shops** Levels 0, 1 and 3 selling art books, jewellery, prints and exhibition souvenirs
- 🚻 **Toilets** All levels; baby-changing facilities on Level 0

Above The Millennium Bridge over the Thames links St Paul's and Tate Modern **Left** The heart of Tate Modern is the towering Turbine Hall

Prices given are for a family of four

Waxwork inmate undergoing punishment at the grisly Clink Prison Museum

③ Clink Prison Museum

The original London dungeon

Medieval Southwark was outside the jurisdiction of London's civic authorities, and was a lawless place notorious for bear fights, drinking dens and brothels – all licensed by the bishops of Winchester, whose palace stood here on the south bank of the Thames. A gaol was needed to control the area, and in 1144 the Clink was opened – a place so infamous that its name became a byword for prisons across the land.

Inside the small, dingy cells of this subterranean attraction, waxwork inmates, recorded shrieks and replica torture equipment are used to tell the gory story of crime and punishment up to 1780, when the Clink locked up for the last time. Information boards describe a 12th-century trial by ordeal (walk across red-hot irons without injury and you're innocent)

and the priestly persecutions of Bloody Mary. It is more histrionic than historical, and maybe a bit too spooky for the under-8s. Ghoulish children will enjoy trying on the scold's bridle or placing their head on the executioner's chopping block. Visitors are able to download a picture of their visit afterwards.

Letting off steam

Head south along Bank End Park and Redcross Way to **Little Dorrit Park** (off Little Dorrit Court, SE1), which has play equipment.

The Lowdown

- 🌐 **Map ref** 12 E5
  Address 1 Clink Street, SE1 9DG; 020 7403 0900; www.clink.co.uk
- 🚗 **Train** London Bridge **Tube** London Bridge **Bus stop** Southwark Bridge, Southwark Street, Borough High Street **River bus** Bankside Pier
- 🕐 **Open** Jul–Sep: 10am–9pm daily; Oct–Jun: 10am–6pm Mon–Fri, 10am–7:30pm Sat & Sun
- 💷 **Price** £18
- **Guided tours** Groups only
- 👫 **Age range** 8 plus
- ⏱ **Allow** Up to 1 hour
- ♿ **Wheelchair access** There are nine steps to get down to the musem.
- 🍴 **Eat and drink** Snacks The Rooftop Cafe (28 London Bridge Street, SE1 9SG; www.theexchange.so/rooftop; open Mon–Sat) has great views of London with seasonal selections Real meal Gourmet Burger Kitchen (Soho Wharf, Clink Street, SE1 9DG; www.gbk.co.uk; 11:30am–10pm daily) does mini versions of its burgers for kids.
- 🛍 **Shop** Gift shop selling souvenirs
- 👫 **Toilets** No

Clambering over a steam-train climbing frame in Little Dorrit Park, SE1

Picnic: under £20; **Snacks:** £20–40; **Real meal:** £40–60; **Family treat:** £60 or more (based on a family of four)

④ The *Golden Hinde*

Ahoy there me hearties!

This beautiful replica of a Tudor galleon sits majestically on the river alongside the cafés and office blocks of Bankside, as if moored there just a minute ago by pirates. Indeed, miniature mutineers swarm aboard regularly, during the Pirate Fun Days and sleepovers staged for families.

The *Hinde* is a full-size reproduction of Sir Francis Drake's flagship, which circumnavigated the world in the 1577–80, discovering California and plundering much Spanish loot along the way. Rewards could be high – after one profitable trip, even a lowly cabin boy became the equivalent of a millionaire.

A number-keyed, useful handout describes the decks, rigging and artillery – but aim to visit at the weekend if possible, when excellent

Dressed up and pretending to fire a cannon on the Golden Hinde

tour guides are on board to help. Sit in Drake's chair in the captain's cabin and marvel at how the cramped quarters once accommodated up to 80 crew – even little ones will need to duck down to explore the gloomy gun deck. Most Saturdays there are costumed family fun days: grab a cutlass and eye-patch and learn how to weigh anchor and fire a cannon.

Letting off steam

Head south along Borough High Street to **Little Dorrit Park** (off *Little Dorrit Court, SE1*).

⑤ Southwark Cathedral

Pilgrims, poets and posh provisions

The "archaeology chamber" in Southwark Cathedral's millennium wing is a window on nearly 2,000 years of worship beside London Bridge. A 4th-century Roman religious icon was unearthed here, and there is a stone coffin from the medieval Priory of St Mary Overie.

The church we see today is mostly 14th century. Geoffrey Chaucer's pilgrims in *The Canterbury Tales* began their journey from a nearby tavern, and the fabulous tomb of Chaucer's contemporary John Gower lights up the cathedral's nave with its carousel colours – red, green and gold. Look out for a 500-year-old stone "corpse", emaciated in its shroud – perfect for spooking the children. However, the best known

memorial remembers William Shakespeare, who spent 12 years working at the nearby Globe Theatre – characters from some of his plays cavort in a stained-glass window above.

From Wednesday to Saturday, the stalls of Borough Market (*see p146*) lap around the cathedral railings, adding greatly to the atmosphere of the neighbourhood. London's oldest food market was chartered by Edward III in 1406, although it is unlikely to have sold ostrich burgers or Burmese curry powder back then. The market now specializes in delectable ingredients from across Europe and beyond, and sampling the food is encouraged – but steer clear on Saturday mornings after 10am, when the area gets super-busy.

Letting off steam

The cathedral has an outside area with tables, and beyond that there is a small square beside the river.

Gilded Mary and Jesus, a detail of the Great Screen, Southwark Cathedral

The Lowdown

🌐 **Map ref** 12 E5
Address St Mary Dock, Cathedral Street, SE1 9DE; 020 7403 0123; *www.goldenhinde.com*

🚆 **Train** London Bridge **Tube** London Bridge, Monument **Bus stop** Borough High Street. **River bus** Bankside Pier

🕐 **Open** 9:30am–6pm daily

💲 **Price** £20, under-3s free

🏃 **Skipping the queue** Best to book ahead for a family workshop

🎭 **Guided tours** Costumed tours or pirate dress-up days every Sat (family £20–33, including adm)

👫 **Age range** 4 plus

🤺 **Activities** 2-hour pirate workshops for families most Saturdays (plus some weekdays in school holidays) – come in costume. Also regular Sat sleepovers for ages 5–10, accompanied by an adult (£45pp). Call or check website

⏱ **Allow** 1 hour for self-guided visit

♿ **Wheelchair access** No, due to the steep stairs and low ceilings

🍴 **Eat and drink** *Picnic* Caffè Nero (3 Cathedral Street, SE1 9DE; 7am–8:30pm Mon–Fri; 7:30am–9pm Sat & Sun) overlooks the ship, or try the stalls at Borough Market (*see p146*)

🛍 **Shop** At the ticket shop selling souvenirs

🚻 **Toilets** At the ticket shop

The Lowdown

🌐 **Map ref** 12 E5
Address London Bridge, SE1 9DA; 020 7367 6700; http://cathedral.southwark.anglican.org

🚇 **Train** London Bridge **Tube** London Bridge, Monument **Bus stop** Borough High Street **River bus** Bankside Pier

🕐 **Open** 8am–6pm Mon–Fri, 8:30am–6pm Sat & Sun; services include choral evensong daily. Borough Market: 10am–5pm Mon–Thu, 10am–6pm Fri, 8am–5pm Sat

💲 **Price** Donations

🚩 **Guided tours** Groups only (adults £5.50; under-11s £3); 11am & 1pm Fri, 1pm Sun

Activities Regular concerts

⏱ **Allow** Up to 1 hour

♿ **Wheelchair access** Yes, via lifts or fixed and portable ramps

🍽 **Eat and drink** *Snacks* The café serves lunch and cakes *Real meal* Fish! *(Cathedral St, SE1 9AL; 020 7407 3803; 11:30am–11pm Mon–Thu, noon–11pm Fri & Sat, 10am–10:30pm Sun)* offers seafood

🛍 **Shop** Selling cathedral souvenirs, cards, books and gifts

🚻 **Toilets** At the west end of Lancelot's Link, near the entrance

The small surgeon's table at the heart of the Old Operating Theatre

⑥ The Old Operating Theatre

The church that dripped blood

This macabre museum makes an interesting counterpoint to the London Dungeon *(see p156)*, just around the corner. Whereas the Dungeon is a schlocky horror show, this is an authentic slice of Victorian gore, inside the attic of 300-year-old St Thomas's Church. It shows off Europe's oldest surviving operating theatre, established in 1822 to serve nearby St Thomas's Hospital, where student surgeons once gathered to watch limbs being chopped off poor patients – without anaesthetics.

Howls of real torment once rang through the rafters here, and the museum's entrance could hardly be spookier – it is reached via a spiral staircase in the church's tower. The first chamber to visit is the Herb Garret, storehouse of the hospital apothecary in centuries past, and stacked with musty animal skins and bizarre potions, much like a witch's pantry. Harry Potter fans will adore the vibe here. The operating room is a creepy space too – literally a theatre, with the surgery table as the stage, steeply banked viewing stands, a box of sawdust to soak up the blood of amputees and a corridor of murderous-looking surgical instruments.

Letting off steam

Little Dorrit Park *(see left)* has a small playground for children.

The Lowdown

🌐 **Map ref** 12 E5
Address 9a Saint Thomas Street, SE1 9RY; 020 7188 2679; http://oldoperatingtheatre.com

🚇 **Train** London Bridge **Tube** London Bridge **Bus stop** London Bridge

🕐 **Open** 10:30am–5pm daily

💲 **Price** £14 (up to 3 kids)

Skipping the queue Capacity is tight, so book ahead for events

👫 **Age range** 7 plus

Activities Free demonstrations, at 2pm Mon–Wed or 7pm Thu (age 7 plus), might feature herbal medicine or 19th-century speed surgery. There's an imaginative programme of family activities in the school holidays: call ahead or check website

⏱ **Allow** 1 hour

♿ **Wheelchair access** limited

🍽 **Eat and drink** *Snacks* Frank's Cafe *(132 Southwark Street, SE1 0SW)* is a classic cafe serving breakfast and lunch with a couple of outdoor tables *Real meal* The George Inn *(77 Borough High Street, SE1 1NH; 020 7407 2056; 11am–10pm daily)* serves traditional pub fare

🛍 **Shop** Selling quirky and original gifts and presents with a medical theme

🚻 **Toilets** On entrance level before entering (requires a key)

HMS *Belfast* and around

HMS *Belfast*, the most powerful battle cruiser in Britain's World War II fleet, is now a floating museum. Visiting with kids is an immersive experience, but avoid inclement days, and check the website for kid's activities. Back on shore, this pedestrianized strip of riverside is perfect for families. Youngsters with an eye for flair will enjoy a visit to the Fashion and Textile Museum.

The Fashion and Textile Museum, with its permanent and temporary exhibitions, gives a preview into many aspects of fashion

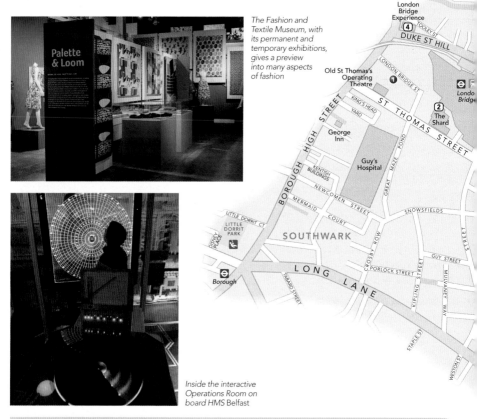

Inside the interactive Operations Room on board HMS Belfast

The Lowdown

🚗 **Train** London Bridge, a five-minute walk away; Tower Gateway (DLR) **Tube** London Bridge, Monument, Tower Hill **Bus** Tooley Street: route numbers 47, 343, 381, RV1; London Bridge: 17, 21, 35, 40, 43, 47, 133, 141, 149, 521 **River bus** London Bridge City Pier, on riverbus route between Woolwich Arsenal and London Eye (0870 781 5049; www.thamesclippers.com)

ℹ️ **Visitor information** City of London Information Centre (*see pp128–9*)

🛒 **Supermarkets** Marks & Spencer Simply Food, 6 More London Place, SE1 2DA; Costcutter, 134 Tooley Street, SE1 2TU **Markets** Borough Market, *see pp144–5*; Bermondsey Market, Bermondsey Square, SE1 3UN (mostly food, plus flowers and garden plants), 6am–2pm Fri

🎪 **Festivals** Thames Festival, music, arts and markets (Sep; www.thamesfestival.org)

➕ **Pharmacies** Boots, 8–11 Hays Galleria, SE1 2HD; 020 7407 4276; 7:30am–7pm Mon–Fri, 10am–6pm Sat, 11am–5pm Sun. For 24-hour pharmacies, visit www.nhs.uk/servicedirectories

🏃 **Nearest playground** Tanner Street Park (*SE1*); Little Dorrit Park (*SE1*); St John's Churchyard (*SE1*); Leathermarket Street Gardens (*SE1*)

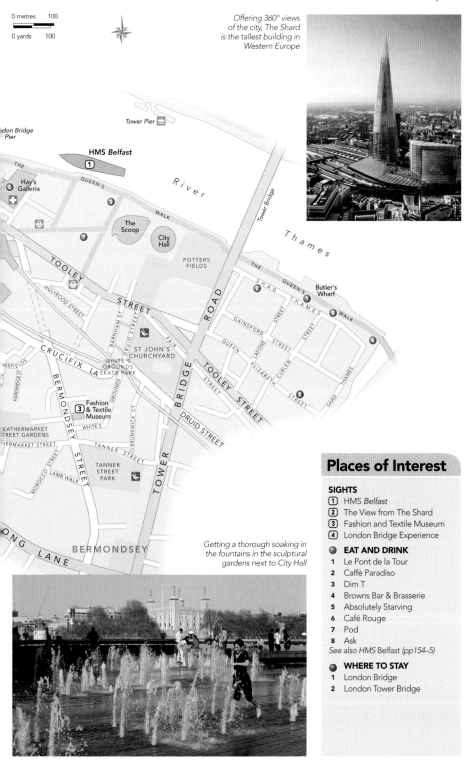

0 metres 100

0 yards 100

Offering 360° views of the city, The Shard is the tallest building in Western Europe

Tower Pier

don Bridge Pier

HMS *Belfast*

①

THE

Hay's Galleria

QUEEN'S

③

WALK

The Scoop

City Hall

⑦

POTTERS FIELDS

River Thames

Tower Bridge

THE

S H A D

QUEEN'S

THAMES STREET

Butler's Wharf

⑧ WALK

④

TOOLEY

STREET

HOLYROOD STREET

BARNHAM ST

DRUID STREET

FAIR

BRIDGE

ROAD

GAINSFORD STREET

LAFONE STREET

CURLEW STREET

SHAD THAMES

QUEEN ELIZABETH STREET

②

St John's Churchyard

WHITE'S GROUNDS SKATE PARK

TOOLEY STREET

CRUCIFIX LA

WSFIELDS

HARDWIDGE ST

BERMONDSEY STREET

③ Fashion & Textile Museum

WHITE'S GROUNDS

BRUNSWICK CT

WHITE'S

DRUID STREET

EATHERMARKET TREET GARDENS

HERMARKET STREET

TANNER STREET

LAMB WALK

MOROCCO STREET

TANNER STREET PARK

TOWER BRIDGE

ONG LANE

BERMONDSEY

Getting a thorough soaking in the fountains in the sculptural gardens next to City Hall

Places of Interest

SIGHTS
① HMS *Belfast*
② The View from The Shard
③ Fashion and Textile Museum
④ London Bridge Experience

● EAT AND DRINK
1 Le Pont de la Tour
2 Caffè Paradiso
3 Dim T
4 Browns Bar & Brasserie
5 Absolutely Starving
6 Café Rouge
7 Pod
8 Ask
See also HMS *Belfast* (pp154–5)

● WHERE TO STAY
1 London Bridge
2 London Tower Bridge

① HMS *Belfast*

Action stations – on one of Britain's great warships

She was built in 1938, in the same Northern Irish shipyard as the *Titanic*, but on a quiet day, HMS *Belfast* feels more like the *Marie Celeste*. What could be more atmospheric than exploring a great warship in battle trim, populated only by visitors and the ghosts of the 800 seamen who once manned her? Generators buzz, orders crackle through the speakers and most areas are accessible to children, who can swarm down ladders and along gangways, into gun turrets and mess decks accompanied by the lively audio guide.

Signalling with semaphore flags

The Lowdown

- 🌐 **Map reference** 12 G5
  Address HMS Belfast, The Queen's Walk, SE1 2JH; 020 7940 6300; www.iwm.org.uk visits/hms-belfast

- 🚗 **Train** London Bridge (a five-minute walk); Tower Gateway (DLR) **Tube** London Bridge, Monument, Tower Hill. **Bus stop** Tooley Street, London Bridge **River bus** London Bridge City Pier, en route between Woolwich Arsenal and London Eye (020 7001 2222; www.thamesclippers.com).

- 🕐 **Open** Mar–Oct: 10am–6pm daily; Nov–Feb: till 5pm (last admission one hour earlier)

- 💲 **Price** £37.05–40.80, under-5s free

- 🎫 **Guided tours** Free audio guide (also in French, German and Spanish); children's audio guide

- 👫 **Age range** 7 plus

- 👪 **Activities** Family drop-in activities take place on selected weekends and during school holidays. Check website for more information

- ⏱ **Allow** 2 hours

- ♿ **Wheelchair access** Limited due to the nature of a warship. See website for details

- ☕ **Eat and drink** *Snacks* The onboard café offers delicious sandwiches, baked goods and drinks

- 🛍 **Shop** In ticket hall

- 🚻 **Toilets** On both the upper and main decks, ask staff for the key to the disabled toilets

Good family value?
For maximum value, make time for the hands-on Life at Sea exhibition on Deck 3, with knots to tie and kitbags to lift.

Key Features

① **Admiral's Cabin** HMS *Belfast* became the flagship of Britain's Far East Fleet, and in the admiral's command room, children can don uniforms and scan for enemy craft.

② **Quarterdeck** The ship's parade ground and exercise yard, this was mainly reserved for officers. It is where visitors board – don't forget to salute!

▮ **Bridge** The compass platform at the front was where the captain controlled the ship.

▮ **Superstructure** This part of the ship held the gun turrets, funnels, life boats, fore mast and main mast.

▮ **Deck Two** This housed a forward mess deck, where the crew would sleep and eat, as well as the officers' mess.

▮ **Deck Three** As well as the staff's cabins, this held the chapel, punishment cells, mail room and laundry.

▮ **Deck Four** This held the shell room and gun guidance system, as well as the ship's wheel and steering gear.

▮ **Deck Five** Home to the forward and aft engine rooms, as well as smaller shells and the submarine detection device.

③ **Anchor** If the electric winch failed, it took 144 men to turn the capstan and raise the ship's main anchor. It is as heavy as an elephant (5.5 tonnes).

⑤ **Operations Room** In the ship's nerve centre, *Belfast*'s finest hour is re-created – when she helped sink the German battleship *Scharnhorst* at the Battle of the North Cape in 1943.

④ **Shell Room** The shells line up like giant bowling pins here. They were loaded into a carousel and then hoisted up to the four main gun turrets.

⑥ **Gun Turret** Swivel in the turret captain's chair and imagine unleashing *Belfast*'s guns on a target 23 km (14 miles) away.

Taking a break in Potters Field Park, right next to Tower Bridge

Letting off steam

Potters Fields Park is a spread of lawn beside Tower Bridge. Behind it, across Tooley Street, **St John's Churchyard**, on Fair Street, has a small play area; at **Tanner Street Park**, further along Tower Bridge Road, is a larger playground. Junior sessions at **White's Grounds Skate Park** *(corner of Crucifix Lane & Druid Street, SE1 3JW)*, cater for ages 11–16: call 020 7525 1102 for details.

Eat and drink

Picnic: £20–30; Snacks: £20–40; Real meal: £45–65; Family treat: £65 or more (based on a family of four)

PICNIC Le Pont de la Tour *(36D Shad Thames, SE1 2YE; 020 7403 8403; www.lepontdelatour.co.uk; noon–11pm Mon–Sat, noon–10pm Sun)* has a great deli with good bread, a cheese counter and gourmet goodies. Grab a picnic and head to nearby Potters Fields Park where there is plentiful rug-spreading space.

SNACKS The designer Docklands haunt of Shad Thames has an array of good eateries, including **Caffè Paradiso** *(45 Shad Thames, SE1 2NJ; 020 7378 6606; www.ristoranteolive lli.co.uk/caffe-paradiso; 7am–7:30pm Mon–Fri, 8am–7pm Sat, 8:30am–7:30pm Sun)*, a Sicilian-style hangout offering excellent brunches and Italian pastries.

REAL MEAL Dim T *(2 More London Place, Tooley St, SE1 2DB; 020 7403 7000; www.dimt.co.uk; noon–11pm Tue–Sat, to 10:30pm Sun & Mon)*, just ashore from HMS *Belfast*, creates a wide range of Asian-fusion dishes, including Thai curries and crispy duck, while children can choose between a bento box or dim-sum selection basket.

FAMILY TREAT There are posher places along Butler's Wharf, but **Browns Bar & Brasserie** *(26 Shad Thames, SE1 2YG; 020 7378 1700; www.browns-restaurants.co.uk; 9am–11pm Mon–Thu, till 11:30pm Thu, till midnight Fri & Sat, 10:30pm Sun)* serves British classics, such as steak and Guinness pie. There's also a two-course children's menu.

Find out more

DIGITAL Learn more about objects from HMS *Belfast*, including photographs of the ship during World War II Arctic Convoy missions, by searching IWM's collections online at *www.iwm.org. uk/collections/search*.

Next stop. . .

CITY HALL Head for the nearby domed glass building of the City Hall (The Queen's Walk SE1; 020 7983 4000; www.london.gov.uk/ city-hall) the headquarters for London's Mayor and the Greater London Authority. The stone amphitheatre outside, known as Scoop, hosts a range of free summer events, including plays, music and cinema screenings.

The stunning façade of the City Hall overlooking River Thames

② The View from The Shard

Amazing 360° views of the London skyline

The tallest building in Western Europe, The Shard was designed by architect Renzo Piano. One of the most recently built skyscrapers to dominate the London skyline, it is 310 m (1,016 ft) high and houses offices, restaurants, the five-star Shangri-La hotel, exclusive residential apartments and the country's highest observation gallery, The View, reached by high-speed lifts. The entrance to The View is via Joiner Street.

Situated near the top of The Shard, on floors 68, 69 and 72, the public galleries feature multimedia displays that provide context to the views. Adults, and especially kids, will enjoy travelling skyward in "kaleidoscopic" lifts that use video screens and mirrors to create the effect of soaring through the iconic ceilings and roofs of London. On arrival at the "cloudscape" on Level 68, head upwards to the triple-height, main viewing gallery at Level 69,

The Shard across the Thames, rising above all London skyscrapers

where unobstructed 360° views of the capital are revealed. The city of London is brought to life through 12 telescopes, enabling people to explore the city around them in real time. These free-to-use instruments also help visitors identify 250 famous landmarks and places of significant interest, while providing information about them in 10 languages. For a profound experience, go to the viewing gallery at Level 72 – the building's highest habitable level. This level is partially open-air, and is considered the highest vantage point in Western Europe. Visitors are surrounded by giant shards of glass that form the top of The Shard and can listen out for the sounds of the bustling city below.

Letting off steam

Walk east along Tooley Street to **St John's Churchyard** *(Fair Street, SE1)*, which has a small playground and grassy areas for picnics.

The Lowdown

- 🌐 **Map ref** 12 F6 **Address** Joiner Street, SE1 9QU; 0844 499 7111; *www.theviewfromtheshard.com*
- 🚃 **Train** London Bridge **Tube** London Bridge **Bus stop** London Bridge: 43, 48, 141, 149, 521
- 🕐 **Open** Apr–Oct: 10am–10pm daily (last entry 8:30pm); Nov–Mar: till 7pm Sun–Wed, till 10pm Thu–Sat
- 💷 **Price** £75–80; book online for a cheaper price. There's concession for disabled guests and free access to a registered carer (bookable only by phone)
- 🚻 **Skipping the queue** Buy tickets online – it's cheaper – or book in advance by phone (extra charge)
- 👫 **Age range** 7 plus
- ♿ **Wheelchair access** Yes
- 🥪 **Eat and drink** *Snacks* Absolutely Starving (51 Tooley St, SE1 2QN; 020 7407 7417; 7am–9pm Mon–Fri, 9am–8pm Sat & Sun) has a hot buffet. *Real meal* Café Rouge (Hay's Galleria, Tooley St, SE1 2HD; 020 7378 0097; 8:30am–11pm Mon–Fri, 9am–11pm Sat, 9am–10:30pm Sun) has a set-price kids' menu
- 🛍️ **Shop** The Sky Boutique
- 🚻 **Toilets** Ground and floor 68 of The View

Prices given are for a family of four

③ Fashion and Textile Museum

A glimpse into the world of high fashion

Occupying a distinctive orange and pink building on trendy Bermondsey Street in London Bridge, this superb museum is the brainchild of British textile designer Zandra Rhodes. Primarily aimed at adults, the museum's vibrant colours will ensure that any kids with even the faintest interest in the world of fashion will enjoy themselves here.

The museum's permanent exhibits explore fashion and textile design from 1950 to the present day. There is also a constantly revolving roster of exhibitions covering all aspects of the fashion industry from specific periods, such as 70s Bohemian Chic, to overviews that have included a display of shoes worn by stars over the last century. Frequent exhibitions dedicated to luminaries of the fashion world such as Zandra Rhodes, Tommy Nutter and Sue Timney are also held here. In addition, the museum offers opportunities to participate in workshops on a variety of fashion-related subjects including pattern cutting, crochet, couture techniques and fashion illustration. The majority of these workshops can be pricey and mostly aimed at adults with serious fashion aspirations but there are occasional events suitable for kids, particularly during the school holidays. Take a look at the museum's website for up to date information on kid-friendly workshops and activities.

The colourful orange-and-pink façade of the Fashion and Textile Museum

The Lowdown

🌐 **Map ref** 12 G6
Address 83 Bermondsey Street, SE1 3XF; 020 7407 8664; www.ftmlondon.org

🚗 **Train** London Bridge **Tube** London Bridge **Bus stop** Tooley Street & Tower Bridge Road **River bus** London Bridge City Pier

🕐 **Open** 11am–6pm Tue–Sat (till 8pm Thu); 11am–5pm Sun (last admission 45 minutes before closing)

💷 **Price** £35, under-12s free

🚻 **Age range** 7 plus

⏱ **Allow** 1 hour

♿ **Wheelchair access** Yes

🍴 **Eat and drink** Picnic Borough Market for delicious takeaway food. Snacks Pod (7 More London Place, SE1 2RT; 020 7407 9048; www.podfood.com; 7am–4:30pm Mon–Fri) offers healthy food such as superfood salads

🛍 **Shop** Near the entrance, offering a covetable range of catalogues from past to present exhibitions

🚻 **Toilets** Near the café

Letting off steam

Walk east to Tower Bridge Road, then up to grassy **Potters Fields Park** (The Queens Walk, SE1 2AA) for great views of Tower Bridge and the Tower of London. The **Butler's Wharf** waterfront is a good place to dash around – it is littered with old anchors that kids will enjoy clambering over.

④ London Bridge Experience
History plus horror for all ages

Housed in the vaults beneath the London Bridge, this tour provides a glimpse into the 2,000-year-old

The London Bridge Experience, considered the scariest in the UK

history of the bridge and promises 'horrifyingly educational fun' for adults and kids alike. Things begin relatively tamely in the first chambers, where actors – interacting with their audience – bring to life the tumultuous local history, from Roman beginnings to the 20th century. Queen Boudica and her army, Jack the Ripper, and the rebels William Wallace, Jack Cade and Wat Tyler have all figured in the bridge's story. The second part of the attraction is the London Tombs, considered the UK's scariest exhibit. With its share of 'zombies, demons and monsters', the tour takes place at a former plague pit and explores its gruesome past. Young visitors under 16s can take the Guardian Angel tour, which offers all the thrills, minus the scare.

Letting off steam

Take the **Tower Bridge Exhibition** (see p126) to explore the history and architecture of this iconic structure. The glass-floor walkways offers spectacular views of London across the Thames. Step inside the Victorian engine rooms to learn about how the bridge functions.

The Lowdown

🌐 **Map ref** 12 E5–F5
Address 2–4 Tooley Street, SE1 2SY; 020 7403 6333; www.londonbridgeexperience.com

🚗 **Train** London Bridge, Cannon Street **Tube** London Bridge **Bus stop** London Bridge **River bus** London Bridge City, Bankside Pier

🕐 **Open** 10am–5pm daily (to 6pm Sat)

💷 **Price** adults £27, under-16s £23; book online for a cheaper price

🚻 **Age range** 5 plus

⏱ **Allow** 2 hours

♿ **Wheelchair access** No

🍴 **Eat and drink** Snacks Caffè Nero (3 Cathedral St, SE1 9DE; 7am–8:30pm Mon–Fri, 7:30am–9pm Sat & Sun) lies a short walk west and serves coffee, sandwiches and small eats, or try the stalls at Borough Market (see p146)

🛍 **Shop** At the exit, selling plenty of kitsch souvenirs

🚻 **Toilets** Just before the shop

Picnic under £20; **Snacks** £20–40; **Real meal** £40–60; **Family treat** £60 or more (based on a family of four)

London Eye and around

Erected in 2000, the London Eye is a genuine wow for kids, especially if approached on foot from Waterloo station. Book ahead to ride – but not before checking the weather forecast, because rain blots out the views. That's good advice for the eclectic South Bank, which can be bleak on a wet day, although it embraces the National Theatre, the London Aquarium and Britain's biggest cinema screen as well as a motley crew of street entertainers.

Southwark and the South Bank

Shakespeare's Globe *p144*

London Eye

HMS *Belfast* *p152*

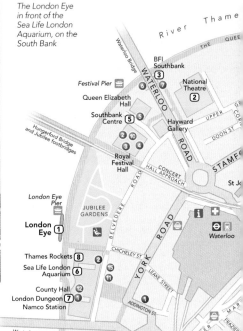

The London Eye in front of the Sea Life London Aquarium, on the South Bank

Places of interest

SIGHTS

1. London Eye
2. National Theatre
3. BFI Southbank
4. Gabriel's Wharf
5. Southbank Centre
6. Sea Life London Aquarium
7. London Dungeon
8. Thames Rockets
9. Imperial War Museum
10. Florence Nightingale Museum

8. House of Crepes
9. Gourmet Pizza Company
10. Skylon Restaurant
11. Ned's Noodle Bar
12. Aji Zen Canteen
13. Café Roma
14. The Garden Café
15. Troia
See also National Theatre (p162), BFI Southbank (pp162–3) and London Film Museum (p165)

EAT AND DRINK

1. Bao Fa Garden
2. Riverside Terrace Café
3. Le Pain Quotidien
4. Canteen
5. Giraffe
6. The Riverfront
7. Wahaca

WHERE TO STAY

1. Park Plaza
2. Premier Inn

Southbank Centre, one of London's popular artistic venues.

| 0 metres | 200 |
| 0 yards | 200 |

The Lowdown

🚗 **Train** Waterloo, a 5-minute walk away **Tube** Waterloo, Westminster, Lambeth North **Bus** Belvedere Road: route number RV1; York Road: 76, 77, 211, 341, 381, 507; Westminster Bridge: 12, 53, 148, 159, 211, 453 **River bus** London Eye Millennium Pier: riverbus services to Woolwich Arsenal (020 7001 2200; *www.thamesclippers.com)*; and to Greenwich via the Tower (020 7740 0400; *www.city cruises.com)*. Also services from Westminster Pier *(see p64)*

ℹ️ **Visitor information** Britain and London Visitor Centre, Waterloo station, SE1 7LY

🛒 **Supermarkets** Costcutter, 17–19 York Road, SE1 7NJ; Sainsbury's, 101 Waterloo Road, SE1 8UL; Iceland, 112–113 Lower Marsh, SE1 7AE **Markets** South Bank Book Market, BFI Southbank, daily; Real Food Market, Royal Festival Hall, Southbank Centre, noon–8pm Fri; 11am–8pm Sat; noon–6pm Sun; Lower Marsh street market, SE1 (mixed stalls), 8am–6pm Mon–Sat (Wed 10am–3pm)

🎪 **Festivals** Coin Street Festival, mixed arts, Bernie Spain Gardens (Jun–Aug); Meltdown Festival, music, Southbank Centre (June); Watch This Space, family arts, National Theatre (Jul–Sep); Thames Festival (Sep); BFI London Film Festival (Oct)

➕ **Pharmacies** Boots, Waterloo Station, SE1 7LY (7am–10pm Mon–Fri; 8am–10pm Sat; 9am–9pm Sun. For a list of 24-hour pharmacies, visit *www.nhs.uk/service directories*

🌿 **Nearest playgrounds** Archbishop's Park *(Lambeth Palace Road, SE1 7LQ)*; Jubilee Gardens *(Belvedere Road, SE1 7XZ)*; Geraldine Mary Harmsworth Park *(Kennington Road, SE11)*; Bernie Spain Gardens *(Duchy Street, SE1 9NL)*

Rockets, planes and armoured cars at the Imperial War Museum

Enthralled by an inquisitive ray at the Sea Life London Aquarium

The Lowdown

- **Map ref** 10 H6
  Address County Hall, Westminster Bridge Road, SE1 7PB; 0871 781 3000, www.londoneye.com

- **Train** Waterloo, a 5-minute walk away **Tube** Waterloo, Westminster **Bus stop** Belvedere Road, York Road, Westminster Bridge **River bus** London Eye Millennium Pier, Westminster Pier

- **Open** Mar: 11am–6pm daily; Apr–Jun: 8:30am–9:30pm; Jun–Aug: 10am–8:30pm; closed 2 weeks in mid-Jan for maintenance; special schedules during Christmas season

- **Price** £90 (book online for 20 per cent discount). Time-flexible and fast-track tickets cost extra

- **Skipping the queue** Jul and Aug are busiest; avoid the 11am–3pm peak and arrive 30 minutes before flight time. Fast-track tickets are the same price for adults and children.

- **Guided tours** 3pm daily (includes fast track entry). £23–26.50 per adult, £19–21.50 for ages 4–15, under 4s free

- **Age range** 5 plus

- **Activities** Free "4D" film experience included in ticket. In winter, the ice-rink in Jubilee Gardens has a separate charge

- **Allow** 1 hour

- **Wheelchair access** Yes (carer can travel for free)

- **Eat and drink** *Family treat* Bao fa Garden, inside County Hall, offers an elaborate menu specializing in traditional Chinese cuisine

- **Shop** At the bottom of the exit ramp, selling souvenirs and visitor photos

- **Toilets** Downstairs at County Hall

Good family value?

It's expensive for 30 minutes, but there's a saving for combined admission to sister attractions Madame Tussauds and London Dungeon. On a budget? Consider the OXO Tower (see p147) instead.

① London Eye
Take a spin over London

How does it feel to be a seagull soaring above London? Find out during a ride on "the world's tallest cantilevered observation wheel". Rising 135 m (443 ft) above the Thames, the London Eye opened as part of the city's millennium celebrations. A serene 30-minute ride in one of its glass capsules offers views stretching 40 km (25 miles) – on a clear day you might even be able to see Windsor Castle!

Key Features

The capsules Each of the 32 capsules weighs 10 tonnes, can hold 25 passengers and rotates at 26 cm (10 in) per second. Celebrity fliers have included Prince Harry, Kate Moss, the Jonas Brothers…and Kermit the Frog!

The spec The wheel cost £70 million, weighs 2,100 tonnes and is supported by two 60-m (197-ft) cables. It was floated up the Thames in sections, assembled and then slowly raised using the cables.

The structure Although no longer the world's tallest observation wheel (the 165-m (541-ft) Singapore Flyer takes that prize for now) it is the largest cantilevered wheel, as it is supported by an A-frame on one side only.

The ride The slow-moving capsules mean the wheel can be boarded without it stopping, and the gentle ascent is entirely unscary.

Extras A 4-minute "4D" cinema show in the ticket hall is free for London Eye travellers. It uses dry ice, bubbles and "real rain" to simulate an aerial journey over London.

The view On a clear day, Windsor Castle, 40 km (25 miles) west of London, is visible – although Wembley Stadium's arch, 12 km (7 miles) away to the northwest, is a better bet.

Imaginative playground at Archbishop's Park, next to Lambeth Palace

Letting off steam

Jubilee Gardens *(Belvedere Road, Southbank SE1 7XZ)*, beside the Eye, has lawns and a playground, and is best for younger children. The colourful **Archbishop's Park** *(Carlisle Lane, SE1 7LE)*, a 10-minute walk away, was designed by children and is probably a better bet. If it's wet, there are hours of mindless pleasure to be had at **Namco Station** inside County Hall *(10am–midnight daily; www.namcofunscape.com)*, which has three beeping, flashing floors of arcade games, dodgem cars and bowling alleys.

Eat and drink

Picnic: under £20; Snacks: £20–40; Real meal: £40–60; Family treat: £60 or more (based on a family of four)

PICNIC For provisions, check out the weekend **Real Food Market** held behind Royal Festival Hall. The hall's **Riverside Terrace Café** *(Royal Festival Hall, SE1 8XX; 020 7921 0758; www.southbankcentre.co.uk; 10am–10:30pm daily)* becomes an outdoor eating space in summer.
SNACKS Le Pain Quotidien *(Festival Terrace, Belvedere Rd, SE1 8XX; www.lepainquotidien.com; 7:30am–11pm Mon–Fri, 8am–11pm Sat, 9am–10pm Sun)* offers superior tartines, salads and snacks.

The stylish Canteen restaurant behind the Royal Festival Hall, South Bank

REAL MEAL Canteen *(Royal Festival Hall, Belvedere Road, SE1 8XX; 0845 686 1122; www.canteen. co.uk; 8am–11pm Mon–Fri, 9am–11pm Sat, 9am–10pm Sun)* serves up a stylish take on English classics (roasts, steak and chips), and its kid's menu offers half portions of most dishes. The restaurant also gives out activity books and there are badges to collect.
FAMILY TREAT Giraffe *(National South Bank Centre, Riverside Level 1, SE1 8XX 020; 7042 6900; www. giraffe.net; 8am–11pm Mon–Thu, to 11:30pm Fri, 9am–11:30pm Sat, 9am–10:30pm Sun)* is the flagship branch of this chain and serves burgers, grills, salads, brunch and has special menu as well as activity books for kids. The food is complemented with world-class music.

Find out more

FILM The Eye has starred in more than one Hollywood blockbuster. It almost comes crashing down in the 2007 comic-book caper *Fantastic Four: Rise of the Silver Surfer*; while in the 2004 movie *Thunderbirds*, Thunderbird 2 lands right beside it in Jubilee Gardens.

A London Duck Tour amphibious vehicle splashing into the Thames

Next stop. . .

SIGHTSEEING TOURS The Eye is high, but there are several unusual ways to see the city at a faster pace. Spin your own wheels by hiring bikes from the **London Bicycle Tour Company** *(from £3.50 per hour; 020 7928 6838; www.londonbicycle. com)*; at Gabriel's Wharf; get soaked on a spray-drenched 40 mph (65 kph) speedboat ride from the London Eye Pier (020 7928 8933; *www.thamesrockets.com*); or see the sights by both land and water on an ingenious, amphibious **London Duck Tour** (020 7928 3132; *www.londonducktours.co.uk*), starting from Chicheley Street, SE1.

② National Theatre

London's top family arts destination

Britain's largest theatre complex was built on the South Bank in 1976. It was designed by Sir Denys Lasdun in the Brutalist architectural style, with lots of concrete and sharp edges, which people seem to either love or hate. Inside are three auditoria showing a terrific mix of classic drama and new writing, providing something for everyone. It's worth just dropping in, too, as the lobby areas embrace many eateries and restaurants, two exhibition spaces (photography figures strongly) and a small stage for free live music before curtain-up most evenings.

Guided tours include a visit to the fan-shaped Olivier Theatre, modelled on ancient Greek theatres, and a glimpse of the scenery workshops backstage, where children can get up close to props from recent plays, such as Alice the mare, a puppet from the smash-hit show *War Horse*, based on Michael Morpurgo's novel for children. The liveliest time to come is June to September, when the theatre hosts a madcap family performance festival, mostly outdoors and largely free.

Enjoying an auditorium tour at the Olivier Theatre, part of the National Theatre

The theatre underwent a six-year, £83m refurbishment project that transformed the theatre's public spaces as well as areas behind the scenes.

Letting off steam

Bernie Spain Gardens (*Upper Ground, SE1 9PP*), just east along the river, offers grassy spaces. **Jubilee Gardens** (*Belvedere Road, SE1 7XZ*), in the opposite direction, has a decent playground.

③ BFI Southbank

Britain's largest big-screen experience

Crouching right under Waterloo Bridge, London's art-house cinema hub opened initially as the National Film Theatre in 1953, and now has four screens, a gallery for celluloid-based art and a very slick cocktail lounge. The programme generally has something for families.

For children who need a screen fix even when sightseeing, there is also the free Mediatheque room: simply choose a booth and access a menu of 2,000 movies and TV shows from the world's biggest screen archive. The children's list spans *Robin Hood* and *The Railway Children* to *Watership Down*. Nearby, the more commercial **BFI IMAX** is contained in a giant glass

The Lowdown

🌐 **Map ref** 11 A5
Address South Bank, SE1 9PX; 020 7452 3000; www. nationaltheatre.org.uk

🚗 **Train** Waterloo or Waterloo East (both a 5-minute walk), Charing Cross (10 minutes). **Tube** Waterloo, Embankment **Bus stop** Waterloo Bridge, Upper Ground, Waterloo Road, Stamford Street **River bus** Festival Pier (Westminster to St Katharine's route; 020 7936 2033; www.crownriver.com); London Eye Millennium Pier; Embankment Pier (across Golden Jubilee Bridges).

🕐 **Open** 9:30am–11pm Mon–Sat, noon–6pm Sun

💲 **Price** Show tickets vary, from £10–45+; standing tickets are sold on the day only, £5

🎭 **Guided tours** Usually 10:15am, 10:30am, 12:15pm, 12:30pm, 5:15pm, 5:30pm Mon–Fri; 10:30am, 12:15pm Sat; 12:30pm Sun. Adults £8.50, under-18s £7.50; call 020 7452 3400

👫 **Age range** All

🤸 **Activities** Foyer concerts 5:45pm Mon–Sat and lunchtimes Sat & Sun (free). The Big Wall in the main foyer has touch-screen clips and information about current shows. Talks and workshops programme, mostly for adults. Watch This Space festival (Jul–Sep) has events Tue–Sun; Playspace programme runs in school summer holiday

⏱ **Allow** Up to 1 hour

♿ **Wheelchair access** Yes

🍴 **Eat and drink** *Snacks* Lyttelton Café (Ground floor) and Olivier Café (Levels 2–3) serve hot and cold dishes pre-theatre *Real meal* Terrace Restaurant (Level 2) offers meze-style bites, with a focus on fresh seasonal ingredients

🛍 **Shop** On the ground floor selling books, texts, programmes, posters, recordings and gifts

🚻 **Toilets** In theatres and foyers

BFI Southbank, a big attraction for film buffs of all ages

drum outside Waterloo Station, where the likes of Harry Potter and Shrek loom 20-m (66-ft) tall on Britain's largest screen. Look out for the monthly Film Funday workshops, where kids get to animate their own movie before the main screening, or dress up as their heroes. A special children's menu is also available at the restaurant.

Letting off steam
Jubilee Gardens (see left).

The Lowdown

🌐 **Map ref** 11 A5
   Address Belvedere Road, SE1 8XT; 020 7928 3232 (IMAX enquiries 020 7928 3232); www.bfi.org.uk

🚗 **Transport** See National Theatre (opposite)

🕐 **Open** 11am–11pm daily (till 11:30pm Fri & Sat); Mediatheque noon–8pm Tue–Sat, 12:30pm–8pm Sun

💲 **Price** Seat prices vary – all tickets cost £6 on Tue. Mediatheque free

🚶 **Skipping the queue** Book ahead for Film Fundays (020 7928 3232)

🏃 **Activities** Film Fundays, usually on last Sun of each month, free with cinema tickets

♿ **Wheelchair access** Yes

🍴 **Eat and drink** Real meal The Riverfront (020 7928 0808; www.riverfrontbarandkitchen.com) does burgers, salads and grills. Family treat Benugo Bar & Kitchen (020 7401 9000; www.benugobarandkitchen.com) is more formal, but offers children's dishes on Film Fundays

🛍 **Shop** Selling postcards, DVDs, BFI merchandise and books, including those for the more serious film connoisseur

🚻 **Toilets** In the foyer

④ Gabriel's Wharf
Boutiques and bicycles

It's heartening that this little oasis of "alternative culture" can thrive in such a go-getting strip of Central London, and that's thanks to Coin Street Community Builders – a gang of residents who banded together in 1984 to save the site from property developers. They've created a perky area of pastel-painted craft studios and cafés right by the Thames, with

appeal for families: it has a giant mural, bicycle hire (see p161), and a bevy of carved wooden beasts, some of them made for tots to ride on. Just beyond looms the Art Deco **OXO Tower**, with a small art gallery on the ground floor, bijou design shops along its balconies and a viewing platform at the summit.

Letting off steam
Bernie Spain Gardens (Upper Ground, SE1 9PP), inland from the main Wharf Plaza, has running-about room.

Some of the pretty, pastel-painted buildings at Gabriel's Wharf

The Lowdown

🌐 **Map ref** 11 A5
   Address 56 Upper Ground, SE1 9PP; 020 7021 1686; www.coinstreet.org

🚗 **Train** Blackfriars, Waterloo **Tube** Southwark, Waterloo **Bus stop** Stamford Street, Blackfriars Bridge, Waterloo Bridge, Upper Ground, Waterloo Road **River bus** Blackfriars Millennium Pier, Bankside Pier

🕐 **Open** Shops, studios and Oxo Gallery 11am–6pm Tue–Sun. Restaurants and cafés till late

💲 **Price** Free, including Oxo Gallery and Oxo Tower Walkway

👫 **Age range** All

🏃 **Activities** Sport and dance drop-in classes are available at the nearby Colombo Centre (34–68 Colombo St, SE1 8DP; 020 7261 1658; www.jubileehalltrust.org/colombo/).

🍴 **Eat and drink** Snacks House of Crepes (56 Upper Ground, SE1 9PP; 020 7401 9816; 10am–3pm) is one of several options at Gabriel's Wharf Real meal Gourmet Pizza Company (59–65 Upper Ground, SE1 9PP; 020 7928 3188; 11:30am–11:30pm daily) serves traditional Italian dishes and tasty pizzas with inventive toppings

🚻 **Toilets** Next to the Studio 6 bar/restaurant

⑤ Southbank Centre

Music, dance, art, poetry, comedy… and purple cows

The Southbank Centre comprises three main venues, the Hayward Gallery, the Queen Elizabeth Hall and the Royal Festival Hall, which together showcase all manner of music, art, dance and performance.

The Hayward Gallery is a contemporary art space that puts on innovative and interactive shows. Following a three-year renovation, it re-opened in 2018, with improved natural lighting for the upper galleries. The Royal Festival Hall, built for the 1951 Festival of Britain, is filled with exhibition, performance and eating areas. Its eclectic line-up includes Friday Lunch, a free gig in the Foyer Bar (Level 2), and family workshops.

Each April the Centre stages a summer arts festival in the Udderbelly, a pop-up theatre in Jubilee Gardens set inside a giant upside-down purple cow. The programme includes family shows, music and theatre.

Letting off steam

Jubilee Gardens (*Belvedere Road, SE1 7XZ; closed Mon*) has a play-ground, and from May–Oct, kids can play in Jeppe Hein's "walk-in fountain" on the Festival Hall terrace.

The Lowdown

- 🌐 **Map ref** 10 H5
  Address Belvedere Road, SE1 8XX; 020 7960 4200; www.southbankcentre.co.uk/venues/hayward-gallery
- 🚆 **Train** Waterloo, Waterloo East, Charing Cross **Tube** Waterloo, Embankment **Bus stop** Waterloo Bridge, Upper Ground, Waterloo Road, Stamford Street **River bus** Festival Pier; London Eye Millennium Pier; Embankment Pier.
- 🕐 **Open** Royal Festival Hall 10am–11pm daily; Hayward Gallery noon–6pm Mon (to 8pm Thu & Fri), 11am–7pm Tue, Wed, Sat & Sun. Queen Elizabeth Hall: 5–11:30pm daily
- 💲 **Price** Performances individually priced, likewise Hayward Gallery exhibitions (reductions for ages 12–16; under-12s free)
- 🎭 **Activities** For the full programme, visit www.southbankcentre.co.uk/find/family.
- ♿ **Wheelchair access** All venues
- 🍴 **Eat and drink** Family treat Skylon Restaurant (Level 3, Royal Festival Hall; 020 7654 7800; noon–2:30pm, 5:30pm–10:30pm Mon–Sat, noon–3:30pm Sun) offers upmarket 'modern British' cuisine; the grill, which is adjacent, is less formal and open till 11pm (10:30 pm Sun).
- 🛍 **Shops** Festival Terrace sells design-led gifts. Royal Festival Hall shop celebrates the artistic programme. Hayward Gallery offers gifts, books and cards.
- 🚻 **Toilets** All venues

⑥ Sea Life London Aquarium

Find Nemo and outstare a shark

It is said that we know more about deep space than we do about the deep oceans. After visiting the London Aquarium, that claim seems entirely plausible. Its three floors of tanks showcase more than 500 marine species, including amazing fish that change colour, fish that change sex, fish that glow in the dark, and fish that look like snowflakes, butterflies or boulders.

The aquarium tunnels under County Hall, its galleries snaking through vaults that echo with ambient music, which can feel a bit claustro-phobic at busy times. A walk-through glass tunnel brings children eye to eye with turtles, rays and murderous-looking sand tiger sharks. In other zones, kids may get to stroke a starfish or help out with the daily fish feeds, though interactivity is limited. The big climax is the Shark Walk, which dares visitors to tiptoe over a glass platform right above the killers.

Mesmerising creatures of the deep in the Sea Life London Aquarium

The Lowdown

- 🌐 **Map ref** 10 H6
  Address County Hall, Westminster Bridge Road, SE1 7PB; 0871 222 6944; www.visitsealife.com/London
- 🚆 **Train** Waterloo **Tube** Waterloo, Westminster **Bus stop** Belvedere Road, York Road **River bus** London Eye Millennium Pier.
- 🕐 **Open** 10am–6pm Mon–Fri, 9:30am–7pm Sat & Sun (last admission: 1 hour earlier)
- 💲 **Price** £79 (15 per cent saving by booking online); under 3s free.
- 👥 **Skipping the queue** Priority Entrance (more expensive) ticket-holders skip most of the queue.
- 👫 **Age range** 3 plus
- 🧑‍🤝‍🧑 **Activities** A variety of feeding sessions available to visitors on Tue, Thu & Sat. Check website for dates, times and fees.
- ⏱ **Allow** Up to 1½ hours
- 🍴 **Eat and Drink** Picnic Ned's Noodle Bar (3E Belvedere Road, SE1 7GQ; 020 7593 0077; noon–11pm Mon–Sat, till 10pm Sun) does kids' noodle boxes Snacks Aji Zen Canteen (County Hall; 020 7620 6117; noon–11pm Mon–Sat, till 10pm Sun) is another tasty option.
- 🛍 **Shop** Selling gifts and souvenirs
- 🚻 **Toilets** All floors

Letting off steam

Try **Jubilee Gardens** (*see left*), or spacious **Archbishop's Park** (*Carlisle Lane, SE1 7LE*), just to the south on Lambeth Palace Road.

⑦ London Dungeon

Gruesome tales of London's grisly past

After 37 years under London Bridge, the Dungeon moved in 2013 to a larger space in the vaults beneath County Hall. The expanded attraction brings 1,000 years of authentic British history to life with talented live actors and special effects. Visitors are ushered into the Dungeon through a gloomy labyrinth of torchlit rooms showcasing dark chapters from the city's past – from the Black Death and Guy Fawkes' conspiracy to blow up Parliament to Sweeney Todd and Jack the Ripper – via dismembered corpses and heads on spikes. There's a generous helping of audience participation: children should stand at the back or expect to be locked in a torture chamber, burnt at the stake or operated on by the butcher surgeon. It's all played for laughs (watch out for chamber pots being emptied from medieval windows) – the young cast act with gusto and the Ripper rooms are especially atmospheric – though younger children might find themselves howling more in terror than delight.

Letting off steam
Jubilee Gardens (see left) and **Archbishop's Park** (see left) have good space for running around and grassy areas for picnics.

The Lowdown
- **Map ref** 10 H6
- **Address** Riverside Building, County Hall, Westminster Bridge Road, SE1 7PB; 0871 423 2240; www.thedungeons.com/london
- **Train** Waterloo **Tube** Waterloo, Westminster **Bus stop** Belvedere Road, York Road, Westminster Bridge **River bus** London Eye Millennium Pier, Westminster Pier
- **Open** 10am–4pm Mon–Wed & Fri (11am–5pm Thu, 10am–6pm Sat & Sun). Times vary in holidays.
- **Price** £74–79; under 4s free (book online for 30% discount)
- **Skipping the queue** Priority entry ticket can be purchased online
- **Age range** All (under-16s need to be accompanied by an adult aged 18 years and over)
- **Allow** 90 minutes
- **Wheelchair access** Yes
- **Eat and drink** Snacks EAT. (Unit 4, Royal Festival Hall) for soups, sandwiches and hotpots Real Meal Giraffe (Belvedere Road, SE1 8XX; 020 7042 6900) for unusual salads and views over Thames.
- **Shop** At the end of the tour
- **Toilets** After the ticket hall

The thrilling speedboat ride, Thames Rockets

⑧ Thames Rockets
Fun fair speedboat ride

This exhilarating speedboat ride takes the family from the London Eye Millennium Pier to Canary Wharf and back in the flash of an eye. It provides the excitement of a fun fair ride and the educational purposes of a tour past some of the city's most famous riverside sights. The guides recount stories about the sights in an engaging and humorous manner, to ensure that kids and adults alike come away with some new-found knowledge, and the afterglow of the adrenalin rush.

The trip on the compact low-lying red vessels is not only a joy in the summer but also enjoyable during the colder months as you are provided with top-notch sailing gear safety equipment, such as lifejackets.

Letting off steam
Jubilee Gardens (see left) has a playground or **Archbishop's Park** (see left) have space for kids to run around.

The Lowdown
- **Map ref** 10 H6
- **Address** London Eye Millenium Pier, Westminster Bridge, southbank SE1 7PB; 020 7982 8933; www.thamesrockets.com
- **Tube** Waterloo
- **Bus Stop** Waterloo Bridge
- **Open** year-round daily departures from 10am–5pm
- **Price** £140; under-5s free
- **Guided tours** No
- **Age range** all ages
- **Allow** 1 hour
- **Wheelchair access** Yes
- **Eat and drink** Picnic Ned's Noodle Bar (3E Belvedere Road, SE1 7GQ; 020 7593 0077; noon–11:15pm Mon–Sat, till 10:15pm Sun) does kids' noodle boxes Real Meal Giraffe (Belvedere Road, SE1 8XX; 020 7042 6900) for unusual salads
- **Toilets** Available for use in The London Eye

Picnic under £20; **Snacks** £20–40; **Real meal** £40–60; **Family treat** £60 or more (based on a family of four)

German Focke Wulf 190, North American P-51 Mustang and British Spitfire at the IWM

⑨ Imperial War Museum (IWM)

War stories and weaponry

Housed in what used to be the Bethlem Royal Hospital, this enormous museum, which tells the stories of people's experiences of war from World War I to the present day, tries hard not to be too gung-ho about its subject. But some kids (and adults) are bound to coo over the vast main hall, literally filled to the rafters with warplanes, tanks, missiles and other deadly hardware. Highlights include British Field Marshall Bernard Montgomery's tank, a Nazi V2 rocket and a one-man submarine.

The IWM makes a real effort to appeal to families through a changing series of well-thought-out galleries and exhibitions. A Family in Wartime highlights the daily struggles of the Allpress family, who lived in Stockwell, London during World War II. Their story has been brought to life through a series of photos and interviews. The displays can be unflinching, but are always accessible, with stories to listen to and games to play such as spot the enemy bomber.

Several galleries explore what life was like at home and abroad during both world wars. On the ground floor, a major permanent exhibition on World War I includes a re-creation of a trench, and many artifacts. An exhibition on the Holocaust, some parts of which might be too graphic for pre-teens (under-11s are not allowed to enter), traces the Nazi persecution and murder of

Up periscope! Children getting hands-on at the Imperial War Museum

Jews, and you can discover the extraordinary stories of bravery behind the Victoria Cross and George Cross in The Lord Ashcroft Gallery. There is also a library with a fascinating archive.

Letting off steam

The IWM is set in **Geraldine Mary Harmsworth Park** (*Kennington Road, SE11*), which has a café, a fine playground, and an indoor play centre for under-5s – or under-12s during school holidays – which is open 1–4pm weekdays.

The Lowdown

🌐 **Map ref** 17 B2
Address Lambeth Rd, SE1 6HZ; 020 7416 5000; www.iwm.org.uk

🚗 **Train** Waterloo, Elephant and Castle **Tube** Lambeth North, Elephant and Castle, Waterloo **Bus stop** Lambeth Road, Kennington Road, St George's Road

🕐 **Open** 10am–6pm daily, last admission: 5:30pm

💲 **Price** Free; temporary exhibitions individually priced

🚩 **Guided tours** Audio guides for adults and children

👫 **Age range** 6 plus, but some exhibitions may be unsuitable for pre-teens

🏃 **Activities** Family activities take place on certain weekends and during school holidays. Check website for the most up-to-date information

⏱ **Allow** Up to 3 hours

♿ **Wheelchair access** Yes, via Park entrance – sometimes parts of exhibitions are not accessible

🍴 **Eat and drink** *Picnic* Café Roma (*Geraldine Mary Harmsworth Park, SE11*) offers ices, shakes and good-value kids' lunch bags. *Snacks* The Garden Café (*Lambeth Palace Rd, SE1 7LB; 020 7401 8865; www.gardenmuseum.org.uk; 10:30am–4:30pm Mon–Fri, till 5:30pm Sat & Sun*) is part of the Garden Museum, set in the former St Mary-at-Lambeth church. The museum has garden history displays and an art cart for children, and the menu at the homely vegetarian café changes daily according to what's in season

🛍 **Shop** Lower ground floor, selling books, CDs, posters and gifts

🚻 **Toilets** All floors except third and fourth

Memorial to the Soviet dead of World War II, Geraldine Mary Harmsworth Park

Prices given are for a family of four

⑩ Florence Nightingale Museum

Throwing light on the Lady With The Lamp

This one-room museum, beside the ambulance bay at St Thomas's Hospital, deserves top marks for making this woman's extraordinary life story so engaging. Florence Nightingale worked as a nurse during the Crimean War (1853–6), and founded Britain's first school of nursing in 1860. The museum is partitioned into three eye-catching "pavilions": the first hemmed by hedgerows to represent Nightingale's gilded youth; the next clad in Turkish tiles, to evoke the Crimean War; the third a mock-up of the bedroom where she spent most of her later life. She was often ill, but became the most popular woman in Victorian England thanks to her tireless campaigning for health reform. Kids can see the figurines that sold by the thousand to Florence's fans, along with her pet owl (stuffed, of course) and that famous lamp.

There are also several gadgets in the museum to help keep kids' attention, not least the ingenious "stethoscope" audio guide. Touch-screen challenges invite children to pack a medicine chest with useful kit for the battlefield, or wash their hands then scan them for germs. Elsewhere, short films bring the history of nursing up to date – including a look at the MRSA menace raging through modern hospitals. The Lady With The Lamp would not approve.

The Lowdown

- 🌐 **Map ref** 16 H1
  Address 2 Lambeth Palace Road, SE1 7EW; 020 7188 4400; www.florence-nightingale.co.uk
- 🚆 **Train** Waterloo **Tube** Waterloo, Westminster **Bus stop** Westminster Bridge, York Road, Lambeth Palace Road **River bus** London Eye Millennium Pier, Westminster Pier
- 🕐 **Open** 10am–5pm daily
- 💷 **Price** £15, under-5s free
- 🚩 **Guided tours** Two tours: one for 7–11 year olds and one for adults. Free audio guides for adults and children aged 7–11
- 🚻 **Age range** 5 plus
- **Activities** Themed art-and-craft activities in school holidays: check website for details. Kids under 7 can follow Florence's story by following the I-Spy trail
- ⏱ **Allow** Up to 2 hours
- ♿ **Wheelchair access** Yes
- 🍴 **Eat and drink** Real meal Troia (County Hall, 3F Belvedere Road, SE1 7GQ; 020 7633 9309; noon–11:30pm daily) does a mix of Turkish and Mediterranean dishes
- 🛍 **Shop** Selling a range of quirky souvenirs
- 🚻 **Toilets** On the ground floor

Letting off steam

Just 3 minutes' walk along Lambeth Palace Road is **Archbishop's Park** (Carlisle Lane, SE1 7LE), with a playground, a nature garden and tennis courts (0845 130 8998) for hire. Later, head for is the **London Fire Brigade Museum** (The Workshop, Lambeth High Street, SE1 7JS) located behind the historical brigade headquarters. It houses photo and video archives alongside modern equipment.

Using a stethoscope to listen to the audio tour at the Florence Nightingale Museum

Picnic under £20; **Snacks** £20–40; **Real meal** £40–60; **Family treat** £60 or more (based on a family of four)

Kensington,
Chelsea & Battersea

With its world-class museums and fine parks, this wedge of West London feels like a purpose-built family entertainment zone. And in the 1850s, that is more or less what it was. A new cultural quarter in Kensington rose from the proceeds of the 1851 Great Exhibition, while across the river, plant-hunter John Gibson created Battersea Park for the masses. Tying the two together is the King's Road, lined with designer shops and restaurants.

Bloomsbury and Regent's Park

The City and the East End

Westminster and the West End

Southwark and the South Bank

Kensington, Chelsea and Battersea

Highlights

Science Museum
If you think science is boring, think again. The galleries here are filled with interactive hi-tech wizardry, and the live science shows are a blast (see pp180–81).

Natural History Museum
This great museum's collection runs to 70 million specimens – animals, insects, fossils, plants and skeletons. But beware: the T rex comes alive (see pp182–3)!

Victoria and Albert Museum
There's a maze of galleries here so it can be hard on the feet. If that's the case, take a break in the palatial paddling pool (see p184).

Battersea Park
Meet the monkeys at Battersea Park Children's Zoo, then ape them at London's wildest adventure playground (see pp188–9).

Kensington Palace
There's nowhere more regal to take high tea than Queen Anne's Orangery at Kensington Palace – they even serve a special child's version (see p176).

Harrods
For everything your child never knew they needed – how about a diamond-encrusted Monopoly set, bespoke rocking-horse or a doll in their own image (see p181)?

Left Wooden pirate galleon, the impressive centrepiece of the Diana Princess of Wales Memorial Playground, Kensington Gardens *Above* Meerkat at Battersea Park Children's Zoo

The Best of
Kensington, Chelsea and Battersea

South Kensington's three famous museums – the Science Museum, the Natural History Museum and the Victoria and Albert Museum (V&A) – represent one of the greatest gatherings of wonders in the world. And they're all free. If the children tire of all this learning, the open spaces of Kensington Gardens and Battersea Park are perfect places to let off steam.

Free for all

This affluent area is one of London's best places for a weekend of free family activities. Start at the **Science Museum** (see pp180–81) on Saturday: arrive at 10am to get first go on the Launchpad gallery's hands-on experiments, then see the auditorium's lively shows; after that, hit the basement picnic zone (cheaper than the cafés). Round off with the 3:30pm tour in the Exploring Space gallery.

On Sunday, take in some pageantry as Her Majesty's horse guards trot under Wellington Arch (see p177) at 10:30am. Afterwards, feed the ducks on the Serpentine lake (see p174) in **Hyde**

Left The Peter Pan-themed Diana Princess of Wales Memorial Playground **Below** Traditional pedalo fun on the Serpentine

Life-size model of a blue whale, the largest-ever creature on the planet, at the Natural History Museum

Park, then leave the park via the playground at Edinburgh Gate and head to the **V&A** *(see p184)*, which runs free drop-in family workshops till 5pm.

Wet, wet, wet ...

Who doesn't love making a splash – whether it's running a hand through the water from a pedalo in **Battersea Park** *(see pp188–9)*, or total immersion at the Serpentine Lido *(see p174)*, which is open from Jun–Sep and has a paddling pool for little ones. Or you could try the Peter Pan paddling pool at the Diana Princess of Wales Memorial Playground *(see p172)* in Kensington Gardens.

The museums get in on the act too: the **V&A** *(see p184)* allows summer paddling in its courtyard, while in the basement playroom at the **Science Museum** *(see pp180–81)*, kids can splash around with water. In winter, when the weather's wet, head for the Chelsea Sports Centre pool *(see p190)* and jump right in.

Encounters with nature

With three great parks and the world's biggest collection of birds, beasts and botany, this area is a great place to introduce children to nature. The main draw is the **Natural History Museum** *(see pp182–3)* – so vast that it warrants a day's exploration. First off, book a place on a behind-the-scenes Spirit Collection Tour and consult the film schedule at the Attenborough Studio. Pick up a free children's backpack from the welcome desk and head off to see prehistoric monsters or cheeky monkeys. From 2:30pm, the Investigate Centre invites families to study real specimens.

There is a meerkat enclosure at **Battersea Park Children's Zoo** *(see p190)*, while just across the Thames, the **Chelsea Physic Garden** *(p191)*

is another hive of animal activity – its holiday workshops include pond-dipping, creepy-crawly handling and herbalism for beginners.

Season by season

In Hyde Park *(see p174)*, spring begins with a bang, with a 41-gun salute on 21 April for the Queen's birthday. From Easter, pedalos and rowing boats glide over the Serpentine, while at the **Natural History Museum** *(see pp182–3)*, they open their wildlife garden and pop-up butterfly house. The Chelsea Flower Show *(see p187)* bursts into bloom in May.

July sees the **Serpentine Galleries** *(see p176)* launch their summer season and entertainers perform at the Diana Princess of Wales Memorial Playground *(see p174)*. The Proms, an eight-week summer season of orchestral concerts, begin at the **Royal Albert Hall** *(see p185)*.

Winter is festival time. November brings fireworks in **Battersea Park** *(see p188–9)* and the city's Christmas bash, Winter Wonderland, in **Hyde Park** *(see p174)*, with Santa, skating and *glühwein*.

A ring-tailed lemur, one of the popular small primates at Battersea Park Children's Zoo

Kensington Gardens, Hyde Park and around

Inspired by the story of Peter Pan, with its pirate galleon and tree full of pixies, the Diana Princess of Wales Memorial Playground in Kensington Gardens is the perfect place to let imaginations run wild. The playground is situated next to the late Princess's Kensington Palace home, with Hyde Park next door for more outdoor fun. Most kids' stuff is concentrated south of the Serpentine swimming lido, making Knightsbridge, on the Piccadilly Tube line, the best route in.

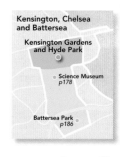

Kensington, Chelsea and Battersea

Kensington Gardens and Hyde Park

Science Museum
p178

Battersea Park
p186

0 metres 200

0 yards 200

The ornate Albert Memorial, Kensington Gardens, commissioned by Queen Victoria after the death of her husband, Albert

Victoria Gate pet cemetery

Places of interest

SIGHTS

1. Kensington Gardens and Hyde Park
2. Kensington Palace
3. Serpentine Galleries
4. Apsley House

● EAT AND DRINK

1. Mount Street Deli
2. Broadwalk Café
3. Serpentine Bar & Kitchen
4. The Cookbook Café
5. Hyde Park Tennis Centre Café
6. Lido Café Bar
7. Hard Rock Café
8. Magazine

See also Kensington Palace (p176)

● SHOPPING

1. Selfridges

● WHERE TO STAY

1. Mandarin Oriental
2. The Parkwood at Marble Arch
3. Royal Garden

Cooling off on a hot day at the Diana Princess of Wales Memorial Fountain

Right *The Serpentine Galleries, built in 1934 as a Tea Pavilion, and now home to modern art*
Far right *Speakers' Corner in Hyde Park, a bastion of public speaking for 150 years*

The Lowdown

🚙 **Rail** Paddington (a 5–10-minute walk) **Tube** Marble Arch, Lancaster Gate, Queensway (all Central Line); Knightsbridge, Hyde Park Corner (both Piccadilly Line) **Bus** Park Lane: route numbers 2, 10, 16, 36, 73, 74, 82, 137, 148, 414, 436; Marble Arch: 6, 7, 23, 98, 113, 159; Bayswater Road: 94, 274, 390; Knightsbridge: 9, 10, 52, 452

ℹ️ **Visitor information** Old Police House, Hyde Park, W2 2UH (*www.royalparks.org.uk*); Victoria Railway Station (*see pp64–5*)

🛒 **Supermarkets** Sainsburys Local, Marble Arch Tower, 55 Bryanston Street, W1H 7AA; West One Food Fayre, 85 Duke Street, W1K 5PG **Markets** Bayswater Road Market (art, jewellery), 10am–6pm Sun; Notting Hill Farmers' Market (food), Kensington Church Street, 9am–1pm Sat; Portobello Market 8am–7pm Mon–Sat (fashion, antiques)

🎏 **Festivals** Royal Gun Salutes, near Speakers' Corner (6 Feb, 21 Apr, 2 Jun, 10 Jun and 14 Nov); Barclaycard British Summer Time, music festival with family day (Jun-Jul); Notting Hill Carnival, Aug Bank Holiday weekend; Winter Wonderland, Christmas festival (Nov–Jan)

➕ **Pharmacies** Bliss Chemists, 5–6 Marble Arch, W1H 7EL (9am–11:30pm daily). For 24-hour pharmacies, visit *www.nhs.uk/ServiceDirectories*

🧹 **Nearest playgrounds** There are three in the parks, at Edinburgh Gate (Hyde Park); Diana Princess of Wales Memorial Playground and Westbourne Gate (both Kensington Gardens)

The Round Pond in Kensington Gardens, popular with wildlife and visitors alike

① Kensington Gardens and Hyde Park
Visit one park and get another one free!

The ever-youthful Peter Pan first sprang to life in Kensington Gardens – his creator JM Barrie lived nearby – and it remains a great place for those who've never really grown up. Along with neighbouring Hyde Park, it offers picnic and play opportunities galore – on both land and water. The LookOut runs arts and crafts programmes inspired by nature, and the Diana Princess of Wales Memorial Walk cleverly links together all the highlights.

Peter Pan statue by the Long Water

Key Features

 Diana Memorial Walk

Kensington Palace *(see p176)*

Peter Pan statue

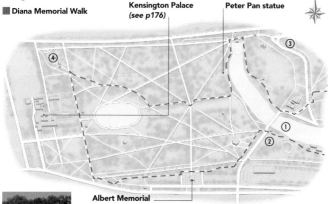

Albert Memorial

① **The Serpentine** Eat beside it, swim in it, row across it, or seek out herons and cormorants in its wilder reaches or swans and geese around its edge.

② **Diana Princess of Wales Memorial Fountain** Created in 2004, in memory of Princess Diana, this is an experiential fountain where kids can dip their toes.

③ **Speakers' Corner** A place for budding orators and eccentrics to address people on any subject they choose. Sunday is the busiest day.

④ **Diana Princess of Wales Memorial Playground** As well as a galleon, there is a music trail and a teepee encampment. Nearby, the ancient Elfin Oak is alive with fairy folk carvings made by Ivor Innes in the 1920s.

The Lowdown

🌐 **Map ref** 8 G4
Address Park Office, Rangers Lodge, W2 2UH; 030 0061 2114; *www.royalparks.org.uk.*

🚌 **Tube** Marble Arch, Queensway, Lancaster Gate **Bus stop** Black Lion Gate; Marlborough Gate; Marble Arch; Hyde Park Corner; Edinburgh Gate; Royal Albert Hall; Palace Gate

🕐 **Open** Hyde Park: 5am–midnight daily; Kensington Gardens: 6am–dusk daily

💷 **Price** Free

📣 **Guided tours** The Royal Parks Foundation run rambles in the parks (*www.supporttheroyalparks. org/shop/experiences/filter/ walks*); 45-minute Albert Memorial tours 1st Sun of month (2pm & 3pm), Mar–Dec (020 7936 2568)

👫 **Age range** All

🏃 **Activities** The Education Centre runs discovery days in the school holidays (*www.supporttheroyal parks.org/learn*). Serpentine Lido (020 7706 3422) and paddling pool open May: 10am–6pm Sat & Sun; Jun–mid-Sep: 10am–6pm daily (adults £4.80, ages 3–15 £1.80, family ticket £12). Hyde Park Tennis & Sports Centre has pay-and-play tennis all year (020 7262 3474). The Boathouse offers boat and pedalo hire, Apr–Oct: 10am–dusk (£34/hour; 020 7262 1330). SolarShuttle boat rides, Mar–Sep: weekends and public hols; Jun–Aug: daily (020 7262 1989; *www.solarshuttle.co.uk*)

⏱ **Allow** Up to a full day

♿ **Wheelchair access** There are

free electric buggies which give half-hour rides around the park.

🍴 **Eat and drink** Serpentine Bar & Kitchen (*see opposite*) or Lido Café Bar (020 7706 8114; *www. benugo.com/restaurants/ser pentine-bar-kitchen*) does pizzas and other dishes. Snacks at Hyde Park Tennis Centre Café (summer 9am–9pm, winter 10am–4pm; 020 7262 3474) and Broadwalk Café (*see right*), as well as at kiosks

🚻 **Toilets** At Serpentine Road, the LookOut; Palace Gate, Lancaster Gate, Black Lion Gate, Marlborough Gate (Kensington Gardens)

Good family value?
The park and its three playgrounds are free; swimming and tennis are affordable; only boat hire is pricey.

Take cover

If it rains, **Queens** (17 Queensway, W2 4QP; 020 7229 0172; www. queensiceandbowl.co.uk; Mon–Sun 10am–11pm; till midnight Fri & Sat) is a 2-minute walk north of Black Lion Gate, and offers ice-skating (£48; skate hire from £3) and tenpin bowling (£7.50 per person). Alternatively, Kensington's trio of mighty museums (see pp180–84) are just a short walk away via Exhibition Road and entirely free.

Youngsters ice-skating at Queens Ice and Bowl

Eat and drink

Picnic: under £30–45; Snacks: under £20; Family treat: £40–65; Family treat: £70 or more (based on a family of four)

PICNIC Delicatessens are more decadent than usual around here. Try Mayfair's **Mount Street Deli** (100 Mount Street, W1K 2TG; 020 7499 6843, www.themountstreetdeli.co.uk; 8am–6pm Mon–Fri, 9am–5pm Sat).

SNACKS Broadwalk Café and Play Café (020 7034 0722; www.royal parks.org.uk; 8am–8pm in summer, 10am–4pm daily in winter), by the Diana Princess of Wales Memorial Playground, has a menu for kids at the Play Café.

The Lido Café Bar, on the banks of the Serpentine

REAL MEAL Serpentine Bar & Kitchen (020 7706 8114; www. royalparks.org.uk/parks/hyde-park/ food-and-drink/serpentine-bar-and-kitchen; 8am–5pm Mon–Fri, till 7pm Sat & Sun) overlooks the lake and

has a kids menu for £5.
FAMILY TREAT The Cookbook Café (1 Hamilton Place, Park Lane, W1J 3QY; 020 7318 8563, www.cook bookcafe.co.uk; 6:30am–10:30am Mon–Fri, 6:30am–11am Sat & Sun; weekend brunch 12.30pm–3:30pm) is cool, casual and costly, with hefty Cold Market Table lunches.

Shopping

The mammoth **Selfridges** department store is nearby (400 Oxford Street, W1A 1AB; 0800 123400, www.selfridges.com).

Find out more

DIGITAL A self-guided walk around Hyde Park can be downloaded at www.royalparks.org.uk/parks/ hyde-park/things-to-see-and-do/ self-guided-walks.
FILM The biopic *Finding Neverland* (2004), starring Johnny Depp, used the real Kensington Gardens for the scenes where author JM Barrie first enchanted children with tales of Peter Pan, Wendy and Captain Hook.

Next stop. . .

PORTOBELLO ROAD MARKET
If it's Saturday, walk west from Black Lion Gate to explore Portobello Road Market (9am–7pm; www. portobelloroad.co.uk), reputedly the world's biggest antiques jamboree. Children should seek out Mr Punch's Old Toys (Unit 18, Admiral Vernon Arcade, W11 2DY) and Victoriana Dolls (101 Portobello Rd, W11 2QB).
HYDE PARK STABLES For a canter beside the Serpentine, contact Hyde Park Stables (63 Bathurst Mews, W2 2SB; 020 7723 2813; www. hydeparkstables.com), which offers riding lessons on Rotten Row, the 300-year-old royal carriageway. From £95 per hour, beginners welcome.

Putting a pony and young rider through their paces at Hyde Park Stables

② Kensington Palace

A palace full of princesses

It was in 1689 that Kensington Palace first became a royal home, when William of Orange asked architect Christopher Wren to turn a Jacobean manor into a place fit for a king. On 20 June 1837, 18-year-old Princess Victoria woke in her bed here to discover she was queen, and by the 1930s, so many minor royals were quartered in "Princesses' Court" that Edward VIII called it "an aunt heap". But the palace is best known as the long-time home of Diana, Princess of Wales – and as a showcase for her gorgeous array of gowns. William and Kate, the Duke and Duchess of Cambridge, now have an apartment here, too.

Major refurbishment in the last few years has opened up much of the palace, allowing visitors better access to the elegant courtyards, which they can enjoy before touring the highlights of the Royal Ceremonial Dress Collection, with its 12,000 historic garments. Other exhibitions reveal the public and private lives of queens – Mary II, Anne and especially Victoria – and detail the trials and tribulations that come with being a princess, by exploring the lives of Princess Margaret and, of course, Diana.

Letting off steam

Head to the nearby **Diana Princess of Wales Memorial Playground** for a run around (see p174).

The Lowdown

- 🌐 **Map ref** 7 D5
  Address Kensington Gardens, W8 4PX; 020 3166 6000; www.hrp.org.uk/KensingtonPalace
- 🚇 **Tube** High Street Kensington, Queensway **Bus stop** Bayswater Road, Knightsbridge
- 🕐 **Open** Mar–Oct: 10am–6pm daily; Nov–Feb: 10am–4pm daily (last admission: 1 hour earlier)
- 💷 **Price** £33 (excluding voluntary donation), under-16s free
- 🚶 **Skipping the queue** Book online to dodge the ticket queue
- 👫 **Age range** 5 plus
- 👫 **Activities** Free family craft activities in school holidays. Online "games and makes" zone has creative downloadable craft projects. Bookable day workshops for families (check website for details)
- 🕐 **Allow** Up to 2 hours
- ♿ **Wheelchair access** Yes
- 🍽 **Eat and drink** Snacks The Broadwalk Café (see p175) is lovely when the sun shines Real meal The palace's 300-year-old Orangery is an elegant place for breakfast, a light lunch or afternoon tea (winter: 10am–4pm; summer 10am–6pm). The Palace café offers a special meal box at a discounted price for children
- 🛍 **Shop** Selling gifts and souvenirs
- 🚻 **Toilets** On the ground floor

③ Serpentine Galleries

Art in the gardens

These two outstanding – and often underrated – galleries showcase modern and contemporary art. The original gallery looks, from the outside, like a twee 1930s tea pavilion – but step indoors, and surprises lurk. The four stark whitespaces have held exhibitions by Andy Warhol, Damien Hirst and Jeff Koons. Typically, there are five shows a year, and from July to October the gallery spills onto the surrounding lawns, when it invites big names such as Frank Gehry to design a pavilion to host "Park Nights" – a theatre, music and film performance programme. Meanwhile, an artist-led Family Sunday workshop takes place most months, and includes hands-on craft activities.

The second gallery is housed in the Grade II-listed Palladian-style building across the lake. The Serpentine Sackler gallery, opened in 2013, focuses on young artists, and there is an outdoor Playscape to encourage all ages to play around with art. The wave-form, Magazine restaurant, is a work of art in itself.

The Lowdown

- 🌐 **Map ref** 8 F6
  Address Kensington Gardens, W2 3XA; 020 7402 6075; www.serpentinegallery.org
- 🚇 **Tube** Knightsbridge, South Kensington, Lancaster Gate **Bus stop** Knightsbridge
- 🕐 **Open** 10am–6pm Tue–Sun
- 💷 **Price** Free
- 👫 **Age range** Call ahead to check suitability of current show
- 👫 **Activities** Free Family Sunday workshop most months (noon–5pm). Check website for full programme
- 🕐 **Allow** 1 hour
- ♿ **Wheelchair access** Yes
- 🍽 **Eat and drink** Snacks Hyde Park Tennis Centre Café (020 7262 3474) offers simple snack fare Real meal Magazine Restaurant serves breakfast, lunch and afternoon tea (020 7298 7552; www.magazine-restaurant.co.uk
- 🛍 **Shop** In reception, selling art books and cards
- 🚻 **Toilets** On the ground floor

The grand entrance gates at Kensington Palace

Prices given are for a family of four

Letting off steam

The galleries are surrounded by open, grassy areas, and there's a playground at the nearby **Serpentine Lido** (see p174).

Children's art workshop at the Serpentine Galleries, a major modern art venue

④ Apsley House

At home with Old Nosey

A door-plate outside Apsley House, known as "Number One, London", says: "To the private apartments of the Duke of Wellington." This mansion on Hyde Park Corner is still part-occupied by descendants of Arthur Wellesley, the first Duke of Wellington, Britain's greatest general and the hero of the Battle of Waterloo (1815). The duke bought the house in 1817, two years after his triumph over Napoleon, and it has been restored to the dazzle of its Regency heyday, filled with the paintings, porcelain and silver given to him by kings and emperors.

Diners at the artistic Magazine Restaurant, Serpentine Sackler Gallery

In his day, Wellington was said to be "the most famous man in Europe", though his troops nicknamed him "Old Nosey" – and Apsley's jolly children's trail encourages kids to hunt for his aquiline profile all over the house. A giant statue of Napoleon stands in the stairwell, but the highlight is the Waterloo Gallery – with works by Goya, Rubens and Velazquez – where children can lie supine and scan the painted ceiling.

Apsley's front window looks out to Wellington Arch, commissioned by George IV as a grand gateway to Buckingham Palace. An admission fee buys you access to exhibits and a balcony view of the Household Cavalry en route to the Changing the Guard ceremony (see p70).

Letting off steam

Hyde Park is Apsley's back garden and the nearest playground is at the park's Edinburgh Gate.

The Lowdown

- **Map ref** 9 B6 **Address** 149 Piccadilly, Hyde Park Corner, W1J 7NT; 020 7499 5676; www. english-heritage.org.uk/daysout/ properties/apsley-house
- **Train** Victoria **Tube** Hyde Park Corner. **Bus stop** Hyde Park Corner
- **Open** Apr–Oct: 11am–5pm Wed–Fri; Nov–Mar 10am–4pm Sat & Sun (last admission: 30 minutes before closing). Wellington Arch opens at 10am
- **Price** £21.10. Joint ticket £23.10 (includes Wellington Arch)
- **Skipping the queue** The Horse Guards ride through Wellington Arch most days at 10:30am and 11:30am – come early for a view
- **Guided tours** Free 15-minute gallery talks daily (times vary)
- **Age range** 7 plus
- **Activities** Free audio guide. Free children's trail from visitor desk or downloadable online
- **Allow** 1–2 hours
- **Wheelchair access** No, due to unavoidable steps
- **Eat and drink** Snacks Serpentine Bar & Kitchen (see p175) is great for lunches Real meal Hard Rock Café (150 Old Park Lane, W1K 1QR; 020 7514 1700; www. hardrock.com) is a themed burger joint with an under-11s' menu
- **Shop** On the ground floor, selling specialist books and memorabilia
- **Toilets** In the basement

Science Museum and around

Prince Albert's dream of a new cultural quarter funded by profits from his 1851 Great Exhibition, ballooned into a trio of colossal free museums south of Hyde Park. From South Kensington Tube station, pedestrian tunnels lead directly to the Science Museum and Natural History Museum, while the Victoria & Albert is just across Exhibition Road. The Science Museum is an especially powerful magnet for kids, using every trick of 21st-century technology to bring its subject to life. This area is a great destination in winter, with almost everything under cover (including indoor playrooms and an IMAX cinema).

Kensington, Chelsea and Battersea

Kensington Gardens and Hyde Park
p172

Science Museum

Battersea Park
p186

Captivated by a statue in the Victoria & Albert Museum

Taking part in a demonstration at the Science Museum

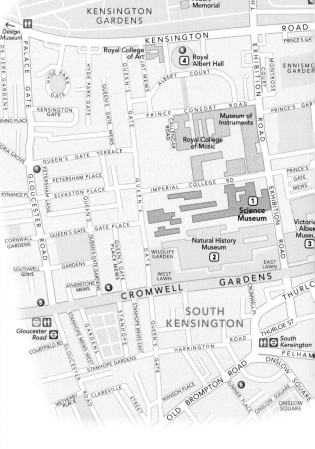

0 metres 200

0 yards 200

Diplodocus skeleton in the Natural History Museum

The Lowdown

🚇 **Tube** South Kensington **Bus** Exhibition Road, South Kensington Tube station: route numbers 14, 49, 70, 74, 345, 414, 430, C1; Kensington Road: 9, 10, 52, 452

ℹ **Visitor information** Victoria Railway Station (see pp64–5)

🛒 **Supermarkets** Waitrose, Gloucester Arcade, 128 Gloucester Rd, SW7 4SF **Markets** South Kensington Farmers' Market, Bute Street, SW7, 9am–2pm Sat

🎊 **Festivals** Kensington Dollshouse Festival, Kensington Town Hall (May); BBC Proms, Royal Albert Hall (Jul–Sep); London Design Festival, Victoria & Albert Museum (Sep); Harvest Festival, Kensington Gardens (Sep); Festival of Remembrance, Royal Albert Hall (Nov); Winter Wonderland, Hyde Park (Nov–Jan)

➕ **Pharmacies** Boots, 203–205 Brompton Road, SW3 1LA (9am–7pm Mon–Sat; 10am–6pm Sun). Harrods Pharmacy, 87–135 Brompton Road, SW1X 7XL (10am–8pm Mon–Sat; noon–6pm Sun). For 24-hour pharmacies, visit www.nhs.uk/ServiceDirectories

🛝 **Nearest playground** Climbing frame at Hyde Park Tennis Centre, near Alexandra Gate; larger playground near Edinburgh Gate

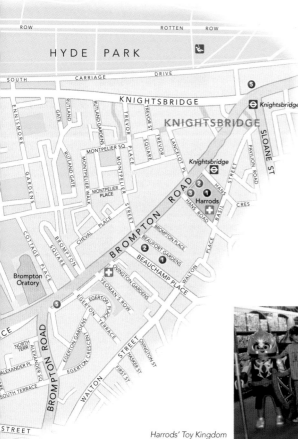

Harrods' Toy Kingdom – guaranteed to excite children young and old

Places of Interest

SIGHTS
1. Science Museum
2. Natural History Museum
3. Victoria & Albert Museum
4. Royal Albert Hall
5. Design Museum

🔴 **EAT AND DRINK**
1. Partridges
2. Ice Cream Parlour
3. The Burger Bar
4. Verdi Italian Kitchen
5. L'Opera

See also Science Museum (p181), Natural History Museum (p183), Victoria & Albert Museum (p184) and Royal Albert Hall (p185).

🔴 **SHOPPING**
1. Harrods

🔴 **WHERE TO STAY**
1. The Beaufort
2. Beaufort House
3. Crowne Plaza
4. Fraser Suites Queens Gate
5. Mandarin Oriental
6. Number Sixteen

① Science Museum
Putting the fizz into physics

Fly with the Red Arrows, fire up a pedal-powered TV set or launch a space probe: the Science Museum offers an explosively entertaining day out. With seven storeys filled with wonders, there's plenty to occupy young and old here. At every turn it's playtime – whether in the Launchpad zone, with its child-friendly experiments, or Antenna, where kids can study scientific breakthroughs. Best of all is the look of the museum – a sci-fi universe of neon-lit galleries that makes just being there an adventure.

Replica of Sir Isaac Newton's telescope

Key features

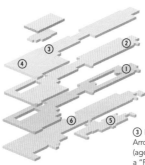

① Who Am I? An intriguing interactive gallery using face-morphing, sex-switching gadgets and personality tests to explore human identity.

② Atmosphere Play games on the tabletops, walk across oceans and see how the environment adjusts in this climate-change hall controlled by its visitors.

③ Fly Zone Soar with the Red Arrows in a "3-D aerobatic experience" (ages 4 plus), or take the controls in a "Fly 360°" simulator (9 plus).

④ Launchpad This kids' gallery has lots of hands-on experiments and science shows with audience participation.

■ **Fifth Floor** Veterinary History, History of Medicine.

■ **Fourth Floor** Glimpses of Medical History.

■ **Third Floor** Launchpad, Flight and the Fly Zone, plus Health and 18th-century medicine.

■ **Second Floor** Energy, Computers, Mathematics, Ships, Docks and Diving, and Atmosphere.

■ **First Floor** Materials, Communication, the Cosmos, Time, Agriculture and Who Am I?

■ **Ground floor** Energy and the power of steam, Exploring Space, Making the Modern World and Pattern Pod for families.

■ **Basement** The Garden gallery and a display on labour-saving gadgets for the home.

⑤ The Garden This basement playroom invites pre-schoolers to get to grips with the material world, via water troughs, junk instruments and a "building site" climbing frame. It's mayhem!

⑥ Eagle capsule This full-size replica of the Apollo 11 craft that put Armstrong and Aldrin on the moon in 1969 is in the Exploring Space gallery.

Letting off steam

The museum's own The Garden playroom (ages 3–6, basement) and Pattern Pod (ages 5–8, ground floor) are both rule-free romping spaces. For alfresco action, head 5 minutes along Exhibition Road into **Hyde Park** for tennis, playgrounds and pedaloes. The area between Rotten Row and the South Carriage Drive is set aside for Frisbee and ball games.

The very open and child-friendly spaces of Hyde Park – perfect for picnics

Prices given are for a family of four

Eat and drink
Picnic: under £20; Snacks: £20–40; Real meal: £40–60; Family treat: £60 or more (based on a family of four)

PICNIC Partridges (17–19 Gloucester Road, SW7 4PL; 020 7581 0535; www.partridges.co.uk; 8am–11pm daily) offers superior cold cuts and nibbles.

SNACKS Ice Cream Parlour (2nd Floor, Harrods, 87–135 Brompton Road, SW1X 7XL; 020 7893 8959; www.harrods.com/content/the-store/restaurants/ice-cream-parlour; noon–9pm Mon–Sat, 11:30am–6pm Sun).

REAL MEAL The Burger Bar (4th Floor, Harrods, 87–135 Brompton Road, SW1X 7XL; 020 7730 1234; www.harrods.com/content/the-store/restaurants/the-burger-bar; 11:30am–9pm Mon–Sat, 11:30am–6pm Sun) is the store's family diner, with burgers and milkshakes to eat.

FAMILY TREAT The Royal Albert Hall's **Verdi Italian Kitchen** (Door 12, SW7 2AP; 020 7070 4401; www.royalalberthall.com/your-visit/food-and-drink/; noon–8:30pm Tue–Sun) is a sleek and grown-up place to dine before (or during) a show. It has free jazz or world music most Friday lunchtimes (noon to 1:30pm) and over Sunday brunch, and a brief menu for under-12s.

The Lowdown

🌐 **Map reference** 14 F2

Address Exhibition Road, SW7 2DD;020 7942 4000; www. sciencemuseum.org.uk

🚗 **Tube** South Kensington **Bus stop** Exhibition Road, South Kensington Tube station: route numbers 14, 49, 70, 74, 345, 414, 430, C1; Kensington Road: 9, 10, 52, 452

🕐 **Open** 10am–6pm daily (until 7pm during school holidays); last admission 5:15–6:15pm; plus 6:45–10pm on last Wed of month (adults only)

💷 **Price** Free. Charges apply for IMAX 3-D cinema (£30), simulator rides and some temporary exhibitions

👪 **Skipping the queue** Launchpad is the big draw for kids, so arrive at 10am and head there first. The gallery is quieter when the live science shows are on

🚩 **Guided tours** Several hour-long and curator-led group tours, £10 per person

Age range All

👫 **Activities** Free 20-minute science shows, seven times daily (ages 7 plus); storytelling (under-7s) weekends at 1:30pm – both in Launchpad. School holiday shows feature Albert Einstein, aviator Amy Johnson and more. Live science experiments sometimes invite

museum-goers to take part in research. World Wonders and Contemporary Art trails for older children are downloadable online. Almost monthly Science Night sleepovers, usually on Saturdays, for ages 7–11 (minimum group size six, including parent/guardian, £55–60 per person)

🕐 **Allow** Up to a day

♿ **Wheelchair access** Yes, all floors

☕ **Cafés** Energy Café serves buffet-style lunches; Deep Blue Diner is a waiter-service family diner – both on ground floor. Shake Bar (Floor 3) specialises in ice cream and shakes and Media Space Café (Floor 2) does salads, wraps and sandwiches. Picnic area around the museum

🛍️ **Shop** On the ground floor, filled with brain-testing games, toys and clever souvenirs

🚻 **Toilets** All floors except 5

Good family value?

The IMAX cinema and flight simulators charge, but with science shows, family tours and hands-on galleries galore, there is more than enough free stuff to fill a day. To avoid being pestered for pennies for the kids' rides, steer clear of the café next to the Fly Zone.

Find out more

There are entertaining and fact-packed digital mini-sites devoted to the museum's galleries online at www.sciencemuseum.org.uk/onlinestuff, which also has more than a dozen brain-expanding computer games: work out how to help the Energy Ninjas beat climate change, or build cuddly "Things" using chromosomes and genes.

Next stop. . .

THE DIANA PRINCESS OF WALES MEMORIAL PLAYGROUND Explore the playground packed with activities including a beach cove with a pirates' galleon, a tree house with walkways and a mermaid's fountain. Many features of the playground are accessible to children with special needs (www.royalparks.org.uk).

HARRODS When little (and big) brains start to ache, there's always Harrods (87–135 Brompton Road, SW1X 7XL), cascading with fairylights. London's most over-the-top department store caters for kids on the fourth floor, with its Toy Kingdom and "children's fashion rooms". The pet department is fun, too, with doggie four-poster beds and cookbooks for cats.

Harrods' Toy Kingdom – where future Formula One stars start out

② Natural History Museum

Life on Earth – in 70 million specimens

Imagine a blue whale rampaging around a cathedral. That's the scene that confronts children entering the hallowed Central Hall of the Natural History Museum – and it's sure to grip them from the start. A giant blue-whale skeleton dominates the lobby, and a sharp left turn from here leads into the dinosaur gallery, stalked by scores of skeletal monsters from prehistoric times.

This is just the beginning of the museum's extraordinary expedition through life on Earth. In other halls, a blue whale dangles from the ceiling, leaf ants scurry and an earthquake simulator shakes. On the lower ground floor, the Investigate Centre has shelf after shelf stacked with exhibits for kids to hold and examine. And don't miss the Darwin Centre, housed in a great white cocoon, which uses wall-to-wall digital wizardry to reveal how the museum collects and conserves its 70 million specimens.

Families should begin their visit at the welcome desk in the Central Hall. The free Explorer backpacks guide under-8s on exciting investigations into the natural world, well-equipped with binoculars, magnifying glass and clue book. There are various Discovery booklets as well, themed on mammals, dinosaurs

Key Features

① **Investigate Centre** This invites children aged 7–14 to grab trays loaded with skins, skulls, rocks and bones, and view them under a microscope. Open 3:30–5pm daily, weekends and holidays 11am–5pm.

③ **Treasures** Home to an amazing display of specimens and objects, such as the dinosaur teeth that sparked the discovery of these giant creatures, each of the 22 exhibits here has a fascinating story to tell.

② **Dinosaur Exhibition** See a giant animatronic Tyrannosaurus rex lunge to life here. The beast was eight times more powerful than a lion, and could have swallowed a human whole.

▓ Second Floor	▓ Ground Floor
▓ First Floor	▓ Lower Ground

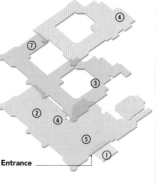

Entrance

⑤ **Central Hall** Under the vaulted arches here, the museum's most astonishing exhibits line up, including its famous replica of a *Diplodocus* dinosaur skeleton and a model of the extinct, flightless giant moa bird.

④ **Quake simulator** Walk into a model of a Japanese supermarket and hold on tight as a re-creation of the 1995 Kobe earthquake shudders the floor. Meanwhile, CCTV screens show scenes from the real thing.

⑥ **The Human Biology Zone** Head here for an entertaining skip through the body and brain. Scan microscopic liver cells, wander inside a womb, and have a go at fun memory tests and optical illusions.

⑦ **Darwin Centre** Journey through the centre's amazing eight-storey white cocoon and discover incredible specimens, exciting displays and shows, and also see leading scientists at work.

Prices given are for a family of four

or rocks for children aged 5–7 and 8–11 (£1 each). For pre-schoolers, there's the Bookasaurus dinosaur trail (free). Kids can do an online investigation of the museum's digital specimen collection at home by visiting www.nhm.ac.uk/natureplus/index.jspa?fromGateway=true allows.

The Darwin Centre's Cocoon is an interactive gallery, which shows visitors how the museum stores and uses its 20 million botanical and entomological specimens. It is open all day and does not require any booking. The timings are same as that of the museum.

Free 30-minute Nature Live shows and talks (for ages 8 and over) run in the Attenborough Studio, daily at 2:30pm, weekends and school holidays at 12:30pm and 2:30pm; the studio also screens nature documentaries daily. Weekly Dino Snores museum sleepovers are open to ages 7–11, though these sell out much in advance.

Check the museum website for the school holiday events programme, which typically includes live actors performing in character as famous figures from science. A tropical butterfly house, a well-established fixture, is erected on the East Lawn (typically

Beehive in the Natural History Museum's Wildlife Garden

Apr–Sep; £5.85 per person or £19.80 family). There is lots to explore on the Kids Only web pages, including nature-cams, games and picture galleries.

Letting off steam

The museum's East and West lawns, on Cromwell Road, welcome picnickers, and the neighbouring Wildlife Garden, with its working beehives, pond and wide variety of other natural habitats is a great place to explore and is open from April to early November (winter by arrangement; 10am–5pm).

The Lowdown

🌐 **Map reference** 14 F2
Address Cromwell Road, SW7 5BD; 020 7942 5000; www.nhm.ac.uk

🚇 **Tube** South Kensington (on Circle, District and Piccadilly lines)
Bus stop South Kensington; Exhibition Road

🕑 **Open** 10am–5:50pm daily; last admission 5:30pm. After Hours opening (till 10:30pm, last Fri of month) offers live music, debates, films and food

💲 **Price** Free. Some temporary exhibitions charge

👫 **Skipping the queue** Spirit Collection tour has limited places: book on arrival at museum, or by phone after 10:15am on the day)

🎫 **Guided tours** Free 30-minute Spirit Collection tour (ages 8 plus) goes backstage at the Darwin Centre up to four times daily. Extended 50-minute tour at 3.15pm weekdays

👫 **Age range** All

🏃 **Activities** Monthly Nature Live Nights open up the museum after hours, mainly for adults (see website)

🕐 **Allow** Up to a day

♿ **Wheelchair access** Yes

☕ **Cafés** The museum's striking galleried restaurant in the Green Zone (11am–3:30pm weekdays, till 4pm weekends and school holidays) serves ploughman's lunches and hot dishes, and offers a hearty children's menu. The Central Café in the Blue Zone does lighter bites and kids' lunch bags, plus there's a basement snack bar and picnic area

🛍️ **Shops** There are three. The main shop near the entrance has imaginative nature-themed gifts; Dino Store and Earth Shop sell dinosaur- and planet-themed items

🚻 **Toilets** On all floors

③ Victoria & Albert Museum

A labyrinth of artistic delights

For a first-time visitor, wandering the 145 galleries of the Victoria & Albert Museum (V&A) can feel like being in a very odd dream: turn a corner, and there's a hall hung with the enormous Raphael Cartoons; climb a staircase, and there's a chamber encrusted with Fabergé gems. Room after room is crammed with the world's most dazzling array of decorative arts – glass, ceramics, sculpture, furniture, textiles, silver and more, spanning five continents and 5,000 years. The Cast Courts, for example, are dominated by a towering 30-m (98-ft) replica of Rome's Trajan's Column, chopped in half to fit under the ceiling.

For children, the V&A can be a little overwhelming, especially since most exhibits are presented very conventionally – don't expect the interactive thrills of the Science and Natural History museums. However, the British galleries on Levels 2 and 4 include a series of ante-rooms with hands-on activities, one for each historical period. These follow a repeating format, with a dressing-up corner (Victorian crinolines, Tudor gauntlets); a design table (weave a

The entrance of the Victoria & Albert Museum, designed by Aston Webb

tapestry, make a bookplate); and a construction puzzle (piece together a chair, build a model of the Crystal Palace). The museum also hosts a number of free activities every day, including storytelling, arts and crafts, tours and treasure hunts. The bookable family workshops give families an opportunity to learn from an experienced artist or designer using quality materials (recommended for kids aged 5–12).

The V&A's toy collection is now held at its sister museum in Bethnal Green (see pp206–7), but by way of

compensation, objects from the defunct Theatre Museum at Covent Garden are displayed in a suite of rooms on Level 3. These are unmissable with kids; they feature backstage film clips from West End shows, a mock-up of pop diva Kylie Minogue's dressing-room, doll-size models of theatrical sets, and flamboyant costumes from *The Lion King*. There are outfits to try on, too.

Letting off steam

The V&A's majestic courtyard garden has lawns and a summer café – plus what must be London's grandest paddling pool, which welcomes waders during warm weather.

④ Royal Albert Hall

Crown prince of concert venues – home of the Proms

Wagner and Verdi; Einstein and Shackleton; Frank Sinatra and Jay Z; Nelson Mandela and the Dalai Lama; the Beatles and the Rolling Stones – they've all appeared here. Does any concert hall in the world have a roster of greats to rival this one? Squatting like a big pink blancmange on the edge of Kensington Gardens, the Royal Albert Hall is the most instantly recognizable performance space in London – and is every bit as iconic on the inside, as its daily front-of-house tours reveal.

The Hall opened in 1871, fulfilling Prince Albert's vision of a venue "for the advancement of the arts and sciences", and improbably, it is still part-supported by profits from his Great Exhibition of 1851, staged across the road in the Crystal Palace. Best known today for the pomp and circumstance of the annual BBC Proms classical music season, it also hosts rock, jazz, comedy and circus performances, film launches and Masters tennis.

Children will love the glamour of the elliptical auditorium, with its dome full of flying saucers (part of the complex acoustics) – especially since the guided tours approach it via the Queen's retiring rooms behind the royal box. Tours also peek into the balustraded "smoking gallery" up in the eaves, where £5 standing tickets can be had on the day of the show. Note that under 5s are not permitted.

The Lowdown

🌐 **Map ref** 14 G2
Address Cromwell Rd, SW7 2RL; 020 7942 2000, www.vam.ac.uk

🚇 **Tube** South Kensington
Bus stop Exhibition Road, South Kensington tube station

🕐 **Open** 10am–5:45pm Sat–Thu; 10am–10pm Fri (selected galleries open late)

💷 **Price** Free; some temporary exhibitions charge (all free for under-12s)

🚶 **Skipping the queue** Advance booking advised for temporary shows or events, available up to 48 hours ahead (www.vam.ac.uk)

🚩 **Guided tours** Free themed tours depart daily from the entrance (www.vam.ac.uk/shop/whatson/index/type/id/2/free-talks-tours)

👫 **Age range** 5 plus

🎒 **Activities** Eight different backpacks for ages 5–12, available till 4pm from the information desk as well as Agent Animal bags for under-5s; plus activity trails devoted to

Tudor and Silver galleries; and Picnic Parties (ages 7–12). Free family Drop-in Design sessions every Sun (10:30am–5pm); free 25-minute Gallery Plays every Sat (11am, 1pm, 3pm). Regular workshops (Fri evening and Sat all day) for ages 11–19 on photography, fashion and theatre (www.vam.ac.uk/create and www.vam.ac.uk/info/young-people)

🕐 **Allow** At least 2 hours

♿ **Wheelchair access** Yes; building is Grade I-listed – lifts are used to visit all areas and levels

🍴 **Eat and drink** *Snacks* L'Opera (241 Brompton Rd, SW3 2EP; 020 7052 9000; www.lopera.co.uk; 10am–11pm), across the road from the museum, is an opulent patisserie-deli *Real meal* The V&A's Café (10am–5:15pm, Fri till 9:30pm), the world's oldest museum restaurant, offers half-price main courses for under-10s

🛍️ **Shop** Gift and bookshop

🚻 **Toilets** On all levels

Letting off steam

The **Kensington Gardens** are across the road – head north past the Round Pond for the Diana Princess of Wales Memorial Playground *(see p174).*

The Lowdown

🌐 **Map ref** 14 F1
    Address Kensington Gore, SW7 2AP; Box Office: 020 7589 8212; *www.royalalberthall.com*

🚇 **Tube** South Kensington, High Street Kensington **Bus stop** Kensington Rd, Queen's Gate, Exhibition Rd

🕐 **Open** Box office 9am–9pm daily. Performance times vary

💲 **Price** Show tickets vary; from £25

🏃 **Skipping the queue** For tours, advance booking recommended

🚩 **Guided tours** There are eight tours of varying duration, some including afternoon tea or a meal. The Behind the Scenes tour is offered a few times a month; £16–20; under-12s not allowed

👫 **Age range** 7 plus on guided tours

🧗 **Activities** Occasional free family concerts during school holidays; regular jazz and comedy shows in the Elgar Room, plus Classical Coffee Mornings most Sundays at 11am (charges apply)

♿ **Wheelchair access** Yes, via ramps and lifts

🍴 **Eat and drink** *Family treat* Coda on the Rausing Circle, Door 1 offers more formal modern British cooking and a cocktail bar

🛍 **Shop** Near box office

🚻 **Toilets** In lobby

⑤ Design Museum

A modern temple to design

Re-opened here in November 2016 after 25 years at Shad Thames, this museum is housed in a modernist monument with a distinctive tent-like parabolic roof. The museum is the first in the world to be devoted solely to contemporary design, and its frequently changing exhibitions explore landmarks in modern design history. The top-floor permanent exhibit 'Designer Maker User' covers everything from typewriters to bicycles to kitchenware.

Letting off steam

The grassy expanses of **Holland Park** await immediately adjacent.

The Lowdown

🌐 **Map ref** 13 B1
    Address 224–38 Kensington High Street, W8 6AG; 020 3862 5937; *www.designmuseum.org*

🚆 **Train** Kensington Olympia **Tube** London Bridge, Tower Hill **Bus stop** The Design Museum

🕐 **Open** 10am–6pm daily (last admission: 5:15pm)

💲 **Price** Free; temporary exhibitions vary – parents plus three kids £22–29; under-6s free

🚩 **Guided tours** There are eight tours of varying duration, some including afternoon tea or a meal. The Behind the Scenes tour is offered a few times a month; £16–20; under-12s not allowed

👫 **Age range** 5 plus

🧗 **Activities** Free activity sheet for under-12s. There are Sunday pm workshops for ages 5–11 most months. School holiday courses for age 12-plus focus on specific design disciplines

⏱ **Allow** 1 hour

♿ **Wheelchair access** Yes, via ramps and lifts

🍴 **Eat and drink** *Family Treat* Parabola (020 7940 8795; *www. parabola.london*), on the rooftop of the Design Museum, offers 'design' platters

🛍 **Shop** On the ground floor

🚻 **Toilets** On the ground floor

The North Porch of the Royal Albert Hall, viewed from the Albert Memorial

Picnic: under £20; **Snacks:** £20–40; **Real meal:** £40–60; **Family treat:** £60 or more (based on a family of four)

Battersea Park and around

Battersea Park boasts a Thames-side promenade, a bucolic boating lake, a miniature zoo and the city's most action-packed adventure playground (in the southwest corner). Approach on foot from Sloane Square Tube station (a 10-minute walk), perhaps diverting along Royal Hospital Road to the National Army Museum, which offers an indoor play zone for younger children – handy when it's wet.

Kensington, Chelsea
and Battersea

Kensington Gardens
and Hyde Park
p172

Science Museum
p178

Battersea
Park

The Chelsea Physic Garden, created in 1673 to help with the identification of medicinal plants

The beautiful surroundings at Battersea Park Lake

Boy with a Dolphin, Cheyne Walk, created by David Wynne in 1975

Places of Interest

SIGHTS
1. Battersea Park
2. Battersea Park Children's Zoo
3. National Army Museum
4. Chelsea Physic Garden

EAT AND DRINK
1. Le Pain Quotidien
2. The Stockpot
3. San Gennaro
4. The Gallery Mess
5. Made in Italy
6. My Old Dutch
See also Battersea Park

(p188), Battersea Park Children's Zoo (p190), National Army Museum (p190) and Chelsea Physic Garden (p191)

WHERE TO STAY
1. Sydney House

0 metres 200
0 yards 200

Sloane Square

Peter Jones

SLOANE SQUARE

LOWER SLOANE ST

SLOANE GDN

KING'S ROAD

CHELTENHAM TER

Saatchi Gallery

WALPOLE ST

ROYAL AVENUE

FRANKLIN'S ROW

TURK'S ROW

ROYAL COURT EAST

CHELSEA BRIDGE ROAD

ST LEONARD'S TERRACE

BURTON'S COURT

The Royal Hospital Chelsea

HOSPITAL ROAD

ROYAL HOSPITAL GARDENS

National Army Museum **3**

PARADISE WALK

DILKE ST

SWAN WALK

CHELSEA EMBANKMENT

Chelsea Bridge

Chelsea Physic Garden **4**

River Thames

Peace Pagoda

CARRIAGE DRIVE NORTH

CARRIAGE DRIVE EAST

NORTH DRIVE

Battersea Park Children's Zoo **2**

Millennium Stadium

QUEENSTOWN ROAD

CARRIAGE DRIVE EAST

Battersea Park **1**

Battersea Park Lake

SOUTH DRIVE

CARRIAGE DRIVE

Battersea Park

PRINCE OF WALES DRIVE

MACDUFF ROAD

LURLINE GARDENS

PRINCE OF WALES DRIVE

BATTERSEA

WARRINER

ALEXANDRA AVE

GARDENS

BATTERSEA PARK ROAD

Above *Getting a taste of life in the trenches at the National Army Museum*
Above right *Brown capuchin monkey at Battersea Park Children's Zoo*

The Lowdown

Rail Battersea Park or Queenstown Road (5-minute walk). **Tube** Sloane Square (10 mins), Pimlico (15 mins) **Bus** Chelsea Bridge: route numbers 44, 137, 452; Battersea Park Station: 156, 344; Chelsea Embankment: 170, 360; Battersea Bridge: 19, 49, 319, 345; King's Road: 11, 22, 211 **River bus** Cadogan Pier, on River Taxi route between Blackfriars and Putney, peak hours only Mon–Fri (01342 820600; www.thamesriver services.co.uk/wpb/thames executivecharters.cfm)

Visitor information Victoria Railway station, (see pp64–5)

Supermarkets Waitrose, 196–198 King's Road, SW3 5XP; Tesco Metro, 275–277 Battersea Park Road, SW11 4LU; Here, 125 Sydney Street, SW3 6NR
Markets Battersea High Street Market (mixed), 9am–4pm Sat; Chelsea Antiques Market, King's Road, 10am–6pm Mon–Sat; Pimlico Road Farmers' Market, Orange Square, 9am–1pm Sat

Festivals BADA Antiques & Fine Art Fair, Duke of York Square (Mar); RHS Chelsea Flower Show, Royal Hospital Chelsea (May); Masterpiece Art Fair, Royal Hospital Chelsea (Jun–Jul); Bastille Day, Battersea Park (Jul); Battersea Park fireworks (Nov)

Pharmacies Healthchem, 166–168 Battersea Bridge Rd, SW11 3AW; 9am–7:30pm Mon–Fri, 9am–6pm Sat. For 24-hour pharmacies, visit www.nhs.uk/ServiceDirectories

Nearest playground Adventure playground and toddler area inside Sun Gate (southwest corner) in the park; St Luke's Park (see p191)

① Battersea Park
London's best adventure playground

It may lack the royal pedigree of Regent's Park or Kensington Gardens, but Battersea Park has its fair share of exotica. Meet monkeys and meerkats at the children's zoo, take tea beside fantastical fountains, hide behind palms in Britain's original sub-tropical gardens and meditate beside a Japanese peace pagoda. What's more, Battersea is the only major city-centre park with a Thames-side promenade, thronging at weekends with baby buggies, roller-skaters and some of the best-dressed joggers in the world.

Pagoda statue

Key Features

① Peace Pagoda Built by Japanese monks in 1984 as a shrine to universal peace, the four gilded sculptures here recount Buddha's path to enlightenment.

Recumbent Cycling Half-bike, half-go-kart, these curious "lie-down" contraptions are rentable for all ages. If that sounds too intrepid, there's a toddlers' train.

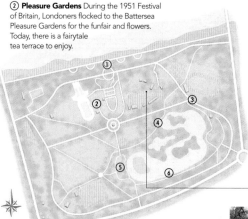

② Pleasure Gardens During the 1951 Festival of Britain, Londoners flocked to the Battersea Pleasure Gardens for the funfair and flowers. Today, there is a fairytale tea terrace to enjoy.

⑤ Sub-Tropical Gardens Created by John Gibson, with finds from his orchid-hunting expeditions in India, this caused a sensation in 1860s London.

⑥ Boating Lake A wooded idyll sprinkled with tree-branch bridges, the lake has sculptures by Henry Moore and Barbara Hepworth, a waterside café and boats for hire.

③ Millennium Arena The park's main sports hub has an eight-lane running track, 19 floodlit tennis courts, all-weather pitches and a gym. It's open to all.

④ Pump House Gallery The Victorian engine house now hosts changing exhibitions of contemporary art.

Children's Zoo *(see p190)*

The Lowdown

Map reference 15 A6
Address Park Offices, Battersea Park, SW11 4NJ; 020 8871 7530, *www.wandsworth.gov.uk/ batterseapark*

Rail Battersea Park or Queenstown Road **Tube** Sloane Square (Circle and District lines) or Pimlico (Victoria line) **Bus stop** Chelsea Bridge, Battersea Park Station, Chelsea Embankment, Battersea Bridge **River** Cadogan Pier

Open 8am–dusk daily

Price Park admission free; charges apply for zoo, boating, cycle hire and sports pitches

Guided tours None; self-guided walk leaflets from Park Office (open weekdays only, 9am–5pm)

Age range All

Activities Adventure Playground 6:30am–10:30pm daily. Land train runs July–August. Cycle hire weekends and holidays from 10am (from £10 per hour; 020 7498 6543, *www. londonrecumbents.co.uk*). Boat hire Easter to September, weekends and school holidays only (£15 per half-hour; 020 7262 1989, *www.solarshuttle. co.uk/battersea.htm*). Frequent school holiday art workshops at Pump House Gallery open 11am–4pm Wed–Sun (020 8871 7572, *www.pumphousegallery. org.uk*). Millennium Arena open weekdays 7am–10pm, 9am–6pm Sat, till 9:30pm Sun (020 8871 7537); tennis bookings

(020 8871 7537). Occasional funfairs in school and bank holidays

Allow Half a day

Cafés Pear Tree Café (*near Rosery Gate, open 8.30am–8pm in summer, winter till 4pm*) opened in 2017 replacing the former Italian eatery. The Tea Terrace Kiosk (*8:30am–7pm*) has snacks; plus weekend sandwich van with picnic tables, outside the adventure playground.

Toilets Near fountains, zoo entrance and adventure playground.

Good family value?
The brilliant playground is free; the zoo, cycling and boating are affordable. What's not to like?

Take cover

The refurbished Adventure Playground, with exciting new equipment, is a fun stop for kids aged 5 to 16 (for opening times, see Lowdown). Just across the river is **Chelsea Sports Centre** *(Chelsea Manor Street, SW3 5PL; 020 7352 6985, www.better.org. uk/leisure/chelsea-sports-centre#/)* with good-value swimming, including junior lessons (pool open weekdays 6:30am–10pm; Sat 8am–8pm; Sun 8am–10pm).

Eat and drink

Picnic: £30–35; Snacks: £30–50; Real meal: £40–60; Family treat: £60 or more (based on a family of four)

PICNIC Le Pain Quotidien *(201 King's Road, SW3 5ED; 020 7486 6154, www.lepainquotidien.co.uk; 7am–9pm Mon–Fri, 8am–9pm Sat, 8am–7pm Sun)* serves a wide selection of breads, cakes, pastries and tarts. The light lunches offered include delicious salads and soups.
SNACKS The endless menu at **The Stockpot** *(273 King's Road, SW3 5EN; 020 7823 3175; www. stockpotchelsea.co.uk; 9am–11pm Mon–Sat, 11:30am–11pm Sun)* should please even the fussiest young palate – there are traditional English dishes as well as a huge range of continental favourites. Takeaways are also available – and it's very cheap for Chelsea.
REAL MEAL South of the park, **San Gennaro** *(22 Battersea Park Road, SW11 4HY, 020 7622 0475, www.sangennaro.co.uk; 5–10:30pm daily)* is a super-authentic, super-friendly pizzeria – evenings only, but half-price before 6:30pm.

Enjoying lunch at the Lemon Tree Café in the Battersea Park Children's Zoo

FAMILY TREAT The Gallery Mess *(Saatchi Gallery, Duke of York's HQ, King's Road, SW3 4RY; 020 7730 8135, www.saatchigallery. com/gallerymess; 10am–11:30pm Mon–Sat, till 7pm Sun)* does deceptively sophisticated comfort food. Daily specials using fresh seasonal ingredients and a constantly changing menu means there is something for everyone. Outdoor dining is available during the summer months. Champion of Damien Hirst and Tracey Emin, the Saatchi is a bastion for provocative new art: while the kids are eating, sneak around the gallery to check if the current show is too shocking for them.

Find out more

DIGITAL Print off a copy of a picture from the colouring gallery, or draw one yourself, and then colour it in to recreate beautiful flowers spotted in Battersea Park: *www.coloring-pictures.net/ misc-flowers.html*

Families enjoying a tour of Stamford Bridge football ground

Next stop. . .

CHELSEA FOOTBALL GROUND
A 20-minute walk via Albert Bridge (or a ride on the number 11 bus from the King's Road) brings the story of association football up to date: from Battersea-based Wanderers FC, who won the first FA Cup back in 1872, to modern-day maestros Chelsea FC. For football lovers, there is the opportunity to have a 1-hour tour of the club's stadium, Stamford Bridge, which run daily from 10am–3pm, except on match-days (£56 and up depending on package, under 5s free; 0871 984 1955, *www.chelseafc.com/tours*). Nearby Brompton Cemetery *(open 8am–6pm daily; closes 4pm in winter)* is worth a look too, for its Beatrix Potter connections.

KIDS' CORNER

Handy plants

The Sub-Tropical Gardens have plants that normally grow in the steamy rainforests of Africa and Asia. If you visit in winter, you'll see them wrapped up to keep out the cold! Find the park information board, and match these tropical plants with things that can be made from them:
1 Euphorbia
2 Bamboo
3 Flax
a Clothing and paper
b Lipstick and shoe polish
c Scaffolding poles and musical instruments

Who's Nutkin?

The writer Beatrix Potter grew up nearby. A lonely girl, she spent her childhood drawing the animals she loved. Where do you think she found the names for her characters Peter Rabbit, Squirrel Nutkin and Jeremy Fisher? From…
a King's Road shopkeepers?
b Brompton Cemetery gravestones?
c Family servants?

Answer at the bottom of the page.

Goal!

If you kick a football around Battersea Park, be sure to play fair. The first game of football under official rules was played here in 1864, and in 1872, a Battersea team called The Wanderers won the first FA Cup. Their kit was pretty ugly – orange, pink and black hoops! Recently, the club started up again, after 120 years. Can you design a more tasteful strip for them?

Answers: **Handy Plants 1**b 2c 3a; **Who's Nutkin?** b gravestones!

② Battersea Park Children's Zoo

Mingle with meerkats and ogle an otter

Chinchillas have the softest fur of any creature on Earth; brown capuchin monkeys smear garlic on their bodies to smell nice; and meerkats can sneak up on scorpions and bite off their stings. This modest menagerie can't compete with London Zoo, with its gorillas and lions, but compensates with intriguing titbits about the behaviour of its cute inhabitants.

The zoo is all about catering for kids – every resident seems to have a name, from Piggle and Wiggle the pigs to Morris and Murray the talking mynah birds – and at weekends children can help feed some of the animals. As well as several small primates, the zoo features child-friendly farm animals, interesting birds from emus to zebra finches, and a Mouse House filled

The ever-popular meerkat enclosure at Battersea Park Children's Zoo

with pet–size animals; there's also a butterfly garden. Stars of the show are the meerkats, and kids get to crawl through a tunnel into their compound, popping their heads up for a closer view.

Two hours is ample time here, even allowing for a long frolic in the excellent playground, which includes a full-size fire engine to "drive", hay bales to clamber on and an enormous sandpit.

Take cover
The zoo is mostly outdoors, so on a really rainy day, flee across the river for a swim, trampoline or jungle gym at **Chelsea Sports Centre** *(Chelsea Manor Street, SW3 5PL).*

The Lowdown

🌐 **Map ref** 15 B6
Address Battersea Park, Chelsea Bridge Gate, SW11 4NJ; 020 7924 5826; www.batterseapark zoo.co.uk

🚗 **Rail** Battersea Park, Queenstown Road **Tube** Sloane Square, Pimlico **Bus stop** Chelsea Bridge, Battersea Park Station, Chelsea Embankment, Battersea Bridge **River bus** Cadogan Pier

🕐 **Open** Apr–Sep:10am–5:30pm daily; Nov–Mar till 4:30pm or dusk (last admission: 30 minutes earlier)

💲 **Price** £28–37

👫 **Age range** 2 plus

🐾 **Activities** Feeding times at weekends and school holidays: otters and meerkats 11am, 2:30pm; monkeys 11:30am, 3pm; farm animals noon and 3:30pm. Storytime Wednesdays in Feb and Mar; drop-in activities during school holidays (check website)

⏱ **Allow** Up to 2 hours

♿ **Wheelchair access** Yes, via ramped entrance

🍽 **Eat and drink** *Snacks* Lemon Tree Café in the zoo serves sandwiches, soup and cakes. *Real meal* La Gondola al Parco (see p188), beside the boating lake, offers hot dishes

🛍 **Shop** Near the ticket office

🚻 **Toilets** Near the gift shop

Prices given are for a family of four

③ National Army Museum

Tiny troops most welcome

Housed in vast new quarters, this museum fills every inch with displays telling the story of the British Army from 1066 to the present. See the skeleton of Napoleon's horse, clamber through a World War I dugout, and light up a toy-soldier war zone to see how Wellington won the Battle of Waterloo. The liveliest areas for children are two Action Zones lined with hands-on kit and quizzes. In Victorian Soldier, a game of chance determines their army rank and whether they'll survive their service. In The World's Army, an interactive map plays out various battles and troop movements from the two world wars. Kids can borrow two prop-packed backpacks themed on World War II spies and military art.

On the face of it, a soft-play area for tots themed on war and conflict is a tricky idea to pull off. Thankfully, the museum's Kids' Zone (for ages 0–8) eschews guns and grenades and sticks to climbing nets, rocking horses and khaki-based dressing-up. It can get a bit manic at weekends, but the room offers a useful safety valve after a tour of the galleries.

Next door to the museum is The Royal Hospital Chelsea, famed as the home of the Chelsea Pensioners since 1682. Christopher Wren's chapel and the Great Hall are free to visit (10am–5pm Mon–Sat; 020 7881 5200; www.chelsea-pensioners.co.uk/visit).

Visitors looking at exhibits at the National Army Museum

The Lowdown

🌐 **Map ref** 15 A5

Address Royal Hospital Road, Chelsea, SW3 4HT; 020 7881 6606; www.nam.ac.uk

🚇 **Tube** Sloane Square **Bus stop** Royal Hospital Road, Chelsea Bridge Road, King's Road **River bus** Cadogan Pier

🕙 **Open** 10am–5:30pm daily

💷 **Price** Free; some temporary exhibitions charge. Kids' zone: £2.50 per child (ages 0–8)

🧍 **Skipping the queue** Free Kids' Zone operates on timed ticket system; it is sometimes reserved for private parties – check online

👫 **Age range** Kids' Play Base, ages 3 and above

🧍 **Activities** Children's activities in the Play Base, Heuristic Play and Treasure Baskets are on offer

⏱ **Allow** Up to 2 hours

♿ **Wheelchair access** Yes

🍽 **Eat and drink** Snacks Base Café, in the museum, offers a short menu of hot dishes and snacks Real meal Made in Italy (249 King's Road, SW3 5EL; 020 7352 1880; www.madeinitalygroup.co.uk; 6–11:30pm Mon, noon–11:30pm Tue–Sat, noon–10:30pm Sun) serves wood-oven pizza by the metre and the usual southern Italian specialities

🛍 **Shop** Selling gifts, toys and books on military topics

🚻 **Toilets** On the Ground and Lower Ground levels

Letting off steam

The Hospital grounds are open 10am – dusk (from 2pm Sun), or cross King's Road to the playground at St Luke's (Cale Street, SW3 3QU), where kids can act out their own play battle.

Pomegranates growing in the Chelsea Physic Garden

④ Chelsea Physic Garden

Calling all plant detectives

"Warning!" says the sign at Chelsea Physic Garden. "Many plants here are poisonous and can kill!" London's oldest botanical garden was opened in 1673 by the Worshipful Society of Apothecaries to study medicinal plants, and includes a Poison Bed, a Tropical Corridor and Perfumery, as well as an 18th-century rockery made from Icelandic lava, in its rambling walled plot beside the Thames. It feels like a charming secret garden.

The ingenious Shelf Life display cultivates nearly 100 plants inside the packaging of food and medicines that are made from them, while the main focus for kids is the inventive family sessions sprinkled through the school holidays. These include garden photography, herbal medicine workshops, paper-making, creepy-crawly handling and (best of all) CSI Chelsea, a crime-solving day looking into forensic pathology.

Letting off steam

Head across the river to **Battersea Park** for plenty of room to play.

The Lowdown

🌐 **Map ref** 15 A5

Address 66 Royal Hospital Road, SW3 4HS; 020 7352 5646; www.chelseaphysicgarden.co.uk.

🚇 **Tube** Sloane Square **Bus stop** Royal Hospital Road, Chelsea Bridge Road, King's Road **River bus** Cadogan Pier

🕙 **Open** Apr–Oct: noon–6pm Tue–Fri, 11am–6pm Sun and Bank Holidays; Nov–Mar: 11am–3pm or dusk (last admission: 30 minutes earlier)

💷 **Price** £21–50 (prices vary by season), under-5s free

📍 **Guided tours** Free most days

👫 **Age range** Most family activity sessions target ages 7 plus

🧍 **Activities** School holiday family programme, themes vary, booking essential (£5.50 per person, including accompanying adult)

⏱ **Allow** 1 hour

🍽 **Eat and drink** Snacks Tangerine Dream Café (open from 12:30pm; 020 7349 6464), in the garden, serves home-made hot lunches and afternoon teas Real meal My Old Dutch (221 King's Road, SW3 5EJ; 020 7376 5650; www.myolddutch.com; 10am–11:30pm Mon–Sat, 10am–10pm Sun) is a cosy creperie

🛍 **Shop** Selling garden-related products

🚻 **Toilets** Beside shop

Beyond
the City Centre

Spread out beyond the city centre are scores of terrifically appealing attractions, including some of London's most-fun museums and its widest, wildest open spaces. For families, several are too good to miss, including toy heaven at the Museum of Childhood, a glimpse into outer space at the Royal Observatory, and the world in one garden at Kew. The Tube, train and bus network makes them all accessible within about an hour.

Highlights

Kew Gardens
Kew invites kids to burrow into a badger's sett, get inside a giant flower, or perch bird-like on the treetop walkway *(see p228)*.

Warner Bros. Studio Tour London – The Making of Harry Potter
Step into the world of Harry Potter and marvel at the sets, costumes and hands-on exhibits *(see p218)*.

Horniman Museum
Among the voodoo shrines and stuffed walruses at this quirky museum, the Music Gallery stands out – touch the table-tops and instruments strike up *(see p222)*.

Wembley Stadium
Touring the stadium is a trip to dreamland for football-crazy kids (and adults), climaxing when they climb those famous steps to view the FA Cup *(see p219)*.

V&A Museum of Childhood
London's noisiest museum? The Museum of Childhood, with its rocking-horse races, Punch & Judy shows and toys *(see pp208–9)*.

Royal Observatory
At the Royal Observatory in Greenwich, kids can mastermind a mission to Venus, dodge a meteorite shower or even watch a big-screen Big Bang *(see p201)*.

Left *Mudchute Park and Farm, a pastoral corner of London in the shadow of the gleaming skyscrapers of Canary Wharf* **Above** *The time ball atop Royal Observatory Greenwich, which dominates Greenwich Park's skyline*

The Best of
Beyond the City Centre

When it comes to visitor attractions, London's riches extend far beyond the Tower of London, Buckingham Palace and Regent's Park. Families who venture out from the centre will be richly rewarded, whether they go east to hip Hoxton, west into well-to-do Richmond and Kew, north to the pleasure grounds of Hampstead Heath or south to the splendours of Greenwich. Here are some itineraries that will help you pick out the plums.

A Greenwich weekend

If Greenwich were outside London, it would vie with Windsor, Oxford and Bath. There is so much to see here by the Thames. An exciting way to arrive is on the Docklands Light Railway (DLR), gliding through the skyscrapers of Canary Wharf. Hop off for the **Museum of London Docklands** (see p202), where there's a programme of events every Saturday. Carry on to Greenwich for lunch at Discover Greenwich (see p200), then ramble through the **Old Royal Naval College** (see p200) and visit the **Cutty Sark** (see p202).

On Sunday, pick up a picnic at Greenwich Market (see see p198) and head for Greenwich Park. When its playground and pedal boats pall, dip into the free Discover Sundays kids' programme at the **National Maritime Museum** (see p200). For a star-studded finish, book family tickets for a blast into the Sky Tonight at the **Royal Observatory** planetarium (see p201).

Life out east

Beyond the eel-pie-and-mash cliché, East London offers a rich mix of multicultural influences and terrific places to see. The starting point for families is the **V&A Museum of Childhood** (see pp208–9) at Bethnal Green – parents can browse the vintage toys while their kids go nuts in play zones scattered about the building.

Just one Tube stop further east, in Mile End, is the **Ragged School Museum** (see p213), offering an eye-opening Victorian classroom experience, while to the west, the **Geffrye Museum** (see p210) is all historical interiors and family action. Get to the Geffrye by bus (26, 48 or 55), or on foot via **Weavers Fields Adventure Playground** (see p209) and **Hackney City Farm** (see p210). On a sunny day, however, most kids would opt for a bus ride north to London Fields (see p211), with its sparkling outdoor lido. Spooky **Sutton House** (see p212) is also within easy reach.

Below Narrowboats moored on the Hertford Union Canal, in Hackney's Victoria Park

Above The Old Royal Naval College, Greenwich, designed by Sir Christopher Wren Middle The Climbers and Creepers indoor playground at Kew Gardens Bottom Horse and pony riding for little ones at Richmond Park

Gods and monsters

The **Horniman Museum** *(see pp222–3)*, a mish-mash of macabre masks and mad musical instruments – is the kind of place that turns kids on to museum-going. It's easy to fill a whole day here: activities include watching the honey bees and harvest mice in the Nature Base and the lively object-handling sessions every weekend afternoon. The museum is free, and nearby **Dulwich Park** *(see p224)*, with its boats, bicycles and café, is great for a lunchtime breather.

The Horniman also combines well with **Crystal Palace Park** *(see pp224–5)*, a 30-minute bus ride south (176 or 197). It is full of Victorian character, with Punch & Judy shows in summer, spooky statues left over from Joseph Paxton's Crystal Palace, and the unmissable Dinosaur Court, 30 life-size monsters beside a lake.

Wilderness diary

Yes, metropolitan London does have wilderness, albeit in child-size chunks. To find some, head southwest, where a trio of natural oases offer year-round treats for wildlife-watchers.

Spring is a great time to visit the **WWT London Wetland Centre** in Barnes *(see p230)*. Sand martins swoop in from sub-Saharan Africa, Easter is full of fluffy ducklings, and there are walks to hear the dawn chorus. In summer, head to **Richmond Park** *(see p232)*, hiring bikes to see Isabella Plantation as the azaleas burst into flaming blooms. In October, the park's red deer spar during their autumn rut. It's never winter inside the steamy glasshouses at **Kew Gardens** *(see pp228–9)*, and its Tropical Extravaganza fills February with spectacular orchid flowers.

Greenwich and around

They don't quite match Manhattan, but the shiny towers of Canary Wharf make a dramatic splash on London's eastern horizon. Once the world's largest port, this docklands quarter was reborn as a hive of business, entertainment and the high life. Arrive on the Docklands Light Railway (DLR) from Bank or Tower Gateway for a futuristic trip through the skyscrapers. Alight at West India Quay for the Museum of London Docklands; or at Mudchute for its city farm. Royal Greenwich, birthplace of Henry VIII, can be reached by DLR or river bus. Packed with museums and markets – all walkable – it's an irresistible summer's day out.

Places of Interest

SIGHTS
1. Greenwich
2. Old Royal Naval College
3. National Maritime Museum
4. Royal Observatory Greenwich
5. Museum of London Docklands
6. Cutty Sark
7. Mudchute Park and Farm
8. Eltham Palace
9. The Fan Museum
10. Thames Barrier

● EAT AND DRINK
1. Royal Teas
2. Paul Rhodes Bakery
3. Trafalgar Tavern
4. Rivington Grill Greenwich
5. Even Keel Café
6. Goddard's at Greenwich

See also Greenwich Park (p198), Old Royal Naval College (p200), Royal Observatory (p201), Museum of London Docklands (p202), Mudchute Park and Farm (p202), Eltham Palace (p204), The Fan Museum (p204) and Thames Barrier (p205)

● WHERE TO STAY
1. Double Tree London Docklands
2. Double Tree London ExCel
3. Fox Apartments
4. Novotel London Greenwich

0 kilometres 1
0 miles 1

An array of colourful puppets on sale at Greenwich Market

Above Vanbrugh Castle – a private residence on the borders of Greenwich Park
Left Making friends with the goats at Mudchute Park and Farm, Isle of Dogs

Thames river bus in front of the Old Royal Naval College, Greenwich

The Lowdown

🚌 **Train** Docklands Light Railway (DLR) runs from Bank and Tower Gateway to Cutty Sark and Greenwich stations, via Canary Wharf/Docklands. Mainline trains run to Greenwich and Maze Hill from Charing Cross **Tube** Canary Wharf and North Greenwich (for the O2) are both on the Jubilee Line **River bus** Services run to Greenwich Pier from Westminster and Embankment and stops en route

ℹ️ **Visitor information** Pepys House, 2 Cutty Sark Gardens, SE10 9LW; 0870 608 2000; www.visitgreenwich.org.uk

🍽️ **Supermarkets** Marks & Spencer Simply Food, 1–2 Cutty Sark Station, SE10 9EJ. **Markets** Greenwich Market (food, crafts, arts) 10am–5:30pm Tue–Sun; Clocktower Market, Greenwich

High Road (vintage, jewellery, books) 10am–5pm Sat–Sun; Blackheath Farmers' Market 10am–2pm Sun

🎉 **Festivals** The London Marathon begins in Greenwich Park (Apr); Greenwich and Docklands International Festival, performance arts (Jun–Jul); Great River Race, starting point (Sep)

➕ **Pharmacies** Pharmacy Meridian, 16 Greenwich Church Street, SE10 9BJ (8:30am–5:30pm Mon–Fri; till 1pm Thu); Duncans, 193–195 Greenwich High Road, SE10 8JA (9am–7pm Mon–Fri; 9:30am–4pm Sat). For 24-hour pharmacies, search at www.nhs.uk/servicedirectories

🎋 **Nearest playgrounds** Greenwich Park Playground; Millwall Park playground

① Greenwich
Where east meets west

As well as periscopes and telescopes, pedaloes and playgrounds, roaming deer, jewelled lizards, exploding stars, the fastest Victorian tea clipper of its day, and Nelson's bloody breeches, Greenwich is also the official home of Greenwich Mean Time since 1847. So there's not a second to waste: climb to the top of the hill and see the glossy lawns of Greenwich Park spread out below, with space for squirrel-chasing, pedal-boating, and plenty of hands-on history.

A ship's figurehead

Key Features

Pavilion Tea House

Playground

Bandstand

① Wildlife Centre
Hides and viewpoints overlook the park's herd of deer, while the Secret Garden Wildlife Centre hosts monthly family open days.

② Boating lake
Boats and pedaloes are available from Easter to October.

③ Greenwich Market From Tuesday to Sunday, the market jumps with stalls selling food, vintage clothing and a variety of arts and crafts.

④ Royal Observatory
Home of Greenwich Mean Time and the Prime Meridian of the World, The Royal Observatory is the official starting point for each new day and year.

⑤ Wernher Collection
Enamelled skulls and an opal-encrusted lizard pendant shine among the paintings and porcelain collected by diamond magnate Julius Wernher (Sunday-Wednesday, www.english-heritage.org.uk).

⑥ Cutty Sark Built in 1869, this Victorian tea clipper was the fastest of its day. Following a six-year conservation project, it has been raised 3 m (10 ft), allowing visitors to walk beneath its copper hull and explore its upper decks.

⑦ Trafalgar Tavern
This atmospheric old pub teetering on a prow of land above the Thames is Greenwich's unofficial figurehead.

The Lowdown

🌐 **Map ref** 18 H3
Address Greenwich Tourist Information, Pepys House, 2 Cutty Sark Gardens, SE10 9LW; 0870 608 2000; www.visitgreenwich.org.uk

🚗 **Train** Greenwich, Maze Hill, or Blackheath (mainline); Cutty Sark or Greenwich (DLR) **Tube** North Greenwich, then bus number 188 **Bus stop** Cutty Sark **River bus** Greenwich Pier: on Embankment to Woolwich Arsenal route (0870 781 5049; www.thamesclippers.com); plus from Westminster (www.thamesriverservices.co.uk; www.citycruises.com)

🕐 **Open** Park: 6am daily (closing times seasonal, 6–9:30pm); closed to traffic 10am–4pm and all day at weekends.Visitor information centre open 10am–5pm daily

💷 **Price** Free

🔫 **Guided tours** From Greenwich Tourist Information Centre, 12:15pm, 2:15pm daily (£7 per adult; under 16s free)

👫 **Age range** All

👟 **Activities** Boat hire (Easter–Oct); playground; pay-and-play tennis and golf putting (020 8293 0276); bandstand concerts on summer weekends (www.royalparks.org.uk/parks/greenwich-park). Family open days at The Wildlife

Centre, 10am–3pm last Sat of month (www.friendsofgreenwich park.org.uk). Full events calendar at www.visitgreenwich.org.uk

⏱ **Allow** At least a day

☕ **Cafés** Pavilion Tea House (see p201) and Cow and Coffee Bean (020 8293 0703), both in Greenwich Park

🚻 **Toilets** At Discover Greenwich, Royal Observatory, children's playground and Blackheath Gate

Good family value?
Excellent. Vast amounts to do, much of it blissfully free.

Letting off steam

Greenwich Park Playground has a Wendy house, scrambling tubes and a sandpit, and the boating lake is right next door. If it rains, the Greenwich Centre *(12 Lambarde Square, SE10 9HB; 020 3795 0600; www.better.org.uk/leisure-centre/london/greenwich/greenwich centre#/)* is close by, with family swimming – phone ahead to check times. Both Greenwich Theatre *(Crooms Hill, SE10 8ES; 020 8858 7755; www.greenwichtheatre.org.uk)* and Greenwich Picture House *(180 Greenwich High Road, SE10 8NN; 0871 902 5732; www.picture houses.com/cinema/Greenwich_ Picturehouse)* have regular family shows and screenings.

Greenwich Park Playground, traditional fun for younger children

Eat and drink

Picnic: £25–35; Snacks: £30–45; Real meal: £55–70; Family treat: £60 or more (based on a family of four)

PICNIC Royal Teas *(76 Royal Hill, Greenwich, SE10 8RT; 020 8691 7240; www.royalteascafe.co.uk)* is a vegetarian café and coffee shop that offers breakfast, baguettes and delicious cakes and scones.
SNACKS Paul Rhodes Bakery *(37 King William Walk, SE10 9HU; 020 8858 8995; www.rhodesbakery.co. uk)*, the artisan baker, does unbeatable sandwiches, pastries and cupcakes.
REAL MEAL Trafalgar Tavern *(Park Row, SE10 9NW; 020 8858*

One of the many enticing artisan food stalls in Greenwich Market

The light, airy and octagonal Pavilion Tea House, Greenwich Park

2909; www.trafalgartavern.co.uk; food served noon–9pm Mon–Thu, noon–10pm Fri, 10am–10pm Sat, 10am–9pm Sun) has been serving whitebait platters since the 1830s. They're still on the menu, alongside many other fresh fish dishes, but no longer caught in the Thames.
FAMILY TREAT Rivington Grill Greenwich *(178 Greenwich High Road, SE10 8NN; 020 8293 9270; www.rivingtongreenwich.co.uk; noon–10pm Mon–Fri, 10am–10pm Sat & Sun)* serves smart seafood and gourmet dishes such as partridge or wild mushroom soup.

Shopping

Greenwich Market *(Durnford St, SE10 9HZ; www.greenwichmarket london.com)* has a mind-boggling spread of hot and cold food, especially at weekends. Alongside all the food stalls are jewellery shops, vintage clothing stores, an array of gift and craft stores and lots of lovely toy shops.

Find out more

DIGITAL In 1515, King Henry VIII had a tiltyard built at Greenwich Palace for jousting tournaments. Find out more about the Tudor joust, and have a go online, at: *www.tudorbritain.org/joust/index.asp*

Next stop...

THE FAN MUSEUM *(12 Crooms Hill, SE10 8ER; 020 8305 1441; www.thefanmuseum.org.uk; 11am– 5pm Tue–Sat, noon–5pm Sun; £14, under 7s free)* This is the only museum in the world devoted to every aspect of fans and fan-making. The museum is home to a collection of more than 3,500 predominantly antique fans from around the world, dating from the 11th century to the present day.

The symmetrical Thameside façade of the Old Royal Naval College

[2] Old Royal Naval College

Home for old sea dogs

Set on riverside lawns, with the silver towers of Canary Wharf rising across the water, Sir Christopher Wren's double-domed palace is the best collection of Baroque buildings in Britain. Except this wasn't a palace, it was a residential home for injured soldiers. Queen Mary II commissioned the complex in the 1690s, and until 1869, seamen spent their days here drinking, gambling and dragging their wooden legs to the river and back.

Today, the college's slick Discover Greenwich visitor centre introduces the place's maritime history – it was the Royal Naval College from 1873–1998 – using lots of tactile gadgetry. There's a dressing-up box, self-guided family trails and crafty children's workshops in the school holidays. Daily guided tours specialize in the kind of horrible history that kids love, including the grisly story of how Horatio Nelson returned from the Battle of Trafalgar in 1805 – preserved inside a barrel of

brandy. Nelson's body lay in state in the Painted Hall, London's answer to Rome's Sistine Chapel, which must be the finest dining hall in Europe – the old sailors once ate their mutton and beans here. Tours also visit the College's underground skittle alley, with its musket ball missiles – and don't miss a peep into the quadrangle now occupied by Trinity Laban Conservatoire of Music, where tubas parp and pianos tinkle from every window.

Letting off steam

Greenwich Park's well-equipped children's playground is nearby, just across Romney Road.

[3] National Maritime Museum

Dive into the depths of Britain's nautical past

Bigger than the average cruise liner, the National Maritime Museum's central hall makes an instant impact on children. Prize exhibits from five centuries of nautical history are here, including Prince Frederick's gilded

barge, which once propelled Georgian monarchs along the Thames. Upstairs are galleries devoted to explorers, cruise travel and the slave trade, while at Level 2, where kids aged 5 to 85 get to hoist flags, load a cargo ship and even fire a cannon. Older children will love the simulation of a sea captain's bridge, which challenges them to steer boats into port. The sea-themed family events schedule divides into sessions for under-5s (Tue) and over-5s (Sat) – both are catered for on Sundays. The museum's Sammy Ofer wing hosts

Playing on one of the huge anchors outside the National Maritime Museum

temporary exhibitions and is also home to a café and shop, along with a more upmarket restaurant serving contemporary British cuisine.

It is the museum's artifacts that most capture the imagination, though: Admiral Nelson's blood-stained breeches, cut from his body after Trafalgar; and the snow boots, part-chewed in hunger, from Sir John Franklin's Northwest Passage expedition, lost in the ice in 1847. The adjoining Queen's House, a Palladian villa from 1614, shows off the museum's nautical art collection, including Canaletto's celebrated view of Greenwich from across the Thames. The addition of the Exploration Wing, with four new galleries, will showcase events from Britain's polar exploration and maritime history.

Letting off steam

There is plenty of space to run around in **Greenwich Park** (see p198).

④ Royal Observatory Greenwich

The world's timekeeper

Dominating Greenwich Park's skyline, the Royal Observatory is a Willy Wonka affair, with green onion domes and a red gobstopper on the roof. The gobstopper is actually the "time ball", which drops daily at 1pm to signal the hour to passing ships. The world has been setting its clocks by Greenwich Mean Time since an international conference fixed the

A favourite photo opportunity – astride the Prime Meridian

line of zero longitude here in 1884, making this the official starting point for each new day and year. Today, visitors queue to have a photo taken astride the Prime Meridian.

The observatory hosts a galaxy of exhibitions, from the intricate to the interplanetary. Watchmaker John Harrison's grapplings with the longitude conundrum will confuse most adults, but the astronomy galleries are much more friendly to children, with a film evocation of the Big Bang and a 4.5 billion-year-old meteorite. In the Astronomy Explorers room kids can man the flight deck and send a virtual space probe to Venus. The most memorable part of the visit, though, is the Peter Harrison Planetarium: tilt back in an armchair and watch as worlds appear, stars detonate and universes collapse on the big screen above.

Letting off steam

Head to **Greenwich Park** (see p198).

The Lowdown

🌐 **Map ref** 18 H4
Address Blackheath Avenue, Greenwich, SE10 8XJ; 020 8858 4422; *www.rmg.co.uk/royal-observatory*

🚂 **Train** Greenwich or Maze Hill, both a 15-minute walk **Bus stop** Romney Road **River bus** Greenwich Pier

🕐 **Open** 10am–5pm daily (last admission 4:30pm)

💷 **Price** £22, under-5s free (astronomy galleries free); Planetarium £26

👪 **Skipping the queue** Book ahead (020 8312 6608; *www.rmg.co.uk/royal-observatory/tickets-prices*)

🚩 **Guided tours** Most weekdays (free, times vary); audio guide (£3.50)

👫 **Age range** 6 plus

👪 **Activities** Kids' trail downloadable from website only. Free monthly Space Explorers workshops (Sat, age 6-plus). Planetarium shows include Space Safari (under-7s), Sky Tonight Live and Asteroid: Mission Extreme (5-plus), (check website for schedule)

🕐 **Allow** 2–3 hours

♿ **Wheelchair access** Yes, but slightly restricted in some buildings

🍴 **Eat and drink** *Snacks* Astronomy Café overlooking Greenwich Park. *Real Meal* The Pavilion Tea House serves hot and cold meals

🛍 **Shop** In Astronomy Centre and near Meridian Line

🚻 **Toilets** In Astronomy Centre and Flamsteed House

Picnic under £20; **Snacks** £20–40; **Real meal** £40–60; **Family treat** £60 or more (based on a family of four)

⑤ Museum of London Docklands

Sailors, slaves and swashbucklers

London's best museum for children? Step forward the Museum of London Docklands which, not content with offering a terrific soft-play area for toddlers, runs weekly Mini Mudlarks sessions for gallery-goers under the age of 2. It shows just how hard the museum tries to engage families.

The museum is set within a Georgian sugar warehouse, built with the profits of the slave trade, and tells the 2,000-year story of wharfside London. Thanks to a series of galleries packed with models, movie clips and touch-screen fun, the place is surprisingly rewarding for children. They will be fascinated by a gibbet cage that was once used to dangle dead pirates above the Thames, and can explore the atmospheric alleyways of Sailortown, a realistic reconstruction of Victorian Wapping, complete with a noisy alehouse and a smelly wild animal emporium.

However, the dedicated children's gallery, Mudlarks, is best saved till last, otherwise it will be impossible to get the children away from its banks of bashing, flashing gadgets and games. Here, they get to hoist cargoes, delve for archaeological finds and even build a scale model of Canary Wharf. Visit on a Saturday, or during school holidays, when the

The Lowdown

🌐 **Address** West India Quay, Canary Wharf, E14 4AL; 020 7001 9844; www.museumoflondon.org.uk/museum-london-docklands

🚗 **Train** West India Quay (DLR). **Tube** Canary Wharf. **Bus** Westferry Circus. **River bus** Canary Wharf Pier, on London Eye–Woolwich Arsenal route (www.thamesclippers.com)

🕐 **Open** 10am–6pm daily

💲 **Price** Free

🚩 **Guided tours** Free highlight tours: ask on arrival

👫 **Age range** All

🧒 **Activities** Mudlarks Children's Gallery open 2–5:30pm weekdays; 10am–5:30pm weekends and school holidays. Free Activity Bags for ages 2–5. Download activity sheets from website. Mini Mudlarks

sessions (6 months–walking) 3:30–4:30pm Wed. Little Mudlarks (walking–age 5) 11am–noon Wed. Under-5s storytime 11–11:45am, 12–12:45pm & 2–2:45pm Wed. Family events Sat and school holidays (check website for full programme) and book ahead.

🕐 **Allow** Half a day

♿ **Wheelchair access** Yes

🍴 **Eat and drink** Picnic Museum café-bar (10:30am–5:30pm daily) serves sandwiches and kids' lunch boxes. Snacks The museum's Rum & Sugar restaurant (11am–11pm Tue–Thu & Sat, to 1am Thu, to midnight Fri, to 6pm Sun) serves heartier fare and often has special kids' offers.

🛍️ **Shop** To left of entrance

🚻 **Toilets** Ground and third floors

museum's family events programme shifts into top gear with a tumult of Caribbean dancing, cookery demonstrations and computer animation workshops.

Letting off steam

Millwall Park (Manchester Road, E14) has a lovely children's playground suitable for all ages.

⑥ Cutty Sark

The classiest tea clipper of all

One of Greenwich's most enduring attractions is back after a complete refurbishment following a

devastating fire in 2007. First launched in 1869 the Cutty Sark was the pride of British sailing ships on the lucrative tea trade route to India and the Far East until they were superseded by steam vessels. It is the last surviving clipper in existence and its presence adds an important touch of authenticity to London's most seafaring corner.

The ship has now been raised by three metres, allowing visitors

The Lowdown

🌐 **Address** King William Walk, Greenwich, SE10 9HT; 020 8312 6608; www.rmg.co.uk/cuttysark

🚗 **Train** Cutty Sark (DLR) or Maze Hill (5-minute walk). **Tube** North Greenwich (Jubilee line). **Bus stop** Cutty Sark. **River bus** Greenwich Pier

🕐 **Open** 10am–5pm daily (last admission 4:15pm)

💲 **Price** £41, under-5s free. Combination ticket with Maritime Museum available

👫 **Age range** All

🧒 **Activities** Family activities (free with admission) in school holidays: check website

🕐 **Allow** Up to 2 hours

♿ **Wheelchair access** Yes

🍴 **Eat and drink** Snacks Even Keel Café offers tea, scones and cakes Real meal Goddard's at Greenwich (020 8305 9612) serves traditional pie and mash.

🛍️ **Shop** Full of stuff for naval enthusiasts.

🚻 **Toilets** Near café on lower deck

Checking out the nautical displays at the Museum of London Docklands

Prices given are for a family of four

Friendly goats lining up for petting at Mudchute Park and Farm

the unique experience of walking underneath the American rock elm hull. The interior has also been refitted to give you the best possible idea of what it was like during its heyday, with all sorts of barrels and other maritime paraphenalia. The outside Main Deck allows you to gaze up at the three huge main masts and admire the intricate rigging.

Lots of interactive features have been added that will delight kids in particular. There is even a theatre on board, where interesting talks and performances take place. Occasional other fun events such as sleepovers are also arranged.

Letting off steam

It's a short walk) to **Greenwich Park** (*see p198*), with its playground, boating lake and picnic lawns.

⑦ Mudchute Park and Farm

Dally with Dalai the llama

It is one of the more surreal sights in London: a llama called Dalai trotting around his paddock, with the Canary Wharf skyscrapers behind. Mudchute is one of Europe's largest city farms, home to every bleating, braying animal from a child's colouring book – plus three llamas and a few rare breeds, too.

Arrive on the Docklands Light Railway (DLR) for a truly space-age journey along elevated tracks in driverless trains – it's best

The Lowdown

🌐 **Address** Pier Street, Isle of Dogs, E14 3HP; 020 7515 5901; *www.mudchute.org*

🚗 **Train** Crossharbour or Mudchute (both DLR). **Bus stop** Crossharbour, Pier Street

🕐 **Open** Farm: 8am–4pm daily; park: open daily

💲 **Price** Free

👫 **Age range** All

🧑‍🌾 **Activities** Duck walk (9am) and animal round-up (4pm). Drop-in sessions Mon–Wed in school holidays; plus seasonal fundays. Riding lessons available (charged).

⏱ **Allow** 2 hours

♿ **Wheelchair access** Yes, but can be difficult if wet

☕ **Eat and drink** *Snacks* Mudchute Kitchen, beside the farmyard, excels at brunch and serves hot snacks. Or take a picnic.

🛍 **Shop** Selling animal feed and sometimes eggs from the hens

🚻 **Toilets** In the courtyard

experienced in the front carriage. The farm's newest donkey, George, sends a rallying call to visitors walking in from Mudchute or Crossharbour stations, and once inside, there are pastures and parkland to explore, riding stables and a courtyard with exotic aviaries and cuddly rabbits and guinea pigs. Stroking is actively encouraged, just ask a friendly farmhand.

Take cover

The multiscreen **Cineworld Cinema** (*0871 200 2000; www.cineworld.co.uk/*), on West India Quay, has afternoon shows through the year on weekends and summer weekdays also, and is the perfect place to sit out the rain. Or head to the lively and engaging **Museum of London Docklands** (*see left*) for some indoors fun.

The beautifully restored Cutty Sark, in the heart of maritime Greenwich

KIDS' CORNER

Quay questions
Try this Museum of London Docklands quiz...

1 How many arches did London Bridge have in 1440?

2 What did whaleboat captains draw in their journal when they killed a whale?

3 Which continent did trading ships import coffee from?

4 In which year was the slave trade banned in Britain?

5 Where would you go to buy rope in London Docklands?

....

Answers at the bottom of the page.

GLORIOUS MUD
In Victorian London, "mudlarks" was the name given to poor children who hunted on the slimy banks of the Thames for things to sell. It was an unpleasant job – in those days, the river was awash with broken glass, toilet waste, even dead bodies!

A pig's tale
Have you heard the story of the Tamworth Two? They were a pair of Tamworth pigs, like those at Mudchute Farm, who got out of their truck on the way to market. The brave porkers made a run for it, crossing a river and hiding out in some woods. Newspapers named them Butch and Sundance, after two famous outlaws. They were eventually captured – but by then they were celebrities, so instead of becoming bacon, they lived happily ever after at an animal sanctuary. Oink!

....

Picnic under £20; **Snacks** £20–40; **Real meal** £40–60; **Family treat** £60 or more (based on a family of four)

⑧ Eltham Palace

Art Deco dream house

With its gold-plated bathroom, self-vacuuming floors and lemur's bedroom, a tour of Eltham Palace is anything but humdrum. Squatting improbably in one of South London's suburbs, the royal palace began life in 1305 as the grand, moated manor of King Edward II, and its 15th-century Great Hall and Tudor bridge look much as they did when the young Henry VIII played in the grounds. Step inside the adjoining house, though, and there's an even bigger surprise – a decadent Art Deco interior from the 1930s, put together with enormous panache by society high-rollers Stephen and Virginia Courtauld.

The Courtaulds lavished their textile fortune on the house, and the whole place screams glamour: the dining room has a shimmering aluminium ceiling and pink leather chairs; Virginia's vaulted bathroom has an onyx tub and gold taps. A built-in "hi-fi" supplied the jazz

The impressive Art Deco interior of Eltham Palace

The Lowdown

🌐 **Address** Court Yard, Eltham, SE9 5QE; 020 8294 2548; www.english-heritage.org.uk/daysout/properties/eltham-palace-and-gardens/

🚆 **Train** Eltham or Mottingham, then 15-minute walk. **Bus stop** Court Road; Eltham High Street. **Car** Free car park off Court Road

🕐 **Open** Apr–Oct: 10am–5pm Sun–Wed; Nov–Mar: 10am–4pm Sun; closed Jan

💲 **Price** £27, under-5s free

🎫 **Guided tours** Free audio guide with admission

👫 **Age range** 5 plus

🎨 **Activities** Children's activity sheets, Time Traveller family days with historical themes in school holidays, plus Easter Egg Hunt and Tudor Jousting weekend (Jun)

🕐 **Allow** 2–3 hours

♿ **Wheelchair access** Yes, but parts of garden are uneven

🍴 **Eat and drink** *Snacks* The palace tearoom (10am–4:30pm) serves light lunches and snacks

🛍 **Shop** Selling gifts and souvenirs

🚻 **Toilets** On the ground floor

The Lowdown

🌐 **Address** 12 Crooms Hill, SE10 8ER; 020 8305 1441; www.thefanmuseum.org.uk

🚆 **Train** Greenwich (mainline), 7-minute walk; Cutty Sark (DLR), 5-minute walk. **Bus stop** Sidcup, Catford and Peckham to the South, Russell Square, Waterloo and Woolwich to the North and East. **River bus** Greenwich Pier. **Car** Pay-and-display car park at Burney Street, Cutty sark Gardens and Greenwich Park North

🕐 **Open** 11am–5pm Tue–Sat, noon–5pm Sun

💲 **Price** £14; under-7s free

🎫 **Guided tours** by appointment

👫 **Age range** 3 plus

🎨 **Activities** Fan-making workshops, first Sat of the month

🕐 **Allow** 2 hours

♿ **Wheelchair access** Yes

🍴 **Eat and drink** *Snacks* The Orangery (020 8305 1441; Tue, Fri, Sat & Sun; booking advised for Tue & Sun) serves traditional afternoon tea, cakes and sandwiches

🛍 **Shop** Selling gifts, souvenirs, books and mementoes

🚻 **Toilets** Yes

soundtrack for their Hollywood-style house parties. Children will be especially captivated by the deluxe living quarters of Mah-Jongg, the couple's pet lemur, who enjoyed such luxuries as central heating and hand-painted wallpaper. Mah-Jongg features heavily in Eltham's activity sheets for kids, and the palace's events programme typically includes Tudor jousting and Art Deco fairs.

Letting off steam

The palace's grounds are a delight, with views over London and lots of places to enjoy a picnic.

⑨ The Fan Museum

For fan enthusiasts!

One of London's most unusual museums – the only one of its kind in the UK – this opened in 1991. It owes its existence and appeal

to the enthusiasm of Helene Alexander, whose personal collection of about 4,000 fans from the 17th century onwards has been augmented by donations. A comprehensive collection of fans and fan leaves belonging to different era, centuries and cultures have been showcased in this museum.

A small permanent exhibition, housed in the ground floor of the museum, looks at types of fans and fan-making. The collection mainly has 18th- and 19th-century European fans. While an extensive collection is rotated in temporary displays and changes thrice in a year. The temporary exhibitions highlight a particular theme in the history of fans.

The beautiful orangery, with murals, overlooks a 'secret' garden in Japanese style. On some days, afternoon tea is served at set timings in the pretty orangery at the back. The afternoon tea, with a selection of macarons,

The delicious spread for afternoon tea at The Fan Museum

tarts, sandwiches and cakes is popular with visitors.

Letting off steam

Head to the **Greenwich Park** (SE10; 0300 061 2380; royalparks. org.uk), which was originally the grounds of a royal palace and still is a Royal Park. There are great river views from the hilltop and on a fine day, most of London can be seen here. There is a playground, a boating lake, sporting facilities and shows for children.

⑩ Thames Barrier

The "sharks" that saved London

London has long been vulnerable to flooding: in 1236 the Thames rose so high that people were able to go boating across Westminster Hall, now part of the Houses of Parliament. But with sea levels inching upwards and tectonic movements tilting the south of England slowly into the sea, something had to be done. The crunch year was 1953, when more than 300 people drowned in floods around the Thames Estuary.

The 520-m- (1,706-ft-) long Thames Barrier became operational in 1982, adding a futuristic new landmark to the riverscape in the form of its seven curvy piers, which line up like shiny steel shark fins advancing on London. The barrier is effectively a tilting dam, swinging up from the riverbed in 10 circular sections whenever surge tides threaten.

The visitor experience is divided by the river. An information centre on the south bank has working models of the barrier in action. To the north, the Thames Barrier Park is a curious landscape of shaped hedgerows, honeysuckle and aerial walkways, perfect for hide-and-seek. Both sides of the river have cafés, playgrounds, and scintillating views,

Above The gleaming Thames Barrier protects London from flooding
Below Among the wave-like manicured hedges at the Thames Barrier Park

but in summer, the fountain plaza tempts most families northwards with its 32 jets of splashing fun.

Letting off steam

There are children's playgrounds on both sides of the river.

The Lowdown

📍 **Address** Information Centre, 1 Unity Way, Woolwich SE18 5NJ; 020 8305 4188; www.gov.uk/ the-thames-barrier. Thames Barrier Park, North Woolwich Road, E16 2HP

🚆 **Train** Charlton, then 15-minute walk (south side) **DLR** Pontoon Dock (north side) **Bus stop** Holborn College Park; North Woolwich Road; Connaught Bridge

🕐 **Open** Information Centre: 10:30am–5pm Thu–Sun) Park: 7am–dusk daily

💲 **Price** £10–15; under-5s free

🤸 **Activities** To see the barrier closed, visit on a maintenance day (dates listed on website); call to book

⏱ **Allow** 1 hour

♿ **Wheelchair access** Information Centre: largely accessible but access to the river front is restricted as steep stairs lead down from the bank. Park: yes

🍽 **Eat and drink** Cafés and picnicking at both sites

🚻 **Toilets** Both sides of river

V&A Museum of Childhood and around

The Cinderella borough of Hackney is finally having a ball, as young professionals move in prompting the opening of hip shopping and dining venues. Especially vibrant are London Fields, home to a lido, and über-trendy Broadway Market. Families will love the V&A Museum of Childhood in nearby Bethnal Green, offering a full day of play for free – and the Central Line brings visitors virtually to the door. Visit on the first Sunday of the month, when the Ragged School Museum, one Tube stop further, stages Victorian lessons.

Places of interest

SIGHTS

1. V&A Museum of Childhood
2. Geffrye Museum
3. Hackney City Farm
4. Hackney Museum
5. Sutton House
6. Discover
7. Ragged School Museum

EAT AND DRINK

1. Broadway Market
2. L'Eau à la Bouche
3. The Gallery Café
4. E Pellicci
5. Frizzante
6. The Grocery
7. Treacle
8. Caffè Theatro
9. Tre Viet
10. King Edward VII
11. The Palm Tree

See also V&A Museum of Childhood (p208), Geffrye Museum (p210), Sutton House (p212), Discover (p212) and Ragged School Museum (p213).

WHERE TO STAY

1. Ace Shoreditch
2. Boundary Rooms
3. Town Hall Apartments

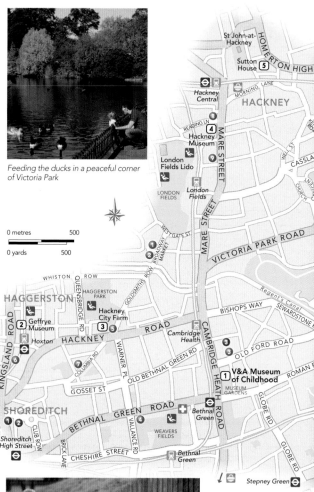

Feeding the ducks in a peaceful corner of Victoria Park

Fashion dolls on display at the V&A Museum of Childhood

Playing on the brightly coloured equipment in Haggerston Park playground

The Lowdown

🚆 **Train** Bethnal Green, Cambridge Heath, London Fields or Hackney Downs (all from Liverpool Street); Stratford **Tube** Bethnal Green, Mile End, Stratford (all Central line) **Bus** number 388 runs to Bethnal Green from Embankment via Liverpool Street; number 254 to Bethnal Green and Hackney from Aldgate

ℹ️ **Visitor information** 020 8356 3500, www.hackney.gov.uk/sports-leisure-parks; www.destinationhackney.co.uk

🏪 **Supermarkets** Tesco, 55 Morning Lane, Hackney, E9 6ND **Markets** Broadway Market (food, fashion, crafts), 7:30am–7pm Sat; Columbia Road Flower Market, 8am–3pm Sun; Backyard Market (vintage fashion, bric-a-brac), 11am–6pm Sat, 10am–5pm Sun

🎪 **Festivals** Great Spitalfields Pancake Race, Dray Walk (Shrove Tuesday); Big Write, Stratford, children's books (www.discover.org.uk; Mar); Bonfire Night, Victoria Park (Nov)

➕ **Pharmacies** Boots, 426 Bethnal Green Road, E2 0DJ (8am–7pm Mon–Fri, 9am–6pm Sat, 11am–5pm Sun). For 24-hour pharmacies search at www.nhs.uk/servicedirectories

🛝 **Nearest playgrounds** Weavers Fields Adventure Playground (Mape St, E2); London Fields (West Side, E8 3EU); Mile End Park (Grove Rd, E3 5BH); Victoria Park playground (Grove Rd, E3 5SN)

One of the many exhibits packed into the Hackney Museum

Playing games at the interactive Discover Children's Story Centre

The mid-20th-century room at the Geffrye Museum

① V&A Museum of Childhood
The grandest playroom in London

Children want to play with toys, not just look at them, and that's tricky when the toys include a queen's doll's house, an 18th-century puppet theatre and the very first Mickey Mouse doll. The Museum of Childhood solves the problem by creating "activity stations" between its display cases, where kids can ride a rocking horse, jump in a sandpit or put together a robot. The impressive building – a huge Victorian pavilion with plenty of space and pink iron balconies – helps set the tone.

Classic Barbie with matching luggage

Key features

First floor This houses the Childhood galleries, which explore the social history of childhood.

Ground floor This floor is divided into two galleries – Moving Toys and Creativity.

① **Queen Mary's Doll's House** Part of a large collection, this was furnished personally by Queen Mary. Look for the tiny telephone – ultra-modern in 1910!

② **Vintage pedal car** A perfect replica of an open tourer, this has working lights, a horn and a turning starter handle. It would have cost a fortune in the 1920s.

③ **Game Boy** Hand-held games took off in 1989 with the Nintendo Game Boy, which sold 118 million units. The Moving Toys gallery looks at toy technology from zoetropes onwards.

④ **Dolls** This collection of over 4,000 dolls dates back to 1300 BC and includes well-known favourites such as Cabbage Patch Kids, Barbie and Tiny Tears.

⑤ **Venetian Puppet Theatre** This huge 18th-century theatre provided entertainment for an aristocratic Venetian family.

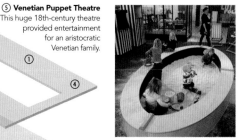

⑥ **Victorian seaside** This gallery has a sandpit for toddlers, overlooked by a 100-year-old Punch & Judy theatre and a booth for kids to stage their own shows.

⑦ **Construction Toys** Meccano, Lego and Mr Potato Head all feature in this impressive collection of 20th-century construction kits.

The Lowdown

Address Cambridge Heath Road, E2 9PA; 020 8983 5200; www.vam. ac.uk

Train Cambridge Heath (five-minute walk) or Bethnal Green (10-minute walk) **Tube** Bethnal Green (Central line) **Bus stop** Cambridge Heath Road

Open 10am–5:45pm daily (last admission 5:30pm)

Price Free

Skipping the queue Major events bookable up to two weeks in advance (check website)

Guided tours Free family tours on Saturdays and Sundays during term time. Daily activities vary

Age range 3 plus

Activities Kids' trails with a variety of themes; drop-in storytelling and art sessions. Montessori Family Packs for under-5s, plus toddler sessions. Tours and activities available every weekend and on school holidays, check the website for details

Allow Half a day

Wheelchair access Yes

Café Benugo Café (daily 10am–5pm), in the main hall, serves lunches and salads. There are picnic tables indoors and outside.

Shop Ground floor, selling books, stationery, gifts and pocket money toys

Toilets Lower ground floor

Good family value?
Excellent – even the temporary exhibitions are free. Bring some change though, as some toys need to be set in motion with a 20p coin.

Prices given are for a family of four

Picnic area within the grounds of the V&A Museum of Childhood

Letting off steam

Museum Gardens, right next door, has lawns but no playground. For a playground, you need **Weavers Fields** *(Viaduct St, Vallance Road, E2 6HD)*, a 10-minute walk away off Bethnal Green Road, where a terrific staffed adventure playground has climbing frames, rope swings, an indoor playroom and tuck shop (3:30–6:30pm Tue–Fri on school days, 11am–6pm Mon–Fri during holidays; plus noon–5pm Sat; noon–3pm Sun). To the east, **Victoria Park** *(Grove Road, Bow, E3 5TB)* is in easy striking range, with its scrumptious lakeside café *(www.towerhamlets.gov.uk/victoriapark)*.

Eat and drink

Picnic: under £20; Snacks: £20–40; Real meal: £20–40; Family treat: £60 or more (based on a family of four)

PICNIC Broadway Market *(south of London Fields, E8 4QL; www.broadwaymarket.co.uk; 9am–5pm Sat)*, a 15-minute walk or a short bus ride north of the museum, is an excellent source of provisions, with over 80 stalls, a cosmopolitan restaurant scene and the French deli **L'Eau à la Bouche** *(at no.35–37; www.labouche.co.uk; open daily)* selling delicious continental classics.
SNACKS The Gallery Café *(21 Old Ford Road, E2 9PL; 020 8980 2092; www.stmargaretshouse.org.uk/thegallerycafe/;*

open daily) is a buzzing, super-cheap veggie and vegan café with good chips and even better cakes.
REAL MEAL Grandest of all the East End "greasy spoon" cafes, **E Pellicci** *(332 Bethnal Green Road, E2 0AG; 020 7739 4873; 7am–4pm Mon–Sat)* has been run by the same Italian family for a century, and is still serving good-value English and Italian dishes. The breakfasts here are deservedly renowned.
FAMILY TREAT Frizzante *(1a Goldsmiths Row, E2 8QA; 020 7739 2266; 10am–4:30pm Tue–Sun plus Thu & Fri evenings)* is a fashionable diner at Hackney City Farm *(see p210)*, with gorgeous rustic Italian cuisine and hip toddlers scurrying underfoot. Its Thursday and Friday dinners are extra special.

Shopping for sweet picnic treats at a stall in Broadway Market.

Find out more

DIGITAL The museum's kids' pages are busy with lots of activities to download, cut out and make. There are kaleidoscopes, thaumatropes, jumping jacks and paper dolls, among others *(www.vam.ac.uk/moc/learning/things-to-do)*.

Next stop...

POLLOCK'S TOY MUSEUM
Unlock another trove of toys from yesteryear at Pollock's Toy Museum in Bloomsbury *(see p104)*.

Enjoying the Italian dishes on offer at Frizzante, Hackney City Farm.

An elegant drawing room at the Geffrye Museum

A flock of geese at the Hackney City Farm

② Geffrye Museum

The ghosts of London past

On paper, it sounds like a bizarre choice for a family day out in London: a procession of roped-off living rooms revealing how carpets, sideboards and wallpaper have evolved from 1600 to the present day. But the Geffrye Museum has one of the hardest-working children's programmes anywhere, from its monthly Saturday Specials with activities such as portrait painting, spider handling and animation workshops, to its five-week Christmas Past season, when the halls are well and truly decked with historical holly. Family audio guides, quiz trails and activity packs are available every weekend, and there's a refreshing commitment to all age groups, from toddlers to teens. Choose a day when there is lots happening, tell the kids they're going to be travelling back in time to Tudor England, and they'll be gripped.

The museum is set in a cute quadrangle of 18th-century almshouses, its front pathway lit by ghostly furniture, the work of installation artist Kei Ito. Indoors, 11 set-dressed rooms chart the changing face of middle-class décor from a 1630 merchant's parlour to a 1998 loft apartment. From April till October, the museum's immaculate period gardens host picnic parties, steel bands and other festivities.

Letting off steam

The Apples & Pears Adventure Playground (28 Pearson Street, London E2 8EL; school days: 3–6pm Tue–Fri; holidays: 9:30am–4pm Mon–Fri; 10am–4pm every Sat; 020 7729 6062) is a supervised play area just a 5-minute walk away.

③ Hackney City Farm

Meet Larry the showbiz donkey

One field does not a farm make, but hats off to the enterprising band of locals who transformed this postage stamp-sized piece of land in one of London's most congested boroughs. Created in 1984 on the site of a derelict lorry park, the farm now has calves, goats, sheep, pigs, rabbits, geese and chickens (not forgetting Larry the donkey, star of the small screen), plus a thriving crafts studio and a cottage garden growing seasonal vegetables.

Feeding time is at 4pm and there's a clutch of courses for all ages, from felt-making and yoga to beekeeping and green living, plus regular afternoon pottery sessions for children. It's worth visiting just for lunch at the sparkling Frizzante café, whose zesty Italian food has made it a dining destination in its own right.

Letting off steam
Haggerston Park (Audrey Street, London, E2 8QH) is on the doorstep, with its pond, ping-pong, BMX track, sports areas and playground.

The Lowdown

🌐 **Map ref** 6 G4
📍 **Address** 136 Kingsland Road, E2 8EA; 020 7739 9893; www. geffrye-museum.org.uk

🚃 **Train** Hoxton, 5-minute walk
Tube Old Street (Northern Line), then number 243 bus or 15-minute walk; Hackney Central and Hackney Downs **Bus stop** Kingsland Road; Hackney Road

🕐 **Open** 10am–5pm Tue–Sun; bank hols (Mon)

💷 **Price** Free; £13–16 per adult for special exhibitions, under-16s free

👫 **Skipping the queue** For Saturday Special activities at 10:30am and 2pm, arrive 30 minutes early to secure a place

🚩 **Guided tours** Audio guide (£4), children free

👫 **Age range** 3 plus

👫 **Activities** Free family audio guide (ages 5–11) and activity backpacks (ages 3–5) only. Free family days first Sat of month (ages 5–16), plus full school holiday programme. Check www. geffrye-museum.org.uk/learning/ children-families/

🕐 **Allow** 1–2 hours

♿ **Wheelchair access** Yes, except for Restored Almshouses Exhibition

☕ **Eat and drink** Picnic The Grocery (54–56 Kingsland Road, E2 8DP) offers upmarket picnic fare
Snacks The museum's café offers a seasonally changing menu of hot dishes and snacks

🛍 **Shop** Selling high-quality gifts and books relating to interiors

👫 **Toilets** On all floors

Enjoying the children's playground at Haggerston Park, Hackney

The Lowdown

🌐 **Address** 1a Goldsmiths Row, E2 8QA; 020 7729 6381; *www.hackneycityfarm.co.uk*

🚃 **Train** Cambridge Heath, 10-minute walk **Tube** Bethnal Green (Central Line), 15-minute walk **Bus stop** Hackney Road

🕐 **Open** 10am–4:30pm Tue–Sun, plus Mon bank holidays

💲 **Price** Free

🧑‍🧒 **Age range** All

🎨 **Activities** Self-guided tour leaflet has animal information and activities (£1). Feeding time 4pm; drop-in pottery twice weekly (£5, 2–4pm Wed or 11am–1pm & 2–4pm Sun). Summer holiday workshops include puppet-making

⏱️ **Allow** 1 hour

♿ **Wheelchair access** Yes; contact Farm Manager beforehand

🍽️ **Eat and drink** *Snacks* Treacle (110-112 Columbia Rd, E2 7RG; 020 7729 0538; www.greatcakeplaces.com; noon–5pm Sat, 9am–4pm Sun), part of Columbia Road flower market, recreates bygone British baking *Real meal* Frizzante cafe (see p209) serves tasty children's dishes.

🚻 **Toilets** On ground floor

④ Hackney Museum
The world on your doorstep

Hackney promises to be the hippest place in London, thanks to its rich stew of cultural influences, and this bright and breezy local museum does a tasty job of stirring the pot, especially for families, though it might be a bit unsafe in

Hands-on exhibits captivate at the Hackney Museum

the evening. The overarching theme of the museum is the 1,000-year history of people who have settled here, and the touchy-feely tone begins with the very first exhibit – a replica Saxon boat that kids can load up with goods. Elsewhere, they get to step into an East End pie-and-mash shop, play conductor on a vintage London bus, and race against the clock to make matchboxes – just as hundreds of poverty-stricken children did in 19th-century Hackney. There are drop-in dance, storytelling and art workshops in school holidays, often coinciding with a temporary show – the summer exhibition is always a hive of hands-on interactivity.

If it's sunny, combine a snoop around the museum with a splash at London Fields Lido, a short walk away via Richmond Road. Open every day, this is the city's only Olympic-size heated outdoor pool.

Letting off steam

As well as the Lido (020 7254 9038; *www.hackney.gov.uk/london-fields-lido*), **London Fields** has tennis courts, ping-pong, a paddling pool and two playgrounds. Also nearby is St John at Hackney Churchyard (*Lower Clapton Road, E5 0PD*), with its neat play area.

The Lowdown

🌐 **Address** 1 Reading Lane, E8 1GQ; 020 8356 3500; *www.hackney.gov.uk/museum*

🚃 **Train** Hackney Central, five-minute walk; Hackney Downs (10 minutes) **Bus stop** Mare Street

🕐 **Open** 9:30am–5:30pm Tue–Fri (Thu till 8pm); 10am–5pm Sat

💲 **Price** Free

🚩 **Guided tours** Free Tea and Tour 3pm Wed. Occasional local history walks (call to check)

🧑‍🧒 **Age range** 3 plus

🎨 **Activities** Interactive exhibits, dressing-up and toddler reading corner. Free drop-in crafts and

storytelling events in school holidays, 2–4pm Wed–Thu

⏱️ **Allow** 1 hour

♿ **Wheelchair access** Yes

🍽️ **Eat and drink** *Snacks* Caffè Theatro (316 Mare Street, E8 1HA) has cool décor, coffees and great cakes *Real meal* Tre Viet (245–249 Mare Street, E8 3NS; 020 8533 7390; noon–11pm Sun–Thu, till 11:30 Fri & Sat) is a good-value Vietnamese eatery

🛍️ **Shop** Selling books, souvenirs and pocket-money toys

🚻 **Toilets** On ground floor

⑤ Sutton House

A Tudor manor in 21st-century London

Oak panelling, echoing flagstones, roaring fires... Sutton House couldn't look more Tudor if Henry VIII himself was at the banqueting table, tossing chicken legs over his shoulder. Built in 1535 by Sir Ralph Sadler, Henry's Secretary of State, it's the last relic of the once-rural Hackney village.

There is plenty to engage kids, including the 16th-century kitchen, with food to handle and smells to sniff, and three "treasure chests" full of hands-on historical goodies – they include Elizabethan codes to crack, Jacobean jigsaws, and even a "dance mat" on which to perfect your 17th-century moves. The Sutton House stewards are ever ready to share a spine-tingling ghost story, while the mechanic's yard has been transformed into the Breaker's Yard, with an imaginative outdoor play space, an old Hackney cab, ice-cream van and art installations.

The Lowdown

- 🌐 **Address** 2 & 4 Homerton High Street, Hackney, E9 6JQ; 020 8986 2264; www.nationaltrust.org.uk/sutton-house-and-breakers-yard
- 🚃 **Train** Hackney Central, 10-minute walk; Hackney Downs, 15-minute walk **Bus stop** Homerton High Street; Lower Clapton Road; Morning Lane
- 🕑 **Open** noon–5pm Wed–Sun
- 💰 **Price** £13.60 (under-5s free)
- 🎫 **Guided tours** First Sun of month, 3pm (free)
- 👫 **Age range** 5 plus
- 🤸 **Activities** Recommended family activities at www.nationaltrust.org.uk/sutton-house-and-breakers-yard/features/top-ten-things-for-families-to-do-at-sutton-house-
- ⏱ **Allow** 2 hours
- ♿ **Wheelchair access** Yes; adapted toilet located close to entrance
- ☕ **Eat and drink** Snacks Enjoy a cup of tea, with cakes and snacks at the Georgian Tearoom, Tudor courtyard or Breaker's yard garden
- 🛍 **Shop** Selling gifts and Trust goods; also second-hand books
- 🚻 **Toilets** Close to entrance

Atmospheric 16th-century room at Sutton House

Admission is cheap by National Trust standards, and free altogether on the last Sunday of the month, when there's a family day themed on music or meals, spooks or squatters (a room of "squatter art" has been preserved from the 1980s). In the summer holidays, there might even be a jousting tournament in the courtyard.

Letting off steam

The house's play area (with picnic tables) is free to all; or head to nearby St John's Churchyard, which has a tots' playground.

⑥ Discover

A stroll in storyland

Shock! Crisis! Emergency! The planet Squiggly Diggly is running out of stories, and a friendly alien named Hootah has been sent to Earth to gather some. That's the backstory for the Discover Children's Story Centre, a one-of-a-kind walk-through wonderland of enchanted towers, secret caves and wishing trees, with lashings of dressing-up and acting-out to

help ensure a happy ending. On the Story Trail, children wander wide-eyed among £6 million-worth of multi-sensory play gear designed to spark the imagination: they might bump into a giant, dress up as a princess, sit down for a tea party, or make

The Lowdown

- 🌐 **Address** 383–387 High Street, Stratford, E15 4QZ; 020 8536 5555; www.discover.org.uk
- 🚃 **Train** Stratford (DLR and mainline trains), 5-minute walk **Tube** Stratford (Central and Jubilee lines), 5-minute walk **Bus stop** Stratford Bus Station; High Street; Stratford Centre
- 🕑 **Open** 10am–5pm Tue–Fri, 11:15am–5pm Sat (open daily during school holidays)
- 💰 **Price** £22, under-2s free
- 🏃 **Skipping the queue** Book ahead for the frequent literature and art events
- 👫 **Age range** 3–11
- 🤸 **Activities** Free storytelling sessions every weekend (11:30am, 2:30pm), and in school holidays (11:30am, 1pm, 2:30pm), plus programme of workshops (see website)
- ⏱ **Allow** 2 hours
- ♿ **Wheelchair access** Yes
- ☕ **Eat and drink** Snacks The centre's café has sandwiches and cakes **Real meal** King Edward VII (47 Broadway, Stratford, E15 4BQ; 020 8534 2313; noon–midnight Mon–Wed, to 9pm Sun) serves traditional British dishes. It is known by locals as King Eddie.
- 🛍 **Shop** Selling pocket-money toys, gifts and classic picture books
- 🚻 **Toilets** On the ground floor

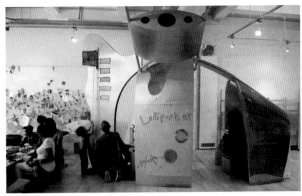
Getting hands-on and stirring imaginations at the Discover Centre

Prices given are for a family of four

Learning the Victorian way at the Ragged School Museum

a spoon puppet and put on a show. Friendly "story builders" are on hand to help them compose their own tall tales; and in case they can't quite believe it themselves, a bank of TV screens shows their progress in storyland.

There is more make-believe in the Story Garden outside, with its pirate ship, space craft, trick mirrors and giant musical instruments; while interactive shows in the Story Studio profile popular kids' characters. Weekend storytelling sessions culminate in the Big Write festival each March, which throngs with well-known writers and illustrators.

Letting off steam
The garden is one big energetic adventure, with a slide and activities.

⑦ Ragged School Museum
Back to school, Victorian style

In Victorian London, children didn't just do without toys and books, they often lacked shoes and a shirt. More than half were illiterate, and one in three funerals were for children under five. A young Dubliner, Thomas Barnardo, was so shocked by the poverty he saw in the East End, he set about rescuing orphans and setting up "ragged schools" to educate them – including this one, in a canalside warehouse in Mile End.

Today, a Victorian education is delivered here again by strict-but-fair Miss Perkins, in full 1870s garb, who scratches the alphabet on her blackboard for pupils aged five to 85. The monthly lessons are a real eye-opener for kids – especially those with poor handwriting, who

may end up standing in the corner wearing a dunce's hat.

The school has also re-created an East End kitchen from 1900, with a mangle, a tin bath and other hands-on hardware. Top marks for interactivity, but the museum must do better on opening times.

Letting off steam
Just along Rhodeswell Road lies **Mile End Park playground** (*Locksley St, Limehouse E14 7EJ*), with its castle to conquer and "riverbed" sandpit. Older kids might favour the swimming pool at Mile End Leisure Centre (*190 Burdett Road, E3 4HL; 020 8709 4420*), just opposite.

The Lowdown

🌐 **Address** 46–50 Copperfield Rd, E3 4RR; 020 8980 6405; www. raggedschoolmuseum.org.uk

🚂 **Train** Limehouse (DLR), 10-minute walk **Tube** Mile End (Central, Hammersmith & City, District lines), 10-minute walk **Bus stop** Ben Jonson Road; Burdett Road; Mile End Road

🕐 **Open** 10am–5pm Wed–Thu, plus 2–5pm first Sun of month

🎫 **Price** Free

👫 **Age range** 5 plus

🎭 **Activities** Free 45-minute history lessons (all ages), 2:15pm and 3:30pm first Sun of month. Free themed activities for under-13s, usually led by eminent Victorians, Wed–Thu in school holidays.

⏱ **Allow** 1 hour

♿ **Wheelchair access** Yes

🍽 **Eat and drink** *Snacks* Greedy Cow (*2 Grove Road, E3 5AX*) offers burgers and steaks *Real meal* The Palm Tree (*127 Grove Road, Mile End, E3 5BH; 020 8980 2918*) is a good pub for a canal-side lunch

🛍 **Shop** Selling vintage toys

🚻 **Toilets** No

Picnic under £20; **Snacks** £20–40; **Real meal** £40–60; **Family treat** £60 or more (based on a family of four)

Kenwood House and around

Aside from its Georgian mansion, Kenwood House, this locale is light on visitor attractions. But there's one compelling reason to make the train ride north: Hampstead Heath, a world of playgrounds, pools and woodland. Kenwood combines well with Golders Hill Park and lunch at The Spaniards Inn (Northern Line to Golders Green, then bus number 210). Or alight at Hampstead, pick up a picnic and hike to the Heath. Consider, too, a visit to Wembley Stadium (Jubilee Line) or the RAF Museum (Northern Line), a little further out of town.

Area of
inset map

Kenwood
House

Central
London

18 km/12 mile

Places of interest

SIGHTS
1. Kenwood House
2. Warner Bros. Studio Tour London – The Making of Harry Potter
3. RAF Museum
4. Wembley Stadium

EAT AND DRINK
1. The Hampstead Butcher
2. Golders Hill Park Refreshment House
3. The Spaniards Inn
4. Gaucho

See also Kenwood House (p216), Warner Bros. Studio Tour London – The Making of Harry Potter (p218), RAF Museum (p218), Wembley Stadium (p219)

WHERE TO STAY
1. Premier Inn, Hampstead
2. Quality Hotel Hampstead
3. La Gaffe

Enjoying the atmosphere at Wembley Stadium

Playing on the landscaped lawns around Georgian Kenwood House

Getting hands-on with the inmates of the Butterfly House, Golders Hill Park

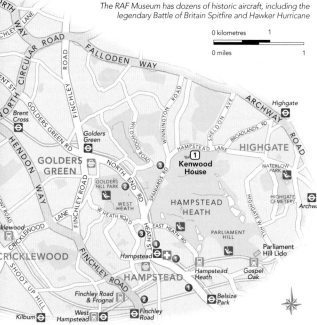

The RAF Museum has dozens of historic aircraft, including the legendary Battle of Britain Spitfire and Hawker Hurricane

0 kilometres 1

0 miles 1

The Lowdown

 Train For Hampstead Village and Parliament Hill (southern side of the Heath), take mainline trains to Gospel Oak and Hampstead Heath from Camden Road station **Tube** For Kenwood House and Highgate, take the Northern Line (High Barnet branch) to Archway, Highgate or Golders Green stations

i **Visitor information** www.lovecamden.org

Supermarkets Tesco Express, 27 Heath Street, Hampstead, NW3 6TR; Sainsbury's, 614 Finchley Road, Golders Green, NW11 7RX **Markets** Hampstead Community Market, Hampstead High Street, 10am–6pm Mon–Sat; Parliament Hill Farmers' Market, Highgate Road, 9am–2pm Sat; Archway Market, Holloway Road (crafts), 10am–5pm Sat

Festivals Hampstead Heath Easter Fair (also at May & August Bank Holidays); Proms at St Jude's (Jun); Hampstead & Highgate Literary Festival (Sep); Hampstead Heath Conker Championships (Oct)

✚ **Pharmacies** Boots, 40 Hampstead High Street, NW3 1QE (8:30am–6:30pm Mon–Sat, 11am–6pm Sun), or see www.nhs.uk/servicedirectories

Nearest playgrounds Parliament Hill (Hampstead Heath); Golders Hill Park (West Heath Avenue, NW11 7QP or North End Road, NW3 7HA); King Edward VII Park; Waterlow Park

Kite-flying on Parliament Hill, Hampstead Heath

① Kenwood House
The big house on the Heath

With its manicured lawns, ornamental lakes, stables and kitchen garden, Kenwood is a gentleman's country estate, 6 km (4 miles) from London's West End. It's an authentic slice of Georgian England, where Robert Adam's Neo-Classical interiors and Humphrey Repton's picturesque park survive more or less intact from the late 1700s. Immediately to the south stretches Hampstead Heath, a hinterland frequented by wild swimmers, kite-fliers, Frisbee-throwers and tree-climbers. It is a big blast of freedom for families.

Picnicking outside Kenwood House

Key Features

The Orangery — Dressing room — The library

The Library, with its ostentatious painted ceiling, colourful friezes and colonnades, is one of Robert Adam's masterpieces.

The Dairy, which was fashionable in that age, was built for the Earl's wife, Louisa. The three restored buildings can be visited to explore the tea room, the dairy room and the living quarters of the dairymaids.

Rembrandt self-portrait (1661) This picture is a highlight of Kenwood's collection of old masters, which also includes Vermeer's *The Guitar Player* and paintings by Hals, Turner and Gainsborough.

The Lowdown

🌐 **Address** Hampstead Lane, NW3 7JR; 020 8348 1286; *www.english-heritage.org.uk/visit/places/kenwood/*

🚆 **Train** Gospel Oak or Hampstead Heath **Tube** Golders Green (Northern line), then bus 210 or H3; or Archway (Northern line), then bus 210 **Bus stop** Hampstead Lane **Car** West Lodge car park (pay-and-display); free parking on Hampstead Lane

🕐 **Open** House: 10am–4pm daily; Estate: from 8am (closing time varies with season)

💲 **Price** Free; some temporary exhibitions charge

🪧 **Guided tours** Yes, times vary (small charge applies)

👫 **Age range** 6 plus

🏃 **Activities** Occasional holiday crafts sessions; Easter Egg trails; bat-spotting walks on summer evenings.

⏱ **Allow** Up to 2 hours

♿ **Wheelchair access** Ground floor and toilets only

☕ **Café** Set in Kenwood's servants' wing, the Brew House Cafe (020 8341 5384; 9am–5pm) serves breakfasts and lunches on the terrace; the Steward's Room serves home-baked bites, cakes, soups and sandwiches for take away only

🏷 **Shop** On the ground floor

🚻 **Toilets** On the ground floor

Good family value?
It's free, and so is the Heath

The park was remodelled in the 1790s under the guidance of Humphrey Repton. Its meandering lakeside walks are designed to spring picturesque "surprises".

Hampstead Heath

First recorded in Saxon times and once the stalking ground of highwaymen, "The Heath" still has a wild streak. A swathe of sandstone hills and wooded glades, it runs from Kenwood House in the north to Parliament Hill, its view of London protected by law. Summer kite-fliers and winter sledgers gather here; at the bottom (near Gospel Oak station), there are playgrounds, a paddling pool and a lido.

Prices given are for a family of four

Sampling the wares at Parliament Hill Farmers' Market

Letting off steam

Kenwood's own grounds have grass to sprawl on and trees to scramble up. Hampstead Heath's best playground (*9am–dusk; 020 7433 1917*) is in the far south, near the Nassington Road entrance, with a sandpit and paddling pool. There is an adventure playground for older children nearby, plus the lido swimming pool – unheated (*open 7am–6pm May–Sep, 7am–noon Sep–Apr*). Accompanied children aged eight and over can also swim in the reedy bathing ponds on the eastern fringe of Hampstead Heath. From Kenwood House, a handy playtime option is **Golders Hill Park** (*West Heath Avenue, NW11 7QP; 020 7332 3511; 7:30am–dusk*), with its petting zoo, deer, butterfly house and playground. Get there via za short bus ride from Kenwood towards Golders Green Station.

Eat and drink

Picnic: under £25; Snacks: £25–40; Real meal: £50–65; Family treat: £70 or more (based on a family of four)

PICNIC The Hampstead Butcher (*56 Rosslyn Hill, NW3 1ND; 020 7794 9210; www. hampsteadbutcher.com*) does good cold cuts, cheeses and ready-to-eat picnic hampers.
SNACKS Golders Hill Park Refreshment House (*020 8455 8010; open 9am–6pm Mon–Sat*) has a terrace, good cakes and home-made ice cream. For a café

on Hampstead Heath, try the one at Parliament Hill Fields (*off Highgate Road; 020 7485 6606; 9am–4:30pm*).
REAL MEAL The Spaniards Inn (*Spaniards Road, NW3 7JJ; 020 8731 8406, www.thespaniards hampstead.co.uk; food daily from noon*) has a large and splendid garden, a traditional British menu and barbecues and hog roasts sizzling away on summer weekends.
FAMILY TREAT Gaucho (*64 Heath Street, NW3 1DN; 020 7431 8222; www.gauchorestaurants.co.uk; noon–11pm Mon–Thu; noon– 11:30pm Fri & Sat; 10am–11:30pm Sun*), between Hampstead Tube station and the Heath, specializes in Argentine steaks that are barbecued outside in good weather.

Find out more

DIGITAL A leaflet with three walking trails on the Heath is downloadable from *www. cityoflondon.gov.uk*: click on "Green Spaces"; "Hampstead Heath"; "Visitor information", then "Trail Maps" under the "Plan Your Visit" heading.
FILM Kenwood House features prominently in the 1999 romantic comedy *Notting Hill*, starring Julia Roberts and Hugh Grant.

Next stop...

POETS' CORNER Two tiny museums south of the Heath add weight to Hampstead's reputation as a hotbed of literature and the arts. Burgh House (*New End Square, NW3 1LT; 020 7431 0144; www.burghhouse.org.uk*) is a Queen Anne mansion once frequented by Rudyard Kipling; while Keats House (*10 Keats Grove, NW3 2RR; 020 7332 3868; www. cityoflondon.gov.uk/things-to-do/ keats-house*) is where the eponymous poet wrote *Ode to a Nightingale*. Both run occasional family events.

Hampstead's 400-year-old, oak-panelled tavern, The Spaniards Inn

② Warner Bros. Studio Tour London – The Making of Harry Potter

A simply wizard tour!

Here at Warner's studio, even though there are no thrilling rides and only a few hands-on interactive gadgetry, children will be spellbound by the original scenery, costumes and props that were used in the filming of all eight Harry Potter movies.

The Making of Harry Potter studio tour is by timed ticket and is largely self-guided, though friendly and knowledgeable staff are always on hand. Among the sets en route are the iconic Great Hall at Hogwarts School of Witchcraft and Wizardry, Professor Dumbledore's study, Hagrid's hut, the Gryffindor common room and Diagon Alley, complete with Ollivanders wand shop and the Weasley brothers' joke emporium. Hagrid's motorcycle and Harry's Nimbus 2000 are also on display. Kids will be delighted to know that

Set of the Great Hall, part of the Warner Bros. Studio Tour, Leavesden Studios

they can ride broomsticks here as well. The tour also offers glimpses into the off-camera world of the film-makers, including how animatronics and green-screen effects brought the monsters and marvels of Harry's world to life.

Letting off steam

The studio has a backlot, which offers plenty of space for kids to run about in. They can also explore the Knight Bus, 4 Privet Drive and Hogwarts Bridge here.

The Lowdown

🌐 **Address** Warner Bros. Studio Tour, Studio Tour Drive, Leavesden, WD25 7LR; 0345 084 0900; www.wbstudiotour.co.uk

🚃 **Train** Watford Junction station, then shuttle buses run every 30 minutes to attraction (£2pp return) **Car** Free parking on site

🕐 **Open** Daily; first tour: 8:30am to 10am, last tour starts at 2:30pm to 7pm (varies with season); closed Dec 25 & Dec 26

💲 **Price** £126, under-4s free (tickets must be bought in advance)

🏃 **Skipping the queue** Book the earliest tour available

👫 **Age range** All ages

🎨 **Activities** Hand-held audio-visual guide available in eight languages includes facts, interviews and unseen footage (£4.95)

⏱ **Allow** 3.5 hours, arrive 20 minutes before the tour starts

♿ **Wheelchair access** Yes

🍴 **Eat and drink** *Snacks* The on-site Studio Café (*9:30am–closing time*) serves soups, salads and sandwiches; the Backlot Café is found midway through the tour

🛍 **Shop** Selling an extensive range of merchandise

🚻 **Toilets** Several throughout

③ RAF Museum

Fighter pilot playtime

Many kids want to be a fighter pilot when they grow up. Few actually make it, so here's the next best thing: a whole hangar full of interactive flying games and challenges at the Royal Air Force Museum in Hendon. Its Aeronauts Centre has 40 hands-on experiments that cunningly disguise principles of science as play: climb into a helicopter cockpit and take the controls; grab a hang-glider bar and manoeuvre through the air; or grapple with pilot aptitude tests.

Getting up close to one of the many planes on display at the RAF Museum

The Lowdown

🌐 **Address** Grahame Park Way, NW9 5LL; 020 8205 2266; www.rafmuseum.org.uk/london

🚃 **Train** Mill Hill Broadway, 15-minute walk **Tube** Colindale (Northern line), 10-minute walk **Bus stop** Grahame Park Way; Lanacre Avenue **Car** Parking on site (from £3 for 0–3 hours)

🕐 **Open** 10am–6pm (to 5pm Nov–Feb). Our Finest Hour show runs hourly, 1–5pm

💲 **Price** Free, except flight simulator (£3) and 4-D theatre (£4)

🚩 **Guided tours** Free volunteer-led tours, times vary. Audio guide to selected galleries available by download only

👫 **Age range** 4 plus; Eurofighter simulator min height 120 cm (4 ft)

🎨 **Activities** Family activity programme focuses on Commonwealth Day (Mar), Armed Forces Day (Jun) and the Battle of Britain (Sep), plus half-term holiday workshops

⏱ **Allow** Half a day

♿ **Wheelchair access** Yes, although getting in aircraft will be difficult

🍴 **Eat and drink** *Snacks* Wessex Café has helicopters and home-made snacks; *Real meal* Echo Alpha Tango serves a health-conscious kids' menu

🛍 **Shop** Selling a variety of aviation-themed gifts

🚻 **Toilets** By the entrance

The museum is spread across the former Hendon Aerodrome, the century-old birthplace of British aviation. Giant hangars house more than 100 full-size flying machines, from Sopwith Camels to cruise missiles, many suspended dogfight-style from the rafters. The Milestones of Flight gallery gives a literal overview of aircraft history from its "control tower" balcony, and other highlights include a sound and light show – Our Finest Hour – bringing alive the Battle of Britain, the a "4-D" theatre experience aboard an American B-17 bomber, and a Eurofighter Typhoon flight simulator, soaring at twice the speed of sound.

Letting off steam
There are lots of grassy picnic grounds at the museum.

④ Wembley Stadium
Ninety minutes of glory

After a controversial £750 million rebuilding, the "new" Wembley Stadium has resumed its mantle as the spiritual home of football, with 90,000 seats and a 133-m (437-ft) arch that curves like a rainbow above the North London skyline. As well as the FA Cup final each May, Wembley hosts or has hosted international rugby, American football, rock concerts and the 2012 Olympic football finals.

For footie-mad kids (and adults), a trip here is akin to a pilgrimage, and the 90-minute guided tours won't let them down. They get to follow in the footsteps of their heroes on matchday – from the England team's dressing-room and warm-up area, through the tunnel to pitch-side, where they'll be greeted by the cacophonous roar of a crowd. After a sit down in the manager's dugout, it's up the famous steps to the Royal Box for a feel of a replica FA Cup. For the adults, there's also a video of historic highlights and a look at some famous

Going behind the scenes at Wembley Stadium

Wembley relics, including the crossbar that helped England win the 1966 World Cup.

Letting off steam
Brought your own ball along? For a good kick-about, head west via Dagmar Avenue to **King Edward VII Park** *(Park Lane, Wembley, HA9 7RX)* which has grassy space, football pitches and a playground.

Out and about on the pathways of King Edward VII Park

The Lowdown

🌐 **Address** Wembley National Stadium, HA9 0WS (booking line: 0800 169 9933); *www. wembleystadium.com/ Wembley-Tours.aspx*

🚗 **Train** Wembley Stadium station. **Tube** Wembley Park (Metropolitan and Jubilee lines) **Bus stop** Olympic Way, Empire Way, Wembley Park Station **Car** Green Car Park, Engineers Way

🕐 **Open** Tours run most days (check website), departing 10am–4pm. Sometimes only a 60-minute "mini tour" is offered, missing out dressing rooms and pitch-side

🎫 **Price** £45, under-5s free

🚻 **Skipping the queue** Advance booking strongly advised; arrive 30 minutes before tour

👫 **Age range** 6 plus

👫 **Activities** Check the website's Groups and School Visits page to explore the events for children

⏱ **Allow** 2 hours

♿ **Wheelchair access** Yes

🍴 **Eat and drink** *Snacks* A café at the entrance serves sandwiches and snacks

🛍 **Shop** Selling football and Wembley souvenirs

🚻 **Toilets** At start of tour

KIDS' CORNER

Handmade Hogwarts
Keep an eye out for the amazing scale model of Hogwarts, which was created by an army of 86 artists. Had it been built by one person, it would have taken 74 years to complete! It is 24 times smaller than the real thing and was used in aerial shots for the films. See if you can spot...
• 2,500 tiny torches and lanterns flickering on and off inside
• Real plants
• Tiny model birds in the owlery
• Real hinges on every door

Is it a bird?
The RAF Museum's aircraft have all sorts of names. As you explore, score points for spotting…
• Names inspired by the wind or the weather
• Names borrowed from birds and animals.

Answers at the bottom of the page.

Wembley in numbers
1 Winning teams must climb 107 steps to collect the trophy. In the "old" Wembley, it was just 39 steps. How many more steps is that?
2 The stadium holds 90,000 fans. If there are 34,000 seats on the bottom tier and 39,000 on the top, how many people can sit in the middle tier?
3 The pitch is 105 metres long and 68 metres wide. What's its total area?

Answers at the bottom of the page.

Answers: **Is it a bird?** Some possible answers – score double points for any **Weather** Hurricane, Chinook, Tempest, Tornado **Birds and animals** Seagull, Harrier, Camel, Bulldog **Wembley in numbers 1** 68 **2** 17,000 **3** 7,140 sq m

---

Picnic under £20; **Snacks** £20–40; **Real meal** £40–60; **Family treat** £60 or more (based on a family of four)

Horniman Museum and around

If the Horniman Museum was in Central London, it would be on every family's must-see itinerary. A treasure chest of strange marvels, it has everything from voodoo charms to mummy cases, live bees to stuffed apes and a skull-covered hat. The museum is near Forest Hill, a 15-minute train ride from London Bridge station. The P4 bus route runs from the Horniman to South London's other star attraction: Dulwich Picture Gallery, whose old masters come to life at ArtPlay family workshops. Better still, walk there across Dulwich Park, where the Pavilion Café is a super sunny-day lunch option.

Picnicking on the lawns surrounding the ornate Victorian conservatory at the Horniman Museum

Enjoying a ride through Dulwich Park on the recumbent bicycles available for hire

Places of interest

SIGHTS

1. Horniman Museum and Gardens
2. Dulwich Picture Gallery
3. Crystal Palace Park

● EAT AND DRINK

1. The Teapot
2. The Pavilion Café
3. The Dartmouth Arms
4. The Herne Tavern

See also Horniman Museum and Gardens (p223), Dulwich Picture Gallery (p224) and Crystal Palace Park (p225)

Getting up close to one of the many life-size dinosaurs that lurk at Crystal Palace Park

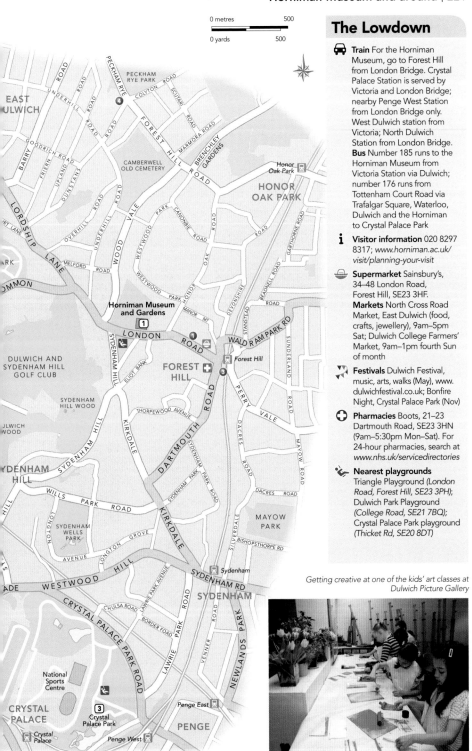

0 metres 500
0 yards 500

The Lowdown

🚗 **Train** For the Horniman Museum, go to Forest Hill from London Bridge. Crystal Palace Station is served by Victoria and London Bridge; nearby Penge West Station from London Bridge only. West Dulwich station from Victoria; North Dulwich Station from London Bridge. **Bus** Number 185 runs to the Horniman Museum from Victoria Station via Dulwich; number 176 runs from Tottenham Court Road via Trafalgar Square, Waterloo, Dulwich and the Horniman to Crystal Palace Park

ℹ️ **Visitor information** 020 8297 8317; www.horniman.ac.uk/visit/planning-your-visit

🛒 **Supermarket** Sainsbury's, 34–48 London Road, Forest Hill, SE23 3HF. **Markets** North Cross Road Market, East Dulwich (food, crafts, jewellery), 9am–5pm Sat; Dulwich College Farmers' Market, 9am–1pm fourth Sun of month

🎆 **Festivals** Dulwich Festival, music, arts, walks (May), www.dulwichfestival.co.uk; Bonfire Night, Crystal Palace Park (Nov)

➕ **Pharmacies** Boots, 21–23 Dartmouth Road, SE23 3HN (9am–5:30pm Mon–Sat). For 24-hour pharmacies, search at www.nhs.uk/servicedirectories

🤸 **Nearest playgrounds** Triangle Playground (London Road, Forest Hill, SE23 3PH); Dulwich Park Playground (College Road, SE21 7BQ); Crystal Palace Park playground (Thicket Rd, SE20 8DT)

Getting creative at one of the kids' art classes at Dulwich Picture Gallery

① Horniman Museum and Gardens
Mummies, magic amulets and a merman

A Victorian tea trader, Frederick Horniman gathered an eclectic collection of objects from across the British Empire. His museum bursts with artifacts from the wildest childhood imagination: a totem pole, magic amulets, mummies, even a merman. Apart from being child-friendly, there is the universally popular Aquarium, and the Butterfly House, opened in 2017, is home to a range of butterfly species. It also hosts some of London's most exotic "Busy Bee" play sessions, which could involve sharks' teeth, ritual masks or thumb pianos.

Goliath Beetle in the Nature Base

Key Features

▨ **First Floor** Natural History Balcony

▨ **Ground Floor** Natural History Gallery, Hands On Base, Education Centre, café and shop

▨ **Lower Ground Floor** Temporary Exhibitions, Music Gallery, African Worlds Gallery and Centenary Gallery

▨ **Basement** An aquarium reveals what lives in ponds, in coral reefs and the Amazon rainforest.

Entrance

① **Haitian voodoo shrine** This gloriously gaudy altar is loaded with strange offerings: make-up, dolls, posters, perfume, skulls. Haitians believe spirits are everywhere, even in discarded objects.

② **Igbo Ijele mask** Piled with figurines and feathers in fantastic colours, this towering mask is Africa's largest. It is worn at the lively ijele ceremony in Nigeria.

③ **Music Gallery** Touch the tabletops to hear sound clips from the dazzling instruments collection.

④ **Tlingit totem pole** Carved in cedar, the Horniman totem pole guards the entrance. It depicts the Alaskan legend of a girl who married a bear.

⑤ **Nature Base** Here you can observe a live honey bee colony, watch the scampering harvest mice and scrutinize beetles under a microscope.

⑥ **Aquarium** The aquarium features 15 displays, from a British pond to a Fijian coral reef. For kids, the seahorses are the stars.

Letting off steam

Draped across the summit of Forest Hill, with panoramic views over London, the museum's grassy grounds include award-winning display gardens, which opened in 2012. Other highlights include the historic bandstand, a picnic area, the animal walk with alpaca and rabbits and the mile-long nature trail on the site of an old railway line. For a traditional playground, cross London Road to the **Triangle**, which has a sandpit, a climbing wall and a tea kiosk.

The vast sandpit at the Triangle, opposite the Horniman Museum

Eat and drink

Picnic: under £20; Snacks: £20–40; Real meal: £40–60; Family treat: £60 or more (based on a family of four)

PICNIC The Teapot (56 London Road, SE23 3HF; 020 8699 2829) is a dapper little tearoom and deli, handily placed halfway between Forest Hill station and the museum.

SNACKS The Pavilion Café in Dulwich Park (College Road, SE21 7BQ; 020 8299 1383; 8:30am–5:30pm, weekends from 9am) is a lovely spot for coffee and home-baked cakes, and their lunchtime specials have an Italian flavour.

REAL MEAL The Dartmouth Arms (7 Dartmouth Road, SE23 3HN; 020 8488 3117; www.thedartmoutharms. com; food served noon–3:30pm, 6pm–9:30pm Mon–Fri, noon–9:30pm Sat, noon–4pm & 5–9pm Sun) is a friendly gastro-pub with several dishes available in smaller portions, ideal for kids. It is near Forest Hill station.

Prices given are for a family of four

The Lowdown

Address 100 London Road, Forest Hill, SE23 3PQ; 020 8699 1872; *www.horniman.ac.uk*

Train Forest Hill, 10-minute walk **Bus stop** London Road; Sydenham Hill

Open 10:30am–5:30pm daily; gardens 7:15am–sunset Mon–Sat, from 8am Sun

Price Free. Aquarium £22; some temporary exhibitions charge

Skipping the queue Busy Bee tickets available at 10:45am, 11:30am & 12:15pm on Wed & Fri, 12:30pm at weekends

Age range 3 plus

Activities Free family activities every weekend afternoon: mix of drop-in "discovery for all" sessions (2–3:30pm) and ticketed art workshops and object-handling (11am, 11:45am, 12:30pm, 1–1:45pm, 1:30–2:15pm, 2:45–3:30pm). Free family storytelling every first Sunday of month (2:15pm & 3:30pm). Frequent sessions on school holiday weekdays, too (check website). Half-hour Busy Bee crafts and story sessions for under-5s every Tue and Wed (10:45am, 11:30am & 12:15pm). Download age-graded activity sheets and learning packs before visiting at: *www.horniman.ac.uk*

Allow At least half a day

Wheelchair access Yes, both museum and gardens

Café The museum's café (9:30am–5pm)has excellent variety for kids; on a sunny day, eat in the ornate Victorian conservatory

Shop Selling toys, musical instruments and books inspired by the museum's collection

Toilets By café and on Lower Ground Floor

Good family value?
Absolutely tremendous. Unlike many London museums, even the café is affordable.

This stuffed walrus dominates the Natural History Gallery

FAMILY TREAT The Herne Tavern *(2 Forest Hill Road, SE22 0RR; 020 8299 9521; www.theherne tavern.co.uk; noon–9pm Tue–Sat; noon–8pm Sun)* is more restaurant than pub, with a children's menu of macaroni and cheese, chicken breast and fries, haddock and fries. It's at East Dulwich: take the 363 bus from the Horniman.

Find out more
DIGITAL The museum's official website *(www.horniman.ac.uk)* has activity packs and trails, including "Animal Fair", "Sea Shapes" and an interactive "Music Gallery".

For behind-the-scenes footage from the Horniman, including an X-ray view of its famous "merman", visit the museum's YouTube channel *(www.youtube.com/user/horniman)*. Find the Horniman on Facebook and Twitter *(@HornimanMuseum)* and follow the walrus himself *(@HornimanWalrus)*.

Next stop...
CRYSTAL PALACE PARK Head here for an afternoon of fun amoung the dinosaurs and playgrounds, or visit the Sports Centre in wet weather.

② Dulwich Picture Gallery

Old masters and leafy grounds

With its cloistered gardens, chapel and mausoleum, this looks precisely the kind of place that wouldn't welcome children, but appearances can be deceptive. London's oldest public gallery is crammed with priceless portraits – from 17th-century saints to 18th-century courtesans – which were gathered in the 1790s for the King of Poland, who was deposed in 1795, leaving his new collection homeless. Architect Sir John Soane (see p94) stepped in, and with his interlinked halls lit by skylights, created the template for art galleries the world over. There are works by Canaletto, Constable, Raphael and Rubens here – and free drawing trails help visitors to unpick their secrets.

The real joy for families, though, is the inspiring array of hands-on art classes that are offered here. On the first and last Sundays of the

The Lowdown

🌐 **Address** Gallery Road, SE21 7AD; 020 8693 5254; www. dulwichpicturegallery.org.uk

🚗 **Train** North Dulwich or West Dulwich, both a 10-minute walk away **Bus stop** College Road; Dulwich College

🕐 **Open** 10am–5pm Tue–Sun (last admission 4:30pm)

💷 **Price** £14, under-18s free; temporary exhibitions extra

👫 **Skipping the queue** Book half-term and after-school courses in advance: 020 8299 8732

👣 **Guided tours** 3pm Sat and Sun (free); multimedia iGuide (£3)

👫 **Age range** 8 plus

👫 **Activities** A range of fun activities for families are offered at www. dulwichpicturegallery.org.uk/learning/for-families/

⏱ **Allow** 1–2 hours

♿ **Wheelchair access** Yes

🍴 **Eat and drink** Real meal The Café offers a full lunch menu (noon–3pm) and picnic boxes for kids. It opens at 8am Tue–Sat and from 9:30am Sun Snacks The Pavilion Café in Dulwich Park (see p222) is also a good bet

🛍 **Shop** Selling art-related gifts, books and toys

🚻 **Toilets** On the ground floor

Left Hanging out paintings to dry at Dulwich Picture Gallery
Below Enjoying the playground in Dulwich Park

month, drop-in ArtPlay sessions encourage grown-ups and their children to work creatively together – drawing cartoons, making bunting or block-printing, perhaps. There is more of the same every Wednesday afternoon in summer, when the gallery gardens are transformed into a giant arty picnic. There are also half-term workshops for ages 6–11, and after-school art clubs for 7–18s.

The 15-minute zip out of town to leafy Dulwich Village feels like a magical journey into the heart of the countryside, and once sated with old masters, children get to cross the road into attractive Dulwich Park, with its boating lake, bike hire and adventure playground.

Letting off steam

The gallery gardens are open for picnics and playtime – no "keep off the grass signs" here. **Dulwich Park** (020 8693 8635; www. southwark.gov.uk/parks-and-open-spaces/parks/dulwich-park) has a playground, cycle hire (020 8299 6636; www.londonrecumbents. co.uk/bikes_we_hire.html#dul; 10am–5pm, last hire 4pm) and turn-up-and-play tennis.

③ Crystal Palace Park

The land that time forgot

Television, theme parks and the Girl Guides – a fine trio of inventions, especially if you happen to be a child, and all were hatched here in one of London's most history-packed parks. So it's great that Crystal Palace may finally get a new lease of life after years in the doldrums, with plans for a makeover that will restore it to something like the popular pomp of its Victorian heyday.

The park was created by master gardener Joseph Paxton (1803–65) to house his mammoth Crystal Palace, which was moved here pane by pane from Hyde Park after hosting the 1851 Great Exhibition. Perched on a ridge overlooking the city, it had extensive pleasure grounds and fountains higher than Nelson's Column, and thousands flocked to visit. However, the Crystal Palace burnt down in 1936: look out for its ghostly terraces, and the odd statue of a sultan or sphinx. But one

Dinosaur-spotting in the Dinosaur Court at Crystal Palace Park

of the park's original wonders is still a huge draw for families – its Dinosaur Court, an army of 30 life-size prehistoric monsters that stalk the boating lake. Installed in 1853 by the sculptor Benjamin Waterhouse Hawkins and the pioneering palaeontologist Richard Owen, these models were a sensation in their day, prefiguring Darwin's *Origin of the Species* and staking a claim for Crystal Palace as the world's first "theme park".

Pick up a guide from the park information centre and go hunting for iguanodons and pterodactyls – dino-mad kids will enjoy pointing out the anatomical errors exposed by 150 years of science. The nearby children's playground boasts a dinosaur climbing frame, and the park also has a small farmyard with alpacas and a reptile room, plus one of the biggest hedge mazes in the country. Add the indoor facilities at the sports centre, the spiritual home of British athletics, and there's easily enough to warrant a train ride out from the city centre. In future, with makeover– the Crystal Palace masterplan promises tropical glasshouses, a treetop walkway, even a revival for one of Paxton's 1850s fountains.

Take cover

The park is dominated by the **National Sports Centre** (Ledrington Road, SE19 2BB; 020 8778 0131; www.better.org.uk/leisure-centre/london/crystal-palace), which has an Olympic-size indoor swimming pool, tennis courts and a climbing wall. The centre's training pool is reserved for 2-hour family-only swimming most days. Alternatively,

visit the museum that tells the story of Paxton's original Crystal Palace (020 8676 0700; www. crystalpalacemuseum.org.uk; open 11am–3pm, Sundays and bank holidays only).

The Lowdown

- 🌐 **Address** Crystal Palace Park, Thicket Road, SE20 8DT; 020 8313 4471; www.bromley.gov.uk. Access via Thicket Rd, Crystal Palace Park Rd and Ledrington Rd
- 🚗 **Train** Crystal Palace, 2-minute walk; Penge West, 5-minute walk
  Bus stop Crystal Palace Station; Penge West Station
- 🕐 **Open** 7:30am–dusk Mon–Fri, from 9am Sat & Sun (to 9pm May–Aug). Information Centre (near Thicket Road entrance) open 9am–5:30pm Mon–Fri
- 💲 **Price** Free
- 🚩 **Guided tours** Dinosaur trail leaflet from information centre, which has a small history display
- 🧍‍♂️🧍‍♀️ **Age range** All
- 🏃 **Activities** Playground and dinosaur area near Thicket Road gate, plus hedge maze (free). Most weekends, keepers at Crystal Palace Park Farm (noon–4pm Mon, Tue & Thu–Sun; 020 8659 2557). Ranger-led pond-dipping and Easter egg hunts in school holidays (call to check). National Sports Centre hosts school holiday activity or sports schools (ages 6–15; www.gll.org/holidayactivities)
- 🕓 **Allow** Up to half a day
- ♿ **Wheelchair access** Yes
- 🍽️ **Eat and drink** Snacks Park café (Thicket Road entrance; 020 8776 5422; 9am–seasonal closing) offers fast food, snacks and drinks
- 🚻 **Toilets** Near Thicket Road entrance

Kew Gardens and around

Glossy, well-groomed and handily located at the end of the District line, Richmond and Kew offer a breath of fresh air for families overcome by the pace of the city. Kids will delight in the gardens' attractions and they will love Richmond Park – especially its deer. For Kew, alight at the tube station, pick up a picnic and tour the gardens on the Explorer Bus. For Richmond Park, take bus number 65 or 371 from Richmond station. Several stately homes are close, too: try the riverside walk from Richmond to haunted Ham House.

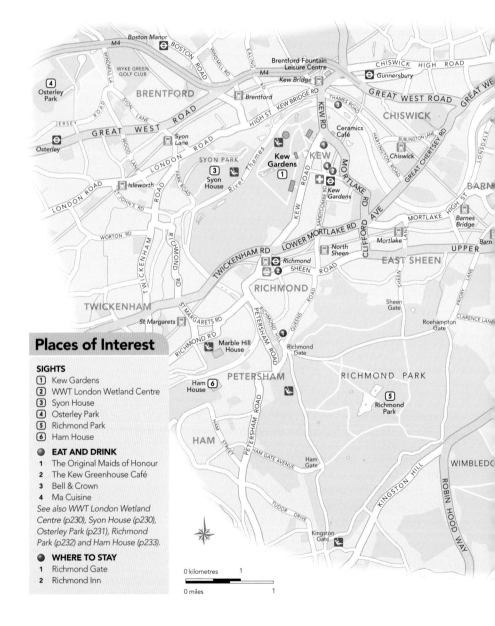

Places of Interest

SIGHTS

1. Kew Gardens
2. WWT London Wetland Centre
3. Syon House
4. Osterley Park
5. Richmond Park
6. Ham House

● **EAT AND DRINK**

1. The Original Maids of Honour
2. The Kew Greenhouse Café
3. Bell & Crown
4. Ma Cuisine

See also WWT London Wetland Centre (p230), Syon House (p230), Osterley Park (p231), Richmond Park (p232) and Ham House (p233).

● **WHERE TO STAY**

1. Richmond Gate
2. Richmond Inn

0 kilometres 1

0 miles 1

Above *The Great Conservatory at Syon House*
Right *Delicious treats on display at The Original Maids of Honour*

Above *Interactive play area, Climbers and Creepers, at Kew Gardens*

Youngsters riding ponies through Richmond Park

The Lowdown

 Train Kew Bridge and Richmond, both served by trains from Waterloo (via Barnes). Richmond and Kew Gardens (North London Line) **Tube** Kew Gardens, Richmond (both District Line)

i **Visitor information** 020 8891 1411; *www.visitrichmond.co.uk*

 Supermarkets Waitrose, 4 Sheen Road, Richmond, TW9 1AE. **Markets** Richmond Foodies' Market, Heron Square, 11am–3pm Sat; *http://duckpondmarket.com/#richmond-foodies*

Festivals Kew The Music picnic concerts (July); Richmond Riverside On The Edge Festival, world music and dance (Aug); Great River Race, finish point (Sep); Richmond Literature Festival (Nov; *www.richmondliterature.com*)

Pharmacies Lloyds, 19–21 Station Parade, Kew, TW9 3PS (8:30am–7pm Mon–Fri, 9am–6pm Sat, 10am–2pm Sun). For 24-hour pharmacies, search at *www.nhs.uk/servicedirectories*

Nearest playgrounds Climbers and Creepers, Kew Gardens (*near Brentford Gate*); Petersham Gate, Richmond Park (*Petersham Rd, TW10 5HS*); Marble Hill Adventure Playground, Marble Hill Park (*Richmond Rd, TW1 2NL*)

① Kew Gardens
The world's most famous garden

Founded in the year 1759, the Royal Botanic Gardens – a treasure trove of lakes, mini-temples, nature trails and playgrounds – is a delightful place to spend time. Kew's Victorian glasshouses offer a botanical world tour, but even better is just dawdling in the dappled glades around Queen Charlotte's Cottage, or admiring the peacocks at the Waterlily Pond. Little visitors can burrow in a badger sett and climb into the treetops – and if that doesn't tire them out, there's an exhilarating plant-themed playhouse.

Oriental Pagoda

Key Features

① **Treetop Walkway** Clamber into the branches of Kew's arboretum for giddying views. The walkway is designed to sway in the wind.

② **Palm House** The tropical plants here drip in the steamy atmosphere of Kew's hottest glasshouse. In the basement aquarium, don 3-D glasses and go "swimming with plankton".

③ **Temperate House** The world's biggest Victorian glasshouse is also home to the world's tallest "house plant", reached via ornate iron balconies.

④ **Climbers and Creepers** Fall prey to the slippery pitcher plant or wriggle into a field-mouse nest in this ingenious indoor playground. Outside, the Treehouse Towers has a zip-wire and rope bridges.

Brentford Gate

Elizabeth Gate

Victoria Gate

Lion Gate

Queen Charlotte's Cottage

Waterlily Pond

⑦ **Badger Sett** Expect muddy kneecaps after a crawl inside this child-size badgers' home. Nearby, the Nature Hide and Stag Beetle Loggery explore more native wildlife.

⑤ **Evolution House** Waterfalls crash and insects hum on this trip through primordial swamps back to the age of the dinosaurs. Watch out for monster millipedes!

⑥ **Princess of Wales Conservatory** Look out for Venus flytraps and the world's largest flower in one of 10 climatic zones. Portholes give a close-up view of the fishponds.

Take cover

Kew's glasshouses, aquariums and indoor playroom offer rainy-day diversions – plus there's a toddler corner in the White Peaks Shop. On nearby Kew Green, the Ceramics Café offers drop-in pottery painting (1A Mortlake Terrace, TW9 3DT; 020 8332 6661, www.ceramicscafe.com/studio -locations/kew; 10am–6pm Tue–Sun), while just south of Kew Gardens, Pools on the Park (Twickenham Rd, Richmond, TW9 2SF; www.richmond. gov.uk/pools_on_the_park) has indoor and outdoor pools (from 6:30am Mon–Fri; 8am Sat & 7am Sun; closing times vary, check website).

Eat and drink

Picnic: under £25; Snacks: £25–45; Real meal: £45–65; Family treat: £60 or more (based on a family of four)

PICNIC The Original Maids of Honour (288 Kew Road, Kew, TW9 3DU; 020 8940 2752, https://

"Maids of Honour" pastries, which gave the popular Kew bakery its name

theoriginalmaidsofhonour.co.uk; 8am–6pm Mon–Fri; from 8:30am Sat & Sun) is a Kew institution, said to date back to Tudor times. It offers tearoom treats, smart lunches and pre-packed picnics of varying extravagance.

SNACKS The Kew Greenhouse Café (1 Station Parade, Richmond TW9 3PS; 020 8940 0183, http:// thekewgreenhousecafe.com; 8am– 5:30pm) is a traditional English café, between the Tube and Victoria Gate, serving pies, quiches, eggs on toast and home-made cakes.

REAL MEAL Bell & Crown (11–13 Thames Road, Strand on the Green

Prices given are for a family of four

The Lowdown

🌐 **Address** Royal Botanic Gardens, Kew, Richmond, Surrey, TW9 3AB; 020 8332 5000; www.kew.org

🚃 **Train** Kew Gardens, 5-minute walk; or Kew Bridge, 10 minutes **Tube** Kew Gardens (District Line) **Bus stop** Kew Gardens, Kew Bridge Station **Car** Parking at Brentford Gate (£6.50 per day) **River bus** Kew Pier, Apr–Sep, four services daily to and from Westminster (020 7930 2062; www.wpsa.co.uk)

🕐 **Open** Apr–Aug: 10am–6:30pm; Sep–Oct: 10am–6pm; Oct–Jan: 10am–4:15pm; Feb–Mar: 10am–5:30pm. Last admission 30 minutes earlier, weekends close an hour later; Evolution House: closed for renovation (check website for details)

💲 **Price** £37.50; under-4s free

🚩 **Guided tours** Explorer Land Train tours the gardens between 11am–3pm (duration 40 minutes, £10–13). Free walking tours daily from Victoria Plaza, 11am and 1:30pm; plus themed tours

🧍 **Age range** All

🏃 **Activities** Climbers and Creepers

(ages 3–9); Treehouse Towers (up to 11). Kids' Kew guidebook (£3.95) has stickers and garden trails. Tropical Extravaganza festival in February (orchids etc); Kew the Music picnic concerts in July

⏱ **Allow** Up to a day

♿ **Wheelchair access** Mostly. Aquarium and top-level galleries not accessible, but garden paths and most buildings are. Explorer Bus can take one wheelchair.

☕ **Café** The Orangery is self-service, with children's portions and afternoon teas; White Peaks Café serves simpler family fare and ice cream next to the play area; Victoria Plaza Café sells sandwiches and snacks. In summer, Pavilion Restaurant has outdoor BBQ and salad buffet. All offer a kids' lunchbox

🛍 **Shop** Selling plant-related and cookery items; children's toy/gift shop near play area

🚻 **Toilets** At main attractions

Good family value? Free admission for under-17s, and there's almost nothing to pay for once inside.

W4 3PL; 020 8994 4164; www.bell-and-crown.co.uk; food: 11am–11pm Mon–Sat, noon–10:30pm Sun) is one of a pleasant strip of popular riverside pubs just across Kew Bridge that boast good pub grub for families.
FAMILY TREAT Ma Cuisine (The Old Post Office, 9 Station Approach, Kew, TW9 3QB; 020 8332 1923, www.macuisine bistrot.co.uk; 11am–10pm Sun–Thu, till 10:30pm Fri & Sat) is a neat French bistro with a very relaxed and welcoming

atmosphere, as well as a Michelin Bib Gourmand for its authentic French food.

Find out more

DIGITAL Check the website www.kew.org/visit-kew-gardens/explore/kids-kew for various attractions and activities for kids up to 10 years of age.

....

Next stop...

KEW PALACE Inside the Royal Botanic Gardens is a playhouse of princesses. Kew Palace (0844 482 7777; www.hrp.org.uk/kewpalace; 10am–5:30pm, from 11am Mon; late Mar–early Oct) looks like an overgrown doll's house – which is apt, since it was bought by King George III as a nursery for his children. It is the smallest surviving royal palace, and its highlights include a 200-year-old "baby house" built by the Georgian princesses themselves. Admission charge is included in the ticket to Kew Gardens.

The "Flying fox" zipwire at Treetop Towers, outside Climbers and Creepers

② WWT London Wetland Centre

London's best duck pond

Opened in 2000, London Wetland Centre has been a conservation triumph – an ugly-duckling pond site transformed into a beautiful wilderness of lagoons and pasture just 6 km (4 miles) from Westminster. Thousands of waterbirds live here, including exotic duck species such as grey-and-gold feathered wigeons, which graze the fields like sheep; and shovelers, which swim in manic circles to create a vortex to bring their food to the surface.

The indoor Discovery Centre is all about engaging children, with its underwater pond camera and poo-shooting exhibit, demonstrating how reed beds filter dirty water. The all-action adventure playground has frogs to bounce on and rubber ducks to race, and kids can wander out into the wetlands to watch for

Whistling ducks by the water at the London Wetland Centre

water voles or otters and admire the reserve's eco-friendly lawnmowers – a trio of cute frizzy-wigged highland cattle. There is warden-led bird feeding each afternoon, while the family events programme fills every weekend and school holiday with nestbox-building, pond safaris and (at Easter) egg candling – a fascinating glimpse inside a duck egg as it develops. But what young ones will appreciate most, perhaps, is the immense feeling of space, and the glorious London skyline stretched across a far horizon.

Take cover

The interactive Discovery Centre, pond zone and "bird airport" observatory offer at least an hour's weatherproof entertainment.

Little dippers looking for waterborne wildlife at the London Wetland Centre

The Lowdown

🌐 **Address** Queen Elizabeth's Walk, Barnes, SW13 9WT; 020 8409 4400; www.wwt.org.uk/wetland-centres/london/

🚃 **Train** Barnes or Barnes Bridge, 15-minute walk. **Tube** Hammersmith, then number 283 bus. **Bus stop** Wetland Centre or Red Lion. **Car** Free parking on site

🕐 **Open** Mar–Oct: 9:30am–5:30pm; Nov–Feb: 9:30am–4:30pm (last admission 1 hour earlier)

💷 **Price** £29–32, under-4s free

🚩 **Guided tours** 11am, 2pm (free), plus noon at weekends

👫 **Age range** All

🏃 **Activities** Bird feeding 3pm daily; otter feeding 11am & 2pm. Free family activities (30–60 mins) weekends and holidays, plus Animal Discovery weekends. Occasional evening bat walks (age 8 plus, £10 per person).

🕐 **Allow** Half a day

♿ **Wheelchair access** Yes, apart from Wildside Hide (steps)

🍴 **Eat and drink** *Snacks* Water's Edge Café sells cakes and hot lunches ; same hours as that of centre

🛍 **Shop** Selling books, eco items, bird feeders/boxes and souvenirs

🚻 **Toilets** Ground floor near café and in the car park

③ Syon House

Costume drama heaven

Gleaming like a gold ingot beside the Thames, this is outer London's last bastion of aristocratic England – still home to the Dukes of Northumberland after more than 400 years. It's easy to imagine the house as a stage set, and on the big screen it has starred in both *Gosford Park* and *The Madness of King George*. Meanwhile, its stellar cast of real-life characters includes Henry VIII and Sir Walter Raleigh, Indian chiefs and Gunpowder Plotters.

Explore the epic suite of rooms designed for the first duke by Robert Adam (1728–92), who gave him the gilded gods, silk hangings and wedding-cake ceilings he had seen in Neo-Classical Italy. There is also the domed Great Conservatory – so grand it inspired Joseph Paxton's Crystal Palace (see pp224–5) – and the extensive grounds landscaped by "Capability" Brown (1716–83). For kids, the ornamental arboretum is especially bewitching during Syon's

The Neo-Classical Northumberland family dining room at Syon House

The Lowdown

🌐 **Address** Brentford, Middlesex, TW8 8JF; 020 8560 0882; www.syonpark.co.uk

🚃 **Train** Kew Bridge, then bus 237 or 267; or Brentford, then 15-minute walk. **Tube** Gunnersbury (District line) then bus 237 or 267. **Bus stop** Brent Lea. **Car** Free car park

🕐 **Open** House: mid-Mar–Oct: 11am–5pm Wed Thu, Sun (last admission 4pm); Gardens: 10:30am–5pm daily

💷 **Price** £28, under-5s free

🚩 **Guided tours** Occasional guided garden walks

👫 **Age range** 8 plus

🏃 **Activities** Garden cinema, Aug; Enchanted Woodland evening openings, Nov; craft fairs

🕐 **Allow** Up to 2 hours

♿ **Wheelchair access** Garden paths are accessible, as is ground floor of the house (via chair lift)

🍴 **Eat and drink** *Snacks* Refectory Café sells a range of snacks and light lunches.

🛍 **Shop** Small gift shop and garden centre

🚻 **Toilets** On the ground floor

The Great Conservatory at Syon House, built of gunmetal, Bath stone and glass

"Enchanted Woodland" season, when it twinkles with more than 1,000 lights. Younger children can be humoured with the promise of a romp at Snakes and Ladders, a soft-play centre in the grounds.

Letting off steam

Syon House has extensive gardens as well as a lake that is a haven for a variety of wildlife. There is also an ice house, which was in use in 1760–61. At that time it took two days to fill it with ice from the lake. The ice was used to make desserts such as ice creams and sorbets.

④ Osterley Park

A very big banker's bonus

In 1761, when wealthy banker Sir Francis Child wanted a flashy new look for his family pile at Osterley Park, there was only one man to call – the style guru extraordinaire, Robert Adam. He didn't just add a Roman portico, stuccoed stairways and the 40-m (131-ft) Long Gallery to the Elizabethan mansion, he

designed new carpets, new furniture, fireplaces and ceilings. The result is a "palace of palaces", a glimpse of how Britain's super-rich bankers lived 250 years ago.

What's great for children is that the rooms "below stairs" at Osterley remain pretty intact, too: in the vaulted servants' hall, they can get to grips with antique kitchen gear, don servants' mob caps and aprons, and watch spooky film projections of Georgian maids and footmen at work. A hand-held audio-visual guide just for kids stars Tweeny the serving girl, who leads the way from room to room, filling fireplaces and fetching water. Osterley's panoramic parkland is open daily all year round – but aim to visit on one of the monthly family discovery days, when it's busy with history trails, crafts and stories.

Letting off steam

The beautiful lake-filled park is prime picnic country: pick up a walks leaflet from the house.

The magnificent mansion at Osterley Park, seen from across the Garden Lake

The Lowdown

🌐 **Address** Jersey Road, Isleworth, Middlesex TW7 4RD; 020 8232 5050; www.nationaltrust.org.uk/osterley-park-and-house

🚂 **Train** Isleworth, 30-minute walk **Tube** Osterley (Piccadilly line), 15-minute walk **Bus stop** Jersey Road (number H28); Hammersmith (H91, 15-minute walk) **Car** Parking £7

🕐 **Open** House Mar–Oct: 11am–5pm daily (till 3:30pm Mar); Nov–mid Dec: noon–3:30pm Sat & Sun (last admission 1 hour earlier). Garden Mar–Oct: 10am–5pm daily; Nov: noon–3:30pm Sat & Sun (last admission: 4:30pm). Park 8am–7:30pm daily

💲 **Price** House and garden: £24.75; park free

🎫 **Guided tours** Audiovisual guide includes family trail; occasional themed tours and parkland walks (charges apply, see website)

👫 **Age range** 6 plus

👫 **Activities** Family Discovery Days last Sun of month, noon–4pm; children's activities on Thu pm in school holidays, 1–4pm; both free with admission

🕐 **Allow** 2 hours

♿ **Wheelchair access** No

☕ **Eat and drink** *Snacks* Stables Café *(10am–5pm daily)* serves home-cooked lunches and teas

🛍 **Shop** Selling gifts; also a farm shop selling flowers and vegetables

🚻 **Toilets** Close to stableyard

⑤ Richmond Park
Hills, hinds and Henry VIII

Gibbet Wood, Bone Copse, Leg of Mutton Pond… the names of the natural features in this park are rich with romance and they describe the place well: it is the wildest tract of country in London. Richmond is the largest royal park and remains much the same as when Charles I put a 13-km (8-mile) wall around it in 1637 and 2,000 deer were released for him to hunt. Some of the oak trees the king knew are here still, and so are the deer: 650 reds and fallows, a great draw for children – though it's best not to get too close, especially during the autumn rut, when they spar for supremacy.

The best way in for families is from Richmond, for the playground at Petersham Gate and Pembroke Lodge Café, set in a Georgian mansion. Walk off the cakes with a hike up Henry VIII's Mound to take in the view to St Paul's Cathedral: some say the king stood watch here for the signal that his marriage to Anne Boleyn had been terminally severed.

A colourful performance at the Polka Theatre in Wimbledon

There is year-round cycle hire inside Roehampton Gate, on the east side, and the park's other sporting options include power-kiting, horse riding and fishing in Pen Ponds. Isabella Plantation, with its azaleas and maze of streams and bridges, looks sensational in spring and autumn, and the hide-and-seek potential goes on for miles.

Take cover

Take the 493 bus from Richmond or Roehampton to the **Wimbledon Lawn Tennis Museum** (Church Rd, SW19 5AE; 020 8946 6131; www.wimbledon.com/visiting/museum; 10am–5pm daily; £42–80, under-5s free, stadium tours included in higher prices), which has interactive exhibits, including the "ghost" of John McEnroe. Or stay on the bus and visit the **Polka Theatre** (240 The Broadway, Wimbledon SW19 1SB; 020 8543 4888; www.polkatheatre. com; 9:30am–4:30pm Wed–Fri, from 10am Sat & Sun; book ahead - check website) for under-14s, with a busy roster of live drama (Wed–Sun), a playground and a dressing-up corner with rocking horses and storybooks.

Above *Children's playground near Petersham Gate, Richmond Park*
Below *Magnificent male red deer under the trees at Richmond Park*

The Lowdown

- 🌐 **Address** Holly Lodge, Richmond Park, Richmond, TW10 5HS; 0300 061 2200; www.royalparks. org.uk/parks/richmond-park

- 🚗 **Train** Richmond, then bus 65 or 371; or Norbiton, then 15-minute walk to Kingston Gate **Tube** Richmond (District Line), then bus. **Bus stop** North side: 33, 190, 337, 391, 419, 485, R68. South: 85, 263, K3. East: 72, 493. West: 65, 371 **Car** Six free car parks

- 🕐 **Open** Park: from 7am Mar–Sep; from 7:30am Oct–Feb (closes half an hour before dusk). Park office: open weekdays 8:30am–4pm. Visitor centre: Pembroke Lodge (Richmond Gate) open 10am–4pm Fri–Sun (till 3pm Nov–Feb)

- 🎟 **Price** Free

- 🚩 **Guided tours** Free garden walks and history rambles most months (dates vary, check website)

- 🧍 **Age range** All

- 🤸 **Activities** Playgrounds at Petersham and Kingston Gates. Cycle hire at Roehampton Gate (10am–5pm Mon–Fri, till 7pm weekends and school holidays; from £4 per hour; 0705 020 9249; www.parkcycle.co.uk). Power-kiting lessons (020 7870 7700; www.kitevibe.com); fishing permits (Jun–Mar; 020 8940 3209); pay-and-play golf (020 8876 1795); for riding stables, see park website

- ⏱ **Allow** Up to a day

- ☕ **Eat and drink** *Snacks* The park's Roehampton Café (9am–5pm daily) sells snacks and ice creams. Plus kiosks at Broomfield Hill and Pen Ponds. *Real meal* Pembroke Lodge Café in the park (020 8940 8207; summer: 10am–5:30pm; winter till dusk) has a full restaurant menu, with children's dishes, and outdoor seating

- 🚻 **Toilets** All main gates

⑥ Ham House

The most haunted house in London?

With its riverside gardens, children's treasure map and gaggle of ghosts, it's hard to think of a more appetizing stately home for families than Ham House. The main draw is its dreamy setting, with lawns running down to an especially bucolic stretch of the Thames. The house itself is a time capsule, little changed since the 1670s, when the ruthless and beautiful Duchess of Lauderdale schemed her way to the top of Stuart society. A prime mover in the secret Sealed Knot society, which restored Charles II to the throne, the duchess filled Ham's halls with exuberant furniture and art.

What will interest kids, though, is not the duchess's legacy, but the fact she may still be in residence. Staff and visitors sometimes hear the tap-tap-tap of her silver cane and glimpse her King Charles spaniel scampering along the corridors. Regular ghost tours complement an imaginative spread of children's stuff here: a dedicated Discovery Room, complete with treasure map for investigating the house; garden trails; and al fresco storytelling, cinema and theatre every summer.

On sunny days, walk to Ham from Richmond station along the Thames Path (download the route at www. nationaltrust.org.uk/hamhouse) or hop on the historic foot-ferry across to the north bank, where Marble Hill House (Richmond Rd, Twickenham, TW1 2NL; 020 8892 5115; www. english-heritage.org.uk/visit/places/ marble-hill-house/) shimmers like a mirage above the water. A Palladian mansion, Marble Hill has a weekend programme for families.

Letting off steam

Children can run wild in the garden's labyrinthine wilderness of hedges and summerhouses.

The Lowdown

🌐 **Address** Ham Street, Richmond, TW10 7RS; 020 8940 1950; www. nationaltrust.org.uk/hamhouse

🚗 **Train** St Margarets or Twickenham, then 10-minute walk and foot ferry (10am–6pm or dusk, Feb–Oct, plus winter weekends); Richmond, then 30-minute riverside walk, or bus 65 or 371 **Tube** Richmond (District Line) **Bus stop** Ham Street, Sandpits Road **Car** Free parking nearby

🕐 **Open** Apr–Oct: noon–4pm daily; Feb, Mar and Nov: guided tours only, 11:30am–3:30pm. Garden, shop and café: 10am–5pm daily

💲 **Price** House and garden: £27.

🎫 **Guided tours** hourly tours from noon–3pm in Feb, Mar and Nov only: 30-minute tours of selected rooms. Garden tours all year round (call for times). "Servants' Tours", Apr–Oct, Tue (charged)

👫 **Age range** All

🏃 **Activities** Interactive Discovery Room, quiz trail and garden trails. Art Cart craft activities Apr–Oct, Sun. Occasional family ghost tours (ages 5 plus; book ahead). Easter egg hunts; summer cinema and theatre in the gardens; Christmas events for families

🕐 **Allow** 2 hours

♿ **Wheelchair access** Limited: steps and narrow doorways inside – lift available; gravel paths outside

🍴 **Eat and drink** Snacks The luscious Orangery Café does its own baking, and has a kids' corner

🎁 **Shop** Selling local and unusual gifts and souvenirs

🚻 **Toilets** In courtyard

The beautifully kept kitchen garden at Ham House

Picnic under £20; **Snacks** £20–40; **Real meal** £40–60; **Family treat** £60 or more (based on a family of four)

Day Trips

London packs in enough history for several cities – but to really breathe the atmosphere of Henry VIII's England, nowhere beats Hampton Court Palace. Families get to dress, act and even eat and drink the period. Windsor, by contrast, is all about the modern monarchy, with a majestic castle, parkland, a school for princes and one of Britain's best theme parks. Do what the Queen does and come for the whole weekend.

Highlights

Play the king
Hampton Court's live history experience includes free cloaks, so kids can dress up and explore Henry VIII's magnificent home (see pp236–7).

Eat like a Tudor
The palace kitchens regularly re-create dishes from 500 years ago – sometimes available to try at the Tiltyard Café (see p237).

Get lost!
People have been losing themselves in Hampton Court Maze for 300 years, and three new forks have made it more fiendish than ever (see p236).

See monarchy in miniature
Displayed at Windsor Castle, Queen Mary's Dolls' House is an exquisite creation and the world's most opulent – a snapshot of royal life in the 1920s (see p238).

Ride with the royals
The royal family love riding in Windsor Great Park. In the absence of horses, saddle up and explore by hiring bicycles from Windsor (see p239).

Visit toyland
Windsor's Legoland is totally geared for pre-teens, with its "pink-knuckle" roller coasters and splashing water rides (see p241).

Left As well as thrilling rides, there are tamer entertainments at Legoland, such as Miniland, a Lego reconstruction of landmarks from around the world
Above A collection of sporting caps in the museum at Eton College

① Hampton Court Palace
Where Henry VIII still rules

Children need to be on their best behaviour at Hampton Court, in case they run into its former owner in one of his tempers. Henry VIII, everyone's favourite bad-boy monarch, caroused here with his 1,000-strong court and his six wives, and still roars through the Great Hall most days, as part of an interactive history experience. As the aroma of roasting meat wafts from the kitchens, families get to dress as 16th-century courtiers in miniature costume dramas – velvet cloaks are available from the Information Centre.

Falconry display in the grounds

Key features

The maze The world's most famous maze was planted for William III in 1690. But don't follow the map at the entrance – it's wrong!

Young Henry VIII Exhibition Sporting hero, musician, dancer… before becoming a bloated tyrant, Henry was a "lusty and brave prince". These hands-on displays trace his early years.

Wine Fountain This was re-created by studying archaeological remains found in Base Court in 2008. As in Henry VIII's day, it can serve wine.

Haunted Gallery It's said Queen Catherine Howard still wails in the corridor through which she was dragged by Henry's guards in 1541.

Great Vine Planted by "Capability" Brown in 1768, this vine produced an amazing 383 kg (845 lb) of sweet black grapes in 2001.

Tudor Kitchens The kitchens had 55 rooms and 200 kitchen hands. On certain weekends, costumed "food archaeologists" re-create banquets based on 500-year-old recipes.

Fountain Court In 1689, William and Mary hired Christopher Wren to execute a Baroque makeover here, in a bid to outdazzle Versailles.

Great Hall Shakespeare's company performed here for James I in 1603. The walls are hung with splendid tapestries of *The Story of Abraham*.

Letting off steam

The grounds go on forever, with the maze, formal gardens and the 20th Century Garden, great for hide-and-seek. For under-5s, there's a soft-play room off Base Court. To the north and within walking distance, **Bushy Park** (Hampton Court Road, Hampton, TW12 2EJ) has a playground, while to the west lies the open-air heated

Deer in Bushy Park, within walking distance of Hampton Court

Prices given are for a family of four

Hampton Swimming Pool *(High Street, Hampton, Middlesex, TW12 2ST; www.hamptonpool.co.uk; open daily).*

Eat and drink
Picnic: under £20; Snacks: £20–40; Real meal: £45–65; Family treat: £60 or more (based on a family of four)

PICNIC There are picnic tables in the 20th-Century Garden, or else spread a rug in the Tiltyard or Wilderness gardens. **The Pheasantry Cafe** *(Woodland Gardens in Bushy Park, TW11 OEQ; 020 8943 1347; summer: 9am–6pm; till 5pm winter)* offers hearty breakfasts, lunch dishes as well as cakes and pastries. **SNACKS** In an area originally used

for jousting by Henry VIII, Hampton Court's **Tiltyard Café** has meal deals on its home-made kids' food. There's also a playroom for younger kids. **REAL MEAL** Jamie's Italian *(19–23 High Street, Kingston, KT1 1LL; 020 3326 4300; www.jamieoliver. com/italian/kingston; noon–10pm Mon–Thu & Sun, till 11pm Fri & Sat)*, stands out among the chain restaurants across the river in Kingston upon Thames, for atmosphere. Extensive menu for kids. **FAMILY TREAT** Jin Jin *(8 Charter Quay, Riverside, Kingston, KT1 1HR; 020 8549 6638; noon–10pm Mon–Thu; till 11pm Fri & Sat; till 9:30pm Sun)* offers flavourful Asian food: the the 'Spicy Pot' menu option, with four small dishes, is best for families.

The Lowdown

Address
East Molesey, Surrey, KT8 9AU; 0844 482 7777; www. www.hrp.org.uk/hampton-court-palace/

Train
Hampton Court Station (trains from London Waterloo) **Bus stop** Trophy Gate, Hampton Court Station **River bus** Services run Apr–Oct from Westminster, Kew and Richmond (www.wpsa.co.uk or www.turks.co.uk) **Car** Park at Hampton Court Palace, Hampton Court Green or Hampton Court Station

Open
Apr–Oct: 10am–6pm; Nov–Mar: 10am–4:30pm (last admission one hour earlier). Maze closes 45min earlier..

Price
£46–57, under-5s free; maze only: £13.60; family ticket admits 2 adults, 3 kids

Skipping the queue
Book ahead online to skip the ticket queue – it's 12 per cent, too.

Guided tours
Costumed tours and dramatic vignettes daily (free, times vary). Four themed audio tours for adults, plus three for children. Regular evening ghosts tours on Sat and Sun (ages 15 plus); £27.50pp

Age range
3 plus

Activities
Range of age-graded children's trails, with prizes; plus audio tours for ages 6 plus (all free). Tudor cloaks in all sizes available from

Information Centre. Cookery weekends in Henry VIII's kitchens (see website for dates), plus additional live interpretations in school holidays, which might include Tudor etiquette, falconry displays, jester shows and jousting. Chapel Royal open for services daily. Hampton Court Music Festival (Jun) and Flower Show (Jul)

Allow
A full day

Wheelchair access
Most of the routes are accessible via a lift. There are some shallow stairs, but doorways are wide. There are scooters for the gardens

Café
Fountain Court Café and Tiltyard Café (see left), in grounds, and Privy Kitchen Coffee Shop, inside the Palace, offer light lunches and a children's menu

Shop
Four – Palace, Tudor Kitchens, Garden and Henry – selling a vast array of themed gifts, books and toys

Toilets
Main car park, Tiltyard Café, Base Court, Fountain Court

Good family value?
It's quite expensive, but apart from the Tower of London, no heritage attraction in Britain does a better job of keeping families entertained all day.

Find out more

DIGITAL
The Palace's website has Tudor crafts and recipes to try, plus interviews with expert curators. Learn how tapestries are conserved, make your own Henry VIII bonnet, or watch a knight donning armour: www.hrp.org.uk/hampton-court-palace/learning/games-and-video/ and www.hrp.org.uk/palace-kid.

the south, is better for younger children. Both parks are big and a whole day is needed when visiting. **The Rose Theatre** (24–26 High St, Kingston, KT1 1HL; 020 8174 0090; www.rosetheatrekingston.org) puts on classy children's shows in school holidays, and has storytelling (under 6s) most Saturdays at 10am & 11am – check website for dates and fees.

Next stop. . .

THEME PARKS AND THEATRE
With a car, two top theme parks are in striking distance. **Thorpe Park** (Staines Road, Chertsey, Surrey KT16 8PN; 0333 321 2001; www.thorpepark.com), 16 km (10 miles) west, has white-knuckle roller-coasters.
Chessington World of Adventures (Leatherhead Rd, Chessington, Surrey, KT9 2NE; 0871 663 4473; www.chessington.com), 10 km (6 miles) to

The Tiltyard Café sometimes serves Tudor dishes, and has a playroom

② Windsor Castle
Her Majesty's fairytale fortress

Bristling with turrets and suits of armour, the world's oldest occupied castle stands theatrically on a hilltop by the River Thames. The Queen stays here regularly – though presumably she doesn't use all 1,000 rooms. Non-royal visitors should pick up a free audio guide (a kids' version is available too) and tour the State Apartments, Chapel and Art Gallery. Children also enjoy the marching guardsmen, carriage rides and all-round holiday atmosphere of the little riverside town of Windsor, below the castle.

Royal Standard

Key Features

Round Tower The oldest part of the castle, this was built of wood in the 1070s by William the Conqueror. A guided tour climbs 200 steps to the top (over-10s only).

Royal Standard When the Queen's flag flies from the Round Tower, Her Majesty is at home.

① **Queen Mary's Dolls' House** The world's most luxurious doll's house was designed by architect Sir Edwin Lutyens in the 1920s, and took 1,500 artists and craftsmen three years to complete.

St George's Chapel This is a Gothic wonder from the 15th century. Light from the stained-glass windows illuminates the tombs of Henry VIII and Charles I.

Changing the Guard Everything stops in Windsor High Street when the castle guard marches through at 10.45am most mornings. The ceremony happens in the castle's Lower Ward.

State Apartments Furnished with gilt, crystal, antiques and armour, these rooms also have priceless art: look out for works by Rembrandt, Rubens, Canaletto and Gainsborough.

② **Long Walk** If the weather is dry, horse-drawn carriages trot along the Long Walk, which leads down to Windsor Great Park (from 12:30pm; Easter–Oct: daily; Nov–Easter: Sat & Sun).

The Lowdown

🌐 **Address** Castle Hill, Windsor, SL4 1NJ; 020 7766 7304; www.royalcollection.org.uk/visit/windsorcastle

🚗 **Train** Windsor & Eton Central, served by trains from Paddington via Slough; or Windsor & Eton Riverside, direct from Waterloo (journey time: 40 minutes–1 hour) **Coach** Green Line daily from London's Victoria Coach Station (www.greenline.co.uk) **Car** Use long-stay parking in Windsor town centre (charged)

🕓 **Open** Mar–Oct: 9:45am–5:15pm; Nov–Feb: 9:45am–4:15pm (last admission 75 minutes earlier). State Apartments closed very occasionally (check ahead). St

George's Chapel open Mon–Sat, and for services only on Sun

💲 **Price** £50 (less when State Apartments are closed), under-5s free. Plus £2 per ticket booking fee

👫 **Skipping the queue** Buy tickets direct from the Royal Collection (online or from castle ticket office) for one year's free re-admission

🎫 **Guided tours** Free 2-hour audio-tour, plus children's version (ages 7–11). Frequent 30-minute tours of Castle Precincts daily (free with admission). Aug–Sep only: 45-minute Conquer the Tower Tour for ages 11 plus (£68); 30-minute Great Kitchen Tour (£16), check website for dates, pre-booking essential.

👫 **Age range** 5 plus

👪 **Activities** Free kids' audio-guide plus activity sheets for ages 5–7 and 7–11 (also downloadable from website). Art activities in Moat Room, first Sat every month. School-holiday programme may include special children's tours, storytelling, object-handling and armour design (check website). Changing the Guard ceremony: Apr–Jul: 11am daily; Aug–Mar: alternate days; no ceremony on Sun

⏱ **Allow** 2–3 hours

♿ **Wheelchair access** Yes, but there are steps to the main entrance and to St Georges Chapel. There is a lift inside the castle. The outside areas can be uneven.

Prices given are for a family of four

Letting off steam

Playtime and picnicking are not smiled upon inside the castle grounds, though there are endless lawns and trees to run among along the Long Walk, south of the castle. The nearest playground is at **Bachelors Acre**, off Victoria Street.

Eat and drink

Picnic: under £20; Snacks: £20–40; Real meal: £45–65; Family treat: £65 or more (based on a family of four)

PICNIC Cinnamon Cafe *(The Old Booking Hall, Windsor Royal Station SL4 1PJ; 01753 857879; www. cinnamoncafe.com)*, en route from the train station to the castle, whips up delicious breakfasts and cakes.
SNACKS Extreme Motion and Windsor Skate Park Café *(Alexandra Gardens, Alma Rd, Windsor, SL4 5HZ; 01753 830220; www.extrememotion. com/coffee-shop/)* serves sandwiches and pizza. It has rails and ramps for all ages, mini-golf, a bungee trampoline and bike hire – good for exploring Windsor Great Park *(see p240)*.
REAL MEAL Gastropub the **Boatman** *(10 Thames Side,*

Playing cricket on the Long Walk, which runs south from Windsor Castle

Bouncing around on a trampoline in Alexandra Gardens, Windsor

Windsor, SL4 1QN; 01753 620010; boatmanwindsor.com; food: noon–10pm) is a child-friendly option with a lovely Thames-side terrace and a limited menu for under-12s and a two-course special lunch for adults.
FAMILY TREAT Gilbey's *(82–3 High Street, Eton, Windsor SL4 6AF; 01753 854921; www.gilbey group.com/restaurants/gilbeys-eton/; noon–10pm)* serves smart modern-British fare with an emphasis on seasonal ingredients. It also has delicious afternoon teas.

Find out more

DIGITAL Explore Queen Mary's Dolls' House in every tiny detail at this interactive mini-site: *www.royalcollection.org.uk/ queenmarysdollshouse.*

Next stop...

BOAT TRIPS
Among the raft of River Thames cruises offered from Windsor Promenade, 5 minutes from the castle, are 40-minute return trips with **French Brothers** to Boveney Lock, with views of Eton College *(mid-Feb–Oct, plus some winter weekends; 01753 851900; www. boat-trips.co.uk)*. Or try **Salters Steamers** *(01865 243 421, www. salterssteamers.co.uk).*

A leisurely tour down the Thames aboard the French Brothers' boat

Café None on site; ice cream and water available from North Terrace
Shop There are three shops, all selling Royal- and castle-themed souvenirs and gifts
Toilets Courtyard and North Terrace

Good family value?

Far from cheap, but just about worth it when combined with the town and Windsor Great Park *(see p240)*. Aim to visit when children's activities are scheduled, and avoid Sundays, when there's no Changing the Guard and St George's Chapel is closed to visitors. Visit again within 12 months for free.

③ Windsor Great Park

Where the royals ride out

He gallops across the Great Park at midnight on a black stallion, wearing a ghoulish antler headdress and with a pack of hell-hounds in his wake. No, it's not the Duke of Edinburgh, but Herne the Hunter, a legendary ghost from Windsor folklore – and he is not the only exotic apparition in this 13th-century hunting park, which stretches south of the castle. There's also a Canadian totem pole to discover, rising incongruously beside Virginia Water, the park's large ornamental lake. The nearby "Roman temple" was picturesquely assembled in 1818 by George IV, with columns taken from Leptis Magna, a major city of the Roman Empire in what is now Libya.

Windsor Great Park is a vast expanse of woods, ponds and pasture, with deer, formal gardens, the royal polo club and more. The

The Deer Park, just one area of the vast Windsor Great Park

Long Walk stretches south into the park from Windsor Castle – but it's a 1- or 2-hour walk to reach the Savill Garden, where, a visitor centre offers a good café, carriage rides and occasional holiday activities for children. A better bet is to hire bikes from Windsor and cycle here on National Cycle Route 4, which largely avoids busy roads. Or go by car, parking either at the Savill Garden or Virginia Water.

Letting off steam

The park's playground is at **Obelisk Lawn**, near the Savill Garden car park, with a shipwreck to scramble on and a sandpit to jump around in.

④ Eton College

Classes for the upper classes

"Etonians should not be approached, shouted at or photographed", says the Eton College website – though children can be forgiven one small giggle at the tail-coated young gentlemen who promenade like penguins around the School Yard. Founded in 1440 by King Henry VI, Eton is the world's most prestigious boys' school, having produced 19 British prime ministers, including David Cameron. Princes William and Harry also studied here – the fees are close to £30,000 per year.

The college is best approached on foot across the river from Windsor

The Lowdown

🌐 **Address** Windsor, SL4 6DW; 01753 370 100; www.etoncollege.com

🚃 **Train** Windsor & Eton Riverside, then 15-minute walk **Car** Arrive from north via Slough Road, or (preferably) walk from Windsor

🕑 **Open** By guided tour only (no tours until 2016 – check website)

💷 **Price** £24–34

🏁 **Guided tours** 1-hour tours (for individuals and small groups)

👫 **Age range** 8 plus

⏱ **Allow** 1–2 hours

♿ **Wheelchair access** Mostly – there is a chairlift to the chapel and cobbled surfaces outside

🍴 **Eat and drink** Picnic Tastes (92 High St, Eton, SL4 6AF; 01753 641 557; www.tastesdeli.co.uk; 10am–6pm Tue–Sat) is a super deli; eat your picnic in Windsor Park. Snacks Zero 3 (21 High St, Eton, SL4 6BL; 01753 864725) serves good-value food to eat in

🛍 **Shop** In Eton High Street, selling school-related items

🚻 **Toilets** Brewhouse Yard

and through Eton village. Tours are offered twice daily in season, covering the school's stately main quadrangle, cloisters and 15th-century chapel. The highlight is the very first schoolroom, preserved from the 1400s and carved with the graffiti of later students Robert Walpole, Percy Shelley and others. The guides happily field questions about the quirks of college life past and present – and children who fail to pay attention can be pointed towards the little museum at the end of the tour. It displays the cane and "swishing block" employed by infamous headmaster Dr Keate, who once flogged almost the entire school.

The Lowdown

🌐 **Address** The Savill Garden, Wick Road, Englefield Green, Surrey TW20 0UU; 01784 435544; www.windsorgreatpark.co.uk/en

🚃 **Train** Windsor & Eton Central. Egham or Virginia Water for Savill Garden **Car** Free parking on A332 south of Windsor. Pay car parks at Savill Garden (free with garden admission), Valley Gardens, Wick Road, Virginia Water Gate and Blacknest Gate

🕑 **Open** Park: 7am–dusk. Savill Garden: Mar–Oct: 10am–6pm; Nov–Feb: 10am–4:30pm (last admission 1 hour earlier)

💷 **Price** Windsor Great Park free. Savill Garden: £42; under-17s free; free for all in Jan & Feb

🏁 **Guided tours** Groups only

👫 **Age range** All

🎯 **Activities** Seasonal treasure trails and activities for families in some school holidays. Open-air theatre

and opera (Jun–Aug); carriage rides from Savill Garden on selected spring and summer weekends (check website for details)

🕑 **Allow** Half a day

🍴 **Eat and drink** Snacks Try a burger, some desserts or bite into a Royal Farms sausage at the Virginia Water Pavillion by the grassy shore of the pond. Real meal Savill Garden Kitchen (01784 485 402; Mar–Oct: 10am–5:30pm; Nov–Feb till 4pm) has home-made kids' meals and lunchboxes

🛍 **Shop** Savill Garden visitor centre, selling gifts, toys, books, garden items, wildlife and eco products, and the Duchy Original range

🚻 **Toilets** Savill Garden, Valley Gardens, Virginia Water car park

Eton students in tail-coats relaxing in between lessons

Prices given are for a family of four

Viking River Splash ride, one of many attractions at Legoland

Letting off steam

Home Park playground *(Romney Lock Road, off King Edward VII Avenue)*, just across the footbridge in Windsor, was given to the public by Queen Victoria.

⑤ Legoland

Tiny-brick wonderland

Pack swimsuits and sunglasses before heading for Windsor's super-popular brick-themed fun park. The swimsuits are for the assorted splash rides, which include simulated jet skis and a super-fast water slide. The shades are for the sheer multi-coloured intensity of it all: Legoland packs in 10 zones of stunt shows, children's theatre, rollercoasters and model-building, all loosely inspired by the classic toy box building blocks.

The focus is on pre-teens, especially ages 5–10, with a handful of mildly thrilling rides plus lots of junior race-car driving, balloon races and submarine adventures (among real-life sharks). Purists will enjoy Miniland, with its intricate Lego landmarks. The whole thing is fiendishly expensive: seek out online ticket deals, and try not to visit at holiday times, when the queues stretch almost to Denmark.

The Pirates' Training Camp playground at Legoland

Letting off steam

Kids with any energy left should head for the climbing apparatus at Pirates' Training Camp or DUPLO Playtown, both in Legoland.

The Lowdown

🌐 **Address** Winkfield Road, Windsor, SL4 4AY; 01753 626319; www.legoland.co.uk

🚃 **Train** Windsor & Eton Central or Windsor & Eton Riverside, then shuttle bus (charged; from 10am till 30 minutes after park closes) **Coach** Green Line service daily from London Victoria (www.greenline.co.uk) **Car** 3 km (2 miles) from Windsor on B3022; parking fee

🕐 **Open** Mar–Oct: check website (closing time varies with season)

💷 **Price** £120–180; book online for reduced prices

🚹 **Skipping the queue** Book online to skip the ticket queue. Ride queues peak noon–3pm; for a hefty extra charge, Q-Bot devices enable visitors to reserve time slots on selected rides

👫 **Age range** 3–12 years

🤸 **Activities** Stunt performances, puppet plays and 4-D cinema shows in Imagination Theatre. Programme might include events with kids' TV characters, laser spectaculars and Hallowe'en fun and fireworks

🕐 **Allow** A full day

♿ **Wheelchair access** Yes

🍽 **Eat and drink** More than a dozen outlets in park, such as Mexican Cantina and Pirate's BBQ, many offering healthy meal deals for kids

🛍 **Shop** Throughout the park; the Big Shop is at the entrance, selling Lego® products

🚻 **Toilets** In car park and throughout the park

Picnic under £20; **Snacks** £20–40; **Real meal** £40–60; **Family treat** £60 or more (based on a family of four)

Where to Stay in London

London's hotels are much more child friendly than they used to be. Today, even the grandest have family rooms and restaurants with children's menus. As alternatives to traditional hotels, B&Bs or small hotels offer more informal accommodation and apartments can make a flexible and good-value option.

AGENCIES

At Home in London
01474 708701; www.
athomeinlondon.co.uk
This agency specializes in B&B accommodation in private homes in central and suburban London. It has more than 80 homes on its books, all carefully chosen and regularly inspected. The website search engine is organized according to London Transport zones 1 (very central) and zones 2/3 (further out).

London Bed & Breakfast Agency
01474 708701;
www.londonbb.com
An agency offering B&B in private houses, and some apartments, covering central, north (a particularly good selection here), south, west and southwest London. It prides itself on paying attention to visitors' individual requirements. Hosts welcome families with children aged five and over.

London Home to Home
020 8769 3500; www.
londonhometohome.com
This friendly B&B agency offers good quality family accommo-dation in private houses in central, north and especially west London. Rooms are comfortable and well maintained, and rates include a continental breakfast. The usual minimum stay is two nights.

London House
0845 834 0244;
www.london-house.com
Gold-standard service, a wide choice and value for money are at the heart of this online business's success. Its speciality is providing serviced, self-catering apartments in relatively central locations of the city.

Westminster and the West End

HOTELS

Dolphin House
Map 16 E5
Dolphin Square, SW1V 3LX; 020 7834 3800; www.dolphinsquare. co.uk/dolphin-house/
Part of the 1930s Dolphin Square development by the river in Pimlico, this place offers a good choice of apartments. Among the main selling points are the 18-m (59-ft) indoor pool (extra charge) and extensive grounds, which include a tennis court.
💷 **££**

Stylish bedroom in London' oldest hotel, Brown's

Brown's
Map 9 D4
33 Albemarle Street, W1S 4BP; 020 7493 6020; www.roccofortehotels. com/hotels-and-resorts/browns-hotel
The kindly staff at London's oldest hotel go out of their way to make children feel at home. Afternoon tea is a must in the iconic English Tea Room, where Rudyard Kipling wrote *The Jungle Book*. Kids' treats include a Brown's bear to snuggle up with and DVDs to watch.
🍼 **£££**

Duke's
Map 9 D5
35–36 St James's Place, SW1A 1NY; 020 7491 4840; www.dukeshotel.com
This traditional Mayfair hotel offers plenty to keep boredom at bay, from storybooks to designated TV channels and PlayStation games. The special menus are always popular and usually rounded off with Duke's signature Knickerbocker Glory ice cream. Delicious picnic boxes can be supplied for lunch on the move.
🚕 🍼 **£££**

The Goring
Map 15 C2
15 Beeston Place, SW1W 0JW; 020 7396 9000; www.thegoring.com
Owned and run by the Goring family for four generations, this London institution prides itself on giving a warm welcome to its "VI (little) Ps". Treats include a bedtime story library, a gift bag and a visit to the kitchen, where children get to don aprons and chef's hats and decorate cakes.
🚕 🍼 💷 **£££**

Rosewood London Hotel
Map 10 H2
252 High Holborn, WC1V 7EN; 020 7781 8888; www.
rosewoodhotels.com/en/london
This impressive hotel is approached through an imposing arch to a Neo-Classical courtyard. It is well placed for Covent Garden and West End theatre trips. Kids' amenities include wireless monitors, mini-bathrobes, slippers and infant bathtub. Prams are available for a fee.
🚕 🍼 **£££**

The entrance of The Goring hotel, a short walk from Buckingham Palace

BED & BREAKFAST

B&B Belgravia and Studios@82
Map 15 C3

64–66 Ebury Street, SW1W 9QD;
020 7259 8570; www.bb-belgravia.com
Handy for Victoria Station, this popular B&B is conspicuous for its fresh appearance and laid-back approach. Bedrooms are decorated in earthy tones, with smart glass-partitioned bathrooms. Studios@82 next door provides self-catering family accommodation. Hot drinks, fruit and shortbread are on tap. Cots and high chairs available.

££

Lime Tree
Map 15 C3

135–7 Ebury Street, SW1W 9QU;
020 7730 8191; limetreehotel.co.uk
With the same postcode as the Queen (well, Buckingham Palace), this is a brilliantly located, simply furnished and comfortable island of good value. The high-ceilinged rooms often feature fireplaces and are bigger than prices suggest and the welcoming staff give advice on travel, dining and making the most of what London has to offer. Please note, it is not suitable for under-5s.

££

Luna Simone
Map 16 E3

47–49 Belgrave Road, SW1V 2BB; 020 7834 5897; www.lunasimonehotel.com
Fresh looking and contemporary, this hotel was established in 1970 and is now run by the original owner's sons. Rooms are comfortable – there is just enough space for the family to sprawl – and there are shiny bathrooms with power showers. It's a friendly place and a cooked breakfast is included in the price.

££

Strand Palace Hotel
Map 10 H4

372 Strand, WC2R 0JJ; 020 7379 4737; www.strandpalacehotel.co.uk
This large, four-star hotel offers contemporary accommodation in the heart of the West End. Covent Garden, Leicester Square, Piccadilly, Trafalgar Square and Buckingham Palace are all within walking distance. Somerset House is a stone's throw away and an ideal spot for children to run around. Room facilities include Wi-Fi, iPod docking stations and complimentary mineral water. Afternoon tea is served daily.

££

A modern kitchen in the Athenaeum Apartments

Taj 51 Buckingham Gate
Map 16 E1

SW1E 6AF; 020 7769 7766; www.taj51buckinghamgate.co.uk
Close to Buckingham Palace, this suites-and-residences hotel, with its butler service, Michelin-starred Quilon restaurant, spa and stunning courtyard garden, exudes luxury. All units include a clothes washer/dryer, Wi-Fi, DVD player and library, and there is complimentary access to a fitness centre as well. All suites come with fully-equipped kitchenettes.

£££

SELF-CATERING

Citadines Prestige Holborn-Covent Garden
Map 10 H2

94–99 High Holborn, WC1V 6LF;
020 7395 8800; www.citadines.com/
united-kingdom/london/citadines-
holborn-covent-garden-london
What these apartments lack in space, they make up for in quality furnishings (everything sparkles following a comprehensive refurbishment) and a handy location (on the borders of Holborn and Covent Garden). If you don't

wish to self-cater, continental breakfast is served downstairs. Air conditioning makes summer stays more comfortable. Pets are welcome (additional fee).

££

44 Curzon Street Apartments
Map 9 C5

44 Curzon Street, W1J 7RF; 0800 314 7160; www.bymansley.com/location/
44-curzon-street
Built in 1908 as a gentlemen's pied-à-terre, this is one of three salubrious serviced apartment blocks in west-central London under the same ownership. Their style is traditional English and cosy. Some apartments have kitchens, though there's no shortage of local restaurants.

£££

Athenaeum Apartments
Map 9 C6

116 Piccadilly, W1J 7BJ; 020 7499 3464; www.athenaeumhotel.com/
accommodation
They come at a bit of a price, but these roomy apartments benefit from the facilities of the nearby luxurious Athenaeum Hotel, while allowing families total independence. With prior notice, the Kids' Concierge will keep your apartment stocked with children's essentials such as games and age-appropriate DVDs.

£££

Comfortable, contemporary rooms in the Luna Simone hotel

Price Guide
The following price ranges are based on one night's accommodation in high season for a family of four, inclusive of service charges and any additional taxes.

£ Under £150 ££ £150–250 £££ over £250

The kitchen and sitting area of one of the SACO – Holborn apartments

Flemings Apartments   Map 9 C5
7–12 Half Moon Street, W1J 7BH;
020 7016 5647; www.flemings-
mayfair.co.uk
Attached to Flemings Hotel but with their own entrance in Clarges Street, these serviced apartments in the heart of Mayfair are smart without being too precious. Helpful hotel staff are happy to arrange outings, from picnics and cycle rides in Green Park to tickets for Premier League football matches.

£££

Bloomsbury & Regent's Park
HOTELS
Bedford   Map 10 G1
83–95 Southampton Row, WC1B
4HD; 020 7278 7871; www.
imperialhotels.co.uk/en/bedford
If one visit to the British Museum isn't enough, the pick of the Imperial group's six Bloomsbury hotels is just around the corner. Interesting local walks are featured on its website, and sightseeing tours further afield leave from the

Traditional English furnishings in a Mayfair apartment

nearby Royal National Hotel. The Bloom & Willow restaurant offers dishes that appeal to youngsters.

£

Marriott Regent's Park   Map 2 G1
128 King Henry's Road, NW3 3ST;
020 7722 7711; www.marriott.com/
hotels/travel/lonrp-london-marriott-
hotel-regents-park
In leafy north London, within striking distance of Regent's Park, London Zoo, Primrose Hill and Camden Lock Market, this Marriott is perennially popular with families. Reasons include the large, airy bedrooms with sliding patio doors on to small balconies, lovely indoor pool, helpful concierges, and great weekend rates.

££

The Landmark   Map 8 H1
222 Marylebone Road, NW1 6JQ;
020 7631 8000; www.
landmarklondon.co.uk
Well placed for an early start at Madame Tussauds, the Planetarium or Sherlock Holmes Museum, this red-brick Victorian building was originally a railway hotel. It now boasts a stunning atrium with towering palm trees, where afternoon tea is served. Families won't feel cramped because the bedrooms are huge at this five-star hotel.

£££

The Langham   Map 9 D2
1C Portland Place, W1B 1JA; 020
7636 1000; www.langhamhotels.
com/en/the-langham/london
This luxurious West End hotel offers the Family Getaway package (for

up to five people), which includes English breakfast for the whole family, a VIP tour of Hamleys toy store nearby and an adjoining room at half price. If your kids are picky eaters, the one-bedroom residence and the regent apartment have their own kitchenettes.

£££

BED & BREAKFAST
Alhambra   Map 4 G5
17–19 Argyle Street, WC1H 8EJ;
020 7837 9575; www.alhambra
hotel.com
An affordable, hospitable base in the King's Cross area, particularly useful for Eurostar travellers. In an 1840s building with a modern interior, it is a family-run affair and has been since 1950. Rooms are on the small side, but squeaky clean. The owner Francesco cooks irresistible full English breakfasts.

££

Arosfa   Map 10 F1
83 Gower Street, WC1E 6HJ; 020
7636 2115; www.arosfalondon.com
Guests are made to feel like part of the family at this simple Bloomsbury B&B, where the genial staff keep the rooms spotlessly cleans and tidy. Be aware that some bedrooms have minuscule bathrooms. The bar with adjoining garden is a highlight. Four nearby Tube stations bring the whole city conveniently within reach.

££

Compact, neatly appointed guest room at Arosfa

Blandford   Map 9 B1
80 Chiltern Street, W1U 5AF; 020
7486 3103; www.capricornhotels.
co.uk/hotel_blandford/index.php
The most charming of the Capricorn chain is perfectly placed for the shops and a visit to Madame Tussauds. It's next to Regent's Park and the refurbished, well-appointed rooms even have laptop safes. The English breakfast here is a must-try.

££

Welcoming room with contemporary decor at The Hoxton

Euro
Map 4 G5

53 Cartwright Gardens, WC1H 9EL; 020 7387 4321; www.eurohotel.co.uk
This is a good hotel to choose if you have a budding tennis star in the family – guests can use the courts in Cartwright Gardens (reservations at reception). Of the clutch of modest hotels that occupy the fine former merchants' houses in this Georgian crescent, the Euro stands out for its large family rooms, good service and competitive rates.

££

Hart House
Map 9 A2

51 Gloucester Place, W1U 8JF; 020 7935 2288; hart-house-hotel. londonhotelsgb.com
For families seeking fair prices but more character than a chain, this B&B provides plain, reliable accommodation in a Georgian house that once sheltered French nobility during the Revolution. The staff are attentive, and the rooms spotless. If you tire of the shops, the Wallace Collection is nearby.

££

Jesmond Dene
Map 4 G5

27 Argyle Street, WC1H 8EP; 020 7837 4654; www.jesmonddene hotel.co.uk
Mostly small rooms, even smaller bathrooms (some microscopic, some shared) and a few steep stairs to negotiate, but the friendly staff, the cleanliness, the breakfasts (charged extra unless you book directly), the free Wi-Fi and, above all, the price for this central, King's Cross location keep families coming back.

££

Jesmond Hotel
Map 10 F1

63 Gower Street, WC1E 6HJ; 020 7636 3199; www.jesmondhotel.org.uk
Front-facing rooms at this spotless, mid-range hotel are all double-glazed against traffic noise. For

families, there are three quad and two triple rooms. Many rooms sport original fireplaces, while all have modern bathrooms and free Wi-Fi. The basement breakfast room serves full English breakfast.

££

Lincoln House
Map 9 A2

33 Gloucester Place, W1U 8HY; 020 7486 7630; lincoln-house. londonhotelsgb.com
A trustworthy alternative to Hart House – in the same road but closer to Oxford Street. Bedrooms are modest, with tiny bathrooms, but have a number of treats, including five-star Hypnos mattresses, satellite TV, unlimited tea and coffee and free Wi-Fi. Air conditioning has been fitted in two-thirds of the rooms.

££

PUB WITH ROOMS
New Inn
Map 2 G3

2 Allitsen Road, NW8 6LA; 020 7722 0726; www.newinnlondon.co.uk
Close to Regent's Park and the canal, the price, the good-natured welcome and the spotless rooms above this gastro-pub are hard to beat. If sleep before midnight is vital, check the live music forecast before booking (usually at weekends). The pub serves breakfasts, good Sunday roasts and upmarket fare.

££

The New Inn pub, just steps from Regent's Park

SELF-CATERING
23 Greengarden House
Map 9 C3

St Christopher's Place, W1U 1NL; 020 7935 9191; greengardenhouse.com
The pedestrianised St Christopher's Place is distinctive and lined with fashionable shops, restaurants and cafés (many with outdoor tables and chairs). These apartments are in pleasant, modern surroundings, with weekday maid service, double glazing and a first-day survival kit for families.

£££

Europa House
Map 2 E5

79A Randolph Avenue, W9 1DW; 020 7724 5924; www.citybase apartments.com/uk/london/ europa-house-apartments
With children in tow, Little Venice has great appeal – it's away from the hurly-burly and has a colourful canal and pretty bridges. Europa House has 14 comfortable, airy apartments, three acres of communal gardens and a children's playground. Frazzled parents can order groceries, take-aways or an in-house massage.

£££

SACO – Holborn
Map 10 H1

Spens House, 72–84 Lamb's Conduit Street, WC1N 3LT; 117 970 6999; www.sacoapartments.com
Exceptionally comfortable and with all mod cons, these award-winning apartments (up to two or three bedrooms) are in a vibrant part of the city. Eclectic boutiques, restaurants, delicatessens and cafés characterize the area, and children can scamper around the Coram's Fields playground. Not for very light sleepers.

£££

The City & the East End
HOTELS
The Hoxton
Map 6 F6

81 Great Eastern Street, EC2A 3HU; 020 7550 1000; thehoxton.com/ london/shoreditch/hotels
The huge ground-floor space here incorporates a reception, shop, sitting room, bar, the Hoxton Grill restaurant and two blazing fires. The place has a real buzz that characterizes the local area. Working on budget airline principles, the earlier you book, the less you pay. As you'd expect in trendy Shoreditch, each of the three grades of rooms are ultra design-led.

££

Apex City of London
Map 12 G4

1 Seething Lane, EC3N 4AX; 0800 049 8000; www.apexhotels.co.uk/ apex-city-of-london-hotel
Early birds can get to the Tower as soon as the gates open from just minutes away. There are free meals for kids under-12s if parents book a family room, and under-17s can stay free in a family room. The pristine rooms have comfortable beds.

£££

Key to symbols *see back cover flap*

Grange City
Map 12 G4
8–14 Cooper's Row, EC3N 2BQ;
020 7863 3700; www.grangehotels.
com/hotels-london/grange-city/
about-this-hotel
The greatest draw of this hotel is
the fabulous 25-m (82-ft) swimming
pool, something of a rarity in
London, with generous children's
hours, particularly at weekends.
Choose from among the three
on-site restaurants. Grange City is
close to the Tower, with splendid
views of it from some of the rooms.

🛏️🚼 £££

*The reception area of Grange City, close
to the Tower of London*

SELF-CATERING
Hamlet (UK)
Map 12 H5
*Nightingale House, 50 Thomas
More Street, E1W 1UA & Burr
Close, E1W 1ND; 01462 678037;
www.hamletuk.com*
Arriving at the Tower early to avoid
the crowds is painless for guests
staying at this one-bedroom
apartment (accommodating four
people) in St Katharine's Dock.
The area was redeveloped in the
1970s and is now surrounded by
shops and restaurants. Kids will
love the activity of the marina as
the pleasure boats come and go.
Minimum seven-night stay.

🚼 ££

Market View by
BridgeStreet
Map 11 C2
*15 West Smithfield, EC1A 9HY;
0800 278 7338; www.bridgestreet.
com/properties/london/market-view*
Of BridgeStreet's City apartment
buildings, this restored Edwardian
red-brick block provides the best
family accommodation. All the
one- and two-bedroom apartments
have sensible laminate floors and
some wooden furniture, and offer
superb views of the still working
Smithfield Meat Market. Lots of
restaurants in this lively area.

🚼 ££

MiNC Eagle Court
Apartments
Map 11 C1
*10–11 Britton Street, EC1M
5QD; www.hotels.uk.com (online
booking only)*
Clerkenwell is a reinvigorated district
that is fun for families, with child-
oriented restaurants and the Little
Angel (puppet) Theatre in nearby
Islington. These apartments offer
clean, modern accommodation at
excellent rates if booked in advance.
Weekly maid service and 24-hour
phone support.

££

Cheval Calico House
Map 12 E3
*42 Bow Lane, EC4M 9DT; 020 7489
2500; www.chevalresidences.com/
cheval-calico-house/index.html*
Cheval Residences have several
apartment buildings in London;
Calico House offers the best value
for money. The one- and two-
bedroom flats are attractive yet
practical, with little luxuries such
as goose-down duvets and Frette
linen. Close to St Paul's Cathedral,
the location is bustling during the
week and quite peaceful at weekends. Seven days minimum rent.

🚼 £££

Southwark & the
South Bank
HOTELS
Premier Inn London
County Hall
Map 10 H6
*Belvedere Road, SE1 7PB; 020 7902
1601; www.premierinn.com/gb/en/
hotels/england/greater-london/
london/london-county-hall.html*
Two under-16s stay for free when
sharing with their parents in this

*The elegant exterior of the London
Bridge hotel*

well-kept hotel. Geared to family
life, this reasonably priced hotel
offers high chairs, additive-free
kids' meals and activity packs.
It also has an enviable location
opposite Westminster.

🚼 £

Church Street
*29–33 Camberwell Church Street,
SE5 8TR; 020 7703 5984;
churchstreethotel.com*
A lively one-off, this Latin
American-inspired sanctuary in
multi-ethnic Camberwell is owned
and was designed by two artistic
brothers. It has an informal tapas
restaurant, two bars (one of which
is a music venue) and large
colourful rooms, furnished with
wrought-iron beds and Mexican
art. The less-expensive rooms
have shared bathrooms. Buses
176 and 185 go from here to the
excellent Horniman Museum.

££

Comfortable sitting area in one of Market View by BridgeStreet's apartments

Ibis Styles London
Southwark Rose   Map 11 D5
*43–47 Southwark Bridge Road,
SE1 9HH; 020 7015 1480;
www.ibis.com/gb/hotel-7465-
ibis-styles-london-southwark-near-
borough-market/index.shtml*
As the name suggests, this budget
chain hotel features rooms that are
startlingly design-led, as are the
common areas. With the Globe,
the National Theatre and Tate
Modern only minutes away, it is
a perfect choice for families of
culture vultures.

♿ **££**

Park Plaza
County Hall   Map 10 H6
*1 Addington Street, SE1 7RY; 0844
415 6760; www.parkplaza.com/
london-hotel-gb-se1-7ry/gbcounty*
This vast 398-room high-rise giant
is handily located for such must-
visit sights as the London Eye and
Aquarium. Its smart Spectrum Bar &
Café boasts a breathtaking setting
below a 14-storey glass atrium.
Studios, ideal for families of four,
have a living area with plasma TV
and kitchenette.

♿🍴 **££**

London Bridge   Map 12 E6
*8–18 London Bridge Street, SE1
9SG; 020 7855 2200; www.
londonbridgehotel.com*
If the London Dungeon features on
your "to do" list, this welcoming
hotel in an interesting central area
could hardly be better located. The
enticing lobby sets the scene, while
rooms (including a few apartments)
are restful with neat black-and-white
bathrooms. The hotel is much larger
than it appears from the outside
and contains two restaurant/bars.

♿🍴 **£££**

BED & BREAKFAST
69 The Grove   Map 16 H5
*69 Vauxhall Grove, SW8 1TA; 07796
874 677; 69thegrove.com*
Set in a quiet Victorian square close
to Vauxhall Tube station and several
main bus routes into the West End,
this townhouse has excellent travel
connections. The building has been
remodelled to offer a choice of rooms
including apartments for families
and groups of up to eight people.
Free Wi-Fi, toiletries and an iPod
dock/alarm clock all add to the
comfort. Minimum two-night stay.

♿🍴🌿 **££**

Kennington B&B   Map 17 B4
*103 Kennington Park Road, SE11
4JJ; 020 7735 7669; www.
kenningtonbandb.com*
This B&B in an impeccably renovated
Georgian townhouse is a standard
setter: it scores top marks for location,
price, welcome and comfort. It has
adjoining rooms, perfect for families
with young children, and is virtually
on the doorstep of Kennington
Tube station, giving easy access
to the rest of London.

🍴🌿🖼 **££**

SELF-CATERING
London Tower Bridge   Map 12 H6
*The Circle, Queen Elizabeth Street,
SE1 2JJ; 020 8674 7069; www.
londontowerbridgeapartments.co.uk*
It may be tricky to find, but once
you're here, this building offers a
refuge from the bustle. Hard-to-match
prices, complimentary use of a nearby
spa, colourful furnishings and plenty
of space for lounging add to the
appeal of these apartments. Patronize
the local deli, bakery and Borough
Market (Wed–Sat), then cook up a
feast in the well-kitted-out kitchen.

🍴 **££**

*Smart lobby of the Crowne Plaza
Kensington*

Kensington, Chelsea & Battersea
HOTELS
Crowne Plaza
Kensington   Map 14 E2
*100 Cromwell Road, SW7 4ER; 0800
405060; www.ihg.com/crowneplaza/
hotels/gb/en/london/lonke/hoteldetail*
Probably the best-value hotel in
Kensington, this is just a short stroll
from the Science and Natural History
museums and a favourite with
families. Although the Cromwell
Road is a busy thoroughfare, once
inside, or in the large garden, all is
calm. Guests who decide to eat out
are spoiled for choice.

♿🍴🌿 **££**

Mandarin Oriental
Hyde Park   Map 9 A6
*66 Knightsbridge, SW1X 7LA; 020
7235 2000; www.mandarinoriental.
com/london/*
From mini bathrobes, books and
crayons to popcorn on demand,
children want for nothing at this
luxurious Edwardian pile on the edge
of Hyde Park and bang opposite
Harvey Nichols. The interior,
including the ballroom where the
Queen learned to dance during the
1930s has been redesigned to offer
a blend of old-world charm and
modern styling.

♿🍴 **£££**

Rafayel on the Left Bank
*34 Lombard Road, SW11 3RF; 020
7801 3600; www.hotelrafayel.com*
You'll find 65 large rooms with
remarkably comfortable beds in this
glossy, eco-friendly hotel. If the kids
wake up hungry in the night, there's
24-hour room service. There's also
pampering for parents in the spa and
gym; a free shuttle bus to and from
Clapham Junction and Clapham
Common; and the kind staff will
organize cycling and kayaking trips.

♿🍴 **£££**

The luxurious Mandarin Oriental, near Hyde Park and Sloane Street

Key to symbols *see back cover flap*

The elegant, well-furnished interior of The Beaufort hotel

Royal Garden

Map 7 D6

2–24 Kensington High Street, W8 4PT; 020 7937 8000; www. royalgardenhotel.co.uk

Favoured by footballers and rock bands, this is a hotel for celebrity spotting. However, the attraction for families is having Kensington Gardens, with the Diana Memorial Playground, Peter Pan statue and Round Pond, as their backyard. The hotel provides micro-scooters for kids' use in the park, plus welcome packs for children.

£££

BED & BREAKFAST
Amsterdam

Map 13 C3

7 Trebovir Road, SW5 9LS; 020 7370 5084; www.amsterdam-hotel.com

Located in a quiet street around the corner from Earl's Court Road Tube station, this prize-winning townhouse B&B has decent-sized and reasonably priced family rooms accommodating four – these are at a premium in this area, so book early. Breakfast is served by smiling staff in a bright, pretty room with crisp tablecloths. The garden is especially lovely in summer.

£

Hyde Park Rooms

Map 8 G2

137 Sussex Gardens, W2 2RX; 020 7723 0225; hydeparkrooms.com/index.html

In business since the early 1980s, this modest family-run B&B offers no-frills accommodation plus a generous breakfast at unbeatable prices for central London. Guests are guaranteed a warm welcome from the owner and staff, and although rooms are simple and not all have en-suite facilities, they are certainly well maintained.

£

Lavender Guesthouse

18 Lavender Sweep, SW11 1HA; 020 7585 2767; www.thelavender guesthouse.com

Simply decorated and equipped, but squeaky clean and very friendly, this guesthouse is in a quiet suburban area but is only a short walk from Clapham Junction (seven minutes by train from Victoria). Rooms are small (but so are rates) and there is a 3-night minimum stay. The sunny garden is filled with flowers and shrubs.

£

New Linden

Map 7 C3

59 Leinster Square, W2 4PS; 020 7221 4321; newlinden.mayflower collection.com

Not far from Portobello Road, this converted townhouse has 50 pristine and carefully designed rooms. Floors are wooden; walls, plain with the occasional modern painting; and beds have distinctive headboards and colourful covers. The staff couldn't be friendlier, and rooms and family suites are good value, considering that the excellent buffet breakfast is included in the price.

£

The Cranley

Map 14 E3

10 Bina Gardens, SW5 0LA; 020 7373 0123; www.the cranley.com

A night spent here feels more like staying with friends than in a hotel: it's a traditional, luxurious home-from-home with plenty of personal touches, such as an honesty bar and turn-down service. A highlight of the day is afternoon tea, served on the front terrace in summer and by the fire in winter.

££

Darlington Hyde Park

Map 8 G2

111–117 Sussex Gardens, W2 2RU; 020 7460 8800; www.darlingtonhotel.com

The area around Paddington is full of B&Bs, many of them rather dubious. However, here is a superior one – four converted Victorian townhouses well located for the train station, as well as Oxford Street's shops. Although some family rooms are on the lower-ground floor, they still feel bright and breezy. Fridges and safes in the rooms are bonuses.

££

The Nadler Kensington

Map 13 D3

25 Courtfield Gardens, SW5 0PG; 020 7244 2255; www.nadlerhotels.com/kensington.shtml

Occupying a smart townhouse in a rather salubrious corner of Earl's Court, this 65-room, 4-star, boutique hotel offers exceptional value. The deluxe rooms comfortably accommodate a family of four; other categories might prove a bit small. Free Wi-Fi and a mini kitchen in every room.

££

Park City Grand Plaza Kensington

Map 13 D2

18–30 Lexham Gardens, W8 5JE; 020 7341 7090; park-city-grand-plaza-kensington.londonhotelsgb.com

Tucked away behind the busy Cromwell Road, this good-value hotel spreads itself through seven substantial townhouses. Family suites can take in parents plus two kids. Once the little ones are in bed, the grown-ups can enjoy a nightcap in the lobby bar. Babysitting availble for a charge.

££

The Parkwood at Marble Arch

Map 8 H3

4 Stanhope Place, W2 2HB; 020 7402 2241; www.parkwood hotel.com

This is a tranquil oasis close to, but a world apart from, the frenzy of Marble Arch. Tasteful prints hang on the walls of the spacious, cheerfully decorated bedrooms, some of which have handsome iron bedsteads and fireplaces. There are a few family rooms that can accommodate four people.

££

Rhodes
Map 8 F3

195 Sussex Gardens, W2 2RJ; 020 7262 0537; www.rhodeshotel.com
The current owners of the Rhodes have been at the helm since 1978 and take great pride in their friendly, eclectic B&B in an elegant Georgian house, which was first opened before World War II. Double glazing keeps the rooms beautifully quiet; the ones at the top are a fairly steep climb, but there are willing members of staff to help with luggage. The Rhodes offers family rooms fitting up to six – a London rarity.

 ££

Sydney House
Map 14 G3

9–11 Sydney Street, SW3 6PU; 020 7376 7711; www. sydneyhousechelsea.com
Plumb between the shops of the King's Road and the museums of South Kensington, this is a cool but cosy Georgian townhouse that has undergone a chic makeover. Rooms have pale walls, blonde-wood floors, flat-screen TVs and comfy beds; a few have balcony or terrace. It has charming staff and fair prices.

 ££

The Beaufort
Map 14 H1

33 Beaufort Gardens, SW3 1PP; 020 7584 5252; www.thebeaufort.co.uk
This plush hotel offers 29 tastefully decorated rooms and suites, a relaxed atmosphere and a classy Knightsbridge address. Be sure to return from shopping or sightseeing in time for tea and mouth-watering home-made scones, served from

3–5pm and included in the room price. There's also a great choice of excellent restaurants nearby.

 £££

Cosy guest room at The Parkwood at Marble Arch

Indigo
Map 13 C3

34–44 Barkston Gardens, SW5 0EW; 020 7373 7851; www.hotelindigo. com/kensington
Possibly the only boutique hotel in Earls Court, Indigo has various categories of plush rooms. Superior doubles are suite-sized, while family rooms have two double beds and small closets. A cheery ground-floor breakfast area later in the day becomes an Italian restaurant offering two- or three-course set menus.

 £££

Number Sixteen
Map 14 F3

16 Sumner Place, SW7 3EG; 020 7589 5232; www.firmdalehotels. com/hotels/london/number-sixteen/
Tim and Kit Kemp, who own Firmdale Hotels, have the knack of creating places to stay that not only look stunning but are easy going and smooth running.

Number Sixteen is no exception. Extras include 24-hour room service, a DVD library, honesty bar and a kids' menu with allergies and intolerances accommodated.

£££

Royal Park
Map 8 F3

3 Westbourne Terrace, Lancaster Gate, W2 3UL; 020 7479 6600; www.theroyalpark.com
The name is apt: Hyde Park is only a few minutes' walk south from this smart, traditional little hotel. Families can arrange to have interconnecting rooms, where breakfast is served in bed each morning. It may be pricey, but extras, such as Wi-Fi and use of a guest computer are included.

£££

SELF-CATERING
Castletown House
Map 13 A4

11 Castletown Road, W14 9HE; 020 7386 9423; www.castle townhouse.co.uk
If these were a short distance east, inside the Royal Borough of Kensington and Chelsea, prices could be double. Choose between one-, two- or three-bedroom apartments with delightful courtyards. The owners are on hand to welcome and help. Minimum two-night stay.

££

Space Apart Hotel
Map 7 D3

36–37 Kensington Gardens Square, W2 4BQ; www.aparthotel-london. co.uk (online booking only)
These are an outstanding choice for families, with everything on demand, from Wii games to potties. The excellent management are hands-on and the wide-open spaces of Hyde Park are on the doorstep. Triple units fit two adults plus two children and have the latest Bosch appliances, attractive furniture and clever storage.

££

The Apartments
Map 15 A3

36 Draycott Place, SW3 2SA; 0843 218 5060; www.theapartments.co. uk/chelsea-locations
These luxuriously appointed and spacious apartments are ideal for longer stays and families of up to three looking for a more homely feel. The apartments have fully equipped kitchens and other features include iPod docking stations, plus a weekly maid and linen service.

£££

Sydney House, located between the King's Road and the Natural History Museum

Key to symbols *see back cover flap*

Beaufort House
Map 14 H1

*45 Beaufort Gardens, SW3 1PN;
020 7584 2600; beauforthouse.co.uk*

Just a 5-minute hop from Harrods toy department, these exclusive one- to four-bedroom apartments overlook a Knightsbridge cul-de-sac. Each one is handsomely furnished and boasts a top-of-the-range kitchen and bathroom. Facilities include iPod docking stations and an extensive DVD collection, plus free access to the nearby Aquila Healthclub.

🛏 £££

Dolphin House
Apartments
Map 16 E4

*Chichester Street, SW1V 3LX; 01797
253823; www.jandkapartments.com/
property/dolphin-house*

Among the many serviced apartments handled by this UK-based chain, these one-, two- and three-bedroom apartments are some of the nicest ones. They enjoy a quiet but central location and benefit from the on-site gym/spa and extensive gardens. There's a minimum four-night stay.

£££

Fraser Suites
Queens Gate
Map 14 E2

*39B Queen's Gate Gardens, SW7
5RR; 020 7969 3555; london-queens
gate.frasershospitality.com/en*

Ideal for families planning a visit to the Natural History Museum, these refurbished apartments (all equipped with full kitchens include huge two-bedroom ones suitable for families. Breakfast is offered downstairs, while evening meals can be delivered to your suite. Daily maid service and 24-hour reception.

🛏 £££

Beyond the Centre

HOTELS
Ace Hotel Shoreditch
Map 6 G6

*100 Shoreditch High Street, E1 6JQ;
020 7613 9800; www.acehotel.
com/london#!*

This renovated hotel sports eight categories of rooms and suites, reflecting the arty ethos of the neighbourhood. If the on-site restaurant doesn't suit your taste buds, nip around the corner to Leila's Café (17 Calvert Avenue), a Spitalfields institution. With Brick Lane, Columbia Road and Spitalfields all within striking distance, this is a recommended option for market enthusiasts.

🛏 ££

Novotel London
Greenwich
Map 18 E4

*173–85 Greenwich High Road, SE10
8JA; 020 7660 0682; www.novotel.
com/gb/hotel-3476-novotel-london-
greenwich/index.shtml*

This branch of the ubiquitous hotel chain stands out for the warmth of its staff and the comfort and cleanliness of its rooms. The company aims to make families a priority, so there are family rooms for parents and two kids. The splendid breakfast will set you and the family up for a day of sightseeing in Greenwich.

🚌 ££

Premier Inn, Hampstead

*215 Haverstock Hill, NW3 4RB; 0871
527 8662; www.premierinn.com*

Fairly convenient for the sights of the West End (via the Northern Line from Belsize Park tube) and close to the attractive outdoor spaces of Hampstead Heath and Kenwood House, this Premier Inn has smart, contemporary public areas and an on-site Thyme restaurant. Bedrooms are quiet, if slightly smaller than average for this chain. Expect attentive service at reception.

🚌 ££

Richmond Gate

*152–58 Richmond Hill, TW10 6RP;
0330 390 0493; www.richmond
gate.com*

This elegant, 4-star hotel occupies a stunning 18th-century building at the top of Richmond Hill. It has a country-house feel and is steps from London's largest park, the river and the centre of Richmond, with its shops and theatres. Only four poster rooms and suites can accommodate a single child with parents.

🏛 ££

Novotel London Greenwich, close to the Old Royal Naval College

Boundary Rooms
Map 6 G5

*2–4 Boundary Street, E2 7DD; 020
7729 1051; boundary.london*

There is plenty of space to spread out in the bedrooms (12 doubles, five suites) at Terence Conran's stylish converted Victorian printworks in Shoreditch. Have breakfast and snacks in the congenial Albion, a café-cum-bakery (open 8am–midnight) and, in summer, eat on the rooftop (which hums at weekends) with the whole City on display.

🛏 £££

The on-site parking lot at Premier Inn, Hampstead

DoubleTree London
Docklands

*265 Rotherhithe Street, SE16 5HW;
020 7231 1001; doubletree3.hilton.
com/en/hotels/united-kingdom/
doubletree-by-hilton-hotel-london-
docklands-riverside-LONNDDI/
index.html*

With a complimentary ferry service to and from Canary Wharf Tube station, getting around from this riverside hotel in a converted 17th-century wharf building, could hardly be easier. The rather utilitarian family rooms are a decent size, but if you need two because of your children, the second room will be half price. There is also a fitness centre for adults.

🚌 🛏 £££

DoubleTree London ExCel

*ExCeL, 2 Festoon Way, Royal Victoria
Dock, E16 1RH; 020 7540 4820;
doubletree3.hilton.com/en/hotels/
united-kingdom/doubletree-by-
hilton-hotel-london-excel-LONEXDI/
index.html*

Although aimed primarily at ExCel convention goers, the hotel's Queen-category rooms with pull-out sofa can accommodate families. Kids will enjoy watching planes taking off and landing at he nearby London City Airport.

Dining and sitting area of one of the Glenthurston self-catering apartments

The on-site restaurant is open through the day, though there are no dedicated menus for children.

🛏 😊 £££

BED & BREAKFAST
Forest Lodge
70 Drax Avenue, West Wimbledon, SW20 0EY; 020 8946 3253; www. thewimbledonbedandbreakfast.com
Located in a large house, Forest Lodge is a family-run bed and breakfast close to Wimbledon Common. Rooms are bright and sunny with pleasant decor. Breakfast is generous, stretching to scrambled eggs with smoked salmon. Guests can use the indoor pool all year round. Amenities include free Wi-Fi, flat-screen TVs and parking. Cots are also available.

🛏 😊 ££

Quality Hotel Hampstead
5–7 Frognal, NW3 6AL; 020 7794 0101; www.qualityhampstead.com
"Olde Worlde" it is not, but it does have bathrooms with contemporary fittings, decent-sized, comfortable bedrooms, lifts to every floor and free parking. It is also close to Finchley Road tube and bus routes into the centre. Staff are knowledgeable and helpful; breakfasts are generous. A variety of tempting local restaurants are available nearby.

££

Richmond Inn
50–56 Sheen Road, TW9 1UG; 020 8940 0171; richmondinnhotel.com
Aspiring botanists and their parents will enjoy being so close to Kew Gardens, while theatre buffs should know that many West End productions try out in Richmond first. The clean, well-equipped

bedrooms (including family rooms for three or four guests) may be slightly suburban for some but there are elegant marble-clad bathrooms, which are something of a treat. Helpful 24-hour staff, a good choice of local restaurants and free parking.

🛏 ££

SELF-CATERING
Glenthurston
30 Bromley Road, SE6 2TP & 27 Canadian Ave, SE6 3AU; 020 8690 3092; www.londonselfcatering.co.uk
For energy-filled young ones, there are swings, a trampoline and grass to run around on in the gardens of these neighbouring Victorian houses, as well as a pool table and an indoor swimming pool. These simple, cheerful apartments are perfect for families, fitting up to 11 guests in the four-bedroom units. There are direct buses to Greenwich and the Horniman Museum, and a good train service into town. Minimum stays three to seven nights, depending on season.

🍴 😊 ££

Fox Apartments
Warehouse K, Western Gateway, ExCeL Centre, E16 1DR; 020 7558 8859; www.foxapartments.com
A superb conversion of an 1840s warehouse, these apartments are very handy for the DLR. Exposed brickwork, warm neutral colours, small patios and simple stylish fixtures and fittings make these two-bedroom-two-bathroom apartments a great find in Docklands. There is some airport noise, but it's not a huge problem. There's a minimum two-night stay.

£££

Sanctum
Map 1 C3
1 Greville Road, NW6 5HA; 020 7644 2100; www.sanctum-international.com
There is little doubt that you get more space for your money even a short distance out of the centre. A three-minute walk from Kilburn Park Tube station (and a direct route to Oxford Circus), this circular space-age building houses 43 light, handsomely furnished apartments, with well-appointed kitchens and first-class management. The largest apartments accommodate five to seven guests.

£££

Town Hall Apartments
8 Patriot Square, E2 9NF; 020 7871 0460; townhallhotel.com/home
Just a five-minute walk from the V&A Museum of Childhood, the Town Hall Apartments are a happy combination of imposing Edwardian architecture and striking contemporary furnishings. The beautifully designed apartments have state-of-the-art facilities, such as wet rooms, and enjoy those of the hotel, including a naturally lit indoor pool and a gym. Hotel staff are obliging.

🍴 £££

RESTAURANT WITH ROOMS
La Gaffe
107–111 Heath Street, NW3 6SS; 020 7435 8965; www.lagaffe.co.uk
Above its own cheerful family-run Italian restaurant in Hampstead's village atmosphere, near the Heath and Kenwood House, La Gaffe has cosy, pleasing rooms (family rooms fit in three people) with serviceable bathrooms. There are very friendly, hospitable staff, who are prepared to go the extra mile to help, and, of course, wonderful home-cooked Italian food.

🛏 😊 ££

La Gaffe restaurant and rooms in the centre of Hampstead village

Key to symbols *see back cover flap*

The distinctive "Gherkin" building towering over the City of London

London
MAPS

London City Maps

The map below shows the divison of the 18 pages
of maps in this section, as well as the main areas
covered in the sightseeing section of this book.
The smaller inset map shows Greater London
and the areas covered in Beyond the City Centre.

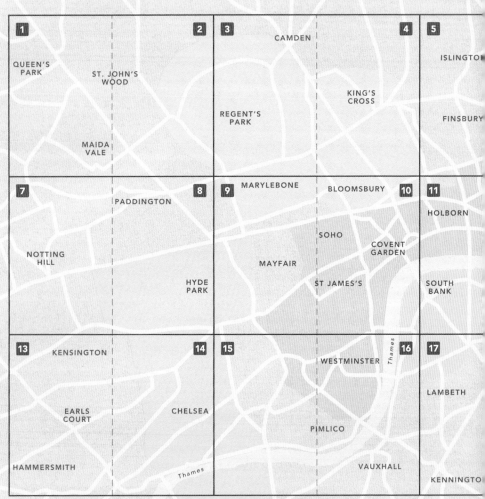

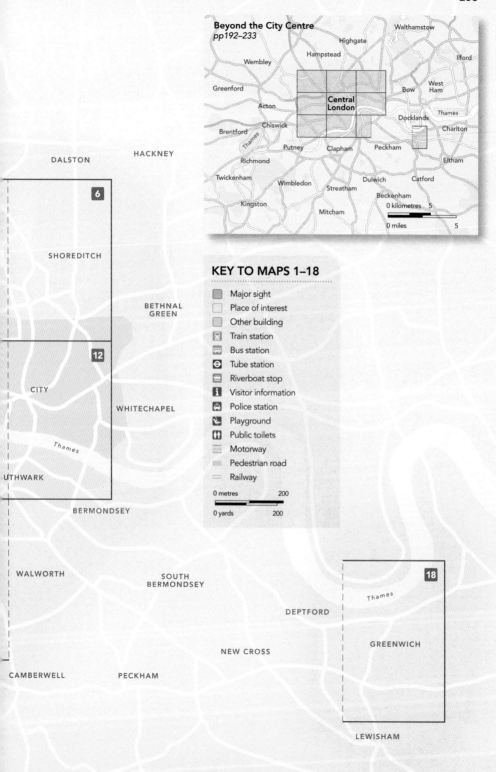

Beyond the City Centre
pp192–233

Walthamstow
Highgate
Hampstead
Wembley
Ilford
Greenford
Bow
West Ham
Acton
Central London
Chiswick
Docklands
Thames
Brentford
Charlton
Thames
Putney
Clapham
Peckham
Richmond
Eltham
Twickenham
Dulwich
Catford
Wimbledon
Streatham
Beckenham
Kingston
0 kilometres 5
Mitcham
0 miles 5

DALSTON
HACKNEY

6

SHOREDITCH

BETHNAL GREEN

12

CITY

WHITECHAPEL

Thames

UTHWARK

BERMONDSEY

WALWORTH
SOUTH BERMONDSEY

DEPTFORD

18

Thames

NEW CROSS

GREENWICH

CAMBERWELL
PECKHAM

LEWISHAM

KEY TO MAPS 1–18

- ⬛ Major sight
- ⬜ Place of interest
- ⬜ Other building
- 🚆 Train station
- 🚌 Bus station
- Ⓔ Tube station
- 🚤 Riverboat stop
- ℹ Visitor information
- 👮 Police station
- 🛝 Playground
- 🚻 Public toilets
- ═ Motorway
- ▒ Pedestrian road
- ╍ Railway

0 metres 200
0 yards 200

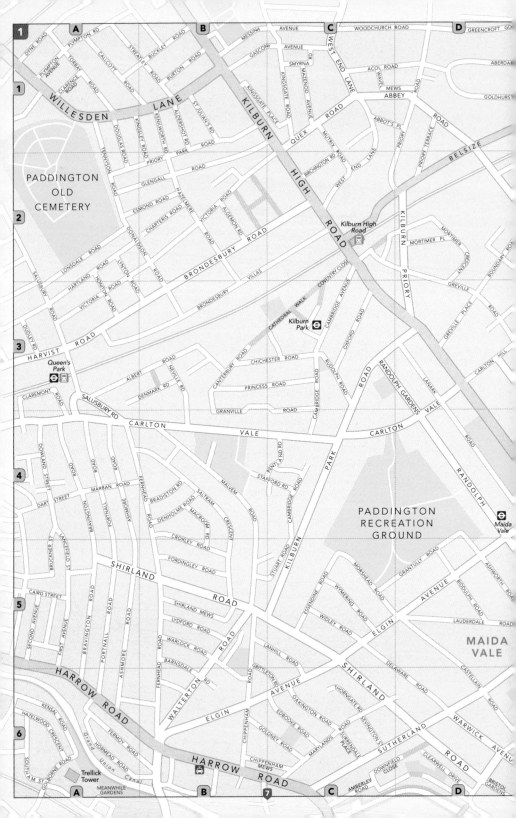

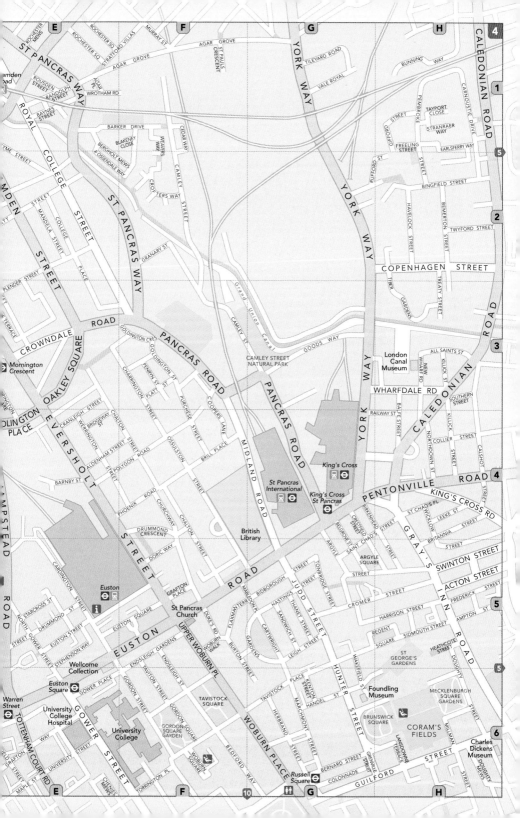

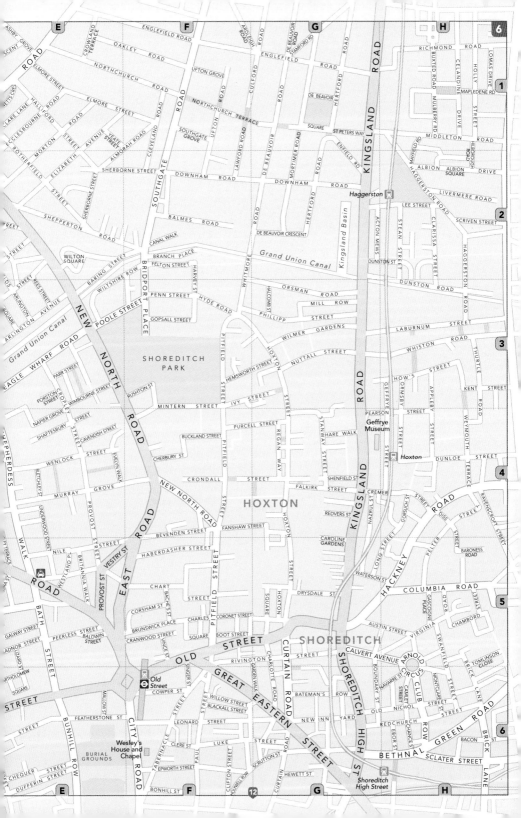

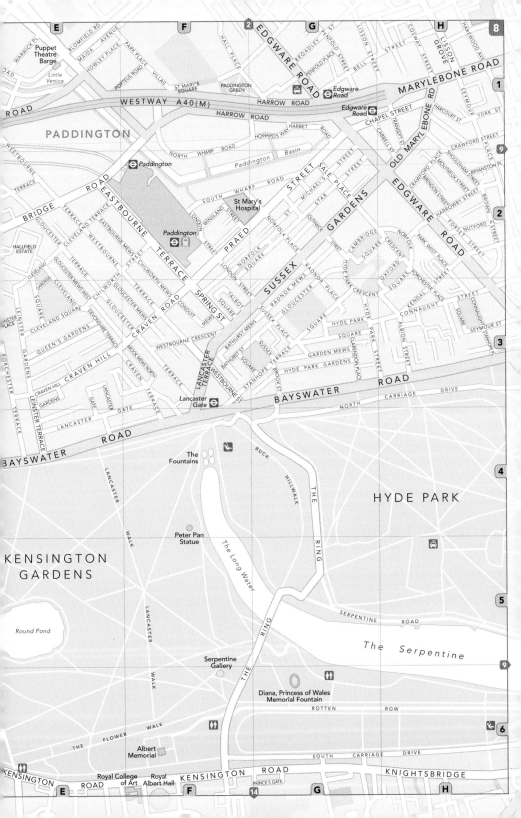

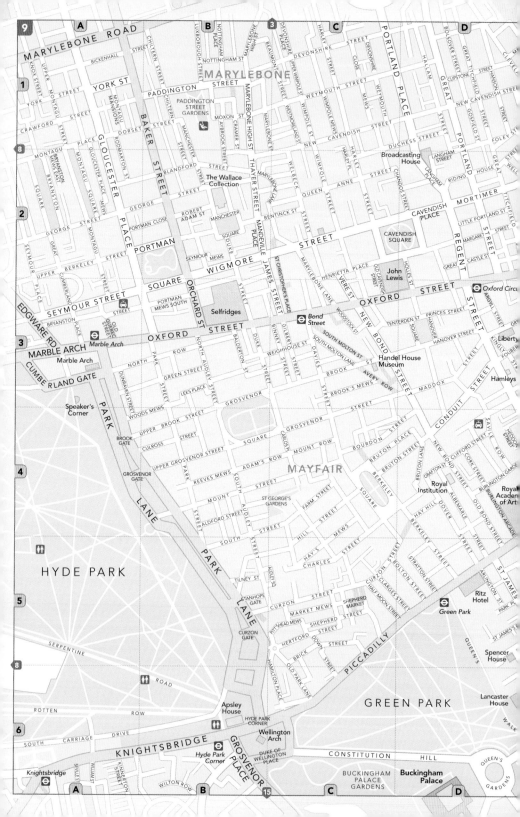

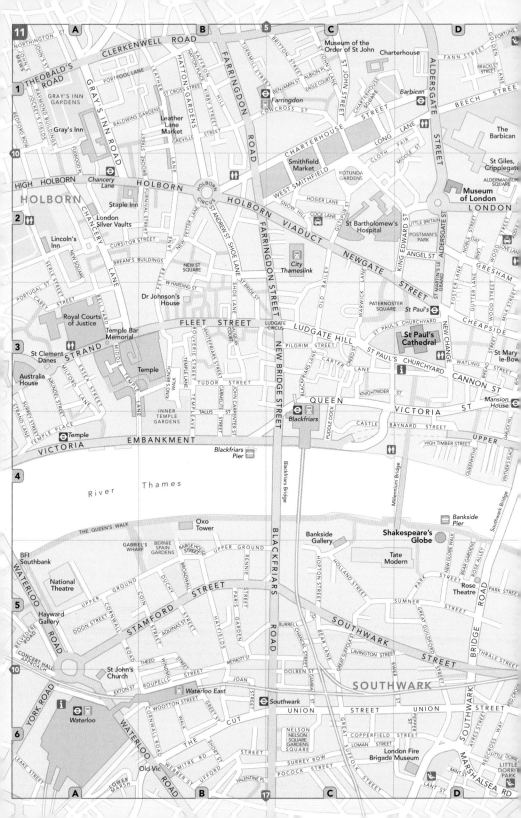

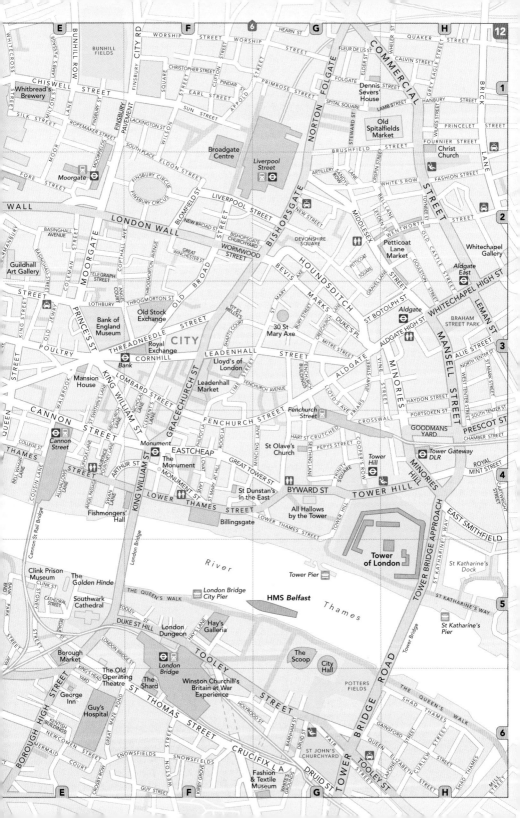

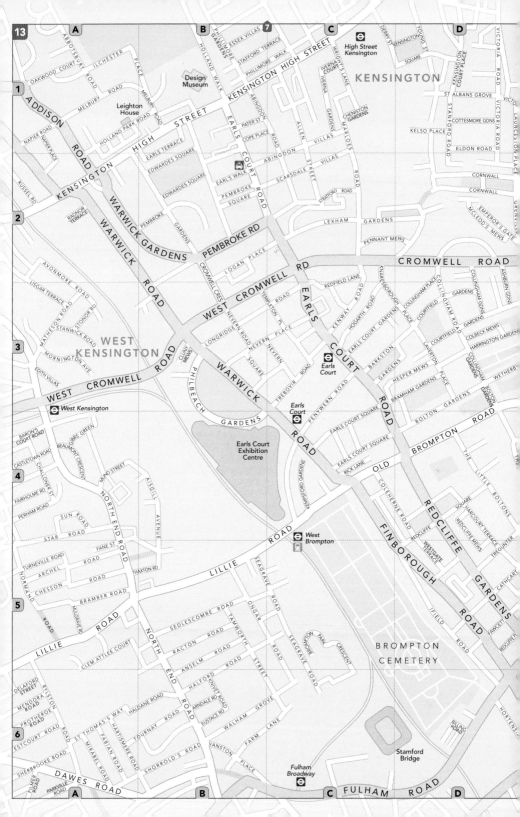

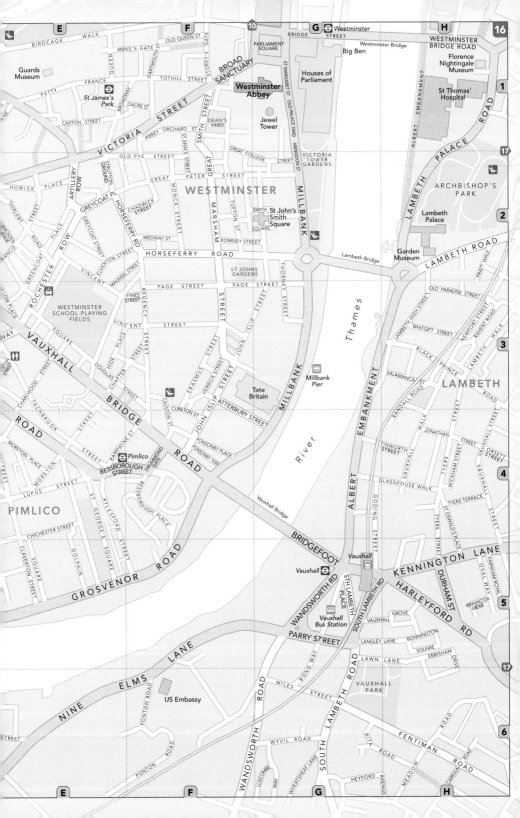

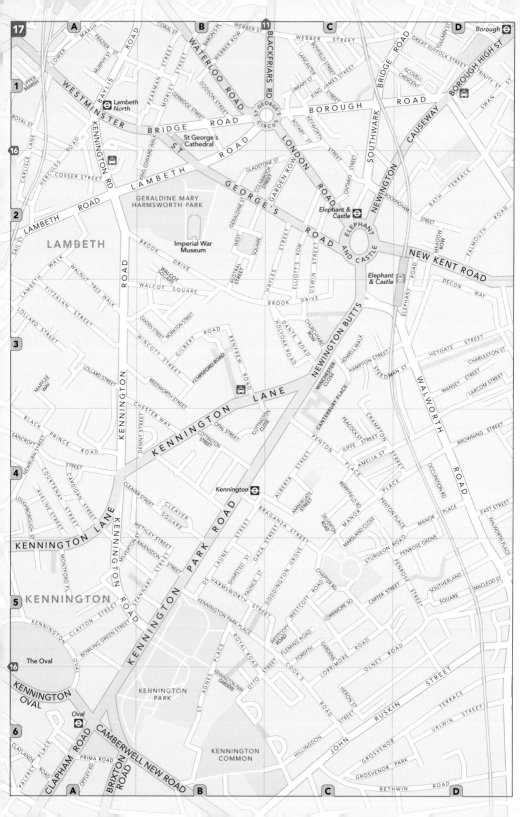

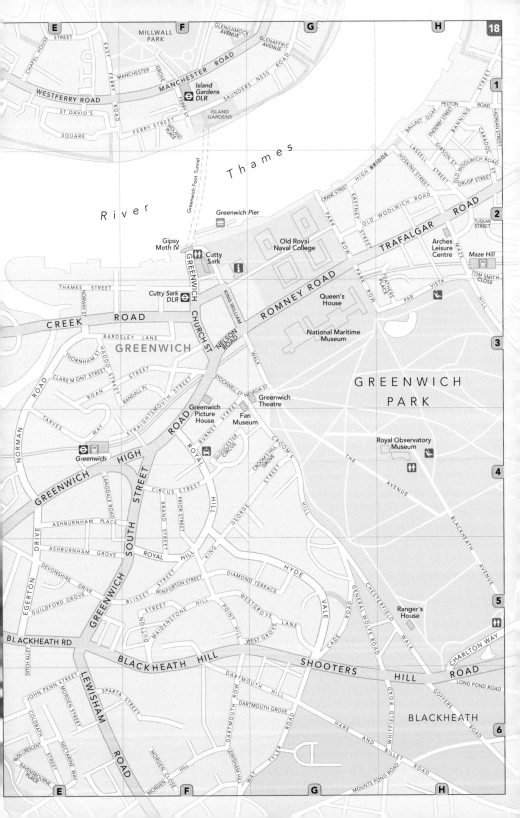

London Maps Index

Index

Page numbers in **bold** type refer to main entries.

Acknowledgments

Dorling Kindersley would like to thank the following people whose help and assistance contributed to the preparation of this book.

Main Contributor
Journalist Vincent Crump, an Oxford English graduate, has worked widely across most spheres of written journalism: on staff for trade magazines, regional newspapers and consumer magazines, and latterly as a freelance writer and editor, principally on travel. Most of his recent work has been as resident UK travel specialist for the *Sunday Times Travel* section and *Sunday Times Travel Magazine*, for whom Vincent has been writing and editing for 10 years. This is his first book.

Introducing London & Where to Stay
Written by Leonie Glass.

Additional Photography
Max Alexander, Demetrio Carrasco, Tim Draper, Steve Gorton, Dave King, Stephen Oliver, Rough Guides/Victor Borg, Chris Stowers.

Cartography
Maps on pages 196–7, 206–7, 214–15, 220–21, 226–7 are derived from © www.openstreetmap.org and contributors, licensed under CC–BY–SA; see creativecommons.org for further details.

Additional Design and Editorial Assistance
ASSISTANT EDITOR Claire Bush
JACKET DESIGN Tessa Blindoss, Louise Dick
ICON DESIGN Claire-Louise Armitt
READERS Scarlett O'Hara, Anna Streiffert
FACT CHECKER Karen Villabona
PROOFREADER Huw Hennessy
INDEXER Helen Peters
With thanks to Douglas Amrine for his help in developing this series.

Revisions Team
Ashwin Raju Adimari, Dipika Dasgupta, Karen D'Souza, Marc Dubin, Maria Edwards, Caroline Elliker, Kaberi Hazarika, Bharti Karakoti, Tanya Mahendru, Catherine Palmi, Susie Peachey, Marianne Petrou, Khushboo Priya, Ankita Sharma, Nikky Twyman, Ajay Verma

Photography Permissions
Dorling Kindersley would like to thank all the museums, galleries, churches and other sights that allowed us to photograph at their establishments.
Terri and Sir Richard Raleigh at 44 Curzon Street Apartments, Apple UK Press Office, Nicolas at Arosfa B&B, Hélène Muron for Barbican Film Sunday, Finoa Vella at Battersea Park Children's Zoo and Lemon Tree Café, Benjamin Pollock's Toyshop, Britain at War, British Music Experience, Paul and Sarah at Brown's Brasserie, Sophie Darley at Browns Hotel, Brunel Museum, Burgh House, Camden Arts Centre, Cartoon Museum, Shannon Hermes at Charles Dickens Museum, Jess Walker at Davis Tanner for Chelsea Football Club and all at the club, The Clink Museum, Crystal Palace Museum, Crystal Palace Sports Center, DR Johnson's House, Lettie McKie at Dulwich Picture Gallery, Faraday Museum and the Royal Institution, Fire Brigade Museum, Florence Knightingale Museum, Gemma Colgan at the Foundling Museum, Lorenzo & Giuseppe at La Gaffe, Garden Museum, Guards Museum, Nancy Loader at Geffyre Museum, Vikki at Giraffe, Golders Hill Butterfly House, Amelia Atkinson at The Goring, Hany Kirollos at Gourmet Burger Kitchen Windsor, Guildhall Art Gallery, Jo Wilkinson and Madeleine McClure at Hamleys, Richard Brindley at Hard Rock Café, Harrods, Tim Powell at Historic Royal Palaces, Sarah Beckett at the Horniman Museum, Household Cavalry Museum, Hunterian Museum, Imperial War Museums, Alison Bledge at Legoland®, Sophie Lilley at The London Eye, London Film Museum, Wendy Neville at London Transport Museum, Nicola Kalimeris at Museum of London, Becca Hubbard at National Army Museum, Claire Gilbey at Natural History Museum, Old Operating Theatre Museum and Herb Garret, Malida at Original Maids of Honour, Gren Middleton at Puppet Theatre Barge, Royal Air Force Museum, Bryony Phillips at Royal Botanic Gardens Kew, Royal Observatory Greenwich, SACO – Holborn, St Paul's Cathedral, Nicola Osmond-Evans at Science Museum, Serpentine Gallery, Snook's Fun Store, Syon House, Theatre Royal Drury Lane, Unicorn Theatre, Joanna Bolitho at V&A Museum of Childhood, Amy Randall at the Wallace Collection, Dean and Chapter of the Collegiate Church of St Peter Westminster, WWT London Wetland Centre, Zoological Society of London (ZSL).

Picture Credits
a = above; b = below/bottom; c = centre; f = far; l = left; r = right; t = top.

The publisher would like to thank the following for their kind permission to reproduce their photographs:

ALAMY IMAGES: The Art Gallery Collection/*The Execution of Lady Jane Grey* 1833 Hippolyte (Paul) Delaroche 80cra; Robert Bird 80tr; Mike Booth 184br; Stephen Chung 33bl; Mark Dunn 216tr; Greg Balfour Evans 20bl; Keith Mayhew 218tc; John Warburton-Lee Photography 178cl; SM Photography 210tr; Marcin Rogozinski 177bl; mauritius images GmbH 216c.

AWL IMAGES: Travel Pix Collection 157tc.

BATTERSEA PARK CHILDREN'S ZOO: 187tl.

THE BRIDGEMAN ART LIBRARY: Index/Bymuseum, Oslo, Norway 54cra.

BRITISH AIRWAYS: Newscast 20–1.

THE TRUSTEES OF THE BRITISH MUSEUM: 103tc, 103cla; Alan Hills 103ca.

THE CHARLES DICKENS MUSEUM: Newangle 106br.

CHESSINGTON WORLD OF ADVENTURES/MERLIN ENTERTAINMENTS GROUP: 49bl.

CORBIS: Demotix/David Mbiyu 46br, /James Gourley 18bl, /P Nutt 18br; EPA/Frantzesco Kangaris 11t; Eurasia Press/ Steven Vidler 55cb; Jason Hawkes 252–3; Heritage Images 78bl; Robbie Jack 91tl; Pawel Libera 58–9; Reuters/A.J. Sisco 17bl; SuperStock/Clive Sawyer PCL 8–9.

DORLING KINDERSLEY: London Canal Museum/ Max Alexander 96–7; Courtesy of The Science Museum 180tr; Park Lane Group Young Artists' Concert 164bl.

DREAMSTIME.COM: Imran Ahmed 180bl; Piero Cruciatti 156tc; Mark Eaton 126tl; Elenachaykina 15br; Irstone 12tl, 26br; Slawek Kozakiewicz 69bl; Tamara Kulikova 203bc; Mariagroth 99bl; Nanisub 193c; Padmayogini 16br, 17br; Jeanette Teare 30bl; Williammacgregor 155bc.

EDF ENERGY LONDON EYE: 160bc.

© ENGLISH HERITAGE PHOTO LIBRARY: 204clb, 216cl, 216cr.

EUROLINES: 21bc.

THE FAN MUSEUM: 204br.

© FASHION AND TEXTILE MUSEUM: 152cla.

GAMBADO CHELSEA: 48br.

GETTY IMAGES: 19br; AFP 62br, /Carl de Souza 19bl; Express/Stan Meagher 57crb; Imagno 80cr; Chris Jackson 72c; Christopher Lee 16bl; Clive Rose 63t; Oli Scarff 15bl; SuperStock 80c; Time & Life Pictures/ Mansell 56tr.

GLENTHURSTON SELF CATERING APARTMENTS: Andrew Hatfield 251tl.

THE GOLDEN TREASURY BOOKSHOP: 43bl.

THE GOVERNOR & COMPANY OF THE BANK OF ENGLAND: 129cr.

IMPERIAL WAR MUSEUMS: 154crb.

WWW.KIDSROLLERBLADINGLESSONS.CO.UK: 13b.

THE KOBAL COLLECTION: Walt Disney Pictures 131bc.

LONDON BOROUGH OF CAMDEN: 48bl.

LONDON CITY AIRPORT: Andrew Baker 20bc.

LONDON RECUMBENTS: 188cl.

MADAME TUSSAUDS/LONDON: 114tc.

MASALA ZONE COVENT GARDEN: 37bc.

NATIONAL ARMY MUSEUM: 190br.

NATIONAL PORTRAIT GALLERY, LONDON: Colin Streater 79tl.

THE NATIONAL TRUST PHOTO LIBRARY ©NTPL: Arcaid/Richard Bryant 233bl; Andrew Butler 231cb; Geoffrey Frosh 212tc; David Levenson 44br.

POLKA THEATRE: © Robert Workman 47br, 232tr.

REGENT'S PARK OPEN AIR THEATRE: Tristram Kenton 14bl. NATURAL HISTORY MUSEUM, LONDON: 182cl.

REX FEATURE: Mark Thomas 24br. RIPLEY'S BELIEVE IT OR NOT: 85tl.

ROYAL ALBERT HALL: © Marcus Ginns 2009 185bl.

THE ROYAL COLLECTION © 2011 HER MAJESTY QUEEN ELIZABETH II: 238cr; John Freeman 74crb; Derry Moore 74cla, 74clb.

ROYAL NATIONAL THEATRE: Simon Annand 162tr.

ROYAL OPERA HOUSE: Sim Canetty–Clarke 45br.

SHAKESPEARE GLOBE TRUST: Pawel Libera 146cl, Rocco Redondo 146cr.

SIR JOHN SOANES MUSEUM: Derry Moore 94tc.

SOMERSET HOUSE: © Gideon Mendel 13tr, 93t.

ST PAUL'S CATHEDRAL: Peter Smith 130cra.

SUPERSTOCK: Photononstop 156br.

THORPE PARK/MERLIN ENTERTAINEMENTS GROUP: 49tl.

TRAVEL PICTURES: Charles Bowman 27clb.

THE VIEW FROM THE SHARD: 153tr.

VISIT GREENWICH: 198cl, 198c.

WESTFIELD LONDON: 41bl.

Jacket images: Front: ALAMY STOCK PHOTO: Anne-Marie Palmer tr; AWL Images: Travel Pix Collection tc; GETTY IMAGES: Pawel Libera tl; ROBERT HARDING PICTURE LIBRARY: Stuart Black cb; Spine: CORBIS: Sylvain Sonnet t.

All other images © Dorling Kindersley
For further information see: www.dkimages.com

SPECIAL EDITIONS OF DK TRAVEL GUIDES
DK Travel Guides can be purchased in bulk quantities at discounted prices for use in promotions or as premiums. We are also able to offer special editions and personalized jackets, corporate imprints, and excerpts from all of our books, tailored specifically to meet your own needs. To find out more, please contact:
(in the United States) **specialsales@dk.com**
(in the UK) **travelguides@uk.dk.com**
(in Canada) **specialmarkets@dk.com**
(in Australia) **penguincorporatesales@penguin randomhouse.com.au**

MAYOR OF LONDON

 tfl.gov.uk

 24 hour travel information
0343 222 1234*

*Service and network charges may apply. See tfl.gov.uk/terms for details.

 Sign
tfl.

© Transport for London   Reg. user No. 17/3152/P   **Improvement works may affect y**